Fireworks® MX:
The Complete Reference

About the Author

Doug Sahlin is an author, graphic designer, and Web site designer living in Central Florida. He is the author of *Flash MX Virtual Classroom*, *How to Do Everything with Adobe Acrobat 5*, and several other books on Web design and graphic design. He has developed and written an online Flash course. His articles and tutorials have appeared in national publications as well as on Internet sites devoted to 3-D design and Web graphics. When not writing books, Doug designs Web sites for his clients. When he manages to find some spare time, he enjoys photography, listens to music, plays his guitar, or just curls up with a good mystery novel.

Fireworks® MX:
The Complete Reference

Doug Sahlin

McGraw-Hill/Osborne

New York   Chicago   San Francisco
Lisbon   London   Madrid   Mexico City
Milan · New Delhi   San Juan
Seoul   Singapore   Sydney   Toronto

McGraw-Hill/Osborne
2600 Tenth Street
Berkeley, California 94710
U.S.A.

To arrange bulk purchase discounts for sales promotions, premiums, or fund-raisers, please contact **McGraw-Hill**/Osborne at the above address. For information on translations or book distributors outside the U.S.A., please see the International Contact Information page immediately following the index of this book.

Fireworks MX: The Complete Reference

1234567890 DOC DOC 0198765432

ISBN 0-07-222456-8

Publisher
Brandon A. Nordin

Vice President & Associate Publisher
Scott Rogers

Acquisitions Editor
Marjorie McAneny

Project Editor
Jenn Tust

Acquisitions Coordinator
Tana Allen

Technical Editor
Deborah Maupin

Copy Editors
Emily Rader, Lisa Theobald

Proofreaders
Linda Medoff, Paul Medoff,
Marian Selig

Indexer
Valerie Robbins

Computer Designers
Apollo Publishing Services

Illustrator
Michael Mueller, Lyssa Wald

Series Design
Peter F. Hancik

This book was composed with Corel VENTURA™ Publisher.

Dedicated to the inner child and creative spirit present in us all.

Contents at a Glance

Contents

Part I

Fireworks Basics

Part II

Creating Artwork for Your Designs

Part III

Modifying Artwork

Part IV

Creating Animations and Interactive Web Pages

Part V

Optimizing and Exporting Documents

Part VI

Appendixes

Acknowledgments

Any project worth doing is worth doing well. When the task at hand is writing a book of this magnitude, the only way to properly do the job is with the support of many. In that regard, I'd like to give thanks to the people who were instrumental in bringing this project from concept to the printed page. Many thanks to all the fine folks at McGraw-Hill/Osborne. Special thanks to Acquisitions Editor Margie McAneny, a card carrying member of the "What Me Worry?" club. Thanks to Project Coordinator Tana Allen for making sure the various parts of this opus were distributed to the right people at the right time. And congratulations on your recent marriage. Thanks to Project Editor Jenn Tust for her words of encouragement and for making sure my E-mail inbox overflowed with chapters to edit, illustrations to revise, and so on. Special thanks to the lovely and talented Emily Rader for manicuring the text in this book to perfection. Enjoy your trip to France. Kudos to Technical Editor Deborah Mauphin for doing a bang-up job of checking the text and illustrations for technical accuracy. Thanks for your insightful comments and suggestions.

Thanks to the talented staff at Macromedia for supporting authors and providing the best graphic design software on the planet. Many thanks to literary agent extraordinaire, Margot Maley Hutchinson, for being a first-class liaison between author and publisher. Thanks to all the talented folks in the Fireworks community for exchanging thoughts, ideas, and lending a helping hand.

As always, thanks to my friends, mentors, and family for your love, humor, and continued support, especially you, Karen and Ted. Thanks to Lisa and Sue for your friendship and giving me a better appreciation of the joys this short life offers us all.

Introduction

Welcome to *Fireworks MX Complete Reference*. This book is designed to be a stand-alone desktop reference for Fireworks MX. In this book, you'll find detailed discussions of the tools, menu commands, and interface elements you use to create a Fireworks document. You'll find detailed step-by-step instructions on how to use Fireworks to create anything from a simple rollover button to a finished design with interactive elements and special effects that will be used as a Web page. The book is written in easy-to-understand language with a minimum of technical jargon. Whether you're new to Fireworks and Web design, or an experienced veteran, you're sure to find valuable information that you can use to streamline your workflow and increase your productivity.

The book is divided into five parts. In Part I, "Fireworks Basics," you'll learn about the new features in the program as well as how to find your way around the workspace.

In Part II, "Creating Artwork For Your Designs," you'll learn to use Fireworks tools and menu commands to create vector and text objects for your documents as well as how to work with bitmap images. Here you'll find two chapters that will show you how to create colorful strokes, fills, textures, and patterns to decorate your vector objects. In this part, you'll also find a thorough discussion of color as it relates to Web design, and you'll learn how to use Fireworks panels to create the optimal color palette for your design.

In Part III, "Modifying Artwork," you'll learn to use Fireworks tools and menu commands to modify various parameters of objects you create. You'll learn to use layers to organize the artwork in your designs as well as how to create reusable artwork. The last two chapters in this part show you how to add interest to your designs by creating special effects and styles.

In Part IV, "Creating Animations and Interactive Web Pages," you'll learn to create animations and interactive elements for your designs. If you've ever wanted to add items like pop-up menus and image swaps to your designs, it's in this part that you'll find detailed information on how to create these elements and more. If your client wants you to add animation to a design in the form of an animated banner, Part IV of this book is where you'll find the information you need to plan and execute the banner.

In Part V, "Optimizing and Exporting Documents," you'll learn how to choose the optimal export method for the document's intended destination. You'll also learn to streamline your workflow by using Fireworks batch processing to eliminate the drudgery of repetitive tasks. If you perform the same actions in the same order on a regular basis, you'll find information in Part V that shows you how to create your own scripts and commands. The final chapter in the book shows you how to integrate Fireworks with other software from the Macromedia graphic design suite, as well as working with other popular Web design and graphic design software.

In Part VI, "Appendixes," you'll find the complete keyboard shortcuts for the two most popular Fireworks keyboard sets as well as Internet resources for Fireworks and Web design.

Conventions Used in This Book

This book was written on the PC. However, Macintosh users will still benefit from this book. When they differ, the commands for both platforms are shown; for example: to open a context menu right-click (Windows) or CONTROL+click (Macintosh).

The path to a menu command is represented in the following manner: Edit | Insert | New Button. The previous example instructs you to choose the New Button command from the Insert menu, which is a submenu of the Edit menu.

In Fireworks, you use panels to perform certain related tasks. For example, the Optimize panel is used to select export settings for the document. The Property inspector is another Fireworks fixture you'll use repeatedly to perform a wide variety of tasks. The Property inspector and frequently used panels have default positions within the Fireworks workspace. When a panel is needed to perform an operation you will be instructed to open it by clicking the arrow to the left of the panel's title; for example, *click the arrow to the left of the word Properties* is the instruction to open the Property inspector from its default position, which is docked at the bottom of the workspace. If you've customized the workspace by hiding one or more panels, or the Property inspector, you'll have to resort to a menu command to open the panel. For example, if you have removed the Optimize panel from the window to the right of the workspace, you would choose Window | Optimize to open the panel.

Throughout the book you'll see two icons: *Note* and *Tip*. Whenever you see the Note icon, it's a reference to further information about the topic of discussion, or an alternative way of performing the task. When you see the Tip icon, you'll find a handy shortcut, information that will help you to perform a task in a simpler matter or streamline your workflow.

With Fireworks you can export documents for use as ASP (Active Server Pages), XML (Extensible Markup Language), XHTML (Extensible Hypertext Markup Language) files and more. You'll learn how to export documents for use in Web pages with these extensions; however, a detailed discussion of each Web page format is beyond the scope of this book. Furthermore, in a text editor, or HTML editor, you can modify the JavaScript Fireworks automatically generates to create certain behaviors. A detailed discussion of JavaScript is also beyond the scope of this book. For more information on JavaScript and other Web design topics, refer to the selection of reference books at www.Osborne.com.

The Complete Reference

Fireworks MX

Part I

Fireworks Basics

Fireworks
MX

Chapter 1

Getting to Know Fireworks MX

Fireworks MX makes it possible for Web designers to optimize graphics for their Web designs and so much more. With the software, you can create sophisticated graphics for Web pages by combining raster (bitmap) images with vector objects. Using the sophisticated editing and image creation tools you can design anything from a simple header to a full-fledged Web page, complete with compelling effects like image swapping, multi-state rollover buttons, and more. Animation is another Fireworks strong suit. You can take advantage of the program's automated animation features or design your own frame-by-frame animation to create animated GIFs and animated banners.

Whether you're new to Fireworks, new to Web design, or an experienced Web professional, you'll find exciting tools in Fireworks MX to streamline your workflow and maximize your productivity. If you shy away from sophisticated Web design effects because you don't know JavaScript, you'll love Fireworks. You supply the graphic objects and choose a special effect (or *behavior*, as it is known in Fireworks), and Fireworks takes care of creating the Hypertext Markup Language (HTML) code and associated JavaScript when you export the document.

Whether you're a novice or a veteran, the quickest way to come to terms with any new software is to install it, pop open the hood, and get some grease under your fingernails. In this chapter, you'll learn what you can do with Fireworks and some of the fundamental concepts behind the software. In addition, you'll learn about the new Fireworks features and how you can use Fireworks to create images, buttons, nav bars, menus, and other items for your Web designs.

Getting Started

Fireworks MX: The Complete Reference is designed to be a standalone desktop reference. While you're reading the book, it's best to have Fireworks open so you can follow the tutorials and examples. You can read the book in linear fashion from cover to cover, or if you're an experienced Fireworks or Web design veteran, read the chapters that interest you the most. Keep the book within arm's reach for ready reference whenever you're designing a Web site.

Minimum System Requirements

Fireworks packs a lot of punch. You use this multifaceted software to optimize your graphic objects for the Web and then export the graphic objects and accompanying HTML. This multitasking does not come without a price, however. In order to properly run Fireworks, you'll need the following hardware:

Windows Minimum System Requirements

- 300 MHZ Intel Pentium Processor (Pentium II or better)
- Windows 98 SE, ME, NT® 4 (Service Pack 6), 2000, or XP

- 64MB (128MB recommended) of available RAM
- 800 × 600, 256-color display (1024 × 768, millions of colors recommended)
- 80MB of free hard disk space
- Adobe Type Manager Version 4, or later, with Type 1 fonts
- CD-ROM Drive

Macintosh Minimum System Requirements

- Power Macintosh Processor (G3 or higher recommended)
- Mac OS 9.1 or later, Mac OS X version 10.1 or later
- 64MB (128MB recommended) of available RAM
- 800 × 600, 256-color display (1024 × 768, millions of colors recommended)
- 80MB of free hard disk space
- Adobe Type Manager Version 4, or later, with Type 1 fonts (OS 9.x only)
- CD-ROM Drive

Note   *These are the minimum requirements needed to run Fireworks. If you plan on taking advantage of round-trip multitasking between Fireworks and other Macromedia software, you should consider upgrading your system to include a faster processor and more memory than the minimum requirements. A high-end graphics card and a 19-inch or larger monitor is another good investment. With better screen resolution and a larger monitor, these additions will give you the maximum available screen real estate for editing your designs while keeping several Fireworks panels open.*

Installing Fireworks

Fireworks MX is designed for both the Windows and Macintosh platforms. To install Fireworks, do the following:

1. Insert the Fireworks CD into your CD-ROM drive.

2. Depending on your platform, do one of the following:

   - In Windows, the installation program should start automatically. If for some reason it doesn't, choose Start | Run. Click Browse and navigate to the setup.exe file on your Fireworks MX CD-ROM. Click OK to begin the installation. Alternatively, you can use Windows Explorer to navigate to the setup.exe file on the CD-ROM and double-click the icon.

   - For Macintosh, double-click the installation icon.

3. Follow the onscreen prompts to enter your serial number and complete the installation.

4. If it's convenient, before exiting the setup, you can log on to the Internet and automatically register your software online.

After you install Fireworks, launch the software by selecting the Fireworks icon from the folder you installed the program in, or select it from the operating system's start menu. If your operating system supports shortcuts, you may find it convenient to add a Fireworks shortcut to your desktop.

Note *If your copy of Firework MX is bundled with other Macromedia software, refer to the installation instructions included with the package.*

What Is Fireworks?

Macromedia Fireworks is software you use to create documents that will be incorporated in a Web design. The documents you create can be comprised of imported raster (bitmap) and vector images. You can add anti-aliased text to your documents and use Fireworks drawing tools to create vector objects. You can also add multi-state buttons, navigation menus, pop-up menus, and sophisticated effects like image swapping. Fireworks features effects that you use to add a drop shadow or a glow around objects, to bevel objects, to add motion blur to objects, and more. When you add an effect (known in Fireworks as a Live Effect) to an object, you can edit it at any time, even after you save a document. If you find the effect is no longer needed, you can delete it to return the object to its original state.

You add the elements to your document working on a canvas in the document window. As you create a document, you can import elements from external sources or create objects with the Fireworks drawing tools. Your artwork can be segregated with layers, and you can add frames to a document for animation. After you create a document, you export it. You can export images by themselves or export images and HTML together. Figure 1-1 shows a document being created in Fireworks.

Fireworks Features

Notice the patterned areas in the right-hand window in Figure 1-1. These are called *slices*. You create a slice when you want to optimize a certain part of a document in a specific format. For example, if you mix bitmaps and text in a document, you can create slices for your bitmap objects and export them optimized in JPEG format; and you can create slices for your text objects and export them in the GIF format. Notice the tabs in the main window (the window where you create the document by adding elements to the canvas and preview the document as it will be exported) in Figure 1-1. You click these tabs to preview the document as it will be exported. You can view and edit all of the

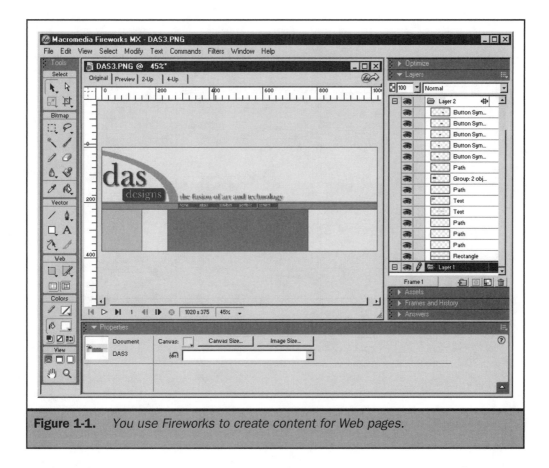

Figure 1-1.   *You use Fireworks to create content for Web pages.*

elements in the document by clicking the Original tab, preview the export as currently optimized by clicking the Preview tab, compare the optimized export to the original by clicking the 2-Up tab, or compare the original against three different optimization methods by clicking the 4-Up tab.

Figure 1-2 shows a Fireworks document being previewed using the 2-Up display. Notice the text at the bottom of the right-hand 2-Up view in Figure 1-2. This shows you the file size using the current optimization method, as well as the download time at a connection speed of 56 Kbps. When you compare documents side by side, you can optimize your graphics so they look good and download quickly, a valuable tool.

The Fireworks Workspace

The Fireworks workspace is laid out so that you can easily access the tools you need to get the job done. The default Fireworks workspace is optimized for 800 × 600 or

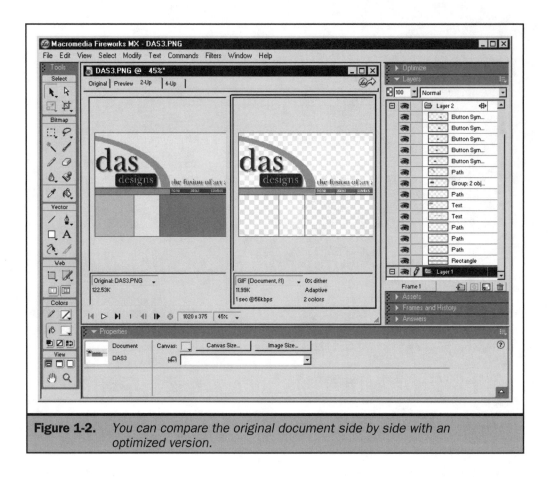

Figure 1-2.   *You can compare the original document side by side with an optimized version.*

higher desktop resolution. However, the workspace is fully customizable. You learn to optimize the workspace to suit your work habits in Chapter 3. Figure 1-3 shows a custom panel set optimized for 800 × 600 with a few floating panels.

The Property Inspector

At the bottom of the workspace you see a window labeled Properties. This multifaceted workhorse is known as the Property inspector. You may recognize this window if you use Macromedia Dreamweaver to edit your HTML pages. The tasks you can perform with the Property inspector vary depending on the type of object you have selected. When you have nothing selected, you can use the Property inspector to resize the document. This timesaving tool will be covered frequently throughout the

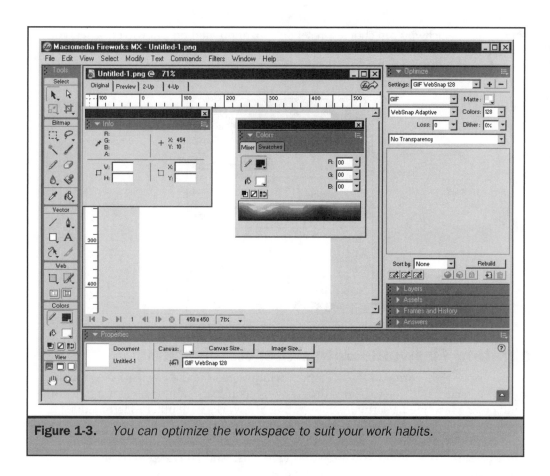

Figure 1-3.   *You can optimize the workspace to suit your work habits.*

course of this book. The Property inspector is shown here with a bitmap object selected in the upper-left pane:

Fireworks Panels

The Property inspector replaced many of the panels you became familiar with in Fireworks 4. However, as efficient as the Property inspector is, you still need to use panels to perform certain tasks. The Property inspector, for example, has a drop-down menu from which you can choose preset optimization methods; however, when you need to fine-tune optimization for a specific document, or an object you intend to export using a different optimization method, you use the Optimize panel shown here:

Integrating Fireworks with Other Applications

In the upper-right corner of the document window, you find a Fireworks icon with an arrow. You click this icon to open a drop-down menu that enables you to use Fireworks with other Macromedia software. Integrating Fireworks with other Macromedia applications will be covered in Chapter 23.

In addition, within other applications, you can edit objects you've created in Fireworks. If, for example, you are working in Flash and you need to resample an image, you can select the image from the Flash document Library, launch Fireworks from within Flash to edit the image, and then return the edited image to Flash.

Creating Your Own Commands

If you perform a certain task in Fireworks on a repetitive basis, you can create a custom command. When you create a new document in Fireworks, every step you take to create a document or modify an image is recorded in the History panel. You can select a single step, or you can select several steps and convert the steps into your own command that appears on a menu bar.

This feature can save you a tremendous amount of time. If, for example, you do work for a client that supplies you with digital images of a certain size and you need to resample them for the Web, in the History panel you can select the steps you previously used to perform the task and save them as a command.

Automating Repetitive Tasks

If you've ever manually performed the same tasks on several images for a client's Web page, you know how time consuming it can be. You can use Fireworks' Batch Processing command to perform the same task on several files at once. After you select Batch Processing, you simply load the files you want to process, select one or more commands, and Fireworks does the rest, rapidly performing the requested command and then saving the files. This frees your valuable time for more creative endeavors.

What's New in Fireworks MX?

If you've used previous versions of Fireworks, you're in for a big surprise the first time you launch the software. The interface has a new look and feel to it. Macromedia is striving to create a common interface for all of its Web publishing software. New to Fireworks is the Property inspector. The Property inspector goes a long way toward making the workspace more productive and user friendly. The tasks handled by the Property inspector pare down the number of panels you have to deal with. The default Fireworks layout integrates key panels with the desktop, neatly tucking them into the panel window on the right side of the Interface.

Your Fireworks toolbox has been enhanced as well. You have new tools for blurring, burning, dodging, sharpening, and smudging bitmap images. You now have a Gradient tool for applying gradients to selections. The toolbox has been compartmentalized; the Bitmap, Vector, and Web tools now have their own sections, making it easier for you to locate a specific tool.

If you frequently use gradients in your work, you now have the ability to vary the opacity of each individual color used to create the blend. Unfortunately, this transparency will not be supported if you export the document as a GIF image.

If you frequently combine several bitmap images and vector objects to create a document, you'll be happy to know you can select them and flatten them into a single bitmap. This new feature makes it easier for you to manage your objects by reducing clutter in the Layers panel.

When you edit slices in Fireworks, dragging a slice guide automatically updates adjacent slice guides. This feature is similar to manually resizing a table in Dreamweaver.

If you frequently end up with objects spanned across several layers, you can now drag them to a layer beyond the visible boundary of the Layers panel as the panel scrolls with you.

You can now move an object while creating it by pressing the SPACEBAR and dragging. This feature works with the Rectangle, Rounded Rectangle, Oval, Polygon/Star, Rectangular Marquee, Oval Marquee, Crop, Text, Hotspot, Slice, and Export Area tools.

You now have the ability to interactively zoom in on an area by selecting the Zoom tool and dragging a marquee around an area of the document you need to magnify. In addition, you have additional magnification presets to choose from.

Fireworks MX makes it easier than ever before to create a pop-up menu. You have additional tabs to work with, as well as the ability to customize how the menu is positioned on the HTML page. You can also change the amount of time for which the menu is visible after a mouseover.

A new menu command makes it possible for you to create a document by reconstituting an HTML table. You can also use this command to re-create a Fireworks document from HTML when the source .png file is no longer available.

An added enhancement in Fireworks MX is the ability to change the text on individual instances of a button without creating a new symbol. This makes it possible for you to edit the original symbol and automatically update all instances of the button, even those with different text on them. This feature is invaluable when you need to edit a *navigation bar,* a device for navigating a Web site, on which you've changed text and assigned unique uniform resource locators (URLs) to each button.

Fireworks now features an Align panel that you can use to align objects to each other or to the document canvas. This panel functions much like the Align panel in Flash and is a tremendous improvement over alignment methods used in previous versions of Fireworks. When you begin using this tool, you'll save time and see a marked improvement in your productivity.

When you add text to a document, it is now handled with the Property inspector. Within the Property inspector, you have additional paragraph controls: first-line indentation, spacing before and after a paragraph, and the capability to select between pixel-leading and percentage-leading control increments. Fireworks also features a spell checker with a user dictionary.

Fireworks Terms

If you're new to Fireworks, there are a few terms that are unique to the software, and other terms you may not be aware of. These terms are used to describe various operations and tasks you perform in Fireworks. The upcoming sections introduce you to terms that will be used throughout the course of this book.

Understanding Slices

When you add interactive elements to a Fireworks document such as multi-state buttons, Fireworks creates a slice for the object. You can also convert a selected object or objects into a slice. When the document is exported, each slice is saved as a separate image file with the optimization method you specify. When you choose an optimization method you specify the file format and when applicable, the amount of compression Fireworks applies to images. You can also assign behaviors to slices. If you export the document as images and HTML, Fireworks creates a table that faithfully reassembles the slices as they will appear when the HTML document is loaded into a browser.

Understanding Hotspots

When you add a hotspot to a document, you define an area to which you can add interactivity. Hotspots are the basic ingredients in an image map. When you create an image map, you create hotspots that are used as links to URLs. You can also use a hotspot for interactive Fireworks elements known as *behaviors*. A hotspot differs from a slice in that a hotspot is not always exported as a separate image, the way a slice is. When you create hotspots for an image map, each hotspot's position, along with the associated URL, is referenced in the HTML document created by Fireworks. In the exported HTML document, each hotspot area is designated by coords (HTML for coordinates) as shown here:

```
<map name="m_homePage_r1_c1">
<area shape="rect" coords="107,84,227,143" href="http://www.dasdesign.net" >
</map>
```

You can create a hotspot by defining an area with one of the Hotspot tools (Rectangle Hotspot tool, Circle Hotspot tool, or Polygon Hotspot tool), or use a menu command to assign a hotspot to an object in your document. Figure 1-4 shows a document that uses a combination of hotspots and slices. You learn how to create hotspots and slices in Chapter 16.

About Behaviors

After you create an interactive area with the Slice or Hotspot tool, you can assign a Fireworks behavior to it. With behaviors, you can add sophisticated effects to your documents such as image swapping, pop-up menus, a status bar message, and more. When you assign a behavior to a hotspot or a slice and then export the document as images and HTML, Fireworks generates the necessary JavaScript to choreograph the effect. You learn to create interactive Web pages using behaviors in Chapter 17.

About Live Effects

You have two different methods for adding special effects to your documents: effects and filters. You add an effect to an object using the Property inspector. When you add an effect such as a drop shadow to text or a bevel to a button, the effect is linked to the object, and Fireworks remembers the settings you choose for the effect. Macromedia refers to the effects you apply with the Property inspector as Live Effects. You can undo a Live Effect or edit it at any time by selecting the object, opening the Property inspector, and then modifying or deleting the effect. When you save the document, the settings for the effect are saved with it. The effect is fully editable the next time you open the document.

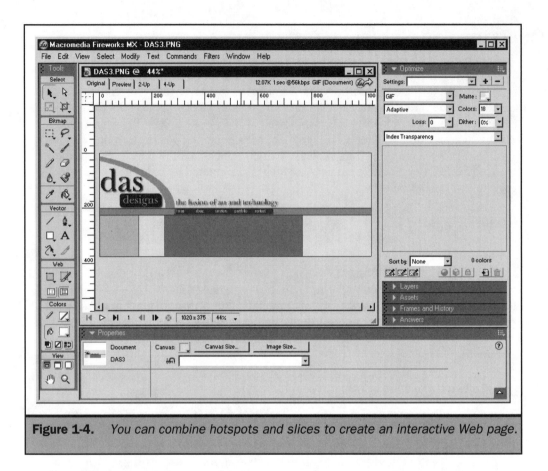

Figure 1-4. *You can combine hotspots and slices to create an interactive Web page.*

When you use a filter on an object, you must undo it. If you add several shapes to the document or perform other edits after applying a filter to an object, you must undo all of the steps you performed after adding the filter to restore the object to its prefilter state. If you apply an external filter (for example a Photoshop-type plug-in) to an object, it must be undone immediately. However, when you use a Live Effect, you can select the object, open the Property inspector and remove the effect at any time, without having to backtrack through numerous steps, even after saving and reopening the document.

About Optimization

When you create graphics for a Web page, your goal is to have a crisp image that downloads quickly from the host Web site. You optimize a document to get the best looking image with the smallest possible file size. You can certainly optimize an image in other image-editing programs, but Fireworks is particularly well suited to this task.

You can apply different optimization methods to different areas, or slices, of a document. For example, if you mix text, vector objects, and bitmap objects in the same document, you can create slices for each type of object, select the object, and then choose the perfect optimization settings for it. As you optimize the document, you can preview the effects of your edits in real time by using one of the preview displays.

Fireworks' default optimization method is the GIF format using 128 colors. This is well suited for vector and text objects; however, bitmaps don't hold up well using this optimization method. Therefore, you choose the default optimization method for the vector and text objects and optimize the bitmap slice as a JPEG file. Optimization will be covered in detail in Chapter 21.

Understanding Bitmaps and Vector Graphics

When you create a Fireworks document, you can combine vector and bitmap (also known as *raster*) graphics; and you can import them into Fireworks.

Bitmap images are comprised of tiny squares of colors known as *pixels*. The number of pixels per inch determines the resolution of the bitmap. The default resolution of a Fireworks document is 72 pixels per inch, the same resolution as most computer monitors. You can import images with higher resolutions, but they will be exported at a resolution of 72 pixels per inch unless you specify otherwise when creating the document.

When you import bitmap objects into a document, you can downsize them with relatively little loss in fidelity. However, when you enlarge a bitmap image, pixels are redrawn; and this results in a loss of fidelity.

The objects you create with the Fireworks drawing tools are vector based. Vector objects are comprised of curved or straight paths that are used to define areas of solid color. A vector graphic is drawn mathematically. When you enlarge or downsize a vector graphic, the paths used to define the vector object are re-created with no loss of fidelity. The only exception to this rule is when you greatly enlarge a vector object with a complex gradient fill. When you export a Fireworks document, the vector objects are rasterized to the document resolution.

About the PNG Format

When you save a Fireworks document, you can only save it in the PNG (pronounced "ping") format. This confuses many first-time Fireworks users who haven't studied the documentation or invested in a book like the one you're reading. Saving your work in Fireworks native format is actually a huge benefit for you. If you import a JPEG image and save the document, your original file is intact. After optimizing the image and adding other elements to it, you can export it as a JPEG with a different filename. You then save the Fireworks document as a .png file, which you can edit at any time. The ability to edit the file at a later date is especially important if you work for clients who frequently change their minds. The Fireworks PNG format is 32 bit—24 bits for color and 8 bits for the alpha (transparency) channel.

Fireworks' Capabilities

New Fireworks users are often unaware of the power lurking in this seemingly innocuous application. Graphic designers accustomed to programs like Photoshop are often baffled when they go to save a document and the only available format is Fireworks' native PNG format. However, after a bit of reading and some experimentation, the true power of Fireworks is revealed. The following sections are a brief overview of what you and Fireworks can accomplish with a bit of diligence, patience, and perseverance on your part.

Creating Images for the Web

When you create a new document in Fireworks, you can populate it with images and vector objects. You can export the file as a single image or add interactivity to the document in the form of buttons, pop-up menus, and behaviors. You then use Fireworks' powerful Optimize panel to ready the image for export. When you use the Optimize panel in conjunction with one of the preview windows, you optimize the document for export as one or more images that download quickly into a viewer's Web browser. You can export the document as images, or as images and HTML. Figure 1-5 shows a document being optimized for Web display.

Creating HTML from Documents

When you create a document with buttons and use the Slice tool or Hotspot tool to create interactive areas, you can apply different optimization methods to the individual slices and assign behaviors , such as image swapping, opening new browser windows, and more, to the hotspots. If you were to try to create this interactivity with a standard HTML editor, you'd have to use JavaScript to pull off these effects. If the HTML editor doesn't have the capability of creating JavaScript on the fly, you have no other choice than to learn enough JavaScript to pull off the effect. You also need to create a table to house all of the individual images you use in the document. When you export a document from Fireworks as images and HTML, the HTML code is created for you. After exporting the document, you can open it in an HTML editor and all of the images are perfectly

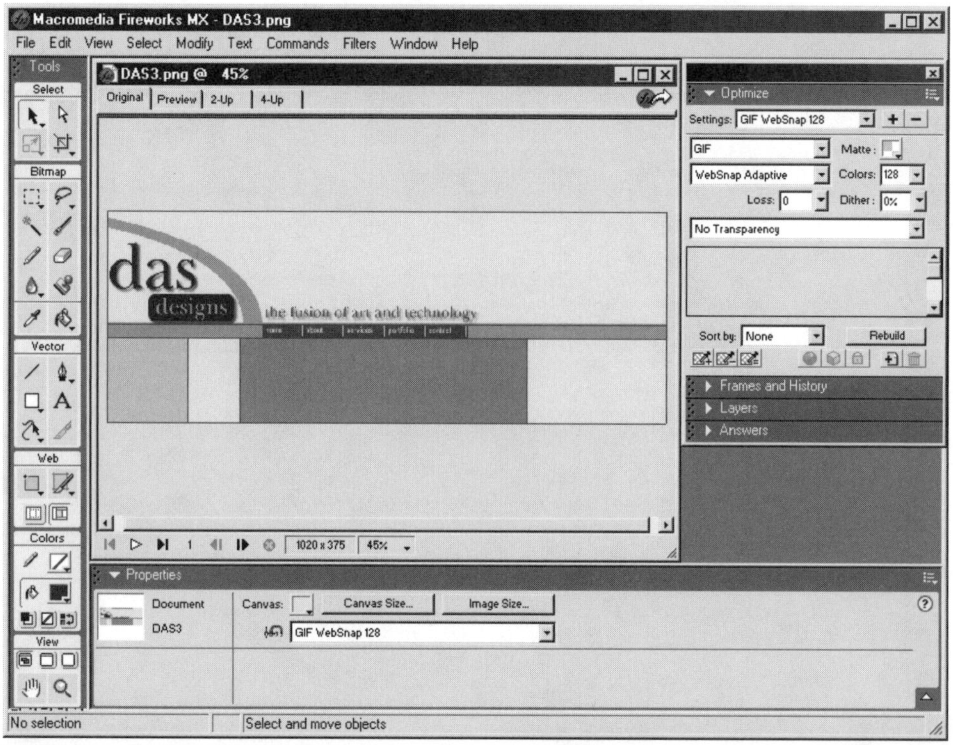

Figure 1-5.   *You optimize a document to create a fast-loading Web page.*

aligned in tables. The JavaScript code Fireworks creates and flawlessly executes the effects you add to the document. Figure 1-6 shows an HTML document created by Fireworks.

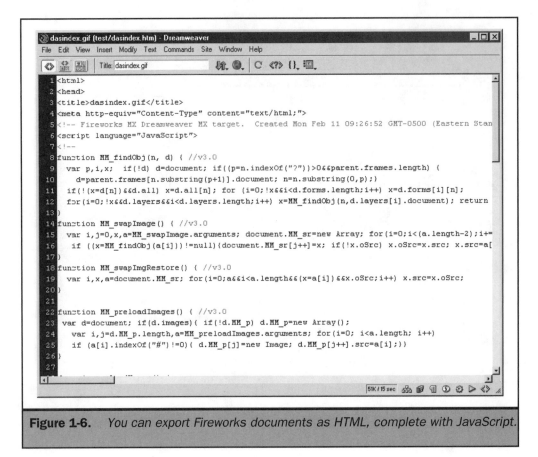

Figure 1-6.   *You can export Fireworks documents as HTML, complete with JavaScript.*

Creating Vector Objects

Fireworks gives you the best of both worlds when it comes to creating a Web design. You can import the bitmaps needed for the page and use the Vector tools to create and edit objects such as banner backgrounds and buttons. After you create a simple vector object such as a rectangle with rounded corners, you can use one of the preset styles to turn it into a thing of beauty. You can apply sophisticated gradient fills to the vector objects you create and border them with custom strokes. Figure 1-7 shows some of the vector objects you can create with Fireworks.

Working with Bitmap Images

There are several photo-editing programs you can use to create images for the Web. However, few give you the capability to combine vector and bitmap images and then export the document in a format you can use on the Web. Fireworks may not have the

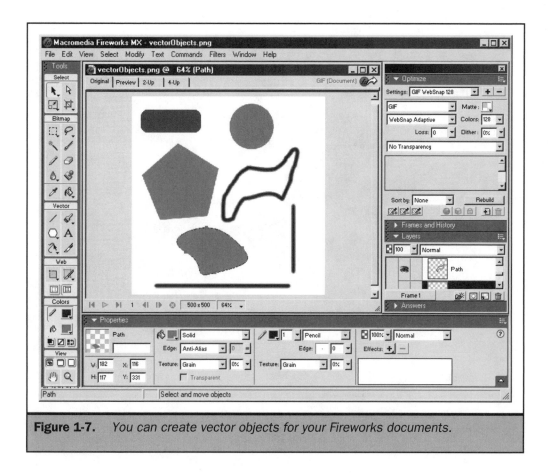

Figure 1-7. *You can create vector objects for your Fireworks documents.*

bitmap-editing power of a program like Photoshop, but it does give you the ability to perform some sophisticated editing to the bitmaps you import into your documents. Within Fireworks you can adjust the color of bitmaps, blur them, sharpen them, and more. You also have the option to use any photo filters you have installed on your machine. Most filters that are compatible with Photoshop will work in Fireworks. Figure 1-8 shows a document containing several bitmap images.

Creating Interactive Web Pages

If your clients need interactive Web pages, Fireworks is the tool to use. As you work your way through this book, you'll learn how to add exciting elements, such as simple rollovers, image swapping, pop-up menus, and more, to your Web designs. And you can preview your work in a Web browser without leaving Fireworks. What's more, you can export that interactivity directly into other Macromedia programs installed on your computer.

Figure 1-8.   *You can use Fireworks to edit bitmap images.*

Working with Other Macromedia Software

When you install Fireworks, the installation program searches your machine for other Macromedia software. When you launch Fireworks, you find a small icon in the upper-right corner of the document window. Click it to reveal a menu that provides links to your other Macromedia software. You can export the objects you create, export HTML, and launch other Macromedia software from within Fireworks. Integrating Fireworks with your other Macromedia software is covered in Chapter 23.

Creating Buttons and Navigation Bars

You can use Fireworks to create all or part of your Web design. You'll find the drawing tools and styles are especially well suited to creating buttons. The buttons you create can be multi-state rollover buttons or simple rollover buttons. After you create a button, you can export it as images and incorporate the button in a Web design you're creating in an HTML editor.

Another item you can create as a standalone object in Fireworks is a navigation bar, or "nav bar" as most designers refer to it. A nav bar is a navigation menu with adjacent buttons aligned vertically or horizontally. To quickly create a nav bar, you create a single button with text and then duplicate the original button for the other items on your navigation menu. After you duplicate the buttons, you can change the text without creating new symbols. If the menu you are creating has more choices than you can comfortably fit on one menu, you can create one or more pop-up menus to create a streamlined menu with several links. The following illustration shows a completed nav bar, complete with a pop-up menu, as previewed in a Web browser.

Creating Web Links

With Fireworks you can easily assign the URL links for buttons, nav bars, hotspots, and image slices. You can use the Property inspector to enter the link, complete with alternate text, as well as specify whether the link opens in the same browser window or a different browser window. As you create the document, Fireworks stores the links in a URL library and on a drop-down menu. You learn to create links and use the URL library in Chapter 16.

Creating Animations for the Web

You have two methods for creating animations in Fireworks. The first method is a menu command driven by a dialog box. You select the object and tell Fireworks how you want it to animate it. After supplying Fireworks the animation parameters, the software either creates frames or duplicates the object in a single frame to imply motion. If you prefer more control over your animations, you can add frames to the document and choreograph the changes from frame to frame. You control the time delay between frames. After you create the animation, you can optimize it as an animated GIF for use in a Web design, or export it as a Flash movie (a .swf file). You learn to create animations in Chapter 18; Chapter 19 is devoted to animated banners.

Creating Documents for Print and Other Applications

Although Fireworks is primarily designed to create graphics for the Web and for HTML documents, you can also take advantage of the software's image-editing commands and other editing features to create images for print and multimedia applications. In addition, you can specify a high resolution for a document that you intend to print on an output device when you first create the document. After arranging the elements of your document, you can choose one of the lossless (no compression is applied to the image, therefore no data is lost) optimization methods with 32-bit color.

Summary

Fireworks MX is a powerful application that you use to create images and HTML documents. You can use the software to import all of the popular image formats and combine them with objects you create in Fireworks. The finished document is optimized for export as images, or images and HTML. This chapter served as your introduction to Fireworks. In Chapter 2, you'll become familiar with the Fireworks workspace.

The Complete Reference

Fireworks MX

Chapter 2

Exploring the Fireworks Workspace

ireworks MX puts a lot of power in your hands. With Fireworks MX you can edit images, create animations, design documents to publish on the Web, and more. Prior to using Fireworks, you probably had to employ two or more software programs to accomplish the same tasks you can with Fireworks. This multitasking is not without a price, however. The Fireworks interface, although well laid out, seems like a busy and foreign environment to the uninitiated.

The Fireworks MX default working environment is conveniently laid out, the interface being divided into a document window, a docked toolbar, a docked Property inspector, and a panel window. The toolbox is subdivided into toolgroups and the document window has four tabs. Within the interface you find a menu bar with a plethora of commands and options—so many commands and options, in fact, that the Fireworks programmers had to add submenus to many of the main menu lists. Many of the menu commands open dialog boxes that you use to modify parameters associated with a command.

The Fireworks working environment may be tailored to suit your working preferences, as you'll discover in Chapter 3. However, before you think about changing the interface, it's important to know what role each part of the working environment plays in your workflow. In this chapter, you'll receive a tour of the Fireworks workspace. You'll also find references to the chapters in which the various tools and menu commands are discussed in detail.

Exploring the Interface

The default Fireworks layout, as shown in Figure 2-1, breaks the interface into five main areas: menu bar, toolbox, document window, Property inspector, and panel window. Within the document window is the canvas. When you create a new document, you specify the canvas dimensions and background color. The canvas is where you create your document by designing and modifying items with the Fireworks tools and/or importing items and modifying them with tools and menu commands.

As you create documents in Fireworks, you can switch back and forth from the canvas to the various interface elements. Many of the tools are duplicated with menu commands, while others are standalone tools—such as the drawing tools. The panel window on the right side of the interface contains the most frequently used Fireworks panels. You can access other panels by using menu commands and then close the panels to reclaim working space when they are no longer needed. As you gain experience in Fireworks, you may find that you use some panels more frequently than others. You can dock frequently used panels in the panel window. You can save a modified workspace as a panel layout, a task you'll learn to perform in Chapter 3.

Using the Menu Bar

After you launch the application, your workflow in Fireworks begins with the menu bar. Here you'll find the commands to create and edit your documents. You can also

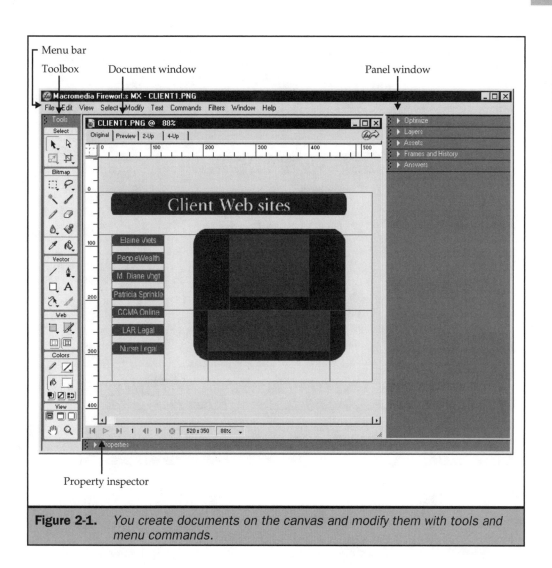

Figure 2-1.   *You create documents on the canvas and modify them with tools and menu commands.*

use menu commands to change your view of the canvas, apply filters to bitmaps, launch panels, summon online help, and more. The Fireworks menu bar is composed of 10 menu items: File, Edit, View, Select, Modify, Text, Commands, Filters, Window, and Help.

As you pass your cursor over the menu bar, each menu item bevels into a button, indicating that the menu can be expanded by clicking the button. After you expand a menu list, you can view the submenus by moving your cursor along the menu bar. After you expand the menu list, click a selection to invoke the command.

Figure 2-2 shows the menu bar with the File menu commands displayed. When you see an arrow to the right of any command, it is an indication that more commands or options are available. Hold your cursor over the command to reveal the additional options.

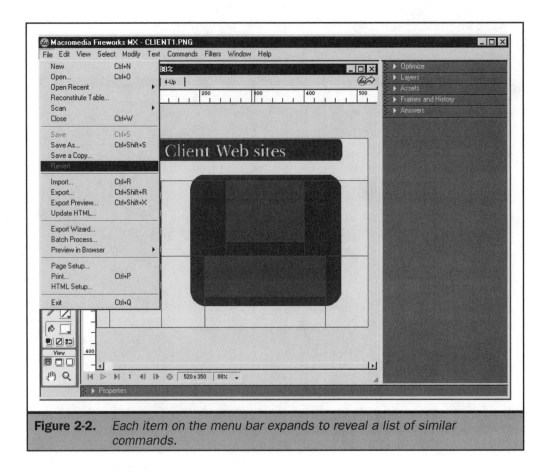

Figure 2-2.   *Each item on the menu bar expands to reveal a list of similar commands.*

In the sections that follow, you'll learn how to use the various menu commands, and you'll find cross references to other chapters where these commands are presented in detail. Note that you can add your own commands to the menu bar and modify them at any time. You cannot, however, delete any Fireworks menu commands.

Using the File Menu

You use the commands on the File menu to create new documents, open existing documents, save documents, import items, export the document, batch process files, and more. Table 2-1 lists the available commands on this menu.

Command	Function(s)	Comments
New	Opens the New Document dialog box	Used to create a new document. See Chapter 4.
Open	Launches the Open dialog box	Used to open existing documents. See Chapter 4.
Open Recent	Displays a list of recently opened documents	Click a document on the list to open it.
Reconstitute Table	Used to re-create a document when the original file is unavailable	
Scan	Used to acquire an image from a TWAIN device attached to the user's computer	See Chapter 6.
Close	Used to close the current document	
Save	Used to save the current document with the current filename	See Chapter 4.
Save As	Used to save the document with a different filename	See Chapter 4.
Save A Copy	Used to save a copy of the current document with the same, or a different filename	
Revert	Used to undo all edits since the document was last saved	Available only after a saved document has been opened and modified
Import	Used to import a file into the current document	
Export	Opens the Export dialog box	Used to export the document as images and/or HTML

Table 2-1.   *File Menu Commands*

Command	Function(s)	Comments
Export Preview	Used to preview the document with current optimization settings	
Update HTML	Updates an exported HTML file while editing the original document	
Export Wizard	Launches a series of dialog boxes to export a document with current optimization	Simplifies and to some extent automates the export process for beginning Fireworks users.
Batch Process	Launches the Fireworks batch processor	See Chapter 20.
Preview In Browser	Enables you to preview the document in a Web browser installed on your system	Includes a submenu that lets you select a primary and secondary Web browser
Page Setup	Opens the Page Setup dialog box	Used to set up a document for print
Print	Opens the Print dialog box	Options let you specify a system printer and page range. See Chapter 4.
HTML Setup	Opens the HTML Setup dialog box	Lets you fine-tune HTML export for a specific HTML editor
Exit	Closes the application	If you choose this command and have unsaved documents open, you are prompted to save the documents.

Table 2-1.   *File Menu Commands* (continued)

Using the Edit Menu

You use the commands in this menu to edit items in your documents, insert objects into your document, set Fireworks Preferences, and modify Keyboard shortcuts. The commands on this menu are listed in Table 2-2.

Command	Function(s)	Comments
Undo	Undoes your last command	You can modify undo levels by changing Preferences.
Redo	Redoes your last command or edit	
Insert	Opens the Insert submenu	Refer to the next section for specific information on the Insert submenu commands.
Libraries	Opens a submenu that lets you access the Fireworks libraries	Libraries are built-in presets of objects, such as animations, buttons, and navigation bars.
Find And Replace	Opens the Find and Replace panel	Find and replace text; find and replace other objects, such as fonts, colors, and URLs used in a document.
Cut	Cuts the currently selected object and pastes it to the clipboard	
Copy	Copies the currently selected object to the clipboard	
Copy Path Outlines	Copies the selected objects to the clipboard as vectors	You can use this command to copy Fireworks vector objects to the clipboard and paste them into other applications, such as Freehand or Flash. This command is used to copy vector objects into older Macromedia software prior to version MX.
Copy HTML Code	Copies the document HTML code, JavaScript, and document images to the clipboard	You can use this command to copy HTML code and images and then paste them into an HTML editor such as Dreamweaver.

Table 2-2.   *Edit Menu Commands*

Command	Function(s)	Comments
Paste	Pastes the contents of the clipboard into the currently selected document	
Clear	Removes the currently selected object(s) from the document without copying it to the clipboard	
Paste As Mask	Pastes a cut object to a selected bitmap as a mask	
Paste Inside	Pastes a cut object inside a selected object	
Paste Attributes	Pastes an object's attributes to another object	
Duplicate	Creates a duplicate of the currently selected object(s), offset from the parent object	
Clone	Creates a duplicate of the selected object, on top of the selected object	
Crop Selected Bitmap	Applies cropping handles to a selected bitmap	
Crop Document	Crops the document to the currently selected object(s)	
Preferences	Opens the Preferences dialog box	You can change preferences to suit your working habits. See Chapter 3.
Keyboard Shortcuts	Opens the Keyboard Shortcuts dialog box	You can create a custom set of keyboard shortcuts or choose an existing keyboard shortcut set. See Chapter 3.

Table 2-2.   *Edit Menu Commands* (continued)

Using the Insert Submenu

If you're a veteran Fireworks user, one of the first things you may notice is the absence of the Insert menu. In order to make room for the Select menu, the Insert menu became a submenu of the Edit menu. Table 2-3 shows the commands available on the Insert submenu.

Command	Function(s)	Comments
New Button	Opens the Button editor	
New Symbol	Opens the Symbol Properties dialog box	After you select a symbol behavior, Fireworks opens the Symbol Editor.
Hotspot	Creates one or more hotspots over the currently selected object(s)	See Chapter 16.
Slice	Creates a slice for the currently selected object(s)	See Chapter 16.
Empty Bitmap	Inserts an empty bitmap object	You can add an empty bitmap to another layer, fill the bitmap with color or gradient, and then filter the bitmap.
Bitmap Via Copy	Copies the current selection into a new bitmap	
Bitmap Via Cut	Cuts the current selection into a new bitmap	
Layer	Adds a layer to the document	See Chapter 12.
Frame	Adds a frame to the document	Frames are used to create animated GIF files. See Chapters 18 and 19.

Table 2-3.   *Insert Submenu Commands*

Using the View Menu

You can modify your view of the canvas with commands from this menu, as well as display the document grid, rulers, and guidelines. Table 2-4 shows the View menu commands.

Command	Function(s)	Comments
Zoom In	Zooms in to the next highest level of magnification	
Zoom Out	Zooms out to the next lowest level of magnification	
Magnification	Displays a drop-down menu of preset magnification levels	You can also click the arrow in the magnification window at the bottom of the workspace.
Fit Selection	Zooms to the selected object(s)	
Fit All	Zooms to display all items on the canvas	
Full Display	Toggles display between showing objects as wireframe outlines or fully textured	Disabling Full Display accelerates redraw when you edit a complex document with many objects.
Macintosh Gamma	Displays the document with Macintosh Gamma	
Hide Selection	Hides the currently selected object	
Show All	Displays all objects	Use this command to display hidden objects again.
Rulers	Toggles ruler display on and off	
Grid	Toggles grid display on and off	
Guides	Toggles guide display on and off	
Slice Guides	Toggles slice guides on and off	

Table 2-4. *View Menu Commands*

Command	Function(s)	Comments
Slice Overlay	Toggles slice overlay on and off	
Hide Edges	Hides or displays edges	When you select objects with hidden edges, the object bounding box is not visible.
Hide Panels	Toggles panel display on or off	Hides panels to gain more workspace.
Status Bar (Windows only)	Toggles status bar display on or off	The Status bar displays information about a currently selected tool or command.

Table 2-4. *View Menu Commands* (continued)

Using the Select Menu

The commands on this menu enable you to select objects and modify selections. You use some commands from this menu on objects and other commands on masks or selections made with the Marquee tools. Table 2-5 displays all the commands on this menu.

Command	Function(s)	Comments
Select All	Selects all objects in the document	
Deselect	Deselects selected objects	You can click outside the canvas or click a blank spot on the canvas to deselect objects.
Superselect	Selects an object group when an individual object in the group is selected	
Subselect	Selects all objects within a selected group	

Table 2-5. *Select Menu Commands*

Command	Function(s)	Comments
Select Similar	Selects areas of color similar to the current selection throughout the document	The color is based on an area you select with one of the Marquee tools, the Lasso tool, or the Magic Wand tool.
Select Inverse	Selects the opposite of the current selection	You use this command on masks created with the Lasso or Magic Wand tool, or on selections made with one of the Marquee tools.
Feather	Opens the Feather Selection dialog box	
Expand Marquee	Opens the Expand Marquee dialog box	Expands a marquee selection by the amount you specify
Contract Marquee	Opens the Contract Marquee dialog box	Reduces the size of a marquee selection by the pixel value you specify
Border Marquee	Opens the Border Marquee dialog box	Creates a border around a marquee by the pixel amount you specify; the border becomes the selection.
Smooth Marquee	Opens the Smooth Marquee dialog box	Samples an area around a marquee by an amount you specify for similar colors and smoothes the selection; useful for bitmap selections made with the Lasso or Magic Wand tool.
Save Bitmap Selection	Saves the current mask or marquee applied to a bitmap	Fireworks can store only one mask as a selection. Bitmap selections are useful when you are working across several layers and need to apply an effect to a bitmap selection you restore on another layer.

Table 2-5. *Select Menu Commands* (continued)

Command	Function(s)	Comments
Restore Bitmap Selection	Restores a previously saved bitmap selection	

Table 2-5. *Select Menu Commands* (continued)

Using the Modify Menu

You use the commands in this menu to modify objects in your document, selections in your document, the document itself, and more. Many of the commands in this menu have submenus that will be discussed in detail in future chapters when they apply to a specific task. Table 2-6 lists all the main commands on the Modify menu.

Command	Function(s)	Comments
Canvas	Opens the Canvas submenu	Use the commands on the submenu to modify canvas size, background color, resolution, and more.
Animation	Opens the Animation submenu	The submenu commands allow you to animate an existing object or modify an existing animation in the document.
Symbol	Opens the Symbol submenu	Use the submenu commands to modify an existing symbol or convert an existing object to a symbol.
Pop-up Menu	Opens the Pop-up menu submenu	The submenu commands are used to modify pop-up menus in your document.

Table 2-6. *Modify Menu Commands*

Command	Function(s)	Comments
Mask	Opens the Mask submenu	Submenu commands are used to modify masks and perform other functions related to masks in your document.
Selective JPEG	Opens the Selective JPEG submenu	Converting a masked area of a bitmap to a selective JPEG lets you optimize the selection at a different optimization level than the rest of the bitmap. See Chapter 6.
Flatten Selection	Converts selected objects into a single object	Flatten objects after you edit them to avoid clutter in the Layers panel.
Merge Down	Merges selected objects into a bitmap	
Flatten Layers	Flattens all layers into a single layer	
Transform	Opens the Transform submenu	Use the submenu commands to resize, skew, or distort a selected object, or to flip and rotate objects.
Arrange	Opens the Arrange submenu	Use the submenu commands to arrange the stacking order of objects in your document.
Align	Opens the Align submenu	Use the submenu commands to align and space objects within your document.
Combine Paths	Opens the Combine Paths submenu	These commands are used on vector objects in your documents, enabling you to combine or otherwise alter overlapping vector objects.

Table 2-6.   *Modify Menu Commands* (continued)

Command	Function(s)	Comments
Alter Path	Opens the Alter Path submenu	Use the submenu commands to reduce the number of points in a path and modify the fill of a closed path.
Group	Combines the selected objects into a group	Grouped objects behave as a single unit and are shown as a single item in the Layers panel.
Ungroup	Ungroups a selected group	

Table 2-6. *Modify Menu Commands* (continued)

Using the Text Menu

When you create text objects for a Fireworks document, you can use any font currently installed on your computer. You use the commands on the Text menu to modify the parameters of a selected block of text. You can also use the Property inspector to perform many of the tasks on this menu—with the exception of calling the Text Editor. When you choose Text on the menu bar, the commands shown in Table 2-7 are available to work with. Creating text objects is presented in Chapter 7.

Command	Functions(s)	Comments
Font	Opens a submenu of all fonts installed on your system	
Size	Opens a submenu of preset font sizes	
Style	Opens a submenu of font styles	Use the submenu commands to create boldface, italic, underlined, or strikethrough text.

Table 2-7. *Text Menu Commands*

Command	Functions(s)	Comments
Editor	Opens the Text Editor	The Text Editor from Fireworks 4 is hiding here. It's a powerful tool for editing text already in your document.
Attach To Path	Attaches a selected block of text to a selected path	Use this command to conform text to an ellipse or curved path.
Detach From Path	Detaches text from a path	
Orientation	Opens the Orientation submenu	Commands on the submenu let you alter the orientation of a selected block of text attached to a path.
Reverse Direction	Reverses the direction of text from left to right or vice versa	
Convert To Paths	Converts selected text to editable paths	When you convert text to a path, the converted text behaves as an editable vector object. You can modify the converted text with any of the Vector tools or related menu commands.
Check Spelling	Checks the spelling of a selected block of text.	A new and welcome feature in Fireworks MX.
Spelling Setup	Opens the Spelling Setup dialog box	Lets you choose a dictionary, edit your personal dictionary, and select from several options.

Table 2-7. *Text Menu Commands* (continued)

Using the Commands Menu

On the Commands menu, you'll find commands to modify the document, add artistic touches to the document, run scripts, and more. If you're familiar with previous versions of Fireworks, you know you can create your own commands to simplify a sequence of frequently performed operations. Your custom commands are stored in this menu. With Fireworks MX, you can also download *extensions* from the Macromedia site. Extensions are commands that have been created by other Fireworks users that automate certain processes or create such things as arrowheads on straight lines. Extensions can be huge time-savers. You manage installed extensions from this menu. Table 2-8 shows the available commands.

Command	Function(s)	Comments
Manage Saved Commands	Opens the Managed Saved Commands dialog box	You can delete and rename saved commands.
Manage Extensions	Launches the Macromedia Extension Manager	If you have the Macromedia Extension Manager installed on your system, you can add new extensions to Fireworks and delete existing ones.
Run Script	Opens the Open dialog box, enabling you to locate and load a saved script	
Creative	Opens the Creative submenu	You can add picture frames to a document or convert selected bitmaps to sepia tone and more.
Data-Driven Graphics Wizard	Opens the Data-Driven Graphics Wizard dialog box	You can assign variables to text, images, and hotspots and export the file as multiple documents with unique information taken from an XML file.
Document	Opens the Document submenu	Use these commands to modify how objects are distributed to layers, reverse frames, and so on.
Panel Layout Sets	Choose from present panel layouts for popular desktip sizes	When you create your own panel sets and save them, they are added to this menu.
Reset Warning Dialogs	Resets all warning dialogs to installed defaults	

Table 2-8. *Commands Menu Commands*

Command	Function(s)	Comments
Save Panel Layout	Opens a dialog box prompting you for a layout name	You can arrange the workspace to suit your preference and save the layout as a menu option.
Web	Opens the Web submenu	

Table 2-8.   *Commands Menu Commands* (continued)

Using the Filters Menu

Previous versions of Fireworks listed this as the Xtras menu. Many Fireworks users use the software for all their image editing. Perhaps this is why this menu now has a more appropriate name. The commands on this menu are used to modify images; for example, you can adjust the color characteristics of an image or sharpen a scanned image. Table 2-9 shows the commands available from the Filters menu. All the commands open submenus that include filters that perform similar functions. These filters will be discussed as needed in conjunction with modifying bitmap images.

Command	Function(s)	Comments
Adjust Color	Opens the Adjust Color submenu	Modify a bitmap's brightness, saturation, contrast, and more.
Blur	Opens the Blur submenu	Use these filters to apply anything from a subtle blur to a Gaussian blur.
Other	Opens a submenu with two filters: Convert to Alpha and Find Edges	
Sharpen	Opens the Sharpen submenu	Use these filters to sharpen a poorly defined image.
Eye Candy 4000 LE	Opens the Eye Candy 4000 LE submenu	Eye Candy is a popular third-party plug-in. The Fireworks version contains a light edition with 3 filters.

Table 2-9.   *Filters Menu Commands*

Command	Function(s)	Comments
Alien Skin Splat LE	Opens a submenu	The Fireworks light edition of Splat contains 1 filter that you use to apply custom effects to edges of a bitmap object such as torn paper.

Table 2-9.   *Filters Menu Commands* (continued)

Tip

When you're creating a document with several bitmap images, you often use the same filter on all images. After you apply a filter to a bitmap, Fireworks remembers the setting you use and a new option appears at the top of the Filters menu: the option to repeat the command. To use the same filter on another bitmap, select the bitmap, open the Filters menu, and choose the command at the top of the menu to apply the previously used filter to the selected bitmap using the same settings.

Using the Window Menu

You use the commands on the Window menu to open and close panels. Commands are also available to arrange the view of multiple windows. Many of the commands have submenus. Table 2-10 shows the available Window menu commands.

Command	Function(s)	Comments
New Window	Opens the current document in a new window	
Toolbars (Windows only)	Opens the Toobars submenu	These commands let you show or hide the common Windows toolbar that includes buttons for printing, saving, opening documents, and so on. You can also show or hide the Windows Status bar that displays information about a selected tool or menu command.

Table 2-10.   *Window Menu Commands*

Command	Function(s)	Comments
Tools	Shows or hides the Fireworks toolbox	
Properties	Shows or hides the Property inspector	
Answers	Shows or hides the Fireworks Answer panel	The Answer panel contains information about the application and a link to tutorials, plus a link to update the panel.
Optimize	Shows or hides the Optimize panel	See Chapter 21.
Layers	Shows or hides the Layers panel	See Chapter 12.
Frames	Shows or hides the Frames panel	Use this panel to add frames to a document that includes animation. See Chapters 18 and 19.
History	Shows or hides the History panel	This command records the steps you use to create a document. You can use it to create your own commands. See Chapter 20
Styles	Shows or hides the Styles panel	Styles are preset effects like beveled edges that you use to modify objects.
Library	Shows or hides the document Library panel	The document Library contains symbols, which are reusable graphics. See Chapter 13.
URL	Shows or hides the URL panel	Open this panel to add any URL used in the document to a button or hotspot.
Color Mixer	Shows or hides the Color Mixer panel	See Chapter 8.
Swatches	Shows or hides the Swatches panel	You use this panel to fill objects with colors from a preset palette.

Table 2-10.   *Window Menu Commands* (continued)

Command	Function(s)	Comments
Info	Shows or hides the Info panel	This panel displays the current coordinates of a selected object as it is being dragged. The panel also displays the current coordinates of the mouse and the color value of the area the mouse is over.
Behaviors	Shows or hides the Behaviors panel	See Chapter 17.
Find And Replace	Opens the Find and Replace panel	Find and replace text; find and replace other objects, such as fonts, colors, and URLs used in a document.
Project Log	Opens the Project Log panel	See Chapter 20
Align	Shows or hides the Align panel	Use this panel to align objects to the document and align selected objects.
Sitespring	Opens the Sitespring panel	Sitespring is a Macromedia utility that is used to manage Web site assets between designers and clients. You must subscribe to the service for the panel to access the various features of Sitespring. For more information, view the Sitespring Web site at: www.macromedia.com/software/sitespring/
Cascade	Displays open documents in cascading fashion	
Tile Horizontal	Displays open documents as horizontal tiles	
Tile Vertical	Displays open documents as vertical tiles	

Table 2-10.   *Window Menu Commands* (continued)

Command	Function(s)	Comments
Documents	Each open document has its own listing.	Click a document title to open that document's window.

Table 2-10.   *Window Menu Commands* (continued)

Using the Help Menu

The last Fireworks menu group has commands that you use to access online help menus, link to the Fireworks Support Center, and link to Fireworks forums, as well as to get additional information about the application. When you open the Help menu, the commands shown in Table 2-11 appear.

Commands	Function(s)	Comments
Welcome	Launches a panel with links to information about using Fireworks for graphics and Web design	Also includes a What's New link
What's New	Launches the What's New section of Fireworks online help	
Using Fireworks	Opens the Fireworks online help document	This command opens a searchable HTML document with information about the application.
Manage Extensions	Opens the Manage Extensions dialog box	Extensions are commands and scripts created by other Fireworks users that you can download from Macromedia's Web site.
Fireworks Support Center	Opens your Web browser and links you to the Fireworks Support Center	You must be logged onto the Internet to use this feature.

Table 2-11.   *Help Menu Commands*

Commands	Function(s)	Comments
Macromedia Online Forums	Provides a link to Macromedia's online forums	Launches your default Web browser and opens the Macromedia Forums page when you are online.
Online Registration	Links you to Macromedia's Online Registration page	You must be logged onto the Internet to use this command.
Print Registration	Prints a copy of the registration form using your system printer	
About Fireworks	Opens a splash screen that displays information about the application, including a list of all members of the development team	

Table 2-11. *Help Menu Commands* (continued)

Viewing Your Work in the Document Window

When you create a new document, Fireworks creates a document window in the middle of the workspace. When you create a new document with a canvas size larger than the available space for the document window, the canvas magnification is adjusted so the entire canvas is visible. The document window has four tabs, each offering a different preview of the document. The document Window tabs, as shown in Figure 2-3, are Original, Preview, 2-Up, and 4-Up. To preview the document in another window, click its tab.

Original Document View

When you create a document, the Original Document view is selected by default. The document is completely editable in this view. You can add, delete, and edit elements in the Original Document view. As you can see in Figure 2-3, all the guides and other editing tools are visible when you create your work. All the elements in the Original Document view are displayed with their original resolutions. You cannot see the effects of your optimization settings on your artwork until you select one of the other preview modes. To preview your document as optimized for export, click the appropriate tab.

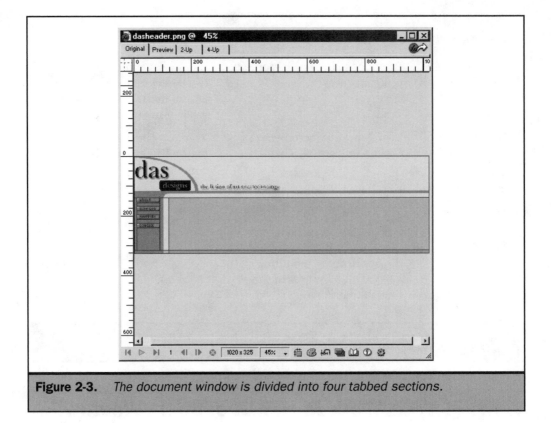

Figure 2-3.   *The document window is divided into four tabbed sections.*

Preview Mode

When you click the Preview tab, you see a preview of the document with the current optimization settings applied. The document, as shown in Figure 2-4, is previewed as it will appear when exported. At the upper-right corner of the window, the file size as optimized is displayed along with the download time at 56 Kbps connection speed. The document in this figure is being previewed with slice guides and overlays hidden.

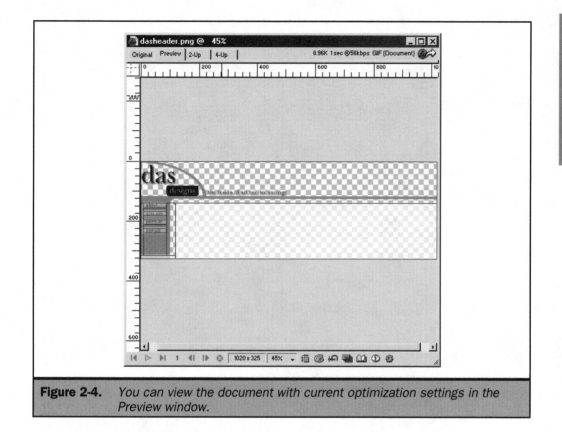

Figure 2-4.   *You can view the document with current optimization settings in the Preview window.*

2-Up Preview Mode

When you click the 2-Up tab, you can compare the document as currently optimized with the original version of the document, as shown in Figure 2-5. The documents are tiled horizontally; the window on the left displays the original document, and the window on the right displays the document as currently optimized. As you tweak the optimization settings, the window on the right updates to reflect your changes. By using this visual side-by-side comparison, you can achieve the optimal compromise between file size and image fidelity.

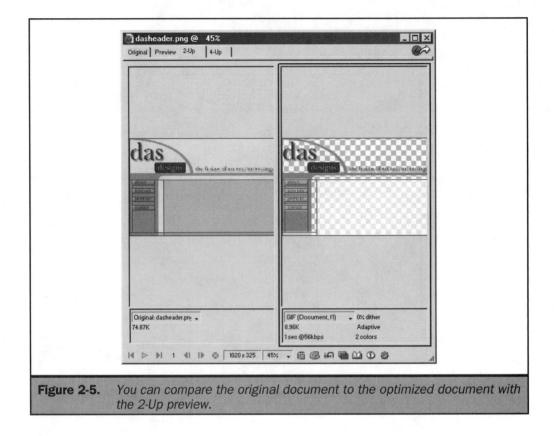

Figure 2-5.   *You can compare the original document to the optimized document with the 2-Up preview.*

Note   *Optimizing documents is covered in detail in Chapter 21.*

4-Up Preview Window

When you click the 4-Up tab, the document window is split into four tiles, each containing a version of your document. When you click the tab, the original document is displayed in the upper-left tile. The other three tiles contain a preview with the current optimization settings applied. Click inside a window and you can change the optimization settings for that preview tile without affecting the optimization settings in the other windows. Working in this manner, you can compare the original against three different optimization settings, as shown in Figure 2-6.

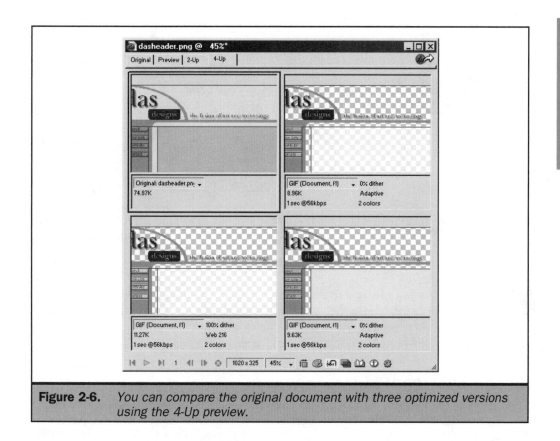

Figure 2-6. *You can compare the original document with three optimized versions using the 4-Up preview.*

Using the Send To Button

When you create a document in Fireworks, you can work interactively with other Macromedia applications installed on your machine. If, for example, you are creating artwork for use in a Dreamweaver document, you can export HTML, update HTML, copy HTML to the clipboard, or launch Dreamweaver all from within Fireworks. To use your Fireworks document, or a selected element from your Fireworks document with another Macromedia application, click the Send To button in the upper-right corner of the document window to open the menu shown below. Integrating Fireworks with other software will be covered in detail in Chapter 23.

Send To button

Send To menu

Caution   *When you work with several applications open at the same time, you put a tremendous strain on your system resources. If you max out your system resources and your computer locks up, you'll lose all your current work. Therefore, before opening another application, it is a good idea to save the document.*

Using the Launcher Bar

The Launcher Bar that was standard with Fireworks 4 is hidden by default in Fireworks MX. You can use the Launcher Bar to open the most frequently used Fireworks panels. To display the Launcher Bar, choose Edit | Preferences, and in the General section of the Preferences dialog box, choose Show Tab Icons. After you choose this preference option, the Launcher Bar is displayed at the bottom of the document window, as shown here:

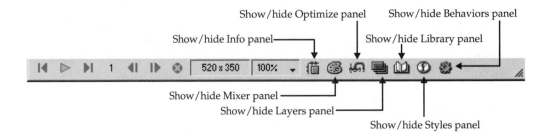

Show/hide Optimize panel

Show/hide Behaviors panel

Show/hide Info panel

Show/hide Library panel

Show/hide Mixer panel

Show/hide Layers panel

Show/hide Styles panel

Creating and Modifying Objects with Tools

After you create a new document, Fireworks creates a blank canvas for you to work on. The canvas is where you create the image you'll eventually optimize and export. You can import objects into the document or create objects with tools from the toolbox. By default, the toolbox is docked on the left side of the interface. The toolbox shown here is divided into six sections: Selection, Bitmap, Vector, Web, Color, and View.

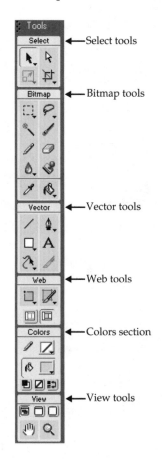

To use a tool, click its icon. When you see an icon with an inverted triangle at its lower-right corner, the icon can be used to access more than one tool. Click the icon to reveal a flyout menu showing all the other tools, as shown below. Throughout this book, individual tools will be discussed in detail as they are used in conjunction with real-world tasks.

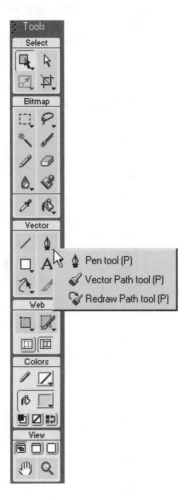

If you're not sure what a particular tool does, pause your mouse over the tool's icon, and soon a tooltip appears with the tool's name and the keyboard shortcut you can use to access the tool quickly.

Using the Select Tools

You use the tools in this section of the toolbox to select individual objects, multiple objects, objects behind other objects, points on a path, or individual items from an object group. To use a tool, click its icon. If the tool is part of a group, the flyout menu appears. Click the desired tool to select it. The Select tools are shown here:

Using the Bitmap Tools

You use the tools in this section of the toolbox to modify selected bitmap images in your documents. Using the tools in this group, you can create marquee and color selections, touch up images, apply gradients to selected areas of an image, and much more. The tools in this group will be presented in detail throughout the book as they apply to a task. By clicking an icon in the bitmap group, shown next, you either select a tool or reveal a tool group's flyout menu.

Using the Vector Tools

You use the tools in the Vector tool group to create vector objects such as circles, rounded rectangles, rectangles, polygons, and paths. In addition a tool to create anti-aliased text and transform vector objects in your document is also available. The Vector tools shown in the following illustration are single tool icons and tool groups. To select a tool, click its icon. To select a tool from a tool group, click the group's icon to expand the flyout menu, and then click the icon of the tool you want. Tools from this group are covered in detail as they apply to the various tasks you'll learn throughout the course of this book.

Using the Web Tools

You use the Web tools to slice a document or create interactive areas known as *hotspots*. Two icons in this section are tool groups. Click the icon to display the group's flyout menu, and then click the appropriate icon to select the tool. The other icons are used to display or hide hotspots and slices. The Web tool section of the toolbox is illustrated here:

Using the Color Wells

When you launch Fireworks for the first time the default *Stroke* (outline or line) color is black and the default *Fill* (solid color) is white. Fortunately, you can use any color you want by clicking the color swatch in either well and then choosing a color from the pop-up palette. The colors in these wells are applied to the objects you create with the Vector tool and certain Bitmap tools. The subject of color is covered in detail in Chapter 8. Fills are covered in Chapter 10, and strokes are discussed in Chapter 9. The Colors section of the toolbox is shown here:

Using the View Tools

You use the tools in this group to change the magnification of the canvas and choose a screen viewing mode. These tools are discussed in detail in Chapter 11. The tools in this group are illustrated here:

Modifying Objects and Tools with Panels

When you edit objects and perform certain operations that require you to change several parameters, you use a panel. The default Fireworks layout houses five panels (Optimize, Layers, Assets, Frames and History, and Answers) in the panel window on the right side of the interface. For most Fireworks users, these are the most frequently used panels. You'll find the other ten panels (Style, Library, URL, Color Mixer, Swatches, Info, Behaviors, Find and Replace, Sitespring, and Align) on the Window menu. Individual panels will be discussed throughout the course of this book as they relate to specific tasks. Figure 2-7 shows floating panels in the workspace as well as the default panels in the panel window.

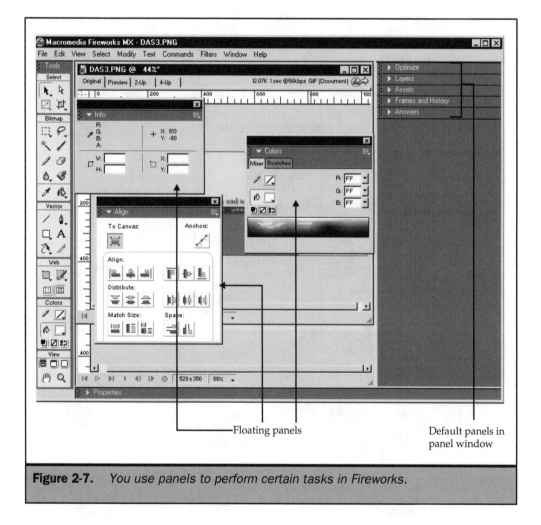

—Floating panels

Default panels in
panel window

Figure 2-7.   *You use panels to perform certain tasks in Fireworks.*

Opening Panels

When you launch Fireworks for the first time, the panels in the panel window are closed. To open a panel, click the arrow to the left of the panel's title. Alternatively, you can choose Window and select the name of the panel in the panel window you want to open.

To open a panel not in the panel window, choose Window and then choose the name of the panel you want to open. When you open a panel from the Window menu that is not docked in the panel window, it appears as a floating window in the workspace. Figure 2-8 shows one open panel in the panel window and one open floating panel.

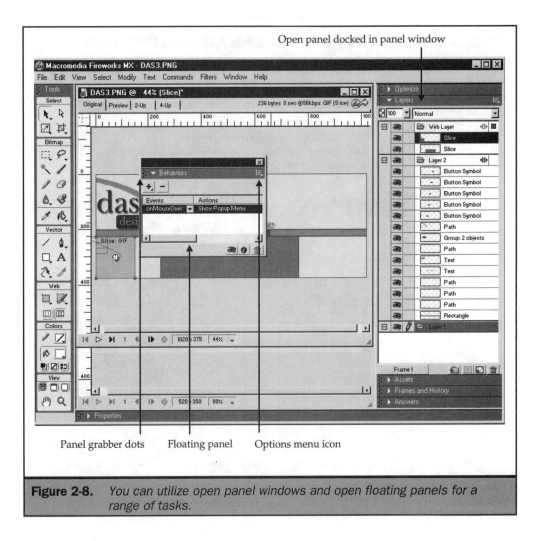

Figure 2-8. *You can utilize open panel windows and open floating panels for a range of tasks.*

Closing Panels

After you perform a task with a panel, you can close it to reduce clutter in the workspace. To close a panel, do one of the following:

- Choose Window and then select the name of the panel you want to close.
- Click the panel's close button.

When you close a floating panel that is part of another group, the entire group closes. If you need to access any panel within a group in the near future, you should collapse the group to gain working space rather than close it.

 You can also close a panel by clicking the icon in the upper-right corner of the panel and then choosing Close Panel from the Options menu.

Collapsing Panels

After you use a panel to perform a task, you can collapse it to gain working space. To collapse a panel, click the arrow to the left of the panel's title. When you collapse a floating panel, it remains in the workspace.

Moving Floating Panels

When you have one or more panels floating in the workspace, you can move them to another location.

To move an open or collapsed panel, do one of the following:

- Click the grabber dots to the left of the panel's title to select the panel. Then drag it to the desired location and release the mouse button.
- Click the solid bar above the panel's title to select the panel. Then drag it to another location and release the mouse button.

As you drag a panel, a ghost image of the panel appears, giving you an indication of the panel's new position.

Docking Panels

You can dock panels to each other, or you can dock additional panels in the panel window. You can also group panels together, a task you'll learn to perform in an upcoming section. After you group two or more panels and close one of the panels, Fireworks remembers the panel group you created and restores it the next time you open either panel. As well, Fireworks remembers your settings when you close the application, and all panel groups you created are restored the next time you launch the application. If you use Fireworks in different capacities, you can save a panel layout and have it appear as a menu option. You'll learn to create custom panel sets in Chapter 3.

To dock one panel to another:

1. Click the grabber dots to the left of the panel's name.

2. Drag the panel to a floating panel or the panel window. As you approach another panel, a highlighted bar appears in the unselected panel, indicating that you can successfully dock the selected panel.

3. Release the mouse button to complete the docking operation.

Using a Panel Options Menu

Each panel has an Options menu that contains certain menu commands relevant to the tasks you'll perform with a selected panel. To open a panel's Options menu, click the Options menu icon shown previously in Figure 2-8. Each panel's Options menu varies depending on the actions you perform with the panel.

Undocking a Panel

You can remove a panel from a docked position at any time. When you float a panel that was docked with another panel, it appears as a separate entity in the workspace.

To undock a panel:

1. Click the grabber dots to the left of the panel's title.

2. Drag the panel beyond the boundary of the panel it is docked with and release the mouse button. As you drag the panel, a ghost image appears indicating its present position.

3. Release the mouse button when the panel is in the desired location.

Creating Panel Groups

When you dock one panel with another each panel has its own title. Another method you can use to optimize workspace is to group one panel with another. When you create a group of one or more panels, they have a single title. An example of this is the Frames and History panel group in the default panel set. You open a panel group by clicking the arrow to the left of the group's name. After you open a panel group, you access an individual panel by clicking its tab.

If you use certain panels in conjunction with each other, you can group them. When you add a panel to a group, its name appears on the group's title bar. For example, if you group the Optimize panel with the Layers panel, the panel's title reads: Layers and Optimize. The following example explains how to group the Optimize panel with the Layers panel. The steps are the same for creating other panel groups; the only difference being the name of the panel in the Options menu command.

To group the Optimize panel with the Layers panel:

1. Click the arrow to the left of the word Optimize. The Optimize panel opens.

2. Click the Options menu icon and from the Options menu choose Group Optimize Panel with | Layers. The Optimize and Layers panel are now a single group called Layers and Optimize. If desired, you can now rename the panel group by choosing Rename Panel Group from the panel's Options menu.

Removing a Panel From a Group

You can also modify the panel layout by removing a panel from a group. This option is handy if you have a panel you use frequently and prefer that it appear in the workspace as a single floating panel.

To remove a panel from a group:

1. Click the arrow to the left of the panel group's name. The panel group opens.

2. Click the tab of the panel you want to remove from the group.

3. Click the Options menu icon and from the Options menu choose Group [*Panel's name*] with | Create New Panel Group. The panel is removed from the group and appears in the workspace as a separate group.

Exploring the Property Inspector

An important new feature of Fireworks is the Property inspector, which serves many functions. It indicates the properties of an object and gives you certain options or parameters you can assign to the selected object. The Property inspector does away with some of the panels you may have become accustomed to in Fireworks 4. For example, the functions of the old Effects panel are now carried out within the Property inspector. The actual fields displayed in the Property inspector vary depending on the object selected when you open the inspector.

By default, the Property inspector is docked at the bottom of the workspace. You can undock the Property inspector and move it to a new location by following the previously outlined steps for undocking a panel. However, the default position of the Property inspector is ideal for most designers. You can expand or collapse the Property inspector by clicking the arrow to the left of the panel's name. When you expand or collapse the Property inspector, it remains in its docked position. You can hide or display the Property inspector by choosing Window | Properties.

Figure 2-9 shows the Property inspector as it appears when a bitmap is selected.

Using the Fireworks Grid

When you create objects and move them about the canvas, you can rely on the Property inspector to display accurate coordinates of an object as you move it. You may also find

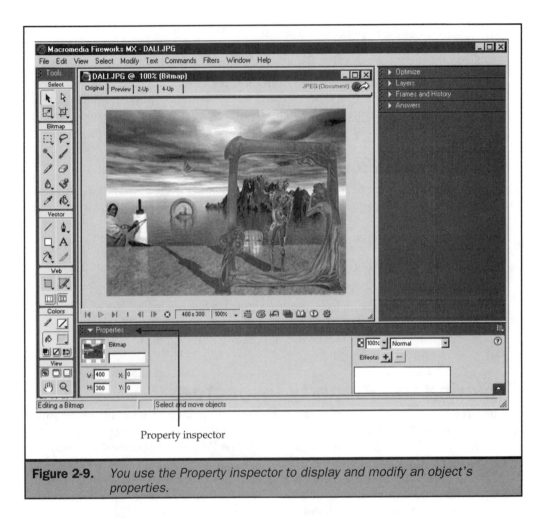

Property inspector

Figure 2-9.   *You use the Property inspector to display and modify an object's properties.*

it is to your advantage to display the grid for visual reference when creating artwork in Fireworks. You can display the grid when needed and hide it when not needed. You can modify the size of the grid spacing as well as enable grid snapping. When you enable grid snapping, objects will snap to grid intersection points as you move them about the canvas. Figure 2-10 shows a document being created with the grid enabled.

Enabling the Grid

By default, the grid is disabled. You can display the grid whenever you need help aligning objects or need a visual reference for other purposes. When you enable the grid, it is displayed when you open existing files or create new documents. If you exit

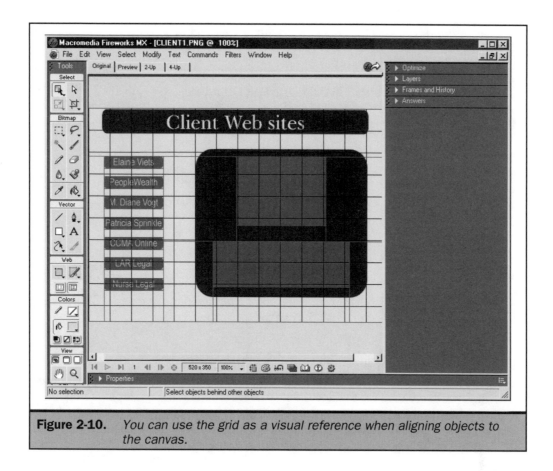

Figure 2-10.   *You can use the grid as a visual reference when aligning objects to the canvas.*

Fireworks with the grid enabled, it is displayed when you next launch Fireworks and open or create a document.

To display the grid, do one of the following:

- Choose View | Grid | Show Grid.

- Choose View | Grid | Edit Grid, and then choose the Show Grid option in the Edit Grid dialog box.

To hide the grid, invoke the Show Grid command again.

Modifying the Grid

The default color for the grid is black, and each grid square is 36 pixels by 36 pixels, which works well for most documents. However, when the default grid setup does not suit the document you are working on (for example, when creating a document with a black background, you cannot see the grid with its default black color), you can modify the grid color and spacing.

Here's how to modify the grid:

1. Choose View | Grid | Edit Grid. The Edit Grid dialog box appears.

2. Click the Color swatch and choose a color from the pop-up palette. Choose a color that contrasts well with the canvas background color.

3. Click the Show Grid option to display the grid.

4. Click the Snap to Grid option to enable grid snapping.

5. Enter a value in the width and height fields to determine grid spacing. Choose a value that works for the document you are creating. For example, if you are modifying a grid for a document that is 600 pixels wide by 20 pixels high that you are using to create a navigation bar with six buttons that measure 100 pixels by 20 pixels, modify the grid so that each space measures 100 pixels by 20 pixels.

6. Click OK to apply the changes.

When you modify the grid, you do not change the color and spacing of the default grid; the modified grid is applied only to the document that was open when you invoked the command. When you save the document, the modified grid settings are saved with it.

Using the Snap To Option

When you enable the Snap To option, objects are attracted to grid intersections. You can take advantage of this feature whether or not the grid is displayed.

To enable grid snapping, do one of the following:

- Choose View | Grid | Snap To Grid.
- Choose View | Grid | Edit Grid, and then choose the Snap To Grid option from the Edit Grid dialog box.

Using Rulers

Another visual aid you can use in your work is a ruler. When needed, you can display a vertical and horizontal ruler. Each ruler is measured in pixels. The individual hash marks for each ruler are spaced in 10-pixel increments. To display rulers as shown in Figure 2-11, choose View | Rulers.

Changing the Ruler Registration Point

By default, the registration point (a measurement of zero pixels) of each ruler is located at the upper-left corner of the canvas. If needed, you can move the registration point for the rulers to any position on the canvas. Note that the change affects the coordinates for the document.

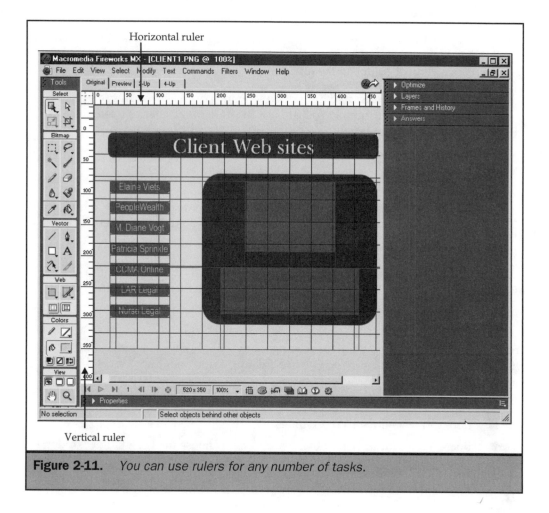

Figure 2-11.   *You can use rulers for any number of tasks.*

To change the registration point for the rulers, do the following:

1. Click the icon that looks like an intersecting vertical and horizontal dashed line at the upper-left corner of the document window and drag it to a new position on the canvas. As you drag, dashed vertical and horizontal lines indicate the position of your cursor.

2. Release the mouse button when the dashed lines are where you want the ruler's registration point to be. After you release the mouse button, document coordinates will be measured beginning at the ruler's new registration point.

To restore the ruler's registration point to the default, double-click the dashed line icon where the rulers intersect.

Creating Guides

After you toggle the ruler display on, you can create guide lines as a further visual aid. You can create as many vertical and horizontal guides as you need to aid your work.

To create a vertical guide, do the following:

1. Click the vertical ruler and drag into the workspace. As you drag, a vertical guide follows your cursor. You can use the horizontal ruler as a reference to place the guide accurately.

2. Release the mouse button when the guide is in the desired position.

To create a horizontal guide:

1. Click the horizontal ruler and drag into the workspace. As you drag, a horizontal guide follows your cursor. Use the vertical ruler as a guide for placement.

2. Release the mouse button when the guide is in the desired position.

You can change the position of any guide by clicking it and dragging it to a new position. After you have the guides aligned properly, you can lock them in place.

Locking Guides

You lock guides to prevent them from being inadvertently selected and moved while you're editing another object. When you're creating a document with several items, it's good practice to lock guides.

To lock guides in their current position, do one of the following:

■ Choose View Guides | Lock Guides.

■ Choose View Guides | Edit Guides, and then choose the Lock Guides option.

To unlock locked guides, invoke the command again.

Modifying Guides

The default color for Fireworks guides works well in most instances. However, when you are creating a document with a background color close to the default guide color, guides become difficult to see. You can easily modify the guide display color to suit the document you are creating by editing the guides.

Here's how to edit guides:

1. Choose View | Guides | Edit Guides. The Guides dialog box opens, as shown here:

2. To change the display guide color, click the Color swatch and choose a color from the pop-up palette. Choose a color that contrasts well with the canvas background color.

3. To show or hide guides, choose the Show Guides option.

4. To enable or disable snapping to guides, choose the Snap To Guides option.

5. To lock guides in place choose the Lock Guides option.

6. To erase guides from a document permanently, click Clear All.

7. Click OK to finish editing guides.

The changes you apply are linked to the document when you save it. The default Fireworks guide parameters are not affected by your edits.

Enabling the Snap To Guides Option

You can modify guides in your document so that objects snap to guides when you move a selected object within the guide's range. This option is handy when you need to align items precisely, for instance a vertical column of navigation buttons.

To enable guide snapping, do one of the following:

- Choose View | Guides | Snap To Guides.
- Choose View | Guides | Edit Guides and then choose the Snap To Guides option from the Guides dialog box.

To disable guide snapping, invoke the command again.

Exploring the Modify Toolbar (Windows Only)

If you work on the Windows platform, you have another toolbar at your disposal. You can use the Modify toolbar to group or ungroup objects, join or split paths, arrange the stacking order of objects in your document, align objects in your document, and rotate and flip objects. The buttons on this toolbar duplicate many of the commands in the Modify menu. If you prefer working from a toolbar, you can duplicate any of these commands by clicking the appropriate button. To display the Modify toolbar shown in the following illustration, choose Window | Toolbars | Modify.

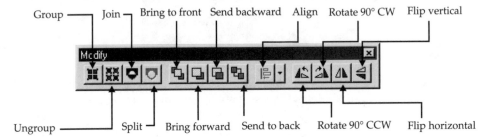

The Modify toolbar is initially displayed as a floating toolbar. You can dock it to the top, bottom, left, or right side of the workspace by clicking its title bar and dragging it to the desired location.

Summary

In this chapter, you learned how the various elements of the workspace are used when creating a Fireworks document. You also learned how to dock and undock panels and how to display the grid and create guides as a visual aid. Now that you know what everything is and what it's used for, you'll be happy to know you can alter the workspace to suit your working preferences, a topic that is covered in Chapter 3.

Chapter 3

Optimizing Your Workspace

N o two designers work alike. Some people like all their tools scattered about the workspace, while others like things neat and tidy, at arm's reach for quick retrieval. No matter what type of designer you are, you can optimize the Fireworks workspace to suit your working habits. You can also modify the keyboard shortcuts; or if you prefer, you can choose from a list of preset keyboard shortcuts. If you are familiar with Adobe Photoshop, you can choose a Photoshop keyboard shortcut set, a handy feature if you're new to Fireworks but intimately familiar with Photoshop. Fireworks MX has enough flexibility built into the software for almost any designer to arrive at an optimal setup. In this chapter, you learn to modify the workspace to suit your habits, modify preferences, and modify keyboard shortcuts.

Modifying Panel Layout

When the Fireworks programmers designed the workspace, they incorporated past versions of the software, their own innate wisdom, and the layout of other Macromedia software to arrive at a compromise they deemed best for their customers. However, they also realized that some people work differently than the average user. If you're a member of that select group, you'll be happy to know you can rearrange the default workspace, shown in Figure 3-1, to your liking.

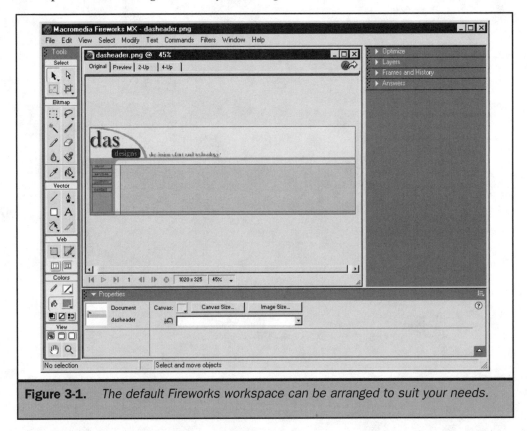

Figure 3-1.   *The default Fireworks workspace can be arranged to suit your needs.*

In Chapter 2, you learned how to move panels, dock panels, create panel groups, and collapse panels. When you exit Fireworks, your settings are saved, and the next time you launch Fireworks, all of the panels are where you last left them. That's great if you use Fireworks in just one capacity. However, if you use Fireworks to its full capacity, you'll be editing bitmap images, creating Web pages, creating graphics, creating animations, and more. You can rearrange the workspace to create an ideal setup when you use Fireworks for a different task than when you last used the program. Alternatively, you can create an optimal setup for a specific task you perform with Fireworks and save the layout as a panel set.

Creating Your Optimal Workspace

You can modify the Fireworks workspace to suit your needs by arranging the various elements. When you create an optimal workspace, you can save it as a panel set. A custom panel set becomes part of the Commands menu. You can launch a panel set at any time by choosing it from the Commands menu.

You can create a custom panel layout by doing the following:

1. Open the panels you'll use when performing the task for which you're creating the panel set.

2. In the panel window, dock panels you use frequently. As an example, if you're generating a panel set for the purpose of creating vector objects, such as buttons and nav bars, open the Mixer panel, and dock it in the panel window.

3. If you prefer to leave panels floating in the workspace, move them to your preferred position. Collapse the panels if you prefer to work with maximum desktop space.

4. Group similar panels together to create one or more panel groups.

5. In the panel window, close any panels not needed for the application (task) for which the panel set is being created. As an example, although the Answers panel is helpful, it is infrequently used, especially when you master Fireworks. If you do have a need for a removed panel, you can always choose Window and then select the panel from the menu.

6. Perform any other modifications you deem necessary to create the optimal panel group for your intended application.

After you create your optimal workspace, you may want to save it as a panel set.

Saving a Panel Set

After you create an optimal workspace, you can save it as a panel set for future use. You can create as many panel sets as you need. When you need to switch from one panel set to another, select a new layout from the Commands menu.

To save a custom panel set, follow these steps:

1. Choose Command | Save Panel Layout. The following dialog box appears.

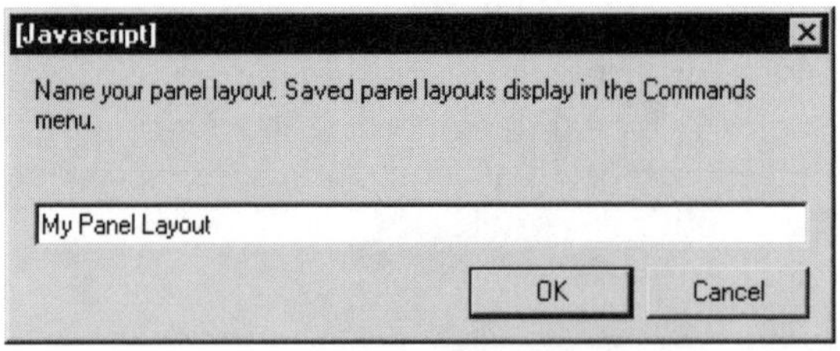

2. Enter a name for the panel layout. Choose a name that reflects the type of operations you perform with the panel layout. If other designers use Fireworks on the same computer, add your initials to the end of the name.

3. Click OK to save the panel layout. Fireworks saves the panel layout, and it appears on the Commands menu.

To rearrange the workspace to the configuration of a custom panel set, choose Commands | Panel Layout Sets and then select the desired layout from the drop-down menu.

Deleting a Saved Panel Set

You can delete a panel set when it has outlived its usefulness. Deleting unused panel sets reduces clutter on the Commands menu.

You can delete a panel set by doing the following:

1. Choose Commands | Manage Saved Commands. The Manage Saved Commands dialog box, shown in the following illustration, appears. The dialog box shows all of the custom panel layouts, as well as other commands you have saved.

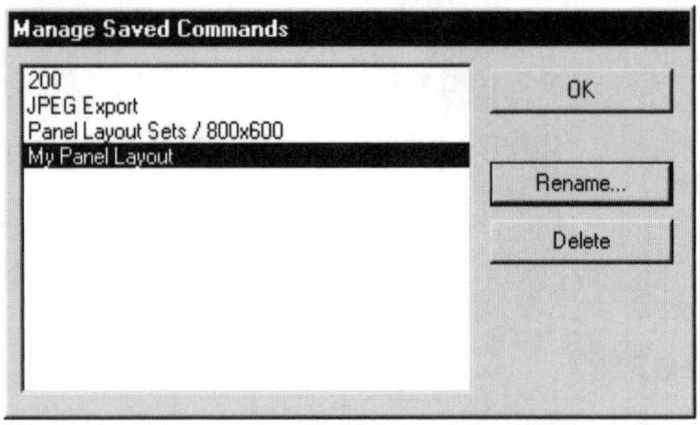

2. Select a panel set and click Delete to remove the panel layout.

You can also rename a panel layout. To rename a panel layout, do the following:

1. Choose Commands | Manage Saved Commands to open the dialog box shown in the previous illustration.

2. Select the panel set you want to rename and then click Rename. The Save Command dialog box, shown here, appears.

3. Enter a new name for the panel set and then click OK. The panel set's new name appears on the Panel Set's Layout Sets menu.

Modifying Preferences

In addition to creating custom panel sets, you can also modify Fireworks preferences. You can change the default colors, the number of undo steps, and much more by modifying preferences. You can modify preferences in five categories: General, Editing, Launch and Edit, Folders, and Import. You can modify every preference category at once, or as the need arises. Every preference category is conveniently located in the Preferences dialog box.

To open the Preferences dialog box, as shown here, choose Edit | Preferences. You can modify preferences in five categories.

Setting General Preferences

You modify General preferences when you need to change the default stroke, fill, or highlight colors, levels of undo, or the bitmap interpolation method. When you open the Preferences dialog box, the General tab is selected by default.

To modify General preferences, do the following:

1. Open the Preferences dialog box, as outlined previously under "Modifying Preferences."

2. Enter a value in the Undo field to change the number of undo steps. You can specify up to 100 levels of undo. When you create a document, Fireworks records and displays as part of the History panel every step you perform, up to the undo level you specify. You can use the History panel to backtrack your steps or save commands. When you exceed the specified undo levels, the oldest command is deleted from the list and from system memory. If you use Fireworks with several applications open at the same time and your system barely meets Fireworks' minimum requirements, you may find it advantageous to specify a low undo level. Setting a low undo level uses less memory and may improve performance. Your new undo setting will not take effect until you relaunch Fireworks.

3. In the color section, you can modify the stroke color (black by default), the fill color (white by default), or the highlight color (light blue by default). Click a swatch, and the pop-up color palette appears. Click a color to select it, and the swatch changes to reflect the new color.

4. In the Interpolation field, you can modify the way Fireworks interpolates pixels when images are rescaled. Click the triangle to the right of the Interpolation field and choose one of the following:

   ■ **Bicubic**   This is the default interpolation method and generally yields the highest image quality.

   ■ **Bilinear**   This interpolation method provides the next best quality when resizing images.

   ■ **Soft**   This method was the default in the first versions of Fireworks. Choose this method, and resized images will be blurred slightly. This method also helps remove unwanted artifacts produced by other interpolation methods.

   ■ **Nearest Neighbor**   This interpolation method produces sharp jagged edges when images are rescaled. Images will have sharp contrast with no blurring of edges.

5. Choose Show Tabbed Icons to display the Launcher Bar and icons for each tabbed section of a panel.

6. Click OK to apply the changes, or click another tab to edit different preferences.

Adjusting Editing Preferences

In the Editing tab, you can modify the appearance of the cursor and certain visual references when editing a document in bitmap mode. In this tab, you can also modify the snapping distance from the grid, guides, and objects.

To modify Editing preferences, do the following:

1. Open the Preferences dialog box.

2. Click the Editing tab to open the dialog box shown here:

3. Choose Precise Cursors, and the cursor is displayed as a crosshair instead of as the icon of the selected tool.

4. Choose Delete Objects When Cropping, and Fireworks permanently deletes pixels and objects that are outside the bounding box of a selection when you choose Edit | Crop Document, or Modify | Canvas Size.

5. Choose Brush-Size Painting Cursors, and when you select the Brush tool or the Eraser tool, your cursor will be resized in accordance with the brush or the eraser size you chose. When you choose this option and use certain multitipped brushes, the cursor will default to a crosshair.

6. Choose Turn Off "Hide Edges" (the default), and with the Hide Edge command invoked, Fireworks will display points at the corners of an unselected object's boundary when you roll over it.

7. Choose Display Striped Border, and Fireworks will display a striped border around the entire canvas when you work in bitmap mode.

8. Choose Show Pen Preview to display a preview of a path as you draw with the Pen tool. The default method only displays the path after you've created the next point.

9. Choose Show Solid Points, and selected points along a path are displayed as hollow, while unselected points are displayed as solid.

10. Choose Mouse Highlight (the default), and objects are highlighted as you move your cursor over them.

11. Choose Preview Drag to display a bounding box of an object's location as you move it across the canvas.

12. Choose Show Fill Handles to display handles that you use to change the location, rotation, and size of an object's fill.

13. In the Pick Distance field, enter the distance the cursor must be from an object before you can select it. Enter a value between 1 and 10.

14. In the Snap Distance field, enter the distance an object must be from a grid intersection or guideline before snapping to it. Snapping must be enabled before this option takes effect. Enter a value between 1 and 10.

Modifying Launch and Edit Preferences

In this section, you can modify how Fireworks handles editing PNG images when Fireworks is launched from an external application.

To modify Launch and Edit preferences, do the following:

1. Open the Preferences dialog box.

2. Click the Launch and Edit tab to reveal the dialog box:

3. Click the triangle to the right of the When Editing From External Application field, and from the drop-down menu choose one of the following:

   ■ **Ask When Launching**   Fireworks prompts you whether to use a source PNG file.

■ **Always Use Source PNG** The source PNG file is loaded and available for editing. After you complete editing and click the Done button to return to the application from which you launched Fireworks, the source file is saved.

■ **Never Use Source PNG** The PNG file as it appears in the application from which you launched Fireworks is loaded and available for editing. When you exit Fireworks, your changes are only applied to the image as used in the other application, and the source file is not modified.

4. Click OK to apply the changes, or click a different tab to modify another preference group.

Setting Folders Preferences

In this section, you can modify the folders in which Fireworks searches for additional materials such as filter and texture files.

To modify Folders preferences, do the following:

1. Open the Preferences dialog box.

2. Click the Folders tab to open the dialog box shown here:

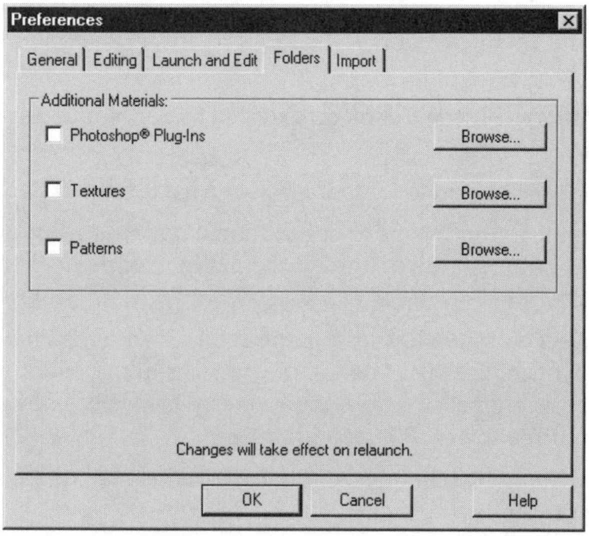

3. Click the Photoshop Plug-Ins checkbox to link external plug-in filters with Fireworks.

4. Click the Browse button to open the Select Photoshop Plug-ins Folder dialog box.

5. Navigate to the folder where your Photoshop plug-ins reside, select the folder, and click Open. The Select button at the bottom of the dialog box changes to reflect the name of the folder you selected.

6. Click the Select button to link the external plug-ins folder with Fireworks. When you next launch the application, the plug-ins will be available from the Filters menu. Applicable filters will be available to add as Live Effects from the Property inspector Effects menu.

7. Click the Textures checkbox to make a folder of images available as textures.

8. Click the Browse button to open the Select An Additional Textures Folder dialog box.

9. Navigate to the folder where your textures are stored and select it. The Select button at the bottom of the dialog box will change to reflect the name of the folder.

Note   *You can use any grayscale image in the PNG, GIF, JPEG, BMP, TIFF, and PICT (Macintosh only) formats as a texture. If images in the folder are in the RGB format, they will be converted to grayscale as they appear on the Textures menu.*

10. Click the Select button to link the texture folder with Fireworks. When you next launch Fireworks, you will be able to apply the textures to objects by selecting them from the Textures menu in the Property inspector. Textures will be covered in Chapter 10.

11. Click the Patterns button to link an external folder of images you want to use as patterns.

12. Click the Browse button to open the Select An Additional Pattern Folder.

13. Navigate to the folder where your additional patterns are stored and select it. The Select button at the bottom of the dialog box changes to reflect the folder's name.

14. Click the Select button to link your pattern folder with the Fireworks application. When you launch Fireworks again, the patterns in the folder will be available when you choose a pattern from the Property inspector Fill Category menu. For more information on fills, see Chapter 10.

15. Click OK to apply the changes, or click a different tab to edit another preference group.

You can deselect any Folders preference by clicking the appropriate checkbox, and when you next launch Fireworks the folders will not be linked to the application; however, the folder location will be listed below the Browse button. You can restore the folder by clicking the checkbox or select a different folder by clicking the Browse button and repeating the preceding steps.

Note   *If you use Fireworks with the Mac OS 9 operating system, you have an additional Folders preference that allows you to choose primary and secondary scratch disk folders. This option is not needed on Mac OS X or any of the Windows operating systems.*

Changing Import Preferences

In this section, you can modify the way Photoshop images are imported into Fireworks. You can specify how Photoshop layers and text are handled within Fireworks.

To modify Import preferences, do the following:

1. Open the Preferences dialog box.

2. Click the Import tab to reveal the dialog box shown here:

3. In the Layers section, choose Convert To Fireworks Objects to import each layer in the Photoshop file as a separate bitmap object on its own layer in Fireworks.

4. In the Layers section, choose Share Layer Across All Frames to copy the Photoshop layers to all frames in the Fireworks document. You must choose Convert To Fireworks Objects to use this option.

5. In the Layers section, choose Convert To Frames to import each layer of the Photoshop file as a separate object on its own frame in Fireworks.

6. In the Text section, choose Editable, and you will be able to edit Photoshop text with the Property inspector or Text Editor.

7. In the Text section, choose Maintain Appearance to import Photoshop text as bitmap objects. If you choose this option, you will not be able to edit any text attributes such as font style, kerning, and so on.

8. Choose Use Flat Composite Image to import the Photoshop file as a flattened image with no layers. This option works only if you save the file from the Photoshop application with a composite image.

9. Click OK to apply the changes, or click another tab to modify different preferences.

Restoring Default Fireworks Preferences

When you modify the default preferences, they are stored as a file. You can restore default preferences at any time by deleting the file.

To restore Fireworks default preferences:

1. Exit Fireworks.

2. Use your operating system features to search for the file named Fireworks MX Preferences.txt. The location of this file varies depending on your operating system and on whether you are a user on a network computer. Use the advanced options feature of your operating system's Search function to search hidden folders. You may end up with more than one file with this name. Choose the file that resides in your application settings folder.

3. After the file is located, delete it.

4. Launch Fireworks, and the default program preferences will have been restored.

Modifying Keyboard Shortcuts

Fireworks MX default keyboard shortcut set is called Macromedia Standard. It is designed for users of other Macromedia products who are using Fireworks for the first time. You can use keyboard shortcuts to select tools and quickly perform menu commands without wading through the menu bar. You can change from the Macromedia Standard keyboard shortcut set to a keyboard shortcut set from another application, or you can create your own custom keyboard set by modifying an existing set.

Selecting a Shortcut Set

If you're familiar with the keyboard shortcuts of another application, you can switch from the Standard Macromedia set to a Fireworks set, a Freehand set, an Illustrator set, or a Photoshop set.

To switch to a different keyboard shortcut set, do the following:

1. Choose Edit | Keyboard Shortcuts. The Keyboard Shortcuts dialog box, shown in the following illustration, opens.

Keyboard Shortcuts

Current Set: Macromedia Standard

Commands: Menu Commands

```
⊞ File
⊞ Edit
⊞ View
⊞ Select
⊞ Modify
⊞ Text
⊞ Commands
⊞ Filters
⊞ Window
⊞ Help
```

Description:

Shortcuts: + | −

Press Key: Change

OK   Cancel

2. Click the triangle to the right of the Current Set field and choose one of the following:

- **Fireworks**   Choose this shortcut set if you're a returning Fireworks user.

- **Freehand**   Choose this shortcut set if you're a veteran user of Macromedia Freehand.

- **Illustrator**   Choose this shortcut set if you prefer the Adobe Illustrator keyboard shortcuts.

- **Macromedia Standard**   Choose this default shortcut set if you're familiar with keyboard shortcuts from other Macromedia applications.

- **Photoshop**   Choose this shortcut set if you prefer the Adobe Photoshop keyboard shortcuts.

3. Click OK to change to the selected shortcut set.

Creating a Custom Shortcut Set

You can create a custom keyboard set by modifying an existing set. This may be to your advantage after you become familiar with Fireworks and repeatedly use a command that is not currently assigned to a keyboard shortcut. You'll also find that a custom keyboard shortcut set is beneficial when you use the History panel to create your own commands.

To create a custom keyboard shortcut set, do the following:

1. Choose Edit | Keyboard Shortcuts to open the Keyboard Shortcuts dialog box.

2. Accept the current keyboard set as a starting point, or click the triangle to the right of the Current Set field and select a different keyboard shortcut, as shown here:

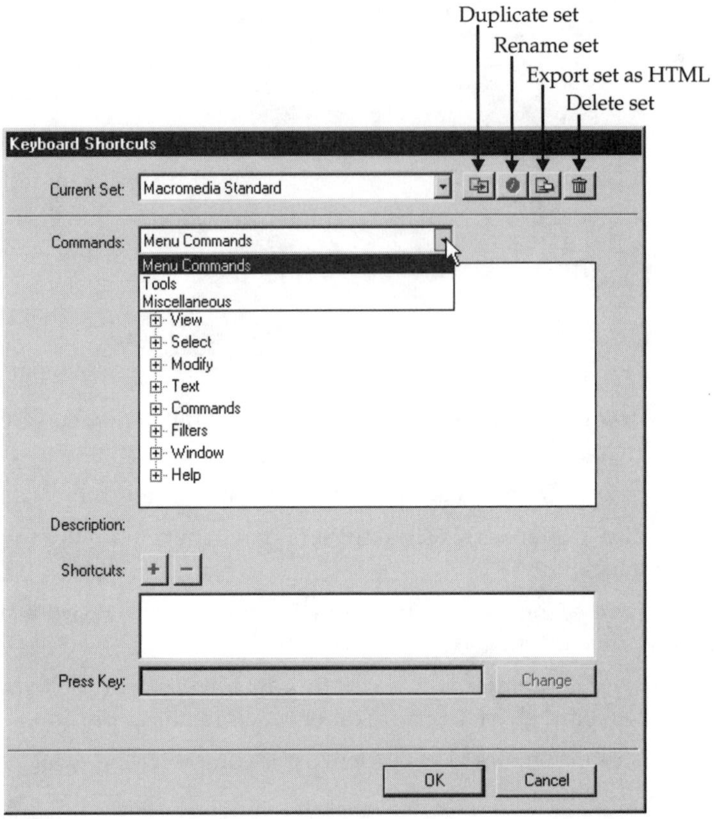

3. Click the Duplicate Set button, positioned to the right of the Current Set field to open the Duplicate Set dialog box shown next.

```
┌─────────────────────────────────────────────┐
│ Duplicate Set                            [X] │
├─────────────────────────────────────────────┤
│    Name: │My Keyboard Shortcut Set         │ │
│                                               │
│              ┌─────────┐   ┌─────────┐       │
│              │   OK    │   │ Cancel  │       │
│              └─────────┘   └─────────┘       │
└─────────────────────────────────────────────┘
```

4. Accept the default name, or enter a name of your own. It is advisable to give the keyboard set a unique name, especially if you aren't the only Fireworks user on that computer.

5. Click OK, and the duplicated keyboard set will become the custom set. Note that you cannot modify any of the preset keyboard shortcuts; you must create a duplicate set.

6. Click the triangle to the right of the Commands field, and choose one of the following:

   ■ **Menu Commands**   This option displays a list of all menu commands, including any custom commands you may have created. The list is set up like the menu bar at the top of the application, listing each menu group. Click the plus sign (+) to the left of a group name to reveal every command on that menu list. Many of the commands have submenus also designated by a plus sign (+) that when clicked reveals the submenu commands. If a command currently has a keyboard shortcut, it is listed in parentheses to the right of the command.

   ■ **Tools**   This option displays every tool in the toolbox. If a tool has one or more keyboard shortcuts, the shortcuts are listed in parentheses to the right of the tool's name.

   ■ **Miscellaneous**   This option displays a list of miscellaneous features that have no tools or menu commands. Each item on this list has a keyboard shortcut in at least one of the keyboard sets. If the keyboard set you duplicated features a shortcut for a feature, it will be listed in parentheses to the right of the feature's name.

7. After selecting a command set, choose an item whose shortcut you want to change.

8. If the item you selected currently has a shortcut, it will be listed in the Shortcuts window and in the Press Key field.

9. Place your cursor in the Press Key field, and from your computer keyboard, enter the keyboard shortcut you want to assign to the item. If the keyboard shortcut you enter conflicts with an existing shortcut, a triangle appears below the Press Key window indicating the command or tool the shortcut is currently

assigned to, as shown in the following illustration. If you don't want to override a current keyboard shortcut, enter another one.

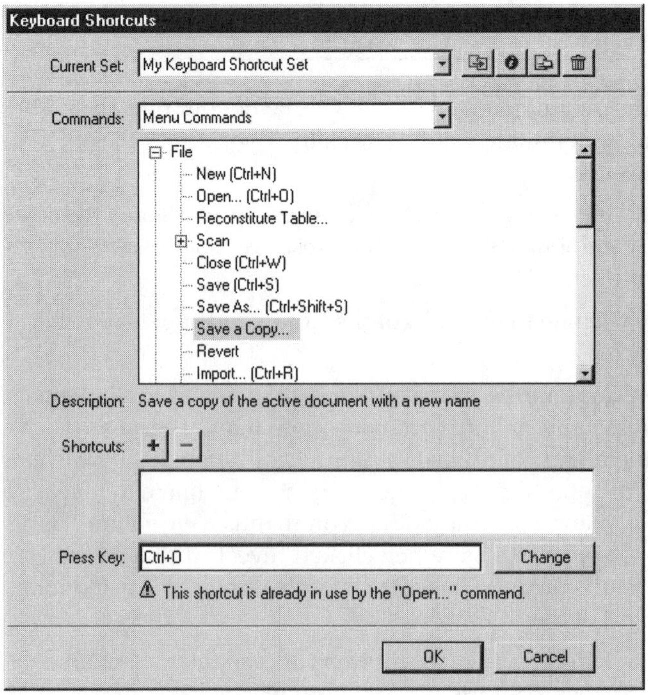

10. Click Change to assign the shortcut to the item. If the shortcut you choose is in conflict with a current shortcut, the warning dialog box shown in the following illustration appears. Click Reassign to override the shortcut, or click Cancel to void the action.

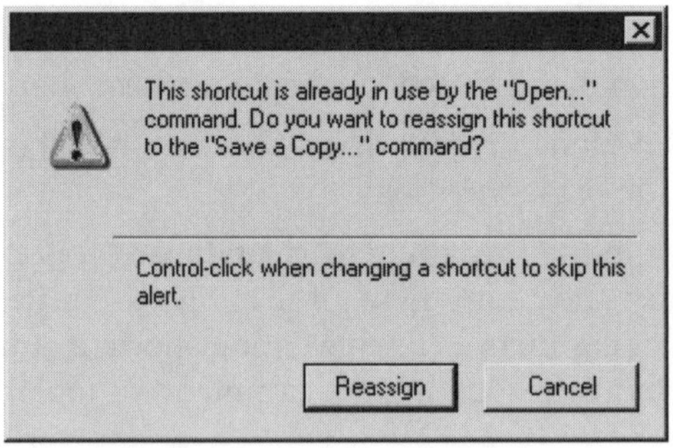

11. Continue modifying the keyboard set by choosing items from a command list and assigning new shortcuts, as shown in the preceding steps. When the keyboard set is just the way you want it, click OK to save the shortcut set.

Creating Secondary Shortcuts

If you need more than one way of accessing a tool or menu command, you can create a secondary shortcut. As you may have noticed, several of the tools have secondary shortcuts. For example, using the default keyboard shortcut set, you can access the Select tool by pressing V or O. This keyboard shortcut is also assigned to the Select Behind tool, which means you can toggle back and forth between the tools by clicking the same keyboard shortcut. You can include versatility like this in your own keyboard shortcut set by assigning the same keyboard shortcut to more than one item, or by creating a secondary keyboard shortcut.

To create a secondary keyboard shortcut, do the following:

1. Choose Edit | Keyboard Shortcuts to open the Keyboard Shortcuts dialog box. If your custom keyboard set is the current step, proceed to step 2; otherwise, click the triangle to the right of the Current Set field and choose a custom keyboard set from the drop-down menu.

2. Select one of the command groups, then select the item to which you want to assign a secondary shortcut or a currently used shortcut.

3. Click the button that looks like a plus sign (+).

4. Place your cursor in the Press Key field, and from your keyboard enter the shortcut you want to add to the item. Certain items require certain characters as keyboard shortcuts; for example, tools require that you use a letter for a shortcut. If you choose an improper keyboard shortcut, Fireworks displays a warning to that effect at the bottom of the Keyboard Shortcuts dialog box. If you choose a keyboard shortcut that conflicts with a system command, the dialog box shown in the previous illustration appears, warning you that the shortcut is being used by another command. Click Reassign to override the current shortcut.

5. Continue adding secondary shortcuts, then click OK to apply the changes to the selected custom keyboard set.

Editing a Custom Keyboard Shortcut Set

After you create one or more custom keyboard shortcuts, you may find it necessary to edit a set as your needs change or as you use the History panel to add new commands to the Commands menu. You can edit a custom keyboard set by adding additional shortcuts, deleting shortcuts, renaming a custom keyboard set, or deleting a custom keyboard shortcut set.

Adding and Deleting Shortcuts from a Set

After you create a custom keyboard shortcut set, you can fine-tune it as you gain more experience using Fireworks. You can add a keyboard shortcut when necessary to streamline your workflow, or delete a keyboard shortcut when it is no longer needed.

To add or delete a keyboard shortcut, do the following:

1. Choose Edit | Keyboard Shortcuts to open the Keyboard Shortcuts dialog box (shown previously in the section "Creating a Custom Shortcut Set").

2. Click the triangle to the right of the Current Set field and select the keyboard shortcut set you need to modify.

3. Click the triangle to the right of the Commands field and choose the list that contains the command you want to delete.

4. Select the item with the keyboard shortcut you want to delete, and click the minus (-) button. The shortcut will be deleted, but the item will still appear on the list in case you want to assign a shortcut to it at a later date.

5. To add a keyboard shortcut, select an item from one of the command lists, place your cursor in the Key Press field, and enter the shortcut from your keyboard.

6. To add a secondary shortcut, select an item that already contains a keyboard shortcut, click the plus (+) button, place your cursor in the Key Press field, and enter the shortcut from your keyboard.

7. Continue editing the shortcut set, or click OK to apply the changes and close the dialog box.

Renaming a Keyboard Set

You can rename a keyboard set at any time. Rename a keyboard set to choose a name that more aptly describes the keyboard set or to choose a more appropriate name if you originally accepted the Fireworks default keyboard set name and now want to change it.

To rename a custom keyboard set:

1. Choose Edit | Keyboard Shortcuts. The Keyboard Shortcuts dialog box appears.

2. Click the triangle to the right of the Current Set field and choose the set you want to rename.

3. Click the Rename Set button. The Rename Set dialog box appears.

Note   *If you select one of the Fireworks preset keyboard sets, the Rename Set button will be grayed out and you will only be able to rename custom keyboard shortcut sets.*

4. Enter a name for the set and Click OK.

5. Click OK to close the Keyboard Shortcuts dialog box.

Deleting a Custom Keyboard Set

You can delete a custom keyboard set when it is no longer needed. You cannot delete any of the Fireworks preset keyboard sets.

To delete a keyboard setup, do the following:

1. Choose Edit | Keyboard Shortcuts to open the Keyboard Shortcuts dialog box.

2. Select the custom keyboard set you want to delete.

3. Click the Delete Set button, which looks like a trash can.

4. Click OK to close the dialog box, or select another set to edit.

Printing a Keyboard Shortcut Cheat Sheet

When you initially learn to use any new program, the learning curve can be fairly steep; Fireworks is no exception. Trying to remember a set of keyboard shortcuts adds to the dilemma. You can alleviate the problem of remembering new keyboard shortcuts by printing out a copy of your currently selected keyboard shortcut set.

To print a copy of your currently selected keyboard shortcut set, do the following:

1. Choose Edit | Keyboard Shortcuts to open the Keyboard Shortcuts dialog box.

2. Select the keyboard shortcut set you want to create a cheat sheet for.

3. Click the Export Set As HTML button, the third button to the right of the Current Set field. The Save As dialog box opens.

4. Navigate to the folder where you want the document saved, and click Save.

5. Close Fireworks and navigate to the folder where you stored the document.

6. Double-click the file's icon to view the exported keyboard shortcut file in your default Web browser. Figure 3-2 shows a custom keyboard shortcut set as displayed in Internet Explorer.

7. Click your browser's Print button to print a hard copy of the shortcut set.

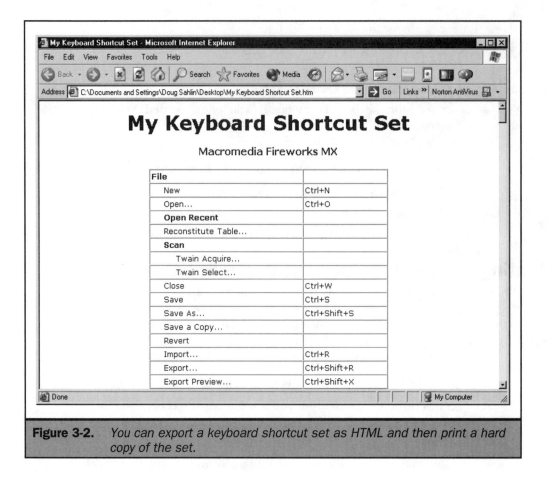

Figure 3-2. *You can export a keyboard shortcut set as HTML and then print a hard copy of the set.*

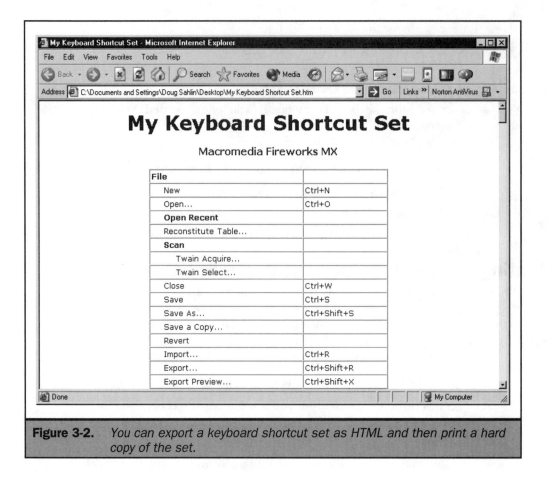

Summary

In this chapter, you learned to customize Fireworks to suit your working preferences. You learned how to save a custom panel set. You also learned how to modify Fireworks preferences to suit your working habits. In the latter part of the chapter, you learned to create custom keyboard shortcut sets and modify them. Chapter 4 will show you the workflow of a typical Fireworks project.

Chapter 4

Exploring Fireworks Workflow

In previous chapters, you were exposed to basic Fireworks concepts; you learned your way around the workspace and optimized it for the way you work. Now that you know a bit about Fireworks and have your workspace in order, it's time to explore how you go about creating a document in Fireworks, adding various elements to the document, exporting it for use in a Web page, and then saving the document for future use.

In this chapter, you'll learn steps involved in creating a document for use in a Web page, or as a standalone Web page. You'll learn how to create a new document. You'll develop an understanding for the workflow in a typical Fireworks project from start to finish. The tools you use to create objects for your documents will be discussed.

Beginning a Project

You always begin a new project at the beginning. Logic may dictate that you begin a project by creating a new document. Some designers can work quite successfully by beginning with a blank canvas and creating content. However, before you start any new project, it's a good idea to know where you're going. This is especially true if you've been hired by a client to design a Web page and are working under deadline.

The first step in any major project is *planning*. If you're working for a client, make sure you understand all of your client's expectations up front. There's nothing more frustrating than spending long hours on a project, and after uploading it to the client's Web site for review, finding out that your client's vision of the project differs from yours.

In addition, if you're working for a client, don't be afraid to request an initial payment before you begin work. This shows good faith on the client's part. Include a provision for extra work in your proposal. Clients can nickel and dime you to death with revisions. Figure for every possible contingency and include it in your proposal. Your client will appreciate knowing everything up front, and you can devote your efforts to creating the Web site rather than concerning yourself with any potential pitfalls of miscommunication.

When you're discussing the project with your client, create thumbnail sketches of the major parts of the site. A quick thumbnail sketch can ensure that you and your client are on the same page. Also, find out as much as you can about the client's target audience. If the majority of your client's viewing audience will view your design with dial-up modems, optimize all documents for the smallest possible file size. However, if the site you are designing will be displayed by employees using a network card on a corporate intranet using a server with a T1 or faster trunk line, you can optimize the document for higher quality graphics without being too concerned about download times.

As part of your preparation for a project, find out who your client's competitors are and get the URLs to their Web sites. This will give you an idea of accepted standards for Web sites in your client's field of endeavor. Use your favorite search engines to find additional Web sites of companies in your client's industry. As you view these Web sites, you'll get an idea of the latitude you'll have when designing the site, and your own creative juices will begin to flow.

When you create thumbnail sketches of a project, you have a point of reference with which to begin working, and you can begin collecting the assets you'll need for the project. Gather all the images and other necessary assets, such as your client's logo, and store them in a project folder on your desktop. If you pay a bit of attention to detail at the beginning of a project, the project will flow smoothly and you won't run into any unexpected snags as you race toward a project deadline.

Creating a New Document

After you do all your wool gathering, you're ready to begin creating documents for the project. When you create a new document, you have a canvas to work with that contains all the objects you use to create a design. If you're creating a document for a Web site that contains several pages that are similar, consider creating a site template that contains all the common elements, such as the site banner and navigation menu.

To create a new Fireworks document, choose File | New to open the New Document dialog box, shown next. Here you specify the canvas size, image resolution, and background color of a new document.

```
┌─ New Document ──────────────────────────────[X]─┐
│ ┌─ Canvas Size: 1.2M ─────────────────────────┐  │
│ │      Width: [760]  [Pixels          ▼] W: 760│  │
│ │     Height: [420]  [Pixels          ▼] H: 420│  │
│ │ Resolution: [72]   [Pixels/Inch     ▼]       │  │
│ └─────────────────────────────────────────────┘  │
│ ┌─ Canvas Color: ─────────────────────────────┐  │
│ │ (•) White                                    │  │
│ │ ( ) Transparent                              │  │
│ │ ( ) Custom        [■▾]                        │  │
│ └─────────────────────────────────────────────┘  │
│                          [    OK    ] [ Cancel ]  │
└──────────────────────────────────────────────────┘
```

Setting Canvas Size

When you create a new document in Fireworks, you specify the canvas size by entering values in the Width and Height fields of the New Document dialog box. By clicking the triangle to the right of each field, you can open a drop down menu that lets you specify whether the value is pixels, centimeters, or inches.

If you're creating a document for a specific size desktop to be viewed in a maximized browser or a specific application, choose the correct document size from Table 4-1.

Desktop Size	Document Size
640 × 480	600 × 300
800 × 600	760 × 420
832 × 624	795 × 470
1024 × 768	955 × 600
WEB TV	544 × 378

Table 4-1. *Document Sizes for Maximized Browsers*

Specifying Canvas Color

After you specify the document size, you can specify the canvas color. The color you choose will serve as the background color for the HTML document when you export the document. Choose a transparent background if you're creating a Web page that uses a tiling background image. The default background color is white. You can choose a different color by following these steps:

1. In the New Document dialog box, click the Custom radio button.

2. Click the color swatch. Your cursor becomes an eyedropper and the following pop-up palette appears.

3. Click one of the color swatches to specify a color from the Web Safe palette, or click the color picker icon to choose a color from the system color picker.

Setting Document Resolution

Most of the documents you create in Fireworks are for publication in a Web page. The default resolution of 72 pixels per inch is ideally suited for displaying images on computer monitors. However, you can also create documents in Fireworks for print. When you create a document for print, specify the resolution size of the output device with which you intend to print the document by entering a value in the New Document dialog box Resolution field.

While setting document resolution, you can change the default resolution unit of measure by clicking the triangle to the right of the Resolution field (in the New Document dialog box), and then choosing Pixels/cm. After you specify the parameters for the new document, the file size of the document is displayed in the upper-left corner of the New Document dialog box.

After specifying the canvas parameters, click OK and Fireworks creates a blank canvas, as shown in Figure 4-1.

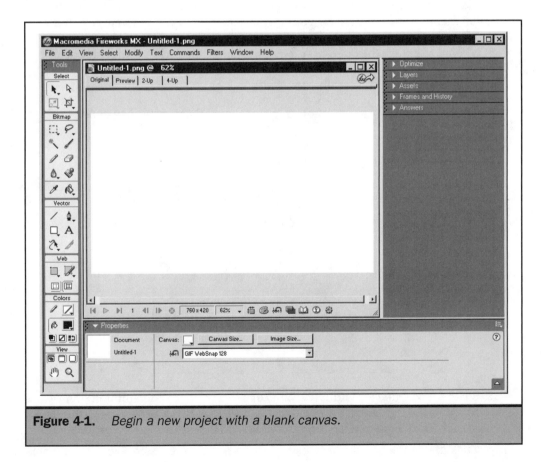

Figure 4-1.   *Begin a new project with a blank canvas.*

Modifying the Canvas

After you begin creating your design, you may find that you need to modify the canvas. You can change the canvas size, canvas color, or resolution on the fly. You can alter the size of the document to specific dimensions using menu commands, crop the document manually using a tool, or size the canvas to fit the elements using menu commands.

Changing the Canvas Size

As you create your document, you may find that the original canvas size no longer suits your needs, or your client may decide to add or delete elements from the document. To accommodate such changes, you can alter the size at any time. You can use four different methods to modify the canvas size.

Changing the Canvas Size Numerically

If you find you need more room on the canvas for additional elements, or to create an additional menu item requested by your client, you can specify the new size of the canvas, as well as how the added pixels are redistributed around the elements in your design when you invoke the operation. You can change the canvas width and height independently; Fireworks does not constrain the proportions.

To resize the canvas numerically, do the following:

1. Choose Modify | Canvas | Canvas Size to open the Canvas Size dialog box shown here:

2. Enter a new value for width (W) and/or height (H). The default unit of measure is in pixels. To choose a different unit of measure, click the triangle to the right of each field, and from the drop-down menu, choose Inches or Centimeters.

3. Click one of the Anchor buttons to specify how Fireworks resizes the canvas around elements already in the document. The default center anchor sizes the

document equally around all sides of the document objects. If you choose the top center anchor, Fireworks resizes the document by adding pixels below the items already in the document.

4. Click OK to resize the document.

Note *You can also access the Canvas Size dialog box by opening the Property inspector with no objects selected and then clicking the Canvas Size button.*

Cropping the Canvas

If you don't need to resize the canvas to a specific dimension, you can manually crop the canvas using the Crop tool. Despite the tool name, you can also increase the size of the canvas with this tool.

To modify canvas size with the Crop tool, use these steps:

1. Select the Crop tool from the toolbar, as shown here:

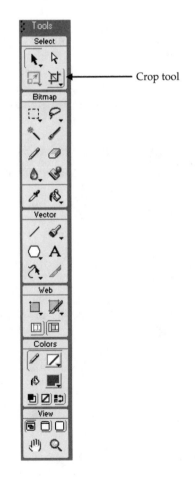

Crop tool

2. Click anywhere on the canvas and drag to define the new canvas size. As you drag, a bounding box appears, designating the current size of the crop area. Release the mouse button when the area is the desired size. Eight handles appear around the cropping box.

3. To move the cropping box, click inside and drag it to a new location.

4. To change the size of the cropping box, drag a handle. The middle handles on the right and left side of the box change the width; the handles on the top center change the height. To resize the width and height in one operation, drag one of the corner handles. To resize the cropping box proportionately, hold down the SHIFT key as you drag one of the corner handles.

5. To increase the size of the document, drag one of the corner handles until the cropping box is the desired size.

6. To complete cropping the canvas, double-click inside the cropping box. Alternately, press ENTER or RETURN.

Trimming the Canvas

You can also resize the canvas by trimming it. When you trim the canvas, you cut away any area around the objects in your document. This command is useful if you create a button or navigation menu and want to shrink the canvas to fit the object(s) (see the next section). To trim the canvas, choose Modify | Canvas | Trim Canvas. When you use this command, Fireworks resizes the document to a rectangular shape that encompasses the borders of the object.

Fitting the Canvas to Objects

If you create a document and some of your items extend beyond the boundary of the original document, you can expand the canvas so that all the items in your design are displayed. To fit the canvas to include all objects in your design, choose Modify | Canvas | Fit to Canvas. If you invoke this command and objects occupy an area smaller than the canvas, the command works like the Trim Canvas command and shrinks the canvas to the objects.

Rotating the Canvas

You can also rotate the canvas at any time. You can rotate the canvas 90 degrees clockwise (CW) or counterclockwise (CCW), as well as rotating the canvas 180 degrees. To rotate the canvas, choose Modify | Canvas, and then choose one of the following: Rotate 180°, Rotate 90°CW, or Rotate 90°CCW.

Changing the Canvas Color

You can change the canvas color any time you feel it's not right for the elements you are adding to your design. You can change the canvas color by choosing one of the color swatches, or you can match the canvas color to a color from an object in your design.

To change canvas color, follow these steps:

1. Choose Modify | Canvas | Canvas Color. The Canvas Color dialog box shown in the following illustration appears.

2. Click one of the radio buttons to choose an option.

3. If you choose the Custom option, click the radio button, and your cursor becomes an eyedropper and the current color palette appears.

4. Click a palette swatch to select a color.

5. Alternatively, you can use a color that you've already included on your canvas. Move your cursor over an object in your document. As the cursor passes over the object, the color swatch changes to reflect the color under your cursor. When you see the color you want, click the mouse, and the object color sampled becomes the background color.

Tip   *To get the hexadecimal value of the custom color, hold your cursor over the color and the value is displayed in a tooltip.*

Creating Objects

After you create a new document, you add the objects needed for your design by creating them with the drawing tools or by importing them. You can import vector objects or bitmap images. You can create objects by using any of the drawing tools in the Vector section of the toolbox. You can create solid objects, outlines, or paths.

Creating Vector Objects

As you learned in Chapter 1, vector objects are composed of paths. Vector objects can be greatly enlarged with little or no loss of fidelity. You can create the following vector objects: rectangles, rounded rectangles, ellipses, and polygons. In addition, you can create open or closed paths. You can also create anti-aliased text for your designs with the Text tool. The drawing tools in the Vector section of the toolbox are shown here:

To select a tool, click its icon, or use a keyboard shortcut. Many of the tools have secondary keyboard shortcuts, while other tools share the same keyboard shortcut making it possible to switch from one tool to another with a keypress.

Many of the tools in the Vector section of the toolbox are tool groups. When a tool group includes more than one tool, you'll see a small triangle at the bottom of the currently displayed tool icon. When you click the triangle next to the currently displayed tool icon, the group expands. You can also expand a tool group by clicking an icon without quickly releasing the mouse button. The following illustration shows the objects the flyout for the tool group used to create objects.

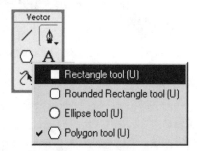

To create an object, select a drawing tool and then click and drag on the canvas. You can also dynamically position the object while creating it by holding down the SPACEBAR and dragging. Release the SPACEBAR when the object is positioned correctly, and continue dragging to finish sizing the object. Fireworks creates a preview of the object as you're creating it; the type of preview depends on the type of object you are creating. Figure 4-2 shows a canvas filled with vector objects created with the drawing tools.

You can edit your vector graphics with a variety of tools. You can move, scale, rotate, and distort vector graphics. When you create vector objects, you can edit the graphic by

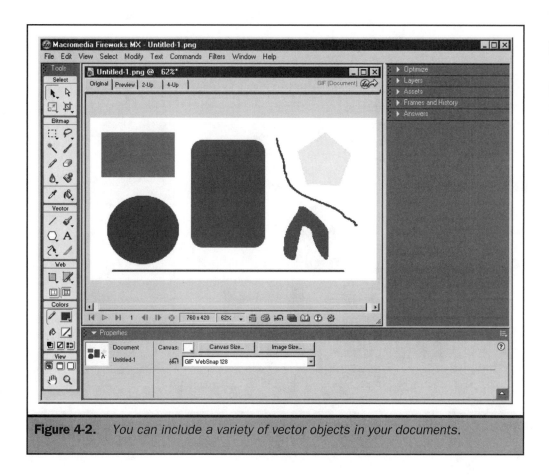

Figure 4-2.   *You can include a variety of vector objects in your documents.*

selecting and manipulating individual points. Creating and editing vector graphics is covered in detail in Chapter 5.

Importing Bitmap Objects

Vector tools are great for creating objects such as buttons, banner backgrounds, and text objects, but most Web sites display bitmap images as well. The amount of bitmap objects you include in your designs will depend on your client's needs and your own tastes. The trick is to find the right balance between the quantity of bitmap images you include in a design with the maximum amount of compression applied to create a suitable file size for downloading from the Internet. With Fireworks, you have a tremendous amount of flexibility when you optimize documents with bitmap images. You can apply different optimization methods to individual graphics, and you can even paste a mask on a bitmap image that lets you apply different compression to the masked area that differs from the rest of the bitmap. Figure 4-3 shows a document in which all the individual bitmaps

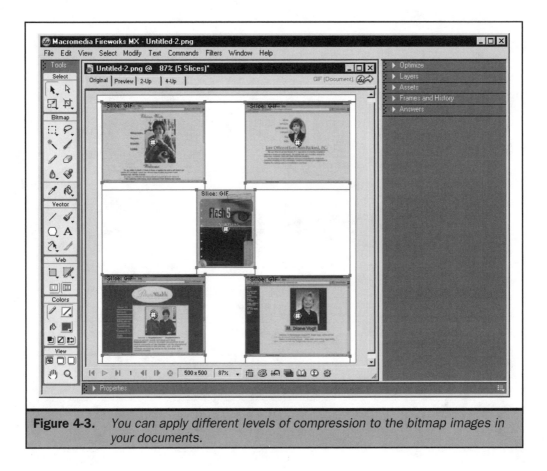

Figure 4-3.   *You can apply different levels of compression to the bitmap images in your documents.*

will be exported as slices. Importing and working with bitmaps images is covered in detail in Chapter 6.

Creating Slices

A document that combines bitmap images and vector objects is dealing with two different animals. Vector objects are often composed of large areas of solid color, whereas bitmap images are made up of dots of color known as *pixels*. As a rule, vector objects display well and have impressively small file sizes when optimized as GIF (Graphic Interchange Format) images. However, when you export a bitmap image as a GIF file, the opposite occurs. The GIF format tries to create the millions of colors in the bitmap from a 256-color palette by combining two colors to create a color in the image, but not in the palette. This process is known as *dithering*. When a bitmap image is dithered, one of two things happens: the file size is bloated beyond belief, or the dithered bitmap looks simply awful. You can export the whole file as a JPEG (Joint Photographic Experts Group) image; however, when you add text to the equation, you create different problems.

Text doesn't compress well as a JPEG file, as *artifacts* appear around the text. If enough JPEG compression is applied, it almost looks as though blurry dots surround the text.

The solution is to export different areas of the document with different optimization methods. You do this by creating *slices*. You can create slices manually with the Slice tool, or you can select an object and then use a menu command to create a slice for the object. You learn to work with slices in Chapter 16.

Working with Live Effects

Most graphics programs allow you to undo multiple actions. However, you often have to undo several actions to remove the unwanted effect from an object, and then redo the actions to include effects you deem necessary for your design. When you add a Live Effect to a vector object or bitmap image, you can edit the effect at any time without altering any other edits applied to the object or the document. You can use Live Effects to adjust a bitmap's color, add a bevel to a button object, create a drop shadow, and more. If you apply two or more effects to an object and like what you see, you can save the effects and have them appear as a style in the Styles panel. The following illustration shows the Live Effects you can add to objects in your design.

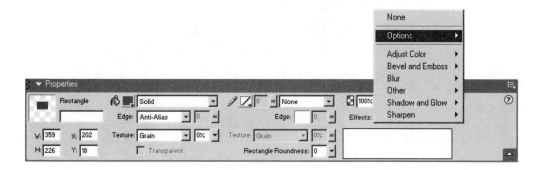

Working with Color

The Internet is bristling with colorful Web designs. You use color judiciously to add interest to your designs and attract a viewer's attention to certain areas of a page. With the proper use of color, you can direct a viewer's attention to different points of interest by using eye-catching color. But like everything else on the Internet, there's a caveat when it comes to color. Read on.

About Web Safe Color

What looks brilliant and vibrant on your monitor may look bland and drab on another monitor. What looks like a lovely aquamarine on your PC, may look like kiwi green on a Macintosh user's computer. Although, in today's day and age, most people have modern equipment, some people surf the Net with computers left over from the Jurassic Commodore 64 era. So, then, how do you design a page that displays the same on your PC and your neighbor's Macintosh or dinosaur machine? The answer is to use the Web Safe 216 palette whenever possible. The Web Safe 216 palette consists of 216 colors that display the same across any platform. These 216 colors comprise the default Fireworks palette.

The Web Safe 216 palette, shown next, is designated in hexadecimal format. The palette is composed of colors that display the same across any platform. You'll learn how to use the Web Safe 216 palette in Chapter 8.

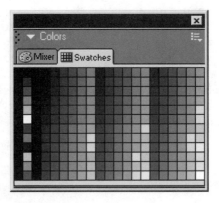

Introducing Strokes and Fills

When you create an object with one of the drawing tools or create a closed path with the Pen tool, the object can be displayed as an outline, a solid object, or a solid object with an outline around it. In Fireworks, an outline or a line is referred to as a *stroke*. A stroke can be a solid line of a given thickness, or you can apply a texture to a line or create a custom line style.

When you create a solid object, the accepted term for the color is *fill*. An object's fill can be either a solid color or a blend of two or more colors, called a *gradient*. The following illustration shows an object with a stroke and no fill, a fill with no stroke, and a stroke and fill. The fill for the third object is a gradient. You'll learn to work with strokes and fills and to create gradients in Chapters 9 and 10.

Adding Interactivity to a Document

With Fireworks, you can add all manner of special effects to your documents. As mentioned, you can create image swapping behaviors. If you create a Web site for a client that needs several linked sections, you can create a pop-up menu that occupies a single space on a navigation bar but expands to display several menu choices. You can also create impressive effects such as displaying a text message in the browser status window when a user rolls a mouse over a button.

Creating Hotspots

When you add interactivity to a design, some change occurs when a user's mouse interacts with a designated area of the document. Areas of interactivity are known as *hotspots*. You can manually create a circular hotspot, a rectangular hotspot, or an irregularly shaped hotspot with the Hotspot tools you find in the Web section of the toolbox. Or you can create a hotspot by selecting a vector or bitmap object and then using a menu command to make it "hot." A hotspot in the document has an aqua blue overlay with a white dot in the center. To add interactivity to the hotspot, you click the white dot to display the menu shown here:

Adding Behaviors

You add a behavior to a hotspot by selecting an item from the drop-down menu that appears when you click the white dot in the hotspot, as shown in the previous illustration. Each behavior has a given set of parameters. For example, a behavior might display a message at the bottom of the browser window when a viewer rolls the mouse over a hotspot. When you add a behavior to a Fireworks document, Fireworks creates the JavaScript to invoke the behavior, saving you the hassle of having to learn how to create JavaScript code.

After you choose a behavior from the drop-down menu, a dialog box appears and guides you through the process of adding the behavior to the hotspot. Behaviors are covered in detail in Chapter 17.

Creating Buttons

One interactive item you'll use repeatedly is the button. Buttons are a integral part of every Web design. They give viewers the choice of what to see and what not to see. When you create a button in Fireworks, it can be a simple rollover button that changes when a user rolls a mouse over the button, or it can be a button that displays a different image when the button is static, rolled over, or clicked. When you create a button, it's a reusable graphic. You can create as many duplicates as you need and then change the text on each button to reflect the button's purpose. You learn to use the Fireworks Button Editor to create buttons in Chapter 17.

Optimizing the Document

After you finish a design, you optimize the document to achieve the smallest possible file size without compromising image quality. Your first step in the optimization process is to compare the original image to the document with the current optimization settings applied. The best way to compare an optimized document to the original is by using the 2-Up or 4-Up display.

With the 2-Up display, you compare the original to an optimized version; with 4-Up, you can compare the original with three different optimized versions. In Figure 4-4, you see a document being previewed in the 2-Up mode. Notice the text in the lower-left corner of the optimized version window, which shows you the current export settings as well as the exported file size and anticipated download time with a connection speed of 56 Kbps. When you optimize, you compare the image quality with the file size and download time. These are your clues as to whether you need to tweak the optimization settings or leave the document as is to export. You can fine tune the export settings with the Optimize panel or the Property inspector.

Using the Optimize Panel

You can use the Optimize panel to apply settings to the entire document, a selected slice, or a selection of slices. When you apply different settings to a slice, the slice is exported with the settings you specify, regardless of the export settings specified for the document. Remember that slices are exported as individual images.

You can choose from among several optimizations methods. The most common export settings for images you use in a Web page are GIF and JPEG. For animations, you export the document as an animated GIF. If you prepare documents for print, or optimize images for use in other applications, you can also optimize the document in the PNG (Portable Networks Graphic), TIFF (Tagged Image File Format), or BMP (bitmap) format. For portable devices, you export documents as WBMP (wireless bitmap) files. Each format has different parameters that you can modify to suit the document's intended destination. If you arrive at an export setting that is ideal for a certain application, you

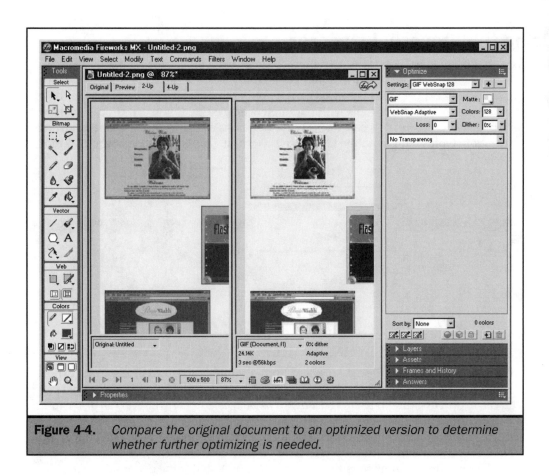

Figure 4-4.   *Compare the original document to an optimized version to determine whether further optimizing is needed.*

can save the settings and they will appear as an option on the Optimize panel Saved Settings menu. The following illustration shows the Optimize panel as used to optimize a document for export as a GIF file.

Using the Property Inspector

You can also use the Property inspector to optimize a document or selected slices. When you use the Property inspector to optimize, you are limited to saved settings that appear on the Default export options menu. You can only modify settings using the Optimize panel. When no objects or tools with parameters are selected, you can choose an export setting from a Property inspector Default export options menu, as shown in the following illustration. Optimizing with the Optimize panel and Property inspector are covered in Chapter 21.

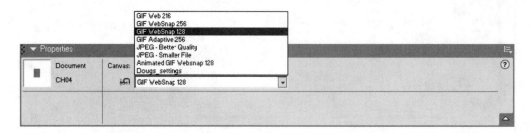

Exporting the Document

After you've completed the artwork and applied what you deem are optimal export settings for the document, you can export the document to its intended destination. You can export documents as images only or as images and HTML. You can also export the document for use in other applications. For example, you can export the file as a Flash .swf file, an Adobe Illustrator 7 file, a Photoshop PSD file, and more. Exporting a Fireworks document is covered in detail in Chapter 22.

Each format has parameters that you can specify to tailor the exported file to suit your intended application. When you export the document as image files with an HTML document, Fireworks creates the JavaScript needed to execute any behaviors you've applied to hotspots and writes the code for the tables needed to compile the slices in the HTML document as they appear in your original Fireworks document.

Setting Up the HTML

When you export a document as images and HTML, you can modify the HTML settings to suit the HTML editor with which you'll modify the document. You can specify the HTML style, choosing to export the document for a specific HTML editor or as generic HTML. You can also specify the way Fireworks codes the tables for the HTML document. If your document includes slices, you can modify the way Fireworks names the slices.

Using the Export Wizard

If you prefer, you can automate the optimization and export process. When you use the Export Wizard, you are guided through a series of steps that let you choose a specific export format, analyze the current optimization settings, or optimize the document to a specific file size. The Export Wizard lets you choose the document destination. After you supply the information, the Export Wizard analyzes your input and then recommends export settings. You can then view the document in the Export Preview window with the recommended settings and choose to export the document or repeat the process, whereupon the wizard launches and you can enter new parameters.

Using the Export Preview

As you create a document, you can preview it in the document window and use the Optimize panel to apply export settings to the document. If you're new to optimizing, Fireworks gives you other options for generating export settings. You can use the Export Wizard to automate the process, or you can use the Export Preview window to preview the document and tweak the export optimization settings. To use the Export Preview window shown in Figure 4-5, choose File | Export Preview.

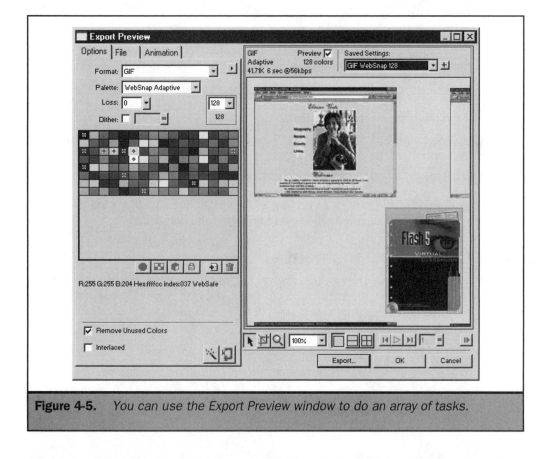

Figure 4-5.   *You can use the Export Preview window to do an array of tasks.*

Saving the Document

After you export the document, you can save the original document. When you save the document, you have only one available file format option: the native Fireworks PNG format. When you save the document, all of the individual objects are preserved as are layers, frames, hotspots, slices, and so on. When you need to edit the document in the future, all the objects in your document are editable when you open the file.

To save a new file, follow these steps:

1. Choose File | Save As. The Save As dialog box, shown next, appears.

2. Enter a filename for the document.
3. Click the triangle to the right of the Save In field and navigate to the folder where you want the document saved.
4. Click Save.

To save an existing file, choose File | Save. Fireworks saves the file using the same filename and folder you specified when you first saved the document.

Saving a Copy of a Document

When you open and close a file repeatedly or perform extensive modifications to a document, data can become corrupt and the original file may not be usable. If you use Fireworks while several other applications are open, you risk the possibility of overtaxing your computer's processor and creating an unstable environment. When this happens, data may become corrupt or Fireworks may become unresponsive and you'll lose your edits. You can prevent the possibility of losing important files due to computer glitches by saving a copy of the file. If for some reason your master file becomes unusable, you can open a copy of the document.

To save a copy of the current document, follow these steps:

1. Choose File | Save A Copy. The Save Copy As dialog box opens.

2. Enter a filename for the copy.

3. Click the triangle to the right of the Save In field and navigate to the folder where you want to store the copy.

4. Click Save.

Opening Existing Documents

When you need to perform edits on an existing document or perform additional edits to a job in progress, you open an existing document. When you open an existing file or work in progress, the elements in your document appear as they were when you last saved the document.

To open an existing document, follow these steps:

1. Choose File | Open. The Open dialog box appears.

2. Click the triangle to the right of the Look In field and navigate to the folder where the file you want to open is located.

3. You can preview files of specific type by clicking the triangle to the right of the Files Of Type field, shown in Figure 4-6.

4. Select a file type or accept the default All Files option. You can specify a file type to speed up a search in a document folder where you have stored several documents of varying file types.

5. Select a file and click Open. Fireworks opens the file.

Tip   *If you're not sure where you saved a file, minimize Fireworks and use your computer operating system's search utility to locate all files of the type you seek. Most search utilities let you limit the number of returns by specifying search criteria, such as which folders to search and when the file was modified.*

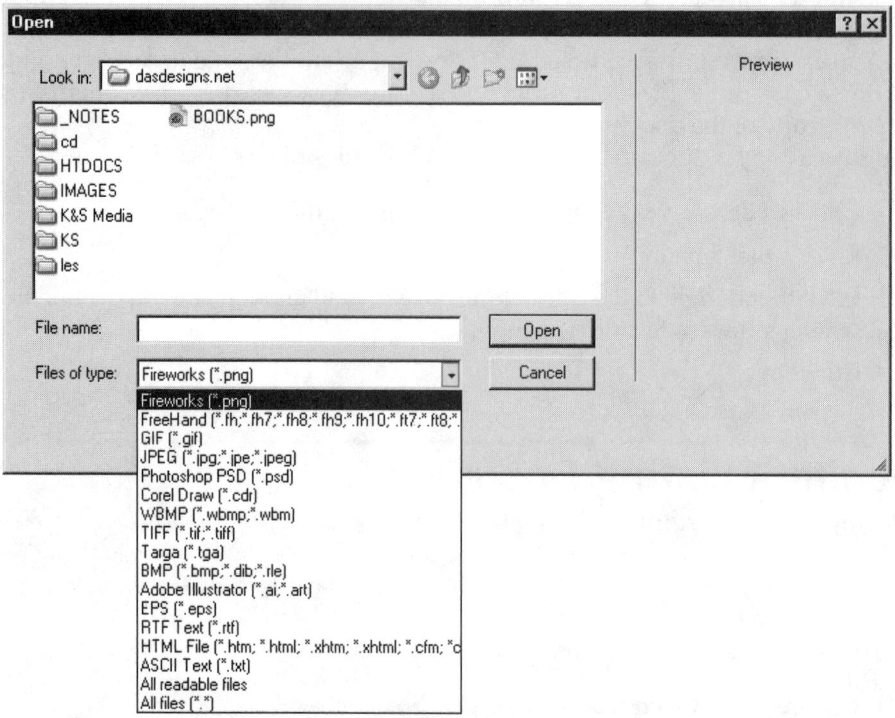

Figure 4-6.   *You click the triangle to the right of the Files Of Type field to preview specific types of saved files.*

Opening Recently Viewed Documents

When you save a document, Fireworks adds the document filename to the Open Recent menu list. Fireworks stores the ten most recently opened documents on this menu list. When you need to open a document you recently saved, choose File | Open Recent and choose the document from the menu list; an example list is shown here:

| File | Edit | View | Select | Modify | Text | Commands | Filters | Window | Help |

New	Ctrl+N
Open...	Ctrl+O
Open Recent	▶
Reconstitute Table...	
Scan	▶
Close	Ctrl+W
Save	Ctrl+S
Save As...	Ctrl+Shift+S
Save a Copy...	
Revert	
Import...	Ctrl+R
Export...	Ctrl+Shift+R
Export Preview...	Ctrl+Shift+X
Update HTML...	
Export Wizard...	
Batch Process...	
Preview in Browser	▶
Page Setup...	
Print...	Ctrl+P
HTML Setup...	
Exit	Ctrl+Q

Open Recent submenu:

1 Web.png
2 CH04.png
3 E:\dasdesigns.net\BOOKS.png
4 I:\MWA pages\meetingbanner.png
5 I:\C+D Proto\title.png
6 I:\CCMA.com\ccmahome.png
7 2DEWOrig.png
8 popUp.png
9 C:\WINDOWS\...\MS3B_2.png
10 C:\WINDOWS\...\MS3B_3.png

Viewing Multiple Documents

When you work on a major project, you often need to access assets from other Fireworks documents. You can open several documents and switch from one document to another from the Window menu, where you select the document you want to view from the list. Alternatively, you can display several documents at one time in their own windows. When you work in this manner, you can drag an asset from one document and drop it into another. You can view multiple documents in cascading fashion or as tiles.

Cascading Documents

When you view multiple documents in cascading fashion, Fireworks arranges the documents so that the title bar of each document is visible in the workspace. To display documents in this manner, choose Window | Cascade. The currently selected document is displayed in its entirety, as shown in Figure 4-7.

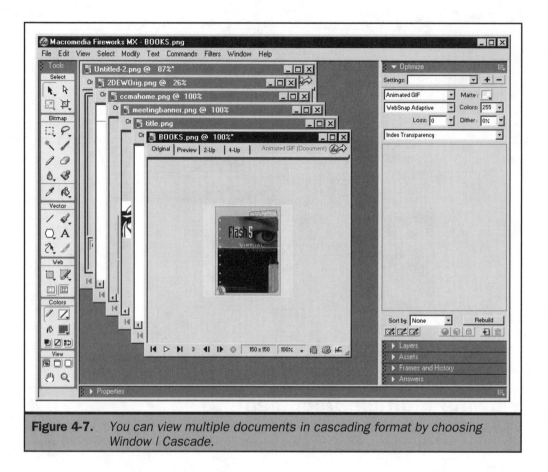

Figure 4-7. *You can view multiple documents in cascading format by choosing Window I Cascade.*

To select another document, click its title bar or any visible part of its window. The document appears at the top of the stack. You can select any element from the current document and choose Edit I Copy to copy it the to clipboard. Click another document to bring it to the top of the stack and choose Copy I Paste to paste the element in that document.

Displaying documents in cascading fashion is convenient when you work with several documents; however, if you work with only two or three documents open, you may find it more convenient to display the documents as vertical or horizontal tiles.

Tiling Documents

When you display documents in tiled fashion, you can see all or part of each document. Displaying documents as tiles is convenient when you want to compare a master copy of a file against your current working version of the document. Working in this fashion, you can immediately compare the results of your edits to the master version of the document. You can display multiple documents as horizontal tiles or vertical tiles.

To display multiple documents as horizontal tiles, choose Window | Tile Horizontal. After you invoke the command, Fireworks arranges your documents as shown in Figure 4-8.

When you want to display documents as vertical tiles, choose Window | Tile Vertical. After choosing the command, your documents are arranged as shown in Figure 4-9.

The method you choose to tile multiple documents is a matter of preference. After you choose either command, you can choose a document by doing one of the following:

- Click a document title bar.

- Click inside a document window.

- Click an item inside a document.

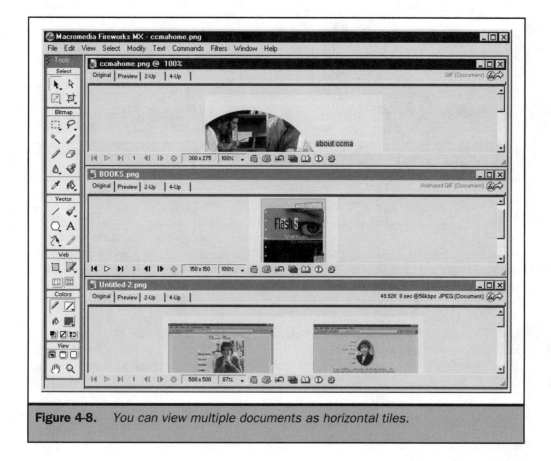

Figure 4-8.   *You can view multiple documents as horizontal tiles.*

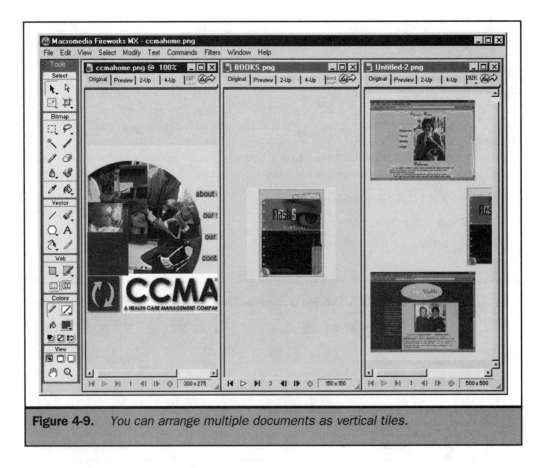

Figure 4-9.   *You can arrange multiple documents as vertical tiles.*

The selected document becomes the currently active document and you can use any tool, menu command, or panel to edit the document. You can also drag an object from one document window into another. This works the same as copying and pasting. The object you selected from the original document is unaffected and you have a copy of the object in another document. Note that if the documents are of different resolutions, Fireworks resamples the object to the resolution of the document into which you drag it.

Tip   *If a document is tiled in a window that's too small to display the entire document, hold down the SPACEBAR to activate the Hand tool. Drag inside the window to pan to another part of the document. Release the SPACEBAR to toggle back to the last used tool.*

Reverting to a Saved Document

When all your best laid plans go to waste and the edits you apply to an existing document just aren't working out as you planned, you can undo all your edits with one menu command. When you undo all of your edits in this way, the document is restored to the previously saved version. This option comes in handy when you have only one version of an important file and current edits aren't to your liking.

To restore a document as you previously saved it, choose File | Revert. After you choose the command, a dialog box is displayed prompting you to revert to the last version of the document or cancel. Click OK to revert the document. This action cannot be undone.

Printing the Document

You can print out a proof copy of a document for a client or print out a final version of the document if intended for print. You can print a document from Fireworks using any installed system printer device. When you choose to print a copy of the document, you can specify the output size and document orientation when setting up the page.

Setting Up the Page

When you print a copy of your document, you can modify the page layout and choose an output device. You can choose the paper size and paper source, modify the margins of the document, and specify the printer device with which to output the document.

Here's how you set up your document for a system printer:

1. Choose File | Page Setup. The Page Setup dialog box, shown in Figure 4-10, appears.

2. Click the triangle to the right of the Size field and choose an option from the drop-down menu. Choose the paper size that matches the paper used by the intended output device.

3. Click the triangle to the right of the Source field and choose a paper source option available for the intended output device.

4. In the Orientation section, accept Portrait (the default) or choose Landscape.

5. In the Margins section, accept the default margin settings or enter different values in the Left, Right, Top, and Bottom fields. The values you enter determine how margins are rendered around the objects in your document.

6. To change the printer, click the Printer button to open a printer Page Setup dialog box.

7. Click the triangle to the right of the Name field and choose a printer from the drop-down menu.

8. Click the Properties button to change output options for the printer device. The options you can modify depend on the system printer you choose. Refer to your printer user manual for specific instructions.

9. If you work on a network, click the Network button and choose a network printer as the intended output device.

10. Click OK to close the printer Page Setup dialog box, and then click OK to apply the settings and close the first Page Setup dialog box.

Tip   *If you have a full version of Adobe Acrobat installed on your system, Acrobat Distiller is installed as a system printer. You can choose Acrobat Distiller for a printer and then print a copy of the document in PDF format. You can attach the PDF file to an e-mail and send the file to a faraway client or a colleague in a different locale.*

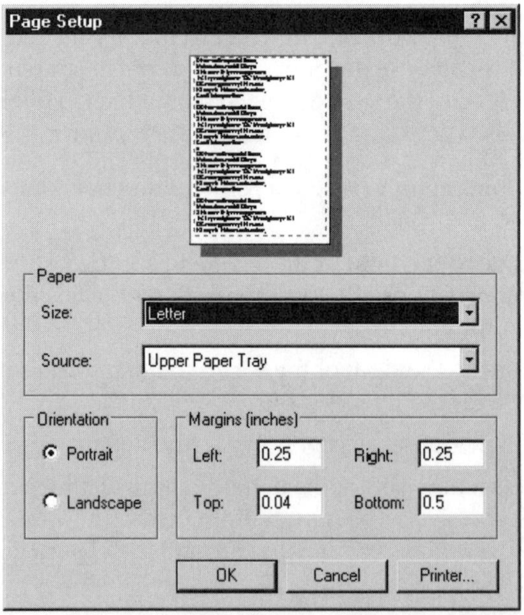

Figure 4-10.   *You use the Page Setup box to set up your document for a system printer.*

Using the Print Command

After you set up the page, you're ready to print the document.

To print the document on a system printer, follow these steps:

1. Choose File | Print. The Print dialog box, shown next, opens.

2. Accept the current printer, or click the triangle to the right of the Name field and choose a printer from the drop-down menu. If you specify a printer using the Page Setup command, the printer is displayed as the current printer.

3. Click the Properties button to modify options for the selected printer.

4. Select an option in the Print Range section. If your document has only one frame, All is the only available option. If the document is a multiple-frame animation, you can specify the range of pages to print by selecting Frames and then entering the starting and ending frame to print.

5. In the Copies area, enter the number of copies to print. Alternatively, you can click the spinner button (the up and down arrows to the right of the field) to specify the number of copies to print.

6. Click OK to print the document.

Summary

In this chapter, you got your first taste of the typical workflow in a Fireworks project. You learned the various steps you apply to take a project from inception to completion. You previewed the various dialog boxes you'll be using when you create your own Fireworks documents. These dialog boxes are discussed in more detail throughout this book when they're needed to complete a specific task. In Chapter 5, you'll learn how to use the vector drawing tools to add objects to your documents.

Fireworks
MX

Part II

Creating Artwork for Your Designs

The
Complete
Reference

Chapter 5

Working with
Vector Objects

Afterter you create a new document, you have a blank canvas to work with. Whether the canvas is sized for a full Web page or a banner, you create the document by importing bitmap images or vector graphics, or by creating vector objects with the Fireworks drawing tools. As you learned previously, vector objects are composed of paths and areas of solid color. Vector objects can be resized with little or no loss in fidelity, which makes them ideal for objects like buttons or banner backgrounds. When you export the document, vector objects are converted to raster (bitmap) images. In this chapter, you'll learn how to import vector graphics created in other programs as well as how to create your own vector objects with the drawing tools.

Importing Vector Drawings

If you use illustration software such as Illustrator, Corel Draw, or Freehand to create illustrations, you can import them directly into Fireworks. If a client supplies you with artwork saved as .ai or .eps files, you can import these art files directly into Fireworks. You can also drag and drop items directly into Fireworks from open documents saved in a supported format. However, certain features, such as textures, or blends may not be supported. This depends largely on the export settings used when the document was saved in its native application.

Adobe Illustrator Files

While working in Fireworks, you can open or import Adobe Illustrator files that are saved in the Adobe Illustrator (AI) or Encapsulated PostScript (EPS) format. When you open an Illustrator document file in Fireworks, you can edit it. When you import a file, Fireworks adds the imported document to the current Fireworks document.

When you import files of these types into Fireworks, you have the option of preserving layers, blends, and objects as editable items in the Fireworks document. You can also scale the image when opening it or importing it.

To open or import an Adobe Illustrator file, follow these steps:

1. Choose File | Open to open a file, or choose File | Import to import a file. The Open dialog box or Import dialog box opens. The dialog boxes are similar; the Open dialog box has two options not applicable to importing files, as shown here:

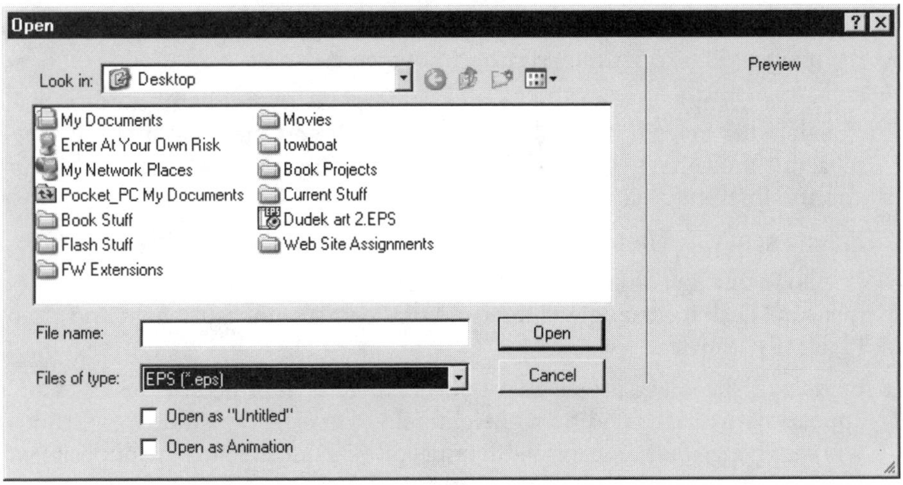

2. Click the triangle to the right of the Files Of Type field and choose Adobe Illustrator (.ai, .art) or EPS (.eps). Alternatively, you can accept the default All Readable Files option.

3. Click the triangle to the right of the Look In field and navigate to the folder where the file is stored.

4. Select the desired File then click Open to open the selected file. A dialog box appears, listing the available options for the selected file type. The options differ according to the type of file you open and are covered in the sections that follow.

Opening .eps Files

When you import or open .eps files, you can change the image size and resolution. You can also specify whether or not to anti-alias the image. When you specify a different image size, you can scale it proportionately or not. To open an .eps file follow these steps:

1. Choose File | Open, select an .eps file and then in the Open dialog box, click Open. The EPS File Options dialog appears, as shown here:

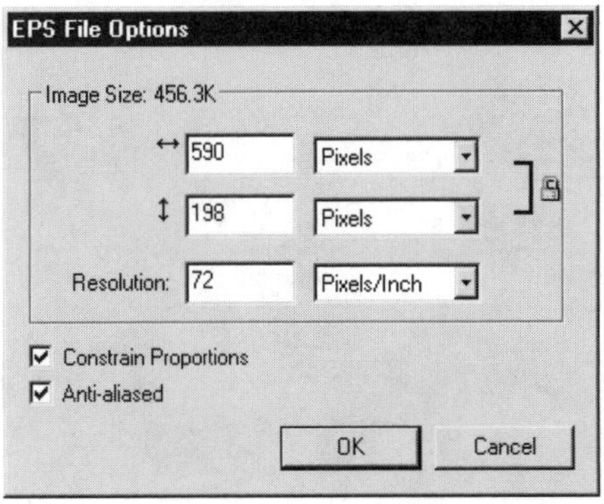

2. In the Image Size section, enter a new value for the width or height. By default, the image will be constrained proportionately.

3. Click the triangle to the right of the unit of measure field and choose Pixels (the default), Percent, Inches, or Centimeters. If you choose a different unit of measure, the value in the window changes to reflect your selection. You can specify different units of measure for width and height.

4. Enter a new value in the Resolution field, or accept the default value of 72.

5. Pixels/Inch is the default unit of measure. To change the Resolution unit of measure, click the triangle to the right of the unit of measure field and choose Pixels/Centimeter.

6. By default, the image is resized proportionately as indicated by the lock icon that appears between the width and height fields. Deselect Constrain Proportions and you can change the value for width or height without affecting the opposite value.

7. By default, Fireworks anti-aliases (smoothes transitions between pixels of different colors) when opening or importing an .eps image. Deselect the Anti-aliased checkbox to open or import the file without anti-aliasing.

8. Click OK to complete importing or opening the file.

Opening .ai Files

When you open or import files saved in the .ai format, you can scale the image by percentage; modify the width or height of the graphic; anti-alias paths and/or text; convert pages to frames; flatten layers; or convert objects, blends, or tiled fills to bitmaps when they exceed a certain value. To open a file saved in the AI format, follow these steps:

1. Choose File | Open, select an .ai file and then in the Open dialog box, click Open to open the Vector File Options dialog box shown here:

2. To resize the image by percentage, enter a value in the percentage field, or drag the slider to select a value. When you choose a value, the image is scaled proportionately, and the Width and Height fields are updated to reflect the size of the image when opened in Fireworks.

3. To resize the image to a given value, enter a number in either the Width or Height field. The image will be resized proportionately. The opposite value will refresh to reflect the size of the image as opened in Fireworks and the Percentage value updates as well.

4. In the Anti-Alias section, choose whether to anti-alias paths, text, or both.

5. If you anti-alias paths and/or text, Fireworks applies a smooth anti-alias by default. Click the triangle to the right of the anti-alias type window and choose Smooth, Crisp, or Strong from the drop-down menu. The Smooth method works well in most instances. Choose Crisp or Strong to sharply define areas of differing colors.

6. In the File Conversion section, you can modify the following:

   ■ If you are importing or opening a multiple-page document, click the triangle to the right of the first field and choose: Open A Page to open a specific page of the document, or choose Open Pages As Frames to open all pages in the file as separate frames in Fireworks.

   ■ If you choose the Open A Page option, the first page is imported by default. To specify a different page, click the triangle to the right of the Page field and choose the desired page from the drop-down menu.

   ■ If the document you are opening or importing has multiple layers, click the triangle to the right of second field and choose one of the following: Remember Layers (the default) to preserve the file's layers in Fireworks, Ignore Layers to flatten the file's layers to a single layer in Fireworks, or Convert Layers To Frames to convert each layer to a frame in Fireworks.

   ■ If the file you are importing or opening has invisible layers, they are not imported unless you choose the Include Invisible Layers option.

   ■ If the file you are importing or opening has a background layer(s), by default it is not imported. Choose Include Background Layers to include the file's background layers as separate layers in Fireworks.

7. When you open or import a file with groups of objects, blends with a large number of steps, or tiled fills with a large number of objects, Fireworks renders these as bitmap images when they exceed a value of 30. To preserve objects of these types in Fireworks, regardless of the number of items in a group, deselect one or more options in this section. Alternatively, you can modify the number of items in a group before Fireworks converts the group to a bitmap. When Fireworks converts a group to a bitmap, it behaves as a single object.

8. Click OK to import the file into Fireworks.

> **Caution** *If you open or import a vector object with groups containing grouped objects, blended fills, or tiled fills with a large number of objects and opt to preserve all objects, the document file size may be exceptionally large.*

Corel Draw Files

If you use Corel Draw to create illustrations, you can open these files in Fireworks or import them into Fireworks documents, provided they are saved as version 8.0 or earlier and have not been compressed. When you import or open a Corel Draw file, you can preserve layers and other objects.

To import a Corel Draw file, follow these steps:

1. Choose File | Open or File | Import. The Open or Import dialog box appears. Both dialog boxes have similar options.

2. Click the triangle to the right of the Files Of Type field and choose Corel Draw (.cdr), or accept the default All Readable Files option.

3. Click the triangle to the right of the Look In field and navigate to the folder where the file is stored.

4. Select the file you want to open or import. Alternatively, you can enter the filename with extension in the File Name field.

5. Click Open. The Vector File Options dialog box appears.

6. In the dialog box, modify the applicable parameters for the file you are opening or importing into a Fireworks document. Refer to the steps in the previous section, "Opening .ai Files," for information on this dialog box.

7. Click OK to open or import the file.

Freehand Files

If you use Macromedia Freehand to create your graphic illustrations, you can open these files in Fireworks or import them into existing Fireworks documents. You can resize the graphic, choose to preserve layers, and set other applicable parameters when you open or import the file in Fireworks. Freehand files open or import into Fireworks with most of the objects preserved. You can open or import files with the .fh (Freehand) or .fht (Freehand Template) extension. To open a Freehand file, or import one into a Fireworks document, choose File | Open, or File | Import, and follow the steps outlined earlier in the "Opening .ai Files" section.

Transferring Vector Objects into Fireworks

You can transfer vector objects from an open file into a Fireworks document in two ways: You can use objects from supported vector file formats that are open in their native applications, or you can use objects from open files in Fireworks.

Using the first method, you copy objects from an open file and then paste them into a Fireworks document. If both documents are open within Fireworks, select the object you want to transfer and then choose Edit | Copy. Click anywhere inside the Fireworks document you want to copy to and then choose Edit | Paste. After the item is copied into the Fireworks document, you can use tools, panels, and menu commands to move or otherwise modify the object.

If the file with the vector object you need is open in another application, use that application's copy command to copy the object to the clipboard. Switch to the Fireworks document you want to copy the object to and choose Edit | Paste. If the document from which you are copying the objects is a different resolution than the Fireworks document, the objects are resampled to the Fireworks document resolution when they are pasted.

Caution	*If you copy the object from its native application, you may lose certain features, such as gradient fills. Other objects may paste into Fireworks bordered by a white rectangle. Objects copied from Freehand and pasted into Fireworks retain most of their Freehand features.*

Another way to get vector objects into Fireworks is to drag them from one document and drop them into the Fireworks document. To drag and drop an object from an open file into a Fireworks document, do the following:

1. Create the Fireworks document, or open an existing document.

2. Choose File | Open and open the file that contains the vector objects needed for the current document.

3. Choose Window | Tile Horizontal or Window | Tile Vertical.

4. Drag the object from the vector file and drop it into the Fireworks document, as shown in Figure 5-1.

Creating Vector Objects

You can use the Fireworks drawing tools in the toolbox to create vector objects for your designs. The vector objects you create can be as simple as a rectangle or as complex as a closed path composed of editable points. Certain parameters of tools can be edited—for example the radius of the corners on a rounded rectangle. You use the Property inspector to modify a tool's parameters and to modify the parameters of an object in the document you are creating.

In this section, you'll learn how to use tools to create objects. To select a tool, you click its icon on the toolbar. If the tool you need is part of a tool group, the icon of last tool selected is displayed on the toolbar. Click the icon and hold down the mouse button until the tool group's flyout menu expands. Then click the tool you need to use. When you select a tool, you can specify the stroke color and fill color for the object you'll create with the tool.

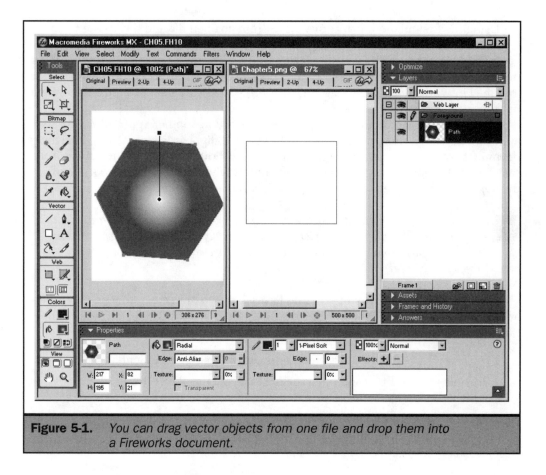

Figure 5-1. You can drag vector objects from one file and drop them into a Fireworks document.

Introducing Strokes and Fills

Every object you create with a closed path can have a stroke (outline), a fill (solid color or gradient that fills the shape with color), or both. When you create an object with the Line tool, it is an open path, which means that the object has a stroke but no fill. When you use the Pen or Brush tool to create an object, you can close the path or keep it open. You can modify stroke and fill parameters with the Property inspector.

Choosing a Stroke Color

After you select a tool, you can specify the stroke color for shapes you create. When you specify a stroke color, it becomes the current stroke color and is applied to all future objects you create with a stroke—until you choose another color. You can specify a stroke color in the Color section of the toolbox or within the Property inspector. The default width for a stroke is 1 pixel.

Here's how to select a stroke color:

1. Select a tool.
2. Click the Stroke icon (the pencil) in the Colors section of the toolbox.
3. Click the No Fill or Stroke icon to create an object with no stroke.
4. Click the color swatch to open the pop-up palette. Your cursor becomes an eyedropper. As you drag your cursor over the swatches, the color window changes to reflect the color over which your cursor is currently positioned. The color's hexadecimal value is noted as well. Alternatively, you can choose a color not on the pop-up palette by clicking the System Color Picker button and then choosing a color from the palette shown here:

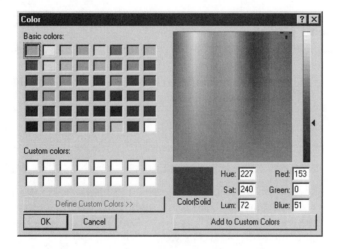

5. Click a color to select it as shown in the following illustration. The Stroke color well refreshes to reflect the color you selected. This color is used on all objects you create until you repeat the previous steps to modify the current stroke color.

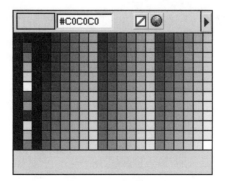

At the bottom of the color palette shown in the previous illustration, notice the Stroke Options button that you can click to modify how the stroke appears on the object.

You can also specify stroke color from within the Property inspector, and you can modify the stroke width and style, tasks you'll learn to perform in Chapter 9. To specify stroke color using the Property inspector, follow these steps:

1. Select a tool.

2. Open the Property inspector.

3. Click the color swatch to the right of the stroke color well. Your cursor becomes an eyedropper.

4. Click a color to select it. The swatch in the stroke color changes to reflect the selected color.

Choosing a Fill Color

To create a solid-looking object, you choose a fill color. You can choose a solid or a gradient fill. You can choose a fill using the fill color well in the Colors section of the toolbox or within the Property inspector. To choose a fill color using the fill color well, use these steps:

1. Select a tool.

2. Click the fill icon (the paint bucket) in the fill color well.

3. To create an object with a transparent fill, click the No Fill Or Stroke button.

4. Click the color swatch to open the pop-up palette. Your cursor becomes an eyedropper. As you move your cursor over a swatch, the color window updates to reflect the swatch over which your cursor is currently positioned. The color's hexadecimal value is displayed as well.

5. Click a color to select it. The swatch in the fill color well refreshes to display the color you selected. The color is applied to all future filled objects you create until you repeat the previous steps to choose a different fill color.

Creating Rectangles

You can add rectangles to your document with the Rectangle tool. You can use rectangles as the basis for many items—for example, as a background for a site banner. Rectangles can be the basis for more complex objects, as you'll learn in Chapter 11. Here's how to add a rectangle to your document:

1. Select the Rectangle tool shown here:

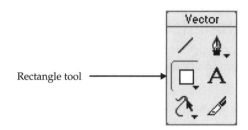

Rectangle tool ⟶

2. Specify a stroke and fill color as outlined previously.

3. Click the point on the canvas where you want the rectangle to appear, and then drag across and down. As you drag, Fireworks creates a bounding box that gives you a preview of the size and position of the rectangle.

4. Release the mouse button when the rectangle is the desired size. Fireworks creates the rectangle, as shown in Figure 5-2.

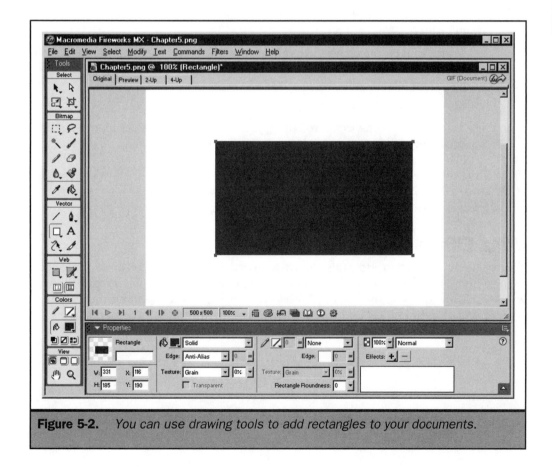

Figure 5-2.   *You can use drawing tools to add rectangles to your documents.*

Creating Rectangles with Rounded Corners

Another useful object you can create for your Fireworks designs is a rectangle with rounded corners. A rectangle with rounded corners can form a button shape or a background for a block of text. Use these steps to create a rectangle with rounded corners:

1. Select the Rounded Rectangle tool shown here:

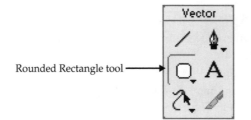

Rounded Rectangle tool ⟶

2. Accept the current stroke and fill colors, or choose different ones as outlined previously.

3. Click the point on the canvas where you want the rectangle to appear, and then drag down and across. As you drag, Fireworks creates a bounding box preview of the rectangle's current size.

4. Release the mouse button when the rectangle is the desired size.

5. Open the Property inspector and drag the rectangle roundness slider to modify the rectangle corner radius, as shown in Figure 5-3.

Tip   *You can change the position of a rectangle, rounded rectangle, ellipse, or polygon as you create it by holding down the SPACEBAR and dragging. Release the SPACEBAR when the object is in the desired position and continue dragging to finish creating the object.*

Creating Ellipses

You use the Ellipse tool to add ovals and circles to a document. You can use a shape you create with this tool as the basis for a more complex object. When you create an object with the Ellipse tool, you can use the Subselection tool to select and move individual points to create a different shape. You'll learn to work with the Subselection tool in Chapter 11.

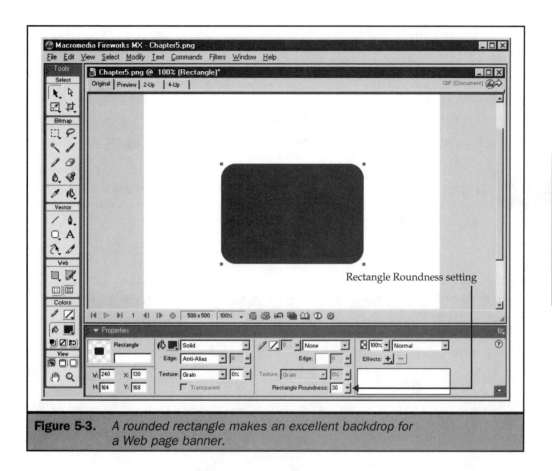

Figure 5-3.   *A rounded rectangle makes an excellent backdrop for a Web page banner.*

Use these steps to add an ellipse to your document:

1. Select the Ellipse tool shown here:

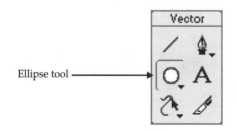

Ellipse tool

2. Specify a stroke and fill color as outlined previously. Remember that you can create an outline by clicking the fill icon and then clicking the No Fill Or Stroke button.

3. Click the spot on the canvas where you want the ellipse to appear, and drag down and across. As you drag the tool, Fireworks creates a preview that shows you the current size and position of the ellipse.

4. Release the mouse button when the ellipse is the desired size, as shown in Figure 5-4.

Tip *To constrain a shape drawn with the Rectangle or Rounded Rectangle tool to a perfect square, hold down the SHIFT key as you create the shape. To constrain a shape created with the Ellipse tool to a round circle, hold down the SHIFT key as you drag the ellipse tool across the canvas.*

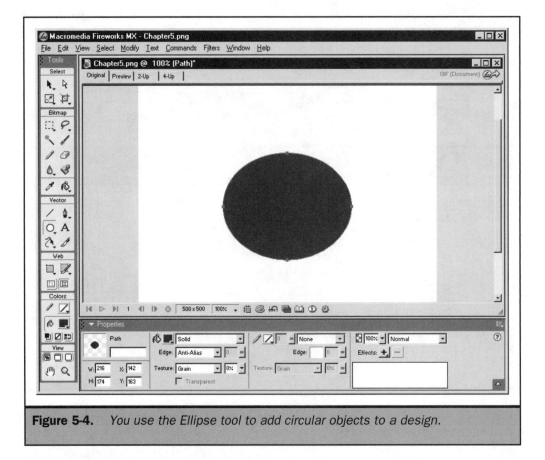

Figure 5-4. *You use the Ellipse tool to add circular objects to a design.*

Creating Polygons

You can add pentagon-like shapes to your designs with the Polygon tool. You can combine polygons with other shapes or use them as standalone objects. To add a polygon to a document, follow these steps:

1. Select the Polygon tool shown here:

Polygon tool   ⟶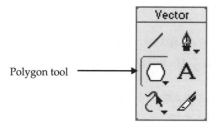

2. Choose a stroke and fill color for the shape as outlined previously.

3. Click a spot on the canvas where you want the polygon to appear, and then drag down and across. As you drag the tool, a preview is displayed, reflecting the current size and shape of the object. Remember that you can press the SPACEBAR momentarily and drag the object to a different position and release it, finishing creating the shape.

4. Release the mouse button when the polygon is the size you want. Fireworks creates the shape, as shown in Figure 5-5.

Creating Straight Lines

You can add straight lines to your designs with the Line tool. Lines have a stroke but no fill. You can modify the thickness of a line using the Property inspector. Here's how to add a line to a document:

1. Select the Line tool shown here:

Line tool   ⟶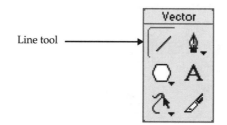

2. Accept the current stroke color, or choose a different color as outlined previously.

3. Accept the default thickness of 1 pixel. To modify the thickness of the line, open the Property inspector and drag the slider to the right of the stroke color well to the desired value.

4. Click the spot on the canvas where you want to create the line and drag. As you drag, a preview appears showing you the current position and shape of the line.

5. To constrain the line, do one of the following:

   ■ Hold down the SHIFT key and drag left or right to constrain the line to the horizontal axis.

   ■ Hold down the SHIFT key and drag down to constrain the line to a vertical axis.

   ■ Hold down the SHIFT key and drag diagonally to constrain the line to a 45-degree angle.

6. Release the mouse button when the line is the desired size. Figure 5-6 shows several lines created with the Line tool.

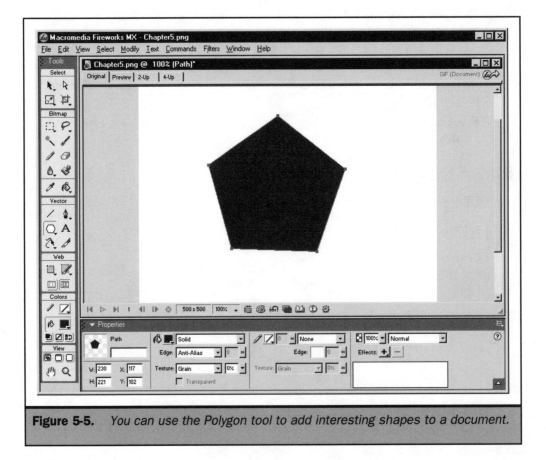

Figure 5-5.   *You can use the Polygon tool to add interesting shapes to a document.*

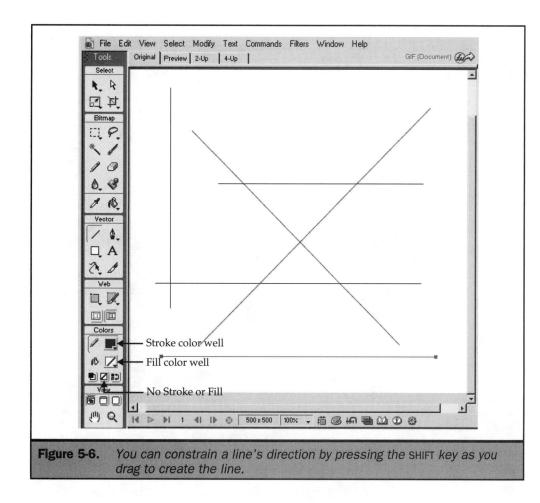

Stroke color well

Fill color well

No Stroke or Fill

Figure 5-6.   *You can constrain a line's direction by pressing the* SHIFT *key as you drag to create the line.*

Using the Pen Tool

You can use the Pen tool to create vector shapes. When you use the Pen tool, you create a path of interconnected points that can be composed of curve points, straight points, or a combination. You can create an open or closed path with the tool. The shapes you create with the Pen tool can be constrained or freeform. Figure 5-7 shows several paths created with the Pen tool.

Creating a Path with the Pen Tool

When you use the Pen tool to create a path, you specify where the points appear on the canvas. If the snap to grid feature is enabled, the points you create will be attracted to

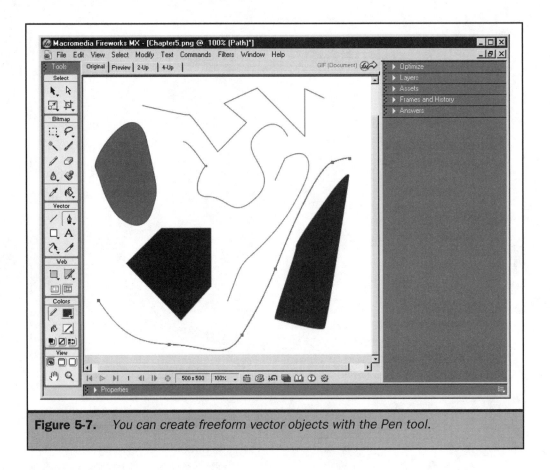

Figure 5-7.   *You can create freeform vector objects with the Pen tool.*

grid intersections when you click near the grid point's intersection. To create a path with the Pen tool, follow these steps:

   1. Select the Pen tool shown here:

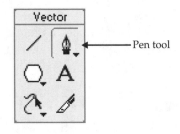

   2. Choose a stroke and fill color as outlined previously. If you create an open path, only the stroke will be used; a closed path will display the stroke and fill you specify.

3. Choose View | Grid | Show Grid to use the grid as a guide when creating a path.

4. Choose View | Grid | Snap To Grid if you want to snap the points you create to nearby grid intersections.

5. Click the point on the canvas where you want the path to begin. After you click, a solid point appears.

6. Click the place where you want the second point to appear. Fireworks joins the two points.

7. Continue adding points to create the path.

8. Double-click the ending point to finish creating the path. The Pen tool is available to create a new path.

Creating Straight Paths

When you click a point on the canvas, the path node (or point) is straight. To create a straight line, click a position on the canvas, move the Pen tool to another spot on the canvas, and then click again. Fireworks combines the points to create a straight path. You can constrain the path as you create it by doing one of the following:

■ To constrain the path to the horizontal axis, create one point and then, while holding down the SHIFT key, click a point to the left or right of the beginning point.

■ To constrain the path to the vertical axis, click to create a point, and then, while holding down the SHIFT key, click above or below the starting point.

About Closed and Open Paths

An open path is a connection of points where the beginning and ending points don't connect. When you create a closed path, you connect the beginning and ending points. When you create a closed path, it can have a stroke but no fill, a stroke and fill, or a fill without a stroke. The following illustration shows an example of an open and closed path.

■ To constrain the path diagonally 45 degrees, click to create one point, and then, while holding down the SHIFT key, click above or below and to the left or right of the beginning point.

You can create a complex multiple-point path, for example, by holding down the SHIFT key and constraining the Pen tool to the vertical axis for one path segment, the horizontal axis for the next path segment, 45 degrees diagonally for the next path segment, and so on. Figure 5-8 shows a path created in this manner.

Creating Curved Paths

You can draw graceful, flowing curved paths with the Pen tool. When you create a curved path segment with the Pen Tool you create path nodes with two tangential handles that can be dragged to modify the shape of the curve. You can define the shape of the curve as you create the path, and after creating it, you can edit the path with the Subselection tool. To create a curved path, do the following:

1. Click and drag the point on the canvas where you want the curved path to begin. As you drag, two tangential handles appear, as shown here:

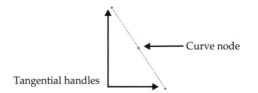

2. Release the mouse button when the tangential handles are the desired length. Note that when you create a curve node as the starting point of a path, you will not be able to see the effect the handles have on the curved segment.

3. Click and drag the point on the canvas where you want to end the curved segment. As you drag, Fireworks creates two tangential handles and displays a preview of the curved path. As you drag, you can move the mouse to control the alignment of the tangential handles. If you hold down the SHIFT key while dragging with the mouse, the tangential handles are constrained to 45-degree increments.

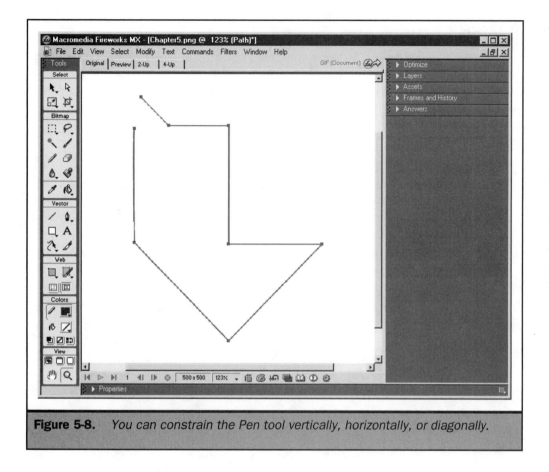

Figure 5-8.   *You can constrain the Pen tool vertically, horizontally, or diagonally.*

4. Release the mouse button when the path is the desired shape. Fireworks creates the curved path as shown here:

Combining Straight and Curved Nodes

You can create wonderfully complex shapes and paths by combining straight and curved nodes. When you create path segments by combining straight and curved nodes, Fireworks creates tangential handles that you can use to modify the path.

To combine straight and curved nodes, do the following:

1. Select the Pen tool and create the beginning point for the path. You can create either a curved or straight node.

2. Click the point on the canvas where you want to create a straight path segment, or click and drag to create a curved path segment. If you're creating a curved segment, drag until the segment curves to your liking. Remember that you can hold down the SHIFT key while creating the point to constrain the path segment vertically, horizontally, or diagonally.

3. Create additional curved or straight points as needed to add curved or straight path segments to your design.

4. Double-click the ending point to finish creating the path. The following illustration shows a path that is a combination of straight and curved segments.

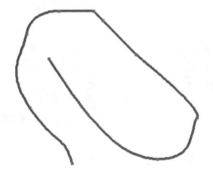

Closing a Path

When you want to create a closed path, you join the beginning and ending path points. You can create a closed path that is an outline or that looks like a solid shape. To create a closed path, do the following:

1. Select the Pen tool.

2. Specify a stroke color and click the No Stroke Or Fill button for the fill if you want the closed path displayed as an outline; or select a stroke color or no stroke color and a fill color to display the closed path as a solid object.

3. Click on the canvas to create the points that define the shape. Remember that you can combine straight and curved nodes to define the shape. As you create the path, Fireworks displays each segment as you create a new point.

4. When the path is the desired shape, click the first point to close the path. Fireworks renders the shape using the stroke and fill colors you specified, as shown here:

Note	*Editing and modifying paths is covered in Chapter 11.*

Setting Pen Tool Preferences

The following section shows you how to set preferences for the Pen tool. For information on setting the other preferences, refer to Chapter 3.

By default, Fireworks displays selected points as solid points and does not generate a preview of paths you create with the Pen tool. You can modify these preferences to suit your working style by doing the following:

1. Choose Edit | Preferences to open the Preferences dialog box.

2. Click the Editing tab to open the Editing section of the dialog box, as shown next. You can set Pen tool preferences to suit your working style.

3. Choose Show Pen Preview to have Fireworks display a preview of a path as you drag across the canvas, but before you click to create the next point in the path. You may find this mode helpful if you use the Pen tool to create complex open and closed paths.

4. Choose Show Solid Points to display selected points as hollow dots and unselected points as solid dots.

5. Click OK to apply the new editing preferences.

Using the Vector Path Tool

You use the Vector Path tool to create freeform painterly paths. With the Vector Path tool, you don't have the point-to-point control of the Pen tool; instead, Fireworks generates the points as you drag the tool across the canvas.

To create a path with the Vector Path tool, do the following:

1. Select the Vector Path tool shown here:

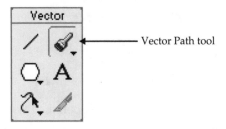

Vector Path tool

2. Select a stroke color as outlined previously.

3. Open the Property inspector.

4. To change the width of the path you create with the tool, click the slider to the right of the stroke color well and drag to specify the path thickness. Alternatively, you can enter any reasonable value in the text field.

5. Click the triangle to the right of the Stroke Category window and choose a setting from the drop-down menu, as shown in the following illustration. Stroke styles modify the shape of the path that you draw with the tool. The default stroke path for the tool creates a path that looks as though it were created with an airbrush. You can choose a different style to create a different look; for example,

click Watercolor and choose one of the options to create a path that looks as though it were created by a watercolor artist's brush. Stroke styles will be covered in greater detail in Chapter 9.

Stroke thickness —————   ————— Stroke thickness slider

Stroke color well —————   ————— Stroke category

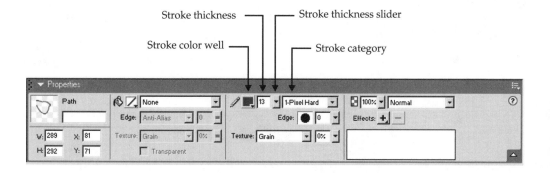

6. Click and drag on the canvas to create the path. As you drag the tool, Fireworks generates a preview of the path. You can constrain the path to the horizontal axis, vertical axis, or a 45-degree diagonal by holding down the SHIFT key as you drag. You can combine different constraints on the same path by halting the mouse where you want to change direction, releasing the mouse, and then pressing the SHIFT key before dragging in a different direction. This can be a bit tricky, however, and won't always produce the results you expect.

7. Release the mouse button when the path is the desired shape. Fireworks renders the path and creates the necessary points. You can create artistic looking paths with the Vector Path tool.

Tip   *You can close a path created with the Vector Path tool by moving your cursor over the beginning of the path and then releasing the mouse button. Fireworks closes the path; no fill is used. With the path still selected, click the fill color well in the toolbox or in the Property inspector and choose a color from the pop-up palette.*

Modifying a Shape's Basic Characteristics

After you create a shape with any of the Fireworks drawing tools, you can perform all manner of modifications on the shape. Editing objects will be covered in detail in Chapter 11. In this section, you'll learn how to move a shape to a new position and change its size.

Selecting an Object

When you have placed several objects on the canvas and need to modify the document, you can select an object and use a tool, menu command, or the Property inspector to make modifications. Here's how you select an object:

1. Select the Pointer tool shown here:

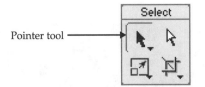

Pointer tool

2. Click an object to select it. To add objects to the selection, hold down the SHIFT key while clicking the objects you want to add. When you select more than one object, you can edit them at once.

Moving an Object

You can move a shape manually by using the Pointer tool, or you can move an object to a specific location using the Property inspector. You can move a single object or a selection of objects.

You can move an object or selection of objects manually by doing the following:

1. Select the object(s) you want to move with the Pointer tool as outlined previously.
2. Drag the object(s) to the desired location and release the mouse button.

You can move an object or a selection of objects numerically using the Property inspector by following these steps:

1. Select the objects you want to reposition with the Pointer tool, as shown previously in this chapter.
2. Open the Property inspector.
3. Enter the desired value in the X and/or Y fields and press ENTER or RETURN. In the following illustration, the objects are moved to the specified location.

Width   X coordinate

Height   Y coordinate

In the previous illustration notice the fields for the width and height of the selected object(s). You can enter values in these fields to resize the object numerically. You can also use other methods to resize objects as well, as you'll learn in Chapter 11.

Arranging Objects

When you create multiple objects for your documents, a stacking order is established. The last shape you create, or the last object you import, is at the top of the stack. Objects on top of the stack eclipse the objects below. As you edit your document, you may find it necessary to arrange the stacking order by bringing objects to the top or bottom of the stack or to a point in between. You arrange the stacking order of objects by using menu commands.

Here's how you rearrange the stacking order of your document:

1. Using the Pointer tool, select the object you want to rearrange.
2. Choose Modify | Arrange, and from the Arrange submenu, choose one of the following commands:

   - **Bring to Front**   Moves the selected object to the top of the stack.
   - **Bring Forward**   Moves the object ahead of the next object in the stack, but behind objects higher in the stacking order.
   - **Send Backward**   Moves the object back one position in the stack, but in front of objects lower in the stack.
   - **Send to Back**   Moves the selected object to the bottom of the stack.

Understanding Blend Modes

When you create and add objects to your document, they appear above objects that were created previously. By default, Fireworks eclipses objects that are lower in the stacking order. This is called the Normal blend mode. You can achieve interesting effects by selecting an object and changing its blend mode.

To change an object's blend mode, do the following:

1. Select the object whose blend mode you want to modify.

2. Open the Property inspector.

3. Click the triangle to the right of the Blend Mode field shown in Figure 5-9, and then choose one of the following:

   - **Normal** The default blend mode. Choose this mode and the selected object is not blended with the objects below it in the stacking order.

   - **Multiply** Choose this blend mode when you want the colors of the selected object multiplied by the colors of the objects beneath. The net effect of this mode creates a blended color that darkens the selected object, and the objects beneath it are visible.

   - **Screen** Choose this mode and the colors of the selected object are multiplied by the inverse color of the objects beneath. This mode effectively lightens the object.

   - **Darken** Choose this mode and pixels of the selected object that are lighter than the colors of objects below are darkened.

   - **Lighten** Choose this mode and pixels of the selected object that are darker than the colors of the objects below are lightened.

   - **Difference** Choose this mode and two different outcomes are possible: If the pixels of the selected object are brighter than the colors beneath, the base color is subtracted; if the pixels of the selected object are darker, the colors from the selected object are subtracted from the underlying colors.

   - **Hue** Choose this blend mode and the hue value of the selected object is combined with the luminosity and saturation of the underlying colors to produce the blending color.

   - **Saturation** Choose this blend mode to combine the saturation of the object's colors with the luminance and hue of the underlying colors to produce the blended color.

   - **Color** Choose this option to combine the saturation of the object's colors with the luminance of underlying colors. When you choose this mode and objects with grayscale colors are beneath the selected object, a tint is applied. If the selected object is grayscale, the underlying colors tint the object.

   - **Luminosity** Choose this mode to combine the luminance of colors in the selected object with the hue and saturation of underlying colors to produce the blend.

- **Invert**   Choose this blend mode and the colors of underlying objects are inverted to create the blend.

- **Tint**   Choose this mode to create a blend by converting the base color to a grayscale value.

- **Erase**   Choose this mode to remove the color pixels from the selected object, including the color pixels of any underlying objects. The net effect erases all color from the selected object.

Figure 5-10 shows several iterations of a vector object placed on top of an underlying bitmap image. A different blend mode has been applied to each object.

You can also achieve interesting effects by varying the opacity of an object with which you've used a different blend mode. To vary a selected object's opacity, click the Transparency slider and drag. As you drag it, you can view the changes in real time. Alternatively, you can enter a value of 0 (completely transparent), 100 (completely opaque), or any value in between to create varying degrees of transparency.

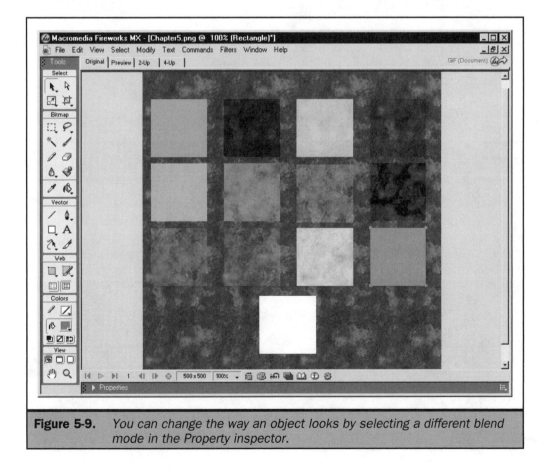

Figure 5-9.   *You can change the way an object looks by selecting a different blend mode in the Property inspector.*

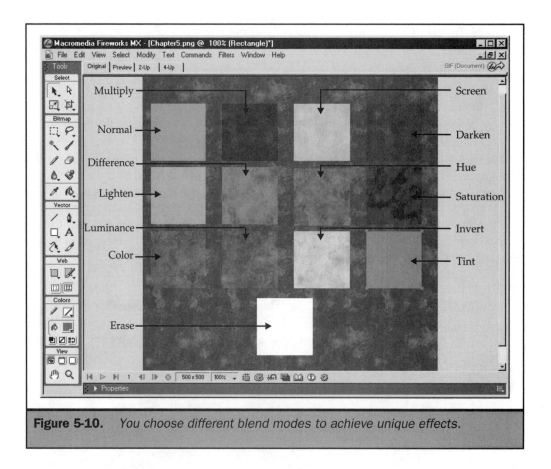

Figure 5-10. *You choose different blend modes to achieve unique effects.*

The following illustration shows three iterations of a bitmap, each with a different transparency level. The image in the middle is at a setting of 100 percent. All images are blended using the Darken mode.

Summary

In this chapter, you learned how to import vector objects into a Fireworks document. You also learned how to create your own vector objects using the Fireworks drawing tools. You were given a brief introduction to modifying objects using the Pointer tool and the Property inspector. Also covered was how to rearrange the stacking order of objects using menu commands. You were shown how to modify an object's appearance by changing its blend mode and transparency. In Chapter 6, you'll be working with bitmap images.

Chapter 6

Working with Bitmap Images

W hen you create a Fireworks document, you can create it for export as a Web page or as a document intended for print. Whichever type of document you create, you can add bitmap images and optimize them for the intended output device. When you work with bitmap images in Fireworks, you can do sophisticated editing such as changing hue and saturation, dodging the image to improve quality, and more. You can also use third-party filters to modify your bitmap images and use Fireworks filters to modify your bitmaps. In this chapter, you'll learn to use Fireworks' powerful bitmap editing features on images you import into your documents and on image files you open for editing.

Understanding Bitmap Images

Although one of Fireworks' main strengths is its use of vector graphics to create images, it is also capable of creating and modifying bitmap images. Vector graphics consist of mathematical formulas that describe the appearance of an image. Bitmap graphics, on the other hand, are composed of dots called pixels (short for *picture elements*).

Understanding Pixels

If you consider a bitmap image as composed of a grid, pixels are the individual spots of color that fill the squares of that grid. Figure 6-1 shows an enlarged view of a bitmap in Fireworks MX. When this grid of colored dots is displayed on a computer screen, our eyes and brains merge all the dots together into a blend that fools us into seeing a picture.

The colored grid technique actually predates the computer age by quite a bit (no pun intended). Take a magnifying glass and look at the Sunday comics, and you'll see that they use the same approach, tiny dots of color assembled to make a continuous image.

When you create a new document in Fireworks MX, you specify the number of pixels in the grid by setting the Width and Height values, as shown in the following illustration. Even if you set the size of the document in inches or centimeters, you are still setting the number of pixels in each dimension when you select how many pixels per inch or centimeter you want in the Resolution value setting.

Figure 6-1.   *You can see the bitmap's grid and pixels in this enlarged view.*

About Image Resolution

The number of pixels per inch (ppi) or pixels per centimeter (ppcm) sets the resolution of an image. The higher the number of pixels per inch (or centimeter), the greater the resolution.

By default, Fireworks uses 72 ppi, a common computer monitor resolution for the Macintosh that is generally accepted as a good resolution for World Wide Web graphics. Some designers set the resolution as high as 96 ppi, which is the accepted norm for PC monitors.

Generally speaking, the more pixels per inch, the better the image quality. The reason for this is that more pixels in the same space means smaller pixels, thus resulting in finer detail. However, as a rule, when you create an image, you set the resolution to match the output device. While a higher resolution results in a better-looking image, it also creates a larger file size. When you're creating a document for export as a Web page or for use as part of a Web design, accept the default resolution of 72 ppi.

Importing Images into a Fireworks Document

The vast majority of images that you work with (clip art, digitized photographs, and so on) are bitmap graphics. Fireworks is capable of handling all the major bitmap graphic file types, either by opening or importing them, or by acquiring new image files using Twain-compliant input devices such as scanners.

Supported Image Formats

Table 6-1 shows the common names and file extensions of the bitmap file formats that Fireworks MX is capable of importing, with the exception of some Illustrator EPS files, EPS files that you open in Fireworks open as bitmaps.

Image Format Name	File Extension(s)
BMP	.bmp, .dib, .rle
Fireworks	.png
FreeHand	.fh, .fh7, .fh8, .fh9, .fh10, .ft7, .ft8, .ft9, .ft10
GIF	.gif
JPEG	.jpg, .jpe, .jpeg
Photoshop	.psd
Targa	.tga
TIFF	.tif, .tiff
WBMP	.wbmp, .wbm

Table 6-1.   *Importable Bitmap File Formats*

Selecting a Twain Device

Before using a Twain-compliant device such as a scanner or digital camera to acquire an image, you need to tell Fireworks MX what the default input device will be when the Scan command is invoked. To select a Twain device, follow these steps:

1. Choose File | Scan | Twain Acquire.

2. In the Select Source dialog box, select the device you want to use as your default Twain source, and then click the Select button; or just double-click the desired device's name.

Scanning Images into Fireworks

The precise series of steps involved in scanning an image into Fireworks MX will vary depending on the software supplied with your scanner. Assuming that you have previously set your scanner as the default Twain device, your scanner's interface opens when you use your scanner to acquire an image. The following shows the process for scanning from a UMAX Astra 2200:

1. Choose File | Scan | Twain Acquire from the menu.
2. Fireworks invokes the scanner software (in this case, UMAX's VistaScan32), shown in Figure 6-2.
3. Make sure the item to be imported is in the scanner.
4. Make any necessary adjustments using the scanner software.

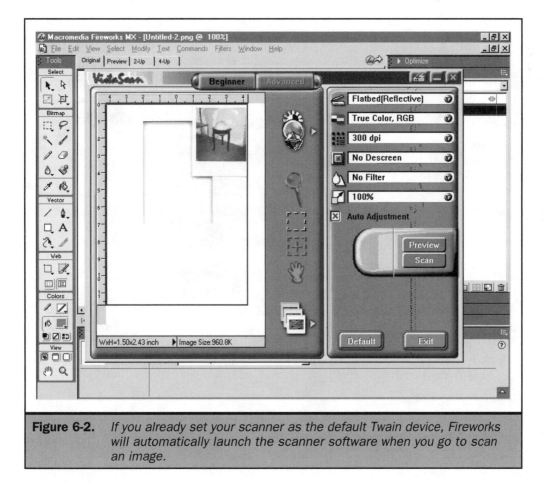

Figure 6-2. *If you already set your scanner as the default Twain device, Fireworks will automatically launch the scanner software when you go to scan an image.*

5. Click the Scan button. The image will be imported directly into Fireworks MX, creating a new document.

6. Click the Exit button.

Capturing Images from Digital Cameras

The process for capturing an image from a digital camera is essentially the same as for capturing one from a scanner. As with scanners, the process can vary depending upon the particular equipment and software. The following steps illustrate how you capture an image from a Logitech QuickCam, assuming that it is already set up as the default Twain device.

1. Choose File | Scan | Twain Acquire from the menu.

2. The camera's software is invoked by Fireworks MX, as shown in Figure 6-3.

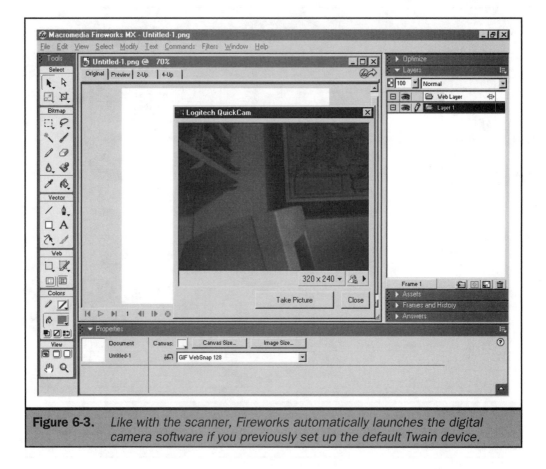

Figure 6-3. *Like with the scanner, Fireworks automatically launches the digital camera software if you previously set up the default Twain device.*

3. Aim and focus the camera.

4. Make any necessary adjustments, such as image size, using the camera's software.

5. Click the Take Picture button, and the image is imported directly into Fireworks MX, creating a new document.

6. Click the Close button.

Inserting New Bitmaps

Bitmaps can be inserted into a document in a few different ways. Of course, you can insert any image already in the clipboard simply by pasting it, but there are other ways. You can add an image from another file by importing the file (as opposed to opening it); and with Fireworks MX, you can also create a new bitmap image by copying or cutting from the same image that you want to insert into.

To insert a bitmap file by importing it, follow these steps:

1. Make sure that the document into which you want to insert the bitmap is open and active.

2. Choose File | Import from the menu.

3. Navigate to the location of the file you want to import.

4. Select the filename and click the Open button (or double-click on the filename).

5. Place the pointer in roughly the upper-left area of the location where you want to insert the imported image in the document, and click.

Here's how you insert a bitmap into a document using the Bitmap Via Copy or Bitmap Via Cut approach:

1. Select an area of a bitmap in the document using one of the Marquee tools.

2. Choose either Edit | Insert | Bitmap Via Copy or Edit | Insert | Bitmap Via Cut from the menu. The only difference between these two methods is that Bitmap Via Copy leaves the original bitmap intact, whereas Bitmap Via Cut leaves a hole in the original bitmap where the selection was cut.

3. The new bitmap appears in the Layers panel, shown here:

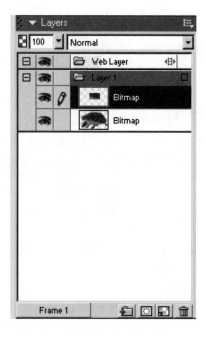

Creating Empty Bitmaps

When you create an empty bitmap, you create an object into which you can paste other bitmap images, or in which you can use any of the drawing tools to create content. You can use any of the bitmap editing tools to modify the bitmap once you have content in it. You can also create an empty bitmap, select part of a bitmap on a lower layer, paste it into the empty bitmap, and then apply filters or live effects to the bitmap to create a special effect.

You can create empty bitmaps using different methods:

1. Create or open a document.

2. Choose Edit | Insert | Empty Bitmap from the menu. Alternatively, click the New Bitmap Image button in the Layers panel, shown here:

New Bitmap
Image button

Once the empty bitmap exists, you can draw inside it using the Pencil or Brush tools, or paste or import bitmap images.

Creating Selections

It is often necessary to select specific areas of an image for various reasons. For example, you may wish to cut or copy a region, fill a particular portion of the image, or apply a filter to a specific area of an image. Many procedures in Fireworks MX depend on the creation of a selection area as the first step.

Creating Rectangular Selections

The most common selections are rectangular selections, and the Marquee tool you use for that purpose is the default bitmap selection tool. To use it, follow these steps:

1. Select the Marquee tool in the toolbox.

2. Place the pointer at the location where you want to establish the corner anchor of the rectangular selection.

3. Click and then drag down and across to define the size of the selection. As you drag the tool, a bounding box appears, giving you a preview of the size and shape of the selection.

4. Release the mouse button when the marquee is the desired size. The selected area will be surrounded by a marquee line, which looks like an army of marching ants. Figure 6-4 shows some rectangular selections.

To make a perfectly square selection, press and hold down the SHIFT *key as you drag the mouse pointer.*

Creating Oval Selections

Rectangles, of course, are not suitable for every selection need you may have. Another common shape used to make selections is the oval.

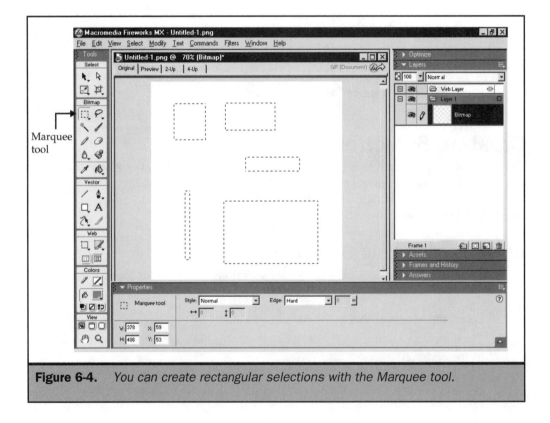

Figure 6-4. *You can create rectangular selections with the Marquee tool.*

To create an oval selection, follow these steps:

1. Click the Marquee tool icon in the toolbox and hold down the mouse button for a moment until the submenu containing the rest of the Marquee tools appears.

2. Select the Oval Marquee tool, shown here:

Oval Marquee tool ⟶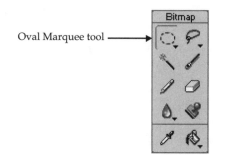

3. Place the pointer at the location where you want to establish the edge of the oval.

4. Click and then drag down and across to define the size of the oval marquee. You can move the selection as you size it by momentarily pressing the space bar. Release the space bar to continue sizing the oval. As you size the selection, a bounding box appears, giving you a preview of the marquee's current size.

5. Release the mouse button when the selection is the desired size. The selected area will be surrounded by a marquee line.

Tip   *To make a perfectly round selection, press and hold down the* SHIFT *key as you drag the mouse pointer.*

Using the Lasso Tool

When the area you need to select won't fit into standard rectangular or oval forms, you can use the Lasso tool to create freeform selections. To create a freeform selection using the Lasso tool, follow these steps:

1. Select the Lasso tool in the toolbox.

2. Place the pointer anywhere along the edge of your desired selection area.

3. Click and hold down the mouse button as you move the pointer around the area you want to select. As you do so, a blue line will follow the pointer, outlining the selection area as you create it.

4. When you have completed drawing the line around the desired selection area, release the mouse button. The selected area will be surrounded by a marquee line. Figure 6-5 shows some freehand selections.

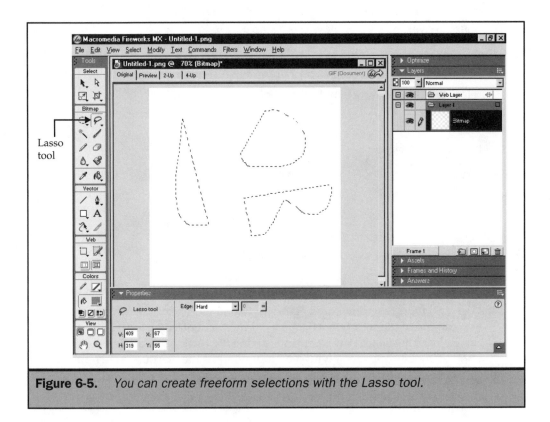

Figure 6-5.   *You can create freeform selections with the Lasso tool.*

<table>
<tr><td>Tip</td><td>*If you release the mouse button before connecting with the starting point, Fireworks MX will automatically close the selection by drawing a line connecting the starting point with the point where you released the mouse button.*</td></tr>
</table>

Using the Polygon Lasso Tool

The Polygon Lasso tool serves a purpose similar to that of the regular Lasso tool. With the Polygon Lasso tool, you can create a selection area that consists of a series of straight line segments, each segment running between points that you have defined on the canvas.

You create a selection with the Polygon Lasso tool as follows:

1. Click the Lasso tool icon in the toolbox and hold down the mouse button for a moment until the rest of the tools in the group appear.

2. Select the Polygon Lasso tool, shown here:

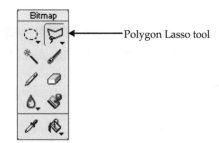

Polygon Lasso tool

3. Place the pointer anywhere along the edge of your desired selection area and click to establish the base point.

4. Move the pointer to the first spot where you need to change direction and click to add another point. As you move the pointer, a straight blue line will follow it, marking the space between the preceding point and the current one.

5. Move the pointer around the selection area, clicking at each point on the canvas where you need to change the direction of the line.

6. When you have completed defining the points around the desired selection area, release the mouse button, and Fireworks closes the selection. The selected area will be surrounded by a marquee line. Use the Polygon Lasso tool to create irregularly shaped selections.

Tip *If you release the mouse button before connecting with the starting point, Fireworks MX will automatically draw a line connecting the starting point with the point where you released the mouse button.*

Using the Magic Wand Tool

You use the Magic Wand tool to create selections based on the similarity of the color values between adjacent pixels. You control the size of the selection by specifying the tolerance level. The tolerance level determines how close in value neighboring pixels must be before they are added to the selection.

The default tolerance value creates a limited selection of pixels. Depending on the color values in a particular image, you may find that this setting fails to select the full range of pixels you desire. If that is the case, you can change the tolerance to a higher value to increase the selection. When you increase the tolerance value, Fireworks is more tolerant of variations in color between neighboring pixels. For example, if you increase the tolerance value and click a red color with the Magic Wand, neighboring pixels don't have to be the exact same shade of red to be included in the selection.

To make a selection with the Magic Wand, do the following:

1. Select the Magic Wand tool in the toolbox.

2. In the Property inspector, set the tolerance to the desired value.

3. Click on the area of the image where you want similar colors to be selected. The area will be surrounded by a marquee line, as shown in Figure 6-6.

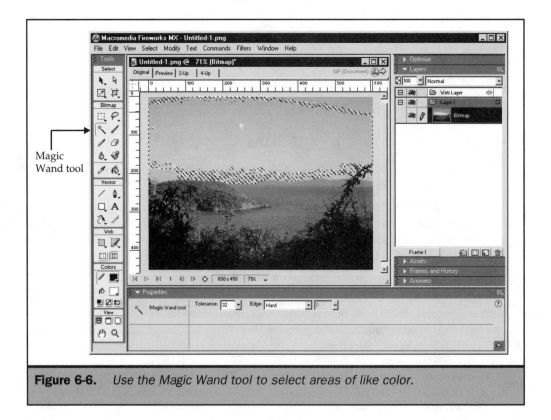

Magic
Wand tool

Figure 6-6.   *Use the Magic Wand tool to select areas of like color.*

4. If the selected area is not what you wanted, adjust the tolerance value in the Property inspector and click on the same area of the image again.

Drawing on Bitmaps

The Pencil tool and the Brush tool are the two tools that can be used to create bitmap images, or draw on existing bitmaps; all the other bitmap tools are used to modify bitmaps.

Using the Pencil Tool

The Pencil tool, shown next, is used to draw a hard line reminiscent of the one created by a lead pencil on paper. Lines created by the Pencil tool are constrained to a width of one pixel.

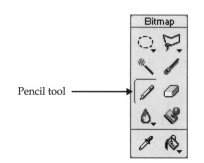

Pencil tool

To use the Pencil tool, follow these steps:

1. Select the Pencil in the toolbox.
2. Open the Property inspector and click the Stroke color swatch to set the stroke color, as shown here:

Opacity

3. If you want the line to be smoothed, click the Anti-aliased checkbox.
4. To prevent the Pencil tool from drawing in transparent areas of the image, click the Preserve Transparency checkbox.
5. To make the Pencil line draw over any fill color it meets, click the Auto Erase checkbox.
6. If you wish, set the opacity of the line by entering a new value in the Opacity box. (The default is 100, or totally opaque.)
7. Place the pointer on the image at the point where you want to begin drawing the line and then drag the tool across the bitmap to define the shape of the line. As you create the tool, a line follows your cursor, giving you a preview of the line's shape.

Note *See Chapter 9 for more information on opacity.*

To constrain the Pencil tool to a straight line, hold down the SHIFT *key as you move the pointer. Straight lines are constrained to 45 degree angles, in the following directions: straight up and down, diagonal, or straight across.*

Using the Brush Tool

The Brush tool is infinitely more flexible and sophisticated than the Pencil tool. By varying the settings in the Brush tool Property inspector, you can create a wide range of brush types and effects. This illustration shows a variety of brush strokes.

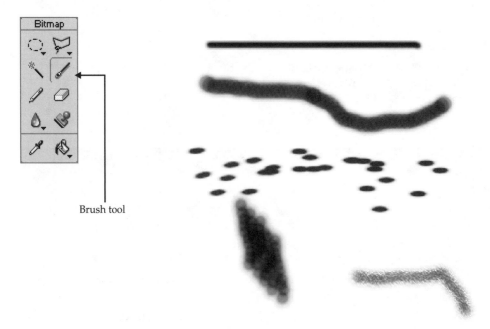

Brush tool

To paint brush strokes, do as follows:

1. Select the Brush tool in the toolbox.

2. Open the Property inspector, and click the Stroke Color well swatch. Select a different color from the palette if you wish, as shown here:

Tip size   Stroke category

Opacity

3. Click and drag the slider to the right of the Tip Size field to select a value. You can also enter a value in the field. The smaller the value, the thinner the line when you paint on an image. The default value is 13.

4. Select a stroke category. The default is Soft Rounded.

5. Set a value in the Edge Softness box. The higher the value, the softer the edge.

6. Set the texture and opacity, if you wish.

7. Click the Preserve Transparency checkbox to prevent the Brush tool from painting in any transparent areas of the image.

8. Place the pointer on the canvas at the point where you want to begin painting and drag the tool across the canvas to create the stroke. As you drag the tool, Fireworks creates a preview of the stroke.

9. Release the mouse button when the brush stroke is as desired.

Note *See Chapter 9 for more information on using textures and opacity.*

Modifying Bitmaps

Bitmaps, whether created entirely by you or taken from some outside source, often require different kinds of modifications. In this section, we'll take a look at the methods Fireworks MX provides for modifying bitmaps, from cropping to smudging.

Cropping Bitmaps

An image, especially an item of clip art, often contains more detail to it than what you want for your purposes. For example, part of the image might be perfect for your document if only you could get rid of the extraneous material. That's where cropping comes in. The Crop tool removes everything outside of the cropping area it covers, leaving only the part of the image you want.

CREATING ARTWORK
FOR YOUR DESIGNS

To size an image with the Crop tool, follow these steps:

1. Select the Crop tool in the toolbox.

2. Place the pointer on the image at the point where you want to select one corner of the rectangular cropping area.

3. Click and then drag down and across to define the shape of the cropping rectangle. As you drag, a bounding box is created, giving you a preview of the cropping rectangle's current size.

4. Release the mouse button when the area you want to preserve has been selected. This illustration shows the cropping rectangle in place.

Crop tool ——

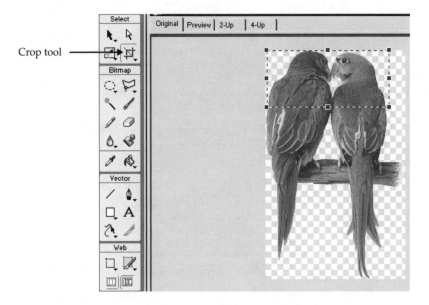

5. Double-click somewhere inside the cropping rectangle. The resulting cropped image is shown here:

Tip   *To resize the cropping rectangle, click and drag one of the eight handles. Drag the middle handles on either side to change the cropping rectangle's width, the center handles on the top and bottom to change height, or one of the corner handles to resize width and height. To resize the rectangle proportionately, hold down the SHIFT key while dragging a corner handle. To move the cropping triangle, click inside it and then drag it to a new location.*

Using the Eraser Tool

Another method for removing material you don't want in a bitmap image is simply to erase it. The Eraser tool is more precise than the Crop tool, and it enables you to erase down to the individual pixel level.

Here's how you use the Eraser tool:

1. Select the Eraser tool in the toolbox, shown here:

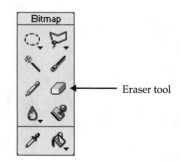

Eraser tool

2. In the Property inspector, set a value for the size of the eraser.

3. In the Edge field, set a value for the edge softness.

4. Choose either the round or square eraser shape. (Round is the default.)

5. If you wish, set the opacity of the eraser by entering a new value in the Opacity box.

Eraser opacity behaves a bit differently than opacity for drawing tools such as the Brush tool. The default value of 100 means that the erasure will be total, while lower values will leave part of the original image intact. The effect of lower values is to lighten the original image where the eraser passes over it. The following two illustrations show these effects. The image on the left is your original image, and the image on the right shows how that same image will look with part of it erased completely (the lower-left side) and part of it erased partially using a low opacity value (the lower-right side).

Note   *See Chapter 9 for more information on opacity.*

Sharpening an Image

You can rescue a slightly blurry image by utilizing Fireworks' sharpening features. Fireworks provides two different ways to manage sharpening: one is to use the Sharpen tool and one is to apply effects.

Using the Sharpen Tool

Sharpen images with the Sharpen tool by following these steps:

1. Click the Blur tool icon in the toolbox. Hold the mouse button down for a moment until the other tools in the group appear.

2. Select the Sharpen tool.

3. In the Property inspector, set a value for the size of the Sharpen tool tip, as shown here:

Tip size

Edge softness   Intensity

4. In the Edge field, set a value for the edge softness.

5. Choose either the round or square shape. (Round is the default.)

6. Click the triangle to the right of the Sharpness field and drag the slider to set a value. Alternatively, enter a value in the text field. Choosing a higher value will increase the sharpening effect.

7. Place the pointer over the area you wish to sharpen.

8. Click and hold down the mouse button as you move the pointer across the image until you have sharpened the desired area

Sharpening with Effects

When you sharpen an image with effects, there are two basic approaches: automatic and manual. The automatic approach has two options, one to sharpen a little bit and one to sharpen the bitmap to a higher degree.

To use the automatic sharpening features, follow this procedure:

1. Select a bitmap.

2. Open the Property inspector and click the Add Effects button (the one with a + sign next to the word "Effects"), as shown here:

Add Effects button

3. From the pop-up menu, choose either Sharpen | Sharpen or Sharpen | Sharpen More.

You can have more control over the sharpening process by using the manual approach:

1. Select a bitmap.

2. In the Property inspector, click the Add Effects button and then choose Sharpen | Unsharp Mask.

3. In the Unsharp Mask dialog box, move the slider to set a value for the sharpen amount. Alternatively, you can enter a value in the text field, as shown here:

4. Drag the Pixel Radius slider to determine the area of sharp contrast surrounding each pixel.

5. Drag the Threshold Slider to set a value for the threshold. Alternatively you can enter a value in the text field. Any pixel having greater contrast than the threshold value will be sharpened.

Blurring Images

The flip side of sharpening an image is to blur an image. While sharpening is more often a repair job than anything else, blurring creates an artistic effect that aims at creating soft areas within a bitmap image.

Using the Blur Tool

The Blur tool works just like the Sharpen tool, except that it produces the opposite effect.

1. Select the Blur tool in the toolbox.

2. In the Property inspector, set a value for the size of the Blur tool tip.

3. Click the triangle to the right of the Edge field and drag the slider to set a value for the edge softness.

4. Choose either the round or square shape. (Round is the default.)

5. Click the triangle to the right of the Intensity field and drag the slider to set the intensity value. You can also enter a value in the text field.

6. Place the pointer over the area you wish to blur.

7. Click and hold down the mouse button as you move the tool across the image, until you have blurred the desired area.

Blurring with Effects

As with sharpening, there are two basic approaches you can take: automatic and manual. The automatic approach has two options, one to blur a little bit and one to blur the image to a higher degree. To use the automatic blurring features, follow this procedure:

■ Select a bitmap. In the Property inspector, click the Add Effects button (the one with a + sign next to the word "Effects") and then choose either Blur I Blur or Blur I Blur More. Fireworks blurs the selected bitmap. Note that you can apply this effect repeatedly to get the desired result.

If you want more control over the sharpening process, use the manual approach:

1. Select a bitmap.

2. In the Property inspector, click the Add Effects button.

3. In the pop-up menu, choose Blur I Gaussian Blur.

4. In the Gaussian Blur dialog box, shown next, move the slider to set a value for the blur radius. The blur radius is the area around each pixel that will be blurred. Higher values produce a more pronounced blurring effect.

Using the Dodge and Burn Tools

If you've ever printed photographic film, you've probably had some experience with dodging and burning. *Dodging* is the process of lightening an area of an image, while *burning* has the opposite effect of darkening an area.

The procedure you use for the Dodge and Burn tools is identical, except that they produce opposite effects:

1. Click the Blur tool icon in the toolbox. Hold down the mouse button for a moment until the other tools in the group appear.

2. Select the Dodge or Burn tool.

3. Open the Property inspector and drag the slider to set a value for the size of the tool tip, shown here:

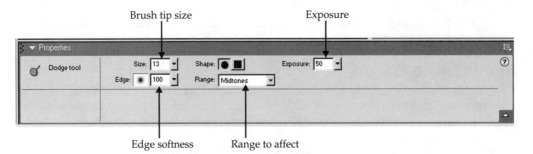

4. Click the triangle to the right of the Edge field and drag the slider to set a value for the edge softness.

5. Choose either the round or square shape. (Round is the default.)

6. Click the triangle to the right of the Range field and from the drop down menu choose Shadows, Midtones, or Highlights.

7. Click the triangle to the right of the Exposure field and drag the slider to set the desired exposure value. The higher the exposure, the more pronounced the dodging or burning effect.

8. Place the pointer over the area you wish to affect.

9. Click and hold down the mouse button as you move the pointer across the image, until you have completed dodging or burning.

Tip   *You can toggle back and forth between dodging and burning by pressing the ALT key (Windows) or the OPTION key (Macintosh) during step 9.*

Using the Smudge Tool

Smudging an image is much like running your finger across a wet painting. The colors the pointer passes over smear in the direction of travel. To use the Smudge tool, follow these steps:

1. Click the Blur tool icon in the toolbox. Hold down the mouse button for a moment until the other tools in the group appear.

2. Select the Smudge tool.

3. Open the Property inspector, click the triangle to the right of the Size field, and then drag the slider to set a value for the size of the Smudge tool tip, as shown here:

Brush tip size   Smudge color swatch

Edge softness   Pressure

4. Click the triangle to the right of the Edge field and drag the slider to set a value for the edge softness. Alternatively, you can enter a value between 0 and 100 in the text field.

5. Choose either the round or square shape. (Round is the default.)

6. Click the Use Entire Document checkbox if you want visible objects on all layers to be smudged as you move over them. Leave it unchecked if you want to smudge only the active object.

7. If you wish, click the Smudge Color checkbox and select a color by clicking the Smudge color swatch and choosing a color from the pop-up palette. This color will begin each smudge you make, creating a mark about one-and-a-half times the size of the tool tip.

8. Click the triangle to the right of the Pressure field and drag the slider to set the desired pressure value. The higher the value, the stronger the smudging.

9. Place the pointer over the area you wish to smudge.

10. Click and hold down the mouse button as you move the pointer across the image until you have completed smudging. Figure 6-7 shows a smudged image.

Note   *You can also use commands from both the Filters and the Effects menus to correct color images in your documents. For more information on changing the color characteristics of bitmaps, refer to Chapter 14.*

Creating a Selective JPEG Mask

File size can be a critical factor, especially when the ultimate destination of the image is the World Wide Web. The larger the file, the longer the download time—and savvy Webmasters are always looking for a way to shorten the download times of their Web pages. By using a selective JPEG mask, you can shrink the size of a file while still maintaining it's high quality.

When you create a selective JPEG mask, you select an area of the image and then specify that this area is to be saved at a different compression than the rest of the image.

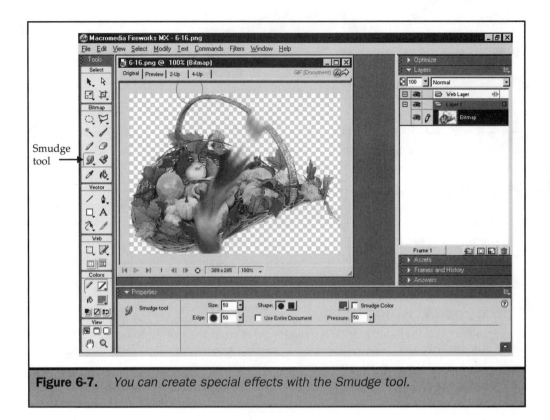

Smudge tool

Figure 6-7. *You can create special effects with the Smudge tool.*

By using this method, the most important parts of an image, such as a person's face, can be saved at a higher quality than the other parts of it.

To create a selective JPEG mask, do as follows:

1. Select a portion of the image using any of the selection tools (Marquee, Lasso, or Magic Wand).

Note *You can select either the portion you want to save at a higher quality or the portion you want to save at a lower quality. It's simply a matter of personal preference, because you can set the quality of the selected area to either a high or a low compression setting.*

2. Choose Modify | Selective JPEG | Save Selection as JPEG Mask from the menu. Alternatively, right-click (Windows) or CONTROL+click (Macintosh) the selection and choose Selective JPEG | Save Selection as JPEG Mask from the context menu. The following illustration shows the selected area (in this case, the area outside the castle), which will be colored.

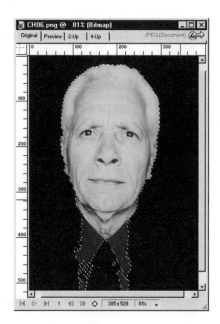

3. In the Optimize panel, make sure JPEG is selected as the file type.

4. Next, click the Edit Select Quality Options button. The Selective JPEG Settings dialog box opens, shown here:

5. Accept the default value of 90, or enter a different value.

6. Click the Preserve Text Quality checkbox (selected by default) to preserve the quality of any text in the mask area.

7. Click the Preserve Button Quality checkbox to preserve the quality of any button symbol in the mask area.

8. If you want to change the color of the mask area click the Overlay color swatch and select a color from the pop-up palette.

9. Click OK to close the dialog box.

10. In the Optimize panel, enter a value in the Quality field. The Quality value affects the unmasked area of the bitmap. Generally you will enter a lower value in this field as the masked area is generally the area where you want the highest quality.

You can change the Selective Quality at any time. If while editing other parts of the document, you find that the higher quality of the masked area is no longer needed, click the Edit Selective Quality Options button and deselect the Enable Selective Quality option.

Touching Up Bitmaps with the Rubber Stamp Tool

You use the Rubber Stamp tool to touch up a bitmap image. For example, if you scan an image into Fireworks that has a noticeable scar such as a tear, you can use the Rubber Stamp tool to fill in the tear with color sampled from neighboring pixels. The Rubber Stamp tool sets up two pointers. The first, called the *sampling pointer,* copies the pixels that lie under it. The copied pixels are duplicated, or *cloned,* at the place where the second pointer, the *cloning pointer,* lies. The Rubber Stamp tool is shown in action in Figure 6-8.

To use the Rubber Stamp tool, follow these steps:

1. Select the Rubber Stamp tool in the toolbox.

2. Open the Property inspector click the triangle to the right of the Size field and drag the slider to set a value for the size of the Stamp tool tip.

3. Drag the Edge Softness slider to set a value for the edge softness.

4. Leave the Source Aligned checkbox selected if you want to duplicate a wide range of pixels. If you simply want to duplicate the area immediately beneath the sampling pointer, deselect the checkbox.

5. Select the Use Entire Document checkbox if you want all visible objects from all layers to be cloned. Deselect the option if you want to clone only the active object.

6. Click the triangle to the right of the Opacity field and drag the slider to set a value. The setting determines the opacity of the cloned pixels. The default setting of 100 produces opaque pixels. Select a lower value and the cloned pixels will exhibit a degree of transparency.

Note   *See Chapter 9 for more information on opacity.*

Tip   *To reset the position of the cloning and sampling pointers to the same location you need to* ALT+*click (Windows) or* OPTIONS+*click (Macintosh) as you move the cloning pointer to a new location and then click to reset.*

Figure 6-8.   *Use the Rubber Stamp tool to clone an image.*

Combining Images (Merge Down Command)

You can merge two or more different bitmap images into a single image with the
Merge Down command.

There are, of course, a number of ways in which you can end up with more than
one bitmap image in a Fireworks MX document—for example, by importing, copying,
pasting, and so on. In the following example, you'll import two bitmaps into a blank
document and then merge them:

1. Choose File | New from the menu.

2. Set a canvas size large enough to accommodate the largest of the bitmap images
   you will be importing.

3. Click OK.

4. Choose File | Import from the menu.

5. Navigate to the directory containing the file you wish to import.

6. Select the filename and click Open, or simply double-click the filename.

7. Click where you want the upper-left corner of the image to appear.

Tip   *If the bitmap image isn't positioned exactly as you want it, you can move it using the arrow keys. Pressing an arrow key will move a selected image one pixel at a time in the direction of the arrow. Holding down the SHIFT key while pressing an arrow key will move the image ten pixels at a time in the direction of the arrow. Alternatively, you can open the Property inspector and enter values in the X and Y fields to accurately position the bitmap.*

8. Repeat steps 4 through 7 for the second bitmap image. Figure 6-9 shows the results.

Figure 6-9.   *Two bitmap images on a canvas*

9. Select the image (or images) you want to merge. To add to the selection, hold down the SHIFT key and click additional images.

10. Choose Modify | Merge Down from the menu.

Note *The images to be merged do not have to be on the same layer. In addition, you can merge one bitmap image onto another one on the underlying layer, as long as it is the top object in that layer. When you use the Merge Down command, the images merge down to a single bitmap object. If you need to edit individual bitmaps, but you need them to behave as a single unit in the document, group them. You can also merge down images in the Layers panel, a technique you'll learn in Chapter 12.*

Masking an Image

Masks are used to selectively hide or show portions of an underlying image. The mask, either through its own transparency or the darkness of the pixels in it, covers some, but not all, of an image.

Caution *The behavior of masking has changed with Fireworks MX, which reverses the behavior of grayscale masking in Fireworks 4. Where black previously showed whatever was underneath the mask and white hid the pixels under it, black now hides and white now shows.*

Fireworks provides several ways to create a mask. You can create a mask using the Layers panel by following these steps:

1. Select a bitmap in the Layers panel.

2. Click the Add Mask button at the bottom of the Layers panel. The mask will appear next to the bitmap in the panel, as shown here:

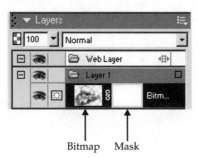

Bitmap   Mask

3. The new mask is automatically selected. Drawing over the bitmap mask will change the mask and reveal bits of the underlying background, or images behind the bitmap the mask is being applied to. When you paint on a bitmap mask, the results vary depending on the grayscale color you choose. Select jet black and all of the underlying images and background are revealed when you paint over the mask. Select a gray color and part of the original image will still be visible. Choosing white has no effect when you paint on a bitmap mask; none of the underlying images or background is revealed. To paint the bitmap instead, select it in the Layer panel, or on the canvas. Figures 6-10 and 6-11 show the original image and the results after modifying the bitmap mask with the Brush tool.

Figure 6-10. *An image with a blank mask over it*

Figure 6-11. *An image after the mask has been painted*

4. Open the Property inspector to show the properties of the mask. By entering values in the boxes, you can alter the width and height of the mask, as well as the X and Y position of the mask's upper-left corner.

5. By default, the Mask To option is set to Grayscale. You can select the Alpha Channel radio button instead if you prefer to use transparency for masking.

To create a mask using the Paste Inside command, simply cut or copy an image to the clipboard, select a bitmap in Fireworks, and choose Edit | Paste Inside from the menu. The pasted image will appear inside the selected bitmap, as shown here:

To create a mask using the Paste as Mask command is a bit more complicated. In this case, you are adding the mask to an existing image rather than using an existing image as a mask. To do so, follow these steps:

1. Paste the bitmap to be used as a mask onto the bitmap to be masked.

Note   *There are, of course, other ways to get more than one bitmap into a single document. This is simply one example of how to do it.*

2. Position the mask-bitmap where you want it to be when the process is completed, as shown here:

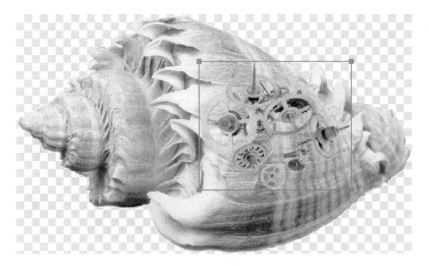

3. Choose Edit | Cut.

4. Click inside the bitmap to be masked, so that it is selected.

5. Choose Edit | Paste as Mask. This illustration shows the mask in place:

Summary

In this chapter, you learned how to use Fireworks to import, create, and modify bitmap images. You discovered that bitmaps are composed of square dots of color known as pixels. You explored how to incorporate images into your documents by importing, scanning, and acquiring them with a digital camera, and you examined how to modify bitmaps using tools and effects. You learned to mask bitmaps to reveal underlying areas, as well as how to use a mask to apply a different level of compression to a masked area. You also learned to merge bitmaps into a single image. In Chapter 7, you'll learn to create text objects.

The
Complete
Reference

Fireworks
MX

Chapter 7

Creating Text Objects

Whenyou create a Web page in an HTML editor, you can add as much text to the document as needed. You can perform some rudimentary formatting by changing the properties of the HTML text, or you can create a cascading style sheet (CSS) to liven up the text. However, many of the truly lovely fonts are not available on every user's system. And then there's the matter of creating text with more than one color, which just doesn't happen when you rely strictly on a HTML editor to create your Web designs. However, when you add Fireworks to the equation, you can create some lively text for banners, buttons, titles for images, and other elements. When you create text in Fireworks and then export the document for use on the Web, all editable text objects are converted to bitmaps. When optimized properly, the text will look as lively in a Web browser as it does when you export it from Fireworks.

You can also create special effects with the text you create in Fireworks. If you decide you want multicolored text for a client's banner, you can create it by taking a quick visit to the Text Editor. If your design calls for text curving around a path, it's possible to accomplish this with a menu command and a bit of tweaking on your part. If you need to mask an image with text, you can quickly get the job done with a few menu commands. You can even modify the amount of anti-aliasing Fireworks applies to your text.

Creating Text Objects

As with most of the objects you create in Fireworks, you have a wide range of latitude when it comes to creating text. You can specify any system font and modify text spacing between letters and much more. Figure 7-1 shows a few examples of the type of effects you can create with text in Fireworks.

Figure 7-1. *You can liven up a document with artistic text.*

You create text objects with the Text tool and then modify them with the Property inspector or the Text Editor. You can create the text object with the Text tool, and then you can set the text parameters such as font style, font color, and kerning. Or you can select the Text tool and open the Property inspector to set the text properties. After you work in Fireworks for a while, you'll know which method best suits your working style. The first step is to select the Text tool shown here:

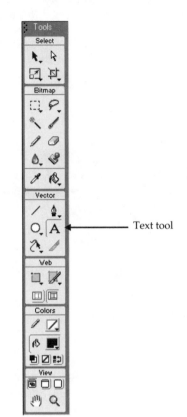

Text tool

Setting Text Parameters

After you create the text, you can use either the Property inspector or the Text Editor to modify your work. If you prefer to set text parameters before creating a block of text, select the Text tool and then open the Property inspector.

If you prefer, you can create the text first and then edit it:

1. Select the Text tool.

2. Click the canvas where you want the text to appear, and type the text.

3. With the Text tool still selected, click and hold down the mouse button on the last letter in the text block; then drag toward the first letter to select all of the text. Alternatively, you can double-click an individual word to select it, and then hold down the SHIFT key and drag to select other words in the text block.

4. Open the Property inspector. When you open the Property inspector after having selected the Text tool or a block of text on canvas, it is configured as shown in the following illustration. After accessing the Property inspector, you can modify a wide range of text parameters, beginning with the font style.

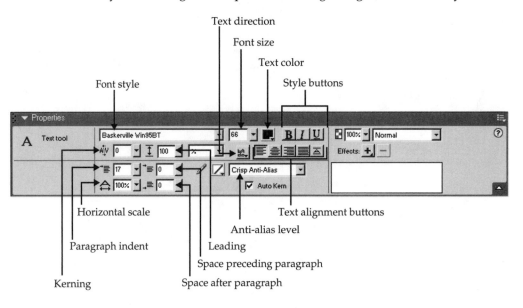

Note   *If you edit a block of text after creating it, you can select the entire block of text with the Pointer tool, open the Property inspector, and change the parameters of every character in the text block. To modify an individual character or a word, double-click the text block and your cursor becomes an I-beam. You can then select one or more characters as described in step 3.*

Selecting a Font Style

After selecting a block of text or the Text tool, you can choose a font style. You can choose any available system font and apply it to the text. When you install Fireworks, the install utility scans your system and records all system fonts.

Here's how you select a font style:

1. Create a block of text as outlined previously, or select the Text tool.

2. Open the Property inspector, and then click the triangle to the right of the Font field to access the font menu.

3. Scroll through the available fonts. As you move your cursor over a font name, a preview appears in a window to the right of the font menu, as shown here:

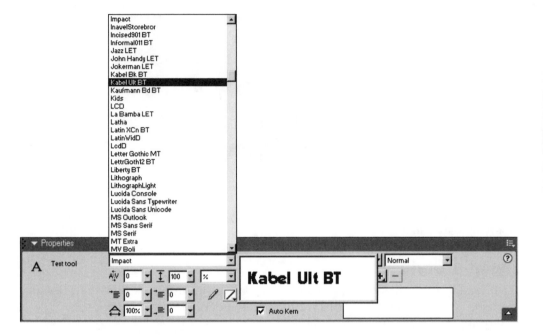

4. Click a font name to select it.

5. After specifying a font style, you can modify a different text parameter—for example, the text color.

Choosing a Text Color

Colorful text is a major ingredient in any successful Web design. When you create text in Fireworks, you can add any color from the currently loaded palette or choose one from the default Web Safe 216 palette. Or, if you or your client prefer, you can choose a color from the system color picker.

Here's how to specify a color for text:

1. Select the Text tool, or select a block of text, as outlined previously.

2. Open the Property inspector.

3. Click the triangle to the right of the color swatch.

4. Select a color from the pop-up palette. Alternatively, click the system color picker button shown in the following illustration to choose a color from the system color picker.

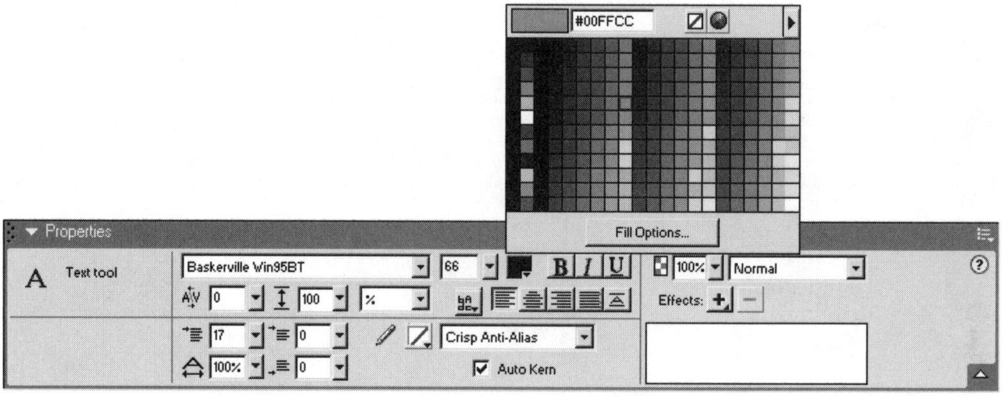

If colorful text alone doesn't suit your design, you can accentuate a block of text by applying a style to it.

Applying a Style

To draw a viewer's attention to a certain item, you can apply a style to the text that describes the item. You can boldface, italicize, or underline a block of text.

To apply a style to text, follow these steps:

1. Select the Text tool, or select a block of text.

2. Open the Property inspector.

3. Click a button to apply one or more styles shown in the following illustration. Choose from boldface, italics, or underline.

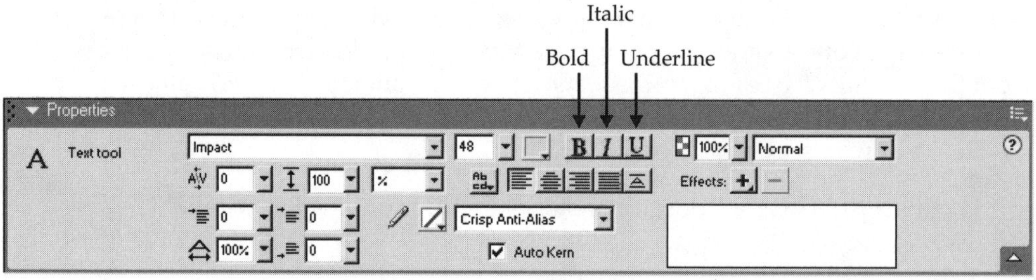

Another modification you can apply to text is spacing between letters, or *kerning*.

Adjusting Text Kerning

Kerning defines the spacing between letters in a block of text. Most fonts feature built-in kerning, but you can adjust the kerning of a text block with the Property inspector.

Here's how you set text kerning:

1. Select the Text tool, or select a block of text as described previously.

2. Open the Property inspector.

3. Drag the slider to the right of the Kerning field, as shown here:

Kerning or Kerning range

4. Drag the slider up to increase the space between letters or down to move them closer together. Alternatively, you can enter a value in the field.

Some fonts have kerning information stored with the font. To use a font's built-in kerning, choose the Auto Kern option, which is selected by default.

Modifying Text Line Spacing

Another text property you can modify is text line spacing, also known as *leading*. When you change this parameter, you modify the space between two lines of text.

Follow these steps to modify text spacing:

1. Select the Text tool.

2. Open the Property inspector.

3. Specify font size, font color, and other attributes that apply to the block of text you want to create.

4. Type a line of text, and then press ENTER or RETURN when you want the text to wrap to another line. Continue typing additional text as needed.

5. In the Property inspector, drag the Leading slider up to increase the space between the lines of text you just created or down to move them closer together. Alternatively, you can enter a value in the field.

6. Release the slider and Fireworks changes the leading between text lines.

When you create a new block of text, the leading value defaults to 100 percent. Note that you can also choose a leading value after you click the Text tool on canvas but before you type a block of text. This option comes in handy when you need to match the leading from one block of text to a new one you're creating. You can also use the Edit | Paste Attributes command to copy attributes from one block of text to another. This command will be presented in Chapter 14.

The default unit of measure for leading is percentage. If you prefer, you can change to pixels by clicking the triangle to the right of the leading units field and then choosing Pixels (px) from the drop-down menu.

Changing the Flow of Text

By default, a block of text flows from left to right. You can modify a block of text and have it flow from right to left, flow vertically from left to right, or vertically from right to left. You can modify a selected block of text or modify the flow parameter in the Property inspector before you type the text.

Here's how you change the flow of text:

1. Select the Text tool, or select a block of text as described previously.

2. Open the Property inspector.

3. Click the button shown in the following illustration and choose one of the following options:

- Horizontal left to right
- Horizontal right to left
- Vertical left to right
- Vertical right to left

You can modify the flow of text to create an interesting animation. Figure 7-2 compares the four types of text flow.

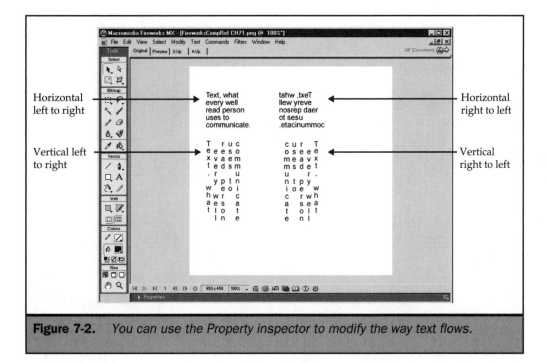

Figure 7-2.   *You can use the Property inspector to modify the way text flows.*

Aligning Text

When you create a block of text that wraps from line to line, you can change the way the text is aligned to the boundary of the text box. For text that flows horizontally, you can choose left, right, justify, or stretch alignment; for vertical text, you can choose from top, center, bottom, justify, and stretch alignment.

To adjust text alignment settings, follow these steps:

1. Select the Text tool, or select a block of text as described previously.

2. Open the Property inspector.

3. If the text box you are creating flows horizontally, the alignment buttons look like those shown in the following illustration. Click a button to choose one of the following alignment options:

   ■ **Left**   Aligns the text with the left side of the text box.

   ■ **Right**   Aligns the text with the right side of the text box.

   ■ **Center**   Aligns all text in the text box.

   ■ **Justify**   Aligns the text flush with the left and right sides of the text box. If you choose this option, the space between words is modified.

■ **Stretch**   Stretches the text to the size of the bounding box if you resize it with either the Pointer or Text tool.

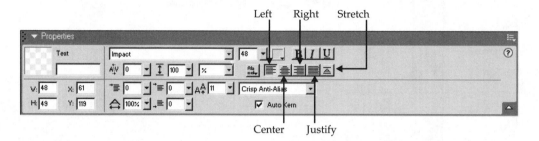

4. If your text flows vertically, the alignment buttons are arranged as shown in the next illustration. Click a button to apply the desired alignment method.

■ **Top**   Aligns the text with the top boundary of the text box.

■ **Center**   Aligns the text with the vertical center of the text box.

■ **Bottom**   Aligns the text with the bottom boundary of the text box.

■ **Justify**   Aligns the text to the top and bottom boundaries of the text box, with no space at the bottom boundary. This alignment method modifies the space between words to align the text evenly with both borders of the text box.

■ **Stretch**   Stretches the text to fit the box when the text box is resized with the Text or Pointer tool.

Shifting the Text Baseline

You can modify where the text appears in relation to the text baseline, where the bottom of the text block rests. You can modify the baseline to make text appear above or below it. You can select one or two letters out of a text block and change the baseline of the selected letters to achieve a special effect.

To modify the baseline of a block of text, follow these steps:

1. Select the Text tool, or select a block of text as described previously.

2. Open the Property inspector.

3. Click the baseline slider, shown in the following illustration, and drag up to raise the text above the baseline or down to place the text below the baseline. Alternatively, you can enter a positive value to raise text above the baseline or a negative value to render text below the baseline.

Baseline shift

If you modify baseline settings of a selected block of text, the selected text is moved as you drag the slider. If you're creating a new block of text, the setting is applied to the new text you create.

Note *You do not have to select the entire text block. You can apply different baseline settings to selected letters. By changing the baseline settings of text on different frames of an animation, you can make text appear to dance.*

Scaling Text Horizontally

You can also scale the letters in a block of text, making them wider or narrower than their default settings. When you scale text, you change the look of the font to spice up an otherwise mundane block of text.

Here's how you scale text:

1. Use the Text tool to type a block of text or select an existing block of text. If you create new text, drag the tool over the letters to select them, or double-click a word to select it.

2. Click the slider to the right of Horizontal Scale field and drag up to make the text wider, or drag down to shrink the width of the letters. Alternatively, you can enter a value between 50% and 300%.

Creating Paragraph Text

When you need to confine text to a particular part of the canvas, you can constrain the width of the text block by selecting the Text tool, clicking the point on the canvas where you want the text to begin and then dragging right or left to define the width of the text block. When you enter text to a fixed-width text block, the text wraps to the next line when it reaches the boundary of the text block.

After you create a block of paragraph text, you can resize it as needed. When you select a fixed-width text box with the Text tool, the bounding box is designated by a square handle in the upper-right corner. Double-click the handle and the text box will convert to auto-size, and the box expands as you enter new text. An auto-size text box is designated by an unfilled circle that appears at the upper-right corner of its bounding box.

Tip   *You can fix the width of a text box to accommodate your design by selecting the Text tool and typing. As you type, the box auto-expands to accommodate the new text. When the box is the desired width, select the Pointer tool and double-click the hollow round handle in the upper-right corner of the box. This converts the box to a fixed width, as designated by a unfilled square handle in the upper-right corner. As you enter additional text, it wraps to the next line.*

Resizing Paragraph Text

Although it might seem logical to assume you can modify the width and height of a block of text by changing the dimension within the Property inspector, doing so not only modifies the size of the text box but also *scales* the text. To change the size of a block of paragraph text, select the Text tool and then click inside the block of text. The text box is highlighted, and six handles appear around the text bounding box, as shown here:

To resize the selected text block, do one of the following:

■ Drag one of the middle handles left or right to change the width of the text block.

■ Drag any of the corner handles up or down to change the height of the text block, or drag left or right to change the width.

■ Drag any of the corner handles diagonally to resize the width and height of the text block simultaneously.

Note _You can also resize the text block using any of these methods after selecting it with the Pointer tool._

Modifying Paragraph Text

When you use the Text tool to create a block of text with multiple lines, you can modify certain parameters, just as you can with word processing software. You can modify the paragraph indent and modify the spacing before and after a paragraph.

To modify the parameters of paragraph text, follow these steps:

1. Select the block of text with the Text tool or Pointer tool.

2. To modify the paragraph indent, click the slider to the right of the paragraph indent field, shown in the next illustration, and drag up to indent the paragraph. Alternatively, you can enter a value in the field. The setting you specify is applied to additional paragraphs that you create by pressing ENTER or RETURN.

3. To modify the space before a new paragraph, drag the space preceding the paragraph slider up. Alternatively, you can enter a value between 0 and 100 in the field.

4. To modify the amount of space after a paragraph, drag the space after the paragraph slider up to specify the amount of space between paragraphs created by pressing ENTER or RETURN. Alternatively, enter a value between 0 and 100 in the field.

Space preceding paragraph

Paragraph indent   Space after paragraph

Anti-Aliasing Text

By default, all text you create for your documents is anti-aliased. When text is anti-aliased, the edges between pixels of differing colors are smoothed to avoid jarring transitions. For instance, when you place black text on a red background, anti-aliasing smoothes the transition between black and red to create a visually pleasing block of text. However, when you apply anti-aliasing to small characters they may appear blurry when the document is exported. The actual font size where text may appear blurry differs depending on the font you use. Click the Preview tab to view the text as it will be exported. If the text appears blurry, follow the upcoming steps and choose Strong Anti-Alias.

You can modify the way text you create is anti-aliased by doing the following:

1. Select the Text tool, or select a block of text.

2. Open the Property inspector.

3. Click the triangle to the right of the anti-alias level field and choose one of the following:

   ■ **No Anti-Alias**   Anti-aliasing is not applied to selected text or text created with the Text tool.

   ■ **Crisp Anti-Alias**   Creates a crisp border between text and surrounding pixels of color.

   ■ **Strong Anti-Alias**   Creates a strong definition between text and surrounding pixels of color. Use this option if small text looks blurry when you preview the document.

   ■ **Smooth Anti-Alias**   Creates a gentle transition between text and the surrounding pixels of color. This option works well in most cases.

Using the Spell Checker

The spell checker is a welcome addition to Fireworks MX. You can check spelling for a selected text block or the entire document. You can specify a dictionary as well as create a custom dictionary of words, phrases, and names you commonly use that are not in the Fireworks dictionary. Before you use the spell checker for the first time, you have to set it up.

Setting Up the Spell Checker

When you set up the spell checker, you can specify the dictionary to use as well as other options, such as whether to ignore duplicate words, whether to ignore letters with numbers, and so on.

Here's how you set up the spell checker:

1. Choose Text | Spelling Setup to open the Spelling Setup dialog box shown in the following illustration. Note that the Macromedia.tlx dictionary always appears at the top of the list.

2. Select a dictionary. For the American and British versions of Fireworks MX, you can choose American English, British English, or both. If you choose more than one dictionary, Fireworks checks both dictionaries during the spell check. For example, if you choose American and British dictionaries, *color* and *colour* are both acceptable.

3. In the Options section, deselect any rules you want Fireworks to disregard. For example, if you deselect Find Duplicate Words, Fireworks will not prompt you to correct a text block that contains "and and."

4. Click OK to complete the setup. The software is now configured to spell check your work.

Working with the Spell Checker

You can spell check a selected block of text or the entire document. When the spell checker locates a misspelled word, you are prompted to replace the word, ignore the suspect word, or add the word to your personal dictionary.

Here's how to use the spell checker:

1. Select a block of text with the Text or Pointer tool. If you do not target a word or text block, the spell checker searches the entire document.

2. Choose Text | Spell Checker to begin checking the selected text or entire document. When the spell checker finds a word that doesn't appear in any of the selected dictionaries, the Check Spelling dialog box opens.

3. In the Check Spelling dialog box, a selection of suggested replacements is displayed. You can choose one of the following options:

- **Add to Personal**   Adds the suspect word to your personal dictionary.

- **Ignore**   Ignores this occurrence of the suspect word.

- **Ignore All**   Ignores all occurrences of the suspect word in the document.

- **Change**   Changes this occurrence of the suspect word with a word you enter in the Change To field, or replaces the suspect word with a word you choose from the Suggestions list.

- **Change All**   Changes this occurrence and all future occurrences of the suspect word with the word you enter in the Change To field or with the word you choose from the Suggestions list.

- **Delete**   Deletes the suspect word from the document.

Editing Your Personal Dictionary

You can add or delete words from your personal dictionary at any time. For example, you can add a term that's unique to an industry you design Web pages for, or you can delete the name of a former client.

To edit your personal dictionary, follow these steps:

1. Choose Text | Spelling Setup. The Spelling Setup dialog box, shown previously, appears.

2. Click Edit Personal Dictionary. The Edit Personal Dictionary dialog box, shown next, appears.

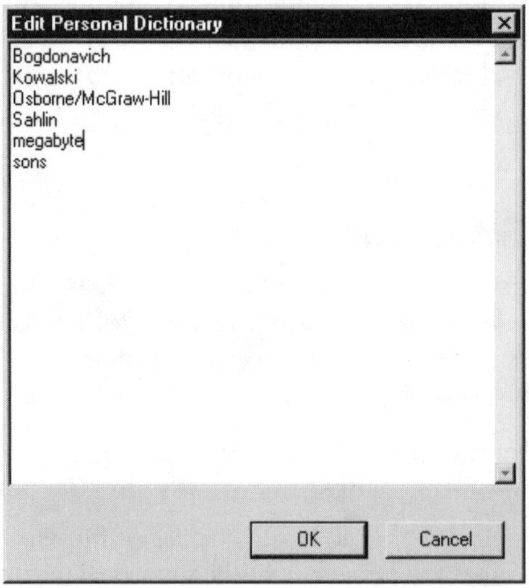

3. To delete a word from your personal dictionary, do one of the following:

- Double-click an individual word to select it, and then press DELETE.

- To delete a multiple-word phrase, place your cursor at the end of the last word, drag backward to select the entire phrase, and press DELETE.

- To delete a single word from a multiple-word phrase, drag your cursor over the word to select it and press DELETE.

4. To add a word to your personal dictionary, click the next available line on the list and enter the word.

> **Tip** *You can select a word from a word processing document, copy it to the clipboard, and then paste it directly into the Edit Personal Dictionary dialog box.*

Editing Text

One of the great things about documents formatted in the PNG (ping) format is that you can edit any part of a document at any time. If you've created a design for a client and four months after you create it, the client's company CEO is replaced, all you need to do to change his name is open the document, edit the text, and export the document again.

Editing Text with the Property Inspector

You perform the vast majority of text formatting with the Property inspector. If you choose, you can also do your editing with the Property inspector. Before you can edit the text, you have to select it. Here's how:

1. Select the Pointer tool or the Text tool and double-click a word to select it.

2. After you select a word, the Text tool becomes the active tool, even if you select the text with the Pointer tool.

3. To select additional words, drag your cursor right or left.

4. If the selected word is the first word in a paragraph, hold down the SHIFT key and click after the last word you want to select. The selection is highlighted and ready for editing.

5. After creating a text selection, open the Property inspector and modify the text as needed.

Editing Text with the Text Editor

In Fireworks 4, you set all the parameters for a text object with the Text Editor. As soon as you selected the Text tool, the editor popped up. With Firework MX, you have the

additional capability of specifying paragraph indent and spacing between lines—
options that are not available in the Text Editor. However, the other text parameters
can all be modified with the Text Editor. As an added bonus, you can select individual
letters from a block of text, modify them, and view the results in real time as the text on
the canvas updates. You can also move the block of text while working in the editor.

To edit a block of text with the Text Editor, follow these steps:

1. Select a block of text by clicking it with the Text tool or Pointer tool.

2. Choose Text | Editor to open the Text Editor shown in the following illustration.
   Alternatively, you can right-click (Windows) or CONTROL+click (Macintosh) and
   choose Editor from the context menu.

3. After you select a block of text, every letter is highlighted. Click anywhere
   inside the editor to deselect the text. When you work inside the Text Editor,
   your cursor is displayed as an I-beam.

4. To edit an individual word, letter, or selection of words, place your cursor in
   front of the first letter you want to select and drag. As you drag, each letter you
   select is highlighted. Release the mouse button to complete the selection.

5. Perform edits as needed. As you can see in the previous illustration, the buttons
   are laid out a bit differently than they appear in the Property inspector; however,
   they perform the same functions. As you perform your edits, the text on

canvas updates to reflect your changes—unlike editing text with the Property inspector, where the selected text on the canvas is highlighted so the results of your edits are not apparent until you deselect the text. If the Text Editor obscures the text you're editing, click the editor's title bar and drag the editor to a new location. You can also move the block of text while editing it. Click the block of text and then drag and drop it at a new location.

6. To apply your current edits and continue working in the Text Editor, click Apply.

7. Click OK to apply your edits and close the Text Editor.

Creating Special Text Effects

You can create interesting designs by applying special effects to the text in your documents. You can attach text to a path that parallels a curve in your document, add a drop shadow to text, or use text as a mask. You can also achieve interesting effects by converting text to an editable object.

Attaching Text to a Path

You can create text that curves, swoops, or undulates by creating a path with any of the drawing tools and then attaching a block of text to the path. When you attach text to a path, you can specify where the text appears on the path, as well as on which side of the path the text appears.

To attach text to a path, follow these steps:

1. Create a block of text with the Text tool.

2. Create a path using any of the drawing tools.

3. Select the Pointer tool, and then select either the text or the path. Then hold down the SHIFT key and click the other item to add it to the selection. Alternatively, you can drag a marquee around both text and path to select them.

4. Choose Text | Attach To Path. After invoking the command, the text is aligned to the path, as shown in Figure 7-3.

Tip *If you create a path with a shape tool, such as the ellipse tool, and the shape has a fill, the fill disappears after you attach the text to the path. If you want to display a filled shape and have text conform to its path, create the filled object, align it on the canvas, and then copy the shape. Attach the text to the path, and then choose Edit | Paste. The filled shape is aligned perfectly with the attached text.*

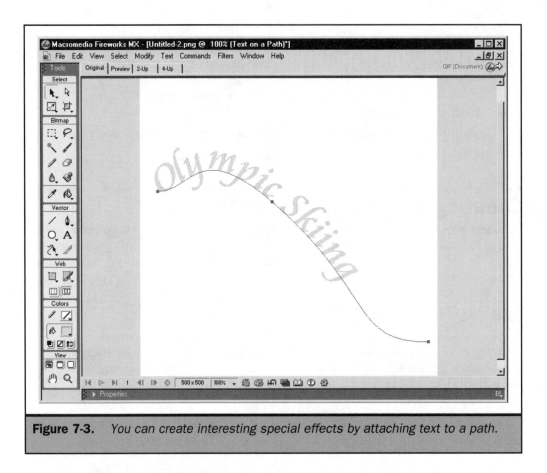

Figure 7-3. *You can create interesting special effects by attaching text to a path.*

Attaching Text to the Opposite Side of a Path

When you attach text to a path, the text appears on top of the path. You can easily display text on the opposite side of a path by doing the following:

1. Select the text with the Pointer tool or Text tool.

2. Choose Text | Reverse Direction. The text is attached to the opposite side of the path, as shown in Figure 7-4.

Changing Text Orientation Along a Path

When you attach text to an open path, each letter is rotated along the path. If this orientation doesn't suit your design, or it doesn't suit the path to which the text is attached, you can change the orientation to skew the text vertically or horizontally along the path.

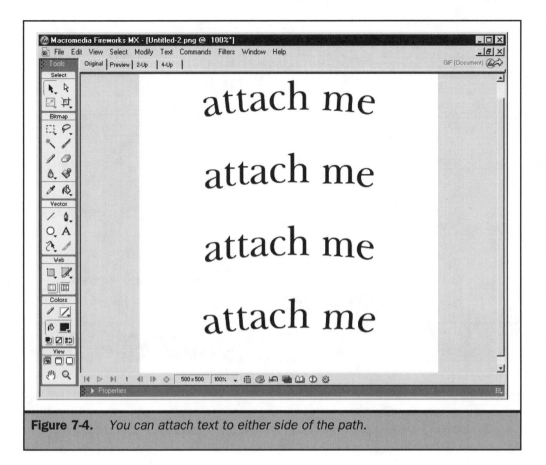

Figure 7-4.   *You can attach text to either side of the path.*

To change the orientation of text attached to a path, do the following:

1. Select the attached text with the Pointer tool or Text tool.
2. Choose Text | Orientation and then choose one of the following:

   ■ **Rotate Around Path**   This is the default option that rotates the text around the path.

   ■ **Vertically**   Aligns each letter perpendicular to the path

   ■ **Skew Vertically**   Aligns the text to the path and then skews each letter vertically

   ■ **Skew Horizontally**   Aligns the text to the path and skews each letter horizontally

Figure 7-5 shows four iterations of text aligned to a circular path, each with a different orientation option applied.

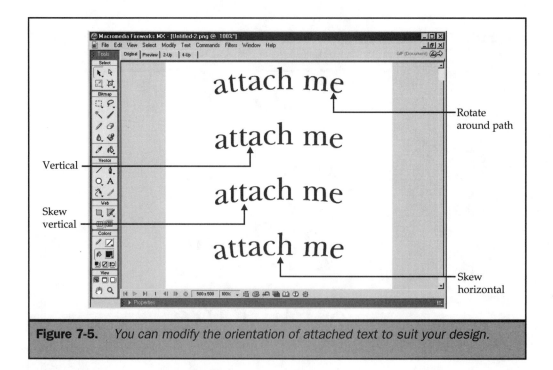

Figure 7-5. *You can modify the orientation of attached text to suit your design.*

Offsetting Text from a Path

When you attach text to an open path, the text is attached at the start of the path. When you attach text to a closed path such as an ellipse, the text is attached and centered in the middle of the path. You can modify the point where the first letter of text appears by changing the offset:

1. Select the attached text using either the Pointer tool or the Text tool.

2. Open the Property inspector.

3. Enter a value in the Text Offset field. This is the value in pixels by which the text will be nudged along the path. If the text is attached to a closed path, entering a negative value will move the text in a counterclockwise direction. The Figure 7-6 shows text attached to an elliptical path being offset by a positive value.

Changing the Distance Text Appears from the Path

Although you can offset the distance along the path at which the text attaches, no settings are available to allow you to modify the distance the text appears from the path. You can achieve this result, however, by modifying the baseline shift of the text and then attaching it to the path.

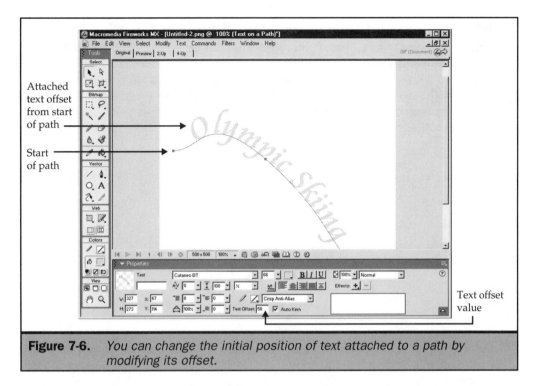

Attached
text offset
from start
of path

Start
of path

Text offset
value

Figure 7-6.   *You can change the initial position of text attached to a path by
modifying its offset.*

To change the distance the text appears from the path, do the following:

1. Create a line of text with the Text tool.

2. Open the Property inspector.

3. Drag the Baseline Shift slider up to modify the baseline shift. Alternatively, in
   the Baseline Shift field, you can enter the distance you want the text to appear
   from the path. This value is in pixels.

4. Select the text and the path with the Pointer tool.

5. Choose Text | Attach To Path. The text appears above the path by the distance
   specified, as shown here:

Attaching Text to Both Sides of an Elliptical Path

When you attach text to an elliptical path, by default it is centered in the middle of the path. You cannot add a second block of text and attach it to the bottom of the ellipse. However, you can use a workaround to achieve the highly desirable effect where text appears on both sides of an ellipse. This section will also introduce you to the Knife tool, which will be covered in detail in Chapter 11.

To attach text to both sides of an ellipse, do the following:

1. Use the Ellipse tool to create an oval shape with no fill.

2. Select the Knife tool, shown here:

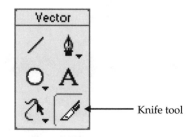

Knife tool

3. While holding down the SHIFT key, drag the tool from one side of the oval past the other, bisecting it in the middle. The knife tool converts the closed path into two open paths.

4. Select the Pointer tool and click anywhere on the canvas to deselect the paths.

5. Use the Text tool to create the text you want to attach to the top of the ellipse.

6. Use the Pointer tool to select the text and the top half of the circle.

7. Choose Text | Attach To Path. The text will attach at the start of the path.

8. Open the Property inspector and enter a value in the Text Offset field to position the text in the center of the path.

9. Use the Text tool to create the text you want to attach to the bottom of the path.

10. Use the Pointer tool to select the text and the bottom half of the ellipse.

11. Choose Text | Attach To path. After you invoke the command, the text is attached to the path; however, it appears inside the ellipse, not below it.

12. Select the Text tool and double-click the block of text attached to the bottom of the ellipse to select it. If you have more than one word in the block of text, select

the first word, hold down the SHIFT key, and then click just beyond the last character to select the entire block of text.

13. In the Property inspector, drag the Baseline Shift slider down to move the text below the baseline. After you release the slider, the text moves below the bottom line of the ellipse. If the distance isn't quite right, drag the slider again to fix it.

14. Enter a value in the Text Offset field to position the text in the middle of the bottom path, as you did when you attached the text to the top of the path. The following illustration shows an example of this technique.

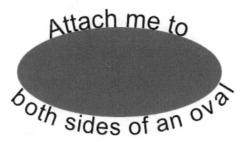

Applying Effects to Text

You can apply effects to text to make it appear as though it is floating above the canvas, as though it is glowing, and much more. After you create a block of text, you can select it and use the Property inspector to apply one or more effects to the text. All of the effects you apply to the text are Live Effects—this means you can modify the settings at any time. Effects are covered in detail in Chapter 14. The following image shows some of the looks you can achieve by applying effects to text.

drop shadow

GLOW

INNER GLOW

INNER SHADOW

Converting Text to Editable Objects

You can also convert text to editable objects. When you convert a text object to an editable object, you can use any of the drawing tools to edit the shape. You learn to modify vector objects in Chapter 11.

To convert a text object to an editable object, select it with the Pointer tool and then choose Text | Convert To Paths. The following illustration shows a letter as a text object side by side with the letter after it is converted to an editable object and modified with the Subselection tool.

Creating a Text Mask

If your design calls for something special, you can create a text object and then paste it over a bitmap image as a *mask*. This technique is useful when you want to create an interesting banner for your design. After you paste a text mask to an image, you can modify it to mask a different area of the image.

Here's how you create a text mask:

1. Import the bitmap you want to mask into the document.
2. Create a block of text, and then position it over the part of the image you want to mask. This technique works well with bold fonts such as Impact.
3. Select the text and choose Edit | Cut.
4. Select the bitmap and choose Edit | Paste As Mask. Figure 7-7 shows a bitmap with a text mask.

To edit the masked bitmap, do the following:

1. Select the masked bitmap with the Pointer tool. A blue bounding box designates the border of the bitmap. The center of the masked bitmap is indicated by a blue dot.
2. To change the position of the bitmap relative to the text mask, click the blue dot and drag it to reposition the bitmap within the text mask.

Figure 7-7.   *You can mask a bitmap with a text object.*

Summary

In this chapter, you learned to create text objects for your documents. You learned to modify the text objects using the Property inspector and the Text Editor. You also learned to attach text to a path and attach text to both sides of an ellipse. Also discussed was how to create special effects for the text in your documents. In Chapter 8, you'll learn to work with color in Fireworks.

Chapter 8

Working with Color

W hen you create a document for the Internet, you create vector objects and text to augment any bitmap images in the design. When you export the document for viewing as a Web page, or as part of a Web page, your work will be viewed by a wide audience using a diverse array of equipment. Your finished product is also viewed using different operating systems and different browsers. In short, what looks perfect on your system may look completely different on someone else's; the green banner background you created may look like blue on someone else's system unless you pay careful attention to color.

So when you create artwork in Fireworks, you have to be mindful of the differences between equipment and operating systems in order for your design to be a success. Fortunately, within Fireworks you have all the tools you need to work with color for the Internet. In this chapter, you'll learn to use the various Fireworks tools to create a finished product that looks the same regardless of the system on which it is viewed.

Working with Color for the Web

Most modern computer monitors are equipped to view millions of colors. However, a document you create might be viewed by someone with a dinosaur of a monitor that only supports 256 colors; and there's also a difference in the way colors appear on a Macintosh system as compared to a Windows-based system.

In order to compensate for these differences, you use the Web Safe color palette. Colors in the Web Safe palette display the same on both Mac and Windows platforms. If you are using full-color bitmaps in your documents, however, using the Web Safe palette is impractical because the colors have to be dithered (mixed) to create a facsimile of the original color using colors from the Web Safe palette. This bloats the file size. When you combine bitmaps and vector graphics in a document, you create slices so that you can export the bitmaps using the JPEG optimization method and export the rest of the document using one of the GIF optimization methods. Optimization is covered in detail in Chapter 21.

For objects other than bitmaps, you can choose one of the 216 colors in the Web Safe palette. If you're careful and don't go overboard and choose every color in the palette, you can export the document with far fewer than 216 colors. In fact, if you're very economical with your use of color, you can create an impressive-looking graphic that exports with fewer than 32 colors. When you export with fewer colors, you cut down on the file size; this means the graphic loads more quickly, which is a windfall if your anticipated audience views the Internet at slow connection speeds.

The Web Safe Color Palette

The Web Safe palette is a universally accepted palette containing 216 colors. These colors display identically whether they are viewed on a Macintosh or on a Windows operating system. The default Fireworks color palette is the Web Safe 216 palette. If you stick to the colors in the default Fireworks palette, your design stands a better chance of looking the same in all browsers on all platforms. Figure 8-1 shows the default Fireworks Web Safe 216 palette.

Understanding the Hexadecimal Color Format

When you work with color for the Web, each color is expressed in hexadecimal format. The format expresses a color using a combination of 6 characters from either the first 6 characters of the alphabet (A through F), or the first 10 numerical characters (0–9). The first 2 characters designate the red (R) component of the color, the second 2 characters represent the green (G) component of the color, and the last two characters represent the blue (B) component of the color. The 6 characters are preceded by the number (#) sign. The combination of the 16 characters can represent 8-bit color depth (16 × 16 = 256 colors). The hexadecimal equivalent for the lowest value of a color component is 00, while FF represents the highest value for a color component. In hexadecimal format, red is #FF0000, green is #00FF00, and blue is #0000FF. Therefore, jet black is #000000, and white is #FFFFFF.

Even though the Web Safe palette consists of 216 colors, you can use the hexadecimal format to refer to any 32-bit color. When you use the hexadecimal format, each color component can have 256 values, multiplied three times (the R, G, and B components), which makes it possible to define 16,777,216 colors using the hexadecimal format.

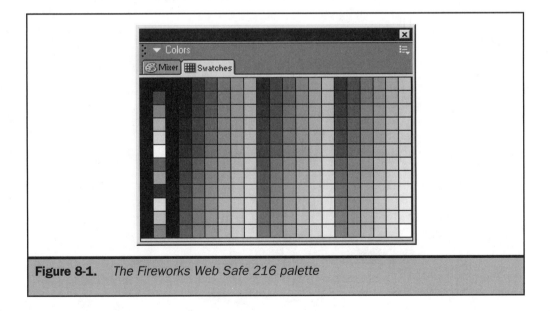

Figure 8-1.   *The Fireworks Web Safe 216 palette*

Using the Swatches Panel

There are different ways to add color to the objects in your document. You can use the Fill Color well or the Stroke Color well. You can also mix a custom color using the Color Mixer panel, a technique you'll learn before the end of this chapter. Alternatively, you can use the Swatches panel. To open the Swatches panel, shown previously in Figure 8-1, choose Window | Swatches.

After you open the Swatches panel, you can perform a number of tasks. You can select a color, add a swatch set to the existing swatches, replace the current swatch set with another, delete a color from a swatch set, or select one of the preset swatches. The following sections cover each task in detail; see "Loading Preset Fireworks Swatch Sets" later in the chapter for more information on preset swatches.

Selecting a Color

After you open the Swatches panel, you can choose any of the colors in the current swatch set as the current fill or stroke color. You can also use a color from the Swatches panel to change the fill color of an object in your document.

To apply a swatch color to an object on the Canvas:

1. Choose Window | Swatches to open the Swatches panel.

2. Select an object on the canvas with a fill and no stroke.

3. Move your cursor over the Swatches panel. Your cursor icon changes to an eyedropper, as shown here:

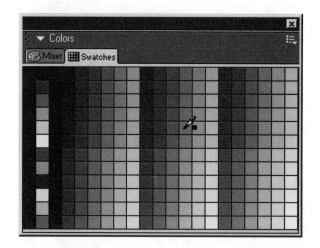

4. Click a swatch to apply the color.

After you apply a fill color to an object in this manner, the selected color becomes the current fill color, and the Fill Color wells in both the toolbox and the Property inspector update to reflect the new color. This fill is applied to all new objects you create until you select another color.

You can also change the current fill color or stroke color using the Swatches panel. This method comes in handy when you have a different color swatch set in the Swatch panel than you do in the Fill and/or Stroke Color wells.

To change a fill or stroke color using the Swatches panel:

1. Open the Swatches panel as outlined previously.

2. Click the color swatch in either the Fill or Stroke Color well. You can use the color wells in the toolbox or in the Property inspector. After clicking a color well, the pop-up color palette appears.

3. Move your cursor toward the Swatches panel. The cursor icon becomes an eyedropper, as shown in the previous illustration.

4. Click the desired color swatch. The swatch in the color well updates to reflect the color you selected.

After selecting a stroke or fill color from the Swatches panel, it becomes the current stroke or fill until you once again select a new color.

Adding a Color to a Swatch Set

When you're working with a swatch set, you may find it necessary to add to the current color swatch a color from a vector or bitmap graphic you have imported; or you might need to add a color from an object you created with one of the Vector tools and filled with a custom color you created with the Color Mixer panel.

To add a color to the currently loaded swatch set:

1. Open the Swatches panel.

2. From the toolbox, select the Eyedropper tool, shown next. Your cursor becomes an eyedropper.

3. Open the Property inspector, and from the Sample menu choose 1 Pixel, 3 × 3 Average, or 5 × 5 Average. This setting designates the size in pixels of the area the Eyedropper tool uses to sample a color value.

4. Drag your cursor across the object, and then click the object to sample the color. The Fill Color well swatch changes to the sampled color.

5. Move your cursor inside and to the edge of the Swatches panel until the cursor icon becomes a paint bucket, as shown here:

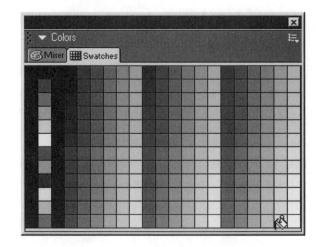

6. Click to add the sampled color to the current swatch set. A new swatch, the same color as the object you sampled, is added to the panel.

Replacing a Swatch Color

In addition to adding colors to a swatch set, you can replace one color with another. This option comes in handy, for example, if a client changes its corporate colors, which you have saved as a swatch set.

To replace one swatch color with another:

1. Open the Swatches panel.

2. Select the Eyedropper tool from the toolbox.

3. Open the Property inspector, and from the Sample menu choose 1 Pixel, 3 × 3 Average, or 5 × 5 Average.

4. Click an object in the document to sample a color.

5. In the Swatches panel, press and hold down the SHIFT key and move your cursor over the swatch color you want to replace. Your cursor becomes a paint bucket.

6. Click the swatch color to replace it with the sampled color.

Deleting a Color from a Swatch Set

Another option you have available is to delete a color from a swatch set. Deleting a color from a swatch set is advisable when you need to work with a limited palette for a particular application.

To delete a color from a swatch set:

1. Open the Swatches panel.

2. Press the CTRL key (Windows) or COMMAND key (Macintosh) while holding your cursor over the swatch you want to delete. Your cursor icon becomes a pair of scissors.

3. Click the swatch to delete the color from the swatch set.

Using the Swatches Panel Options Menu

When you open the Swatches panel, you can perform different tasks by summoning the Swatches panel Options menu. To open the Swatches panel Options menu, shown next, click the icon in the upper-right corner of the panel. In the sections that follow, you'll learn to use commands that pertain to managing the Swatches panel.

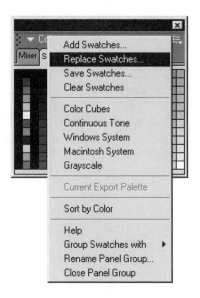

Adding Swatches

If you're working on a document and you need to use colors from a previously saved swatch set, you can add the swatch set to append the colors to the currently loaded swatch set. This is an easy way to add colors to a limited palette.

 Saved color swatches are identified by the .act extension.

To add a saved swatch set to the current set:

1. Choose Add Swatches from the Swatches panel Options menu. The Open dialog box appears.

2. Navigate to the folder where you save swatch sets, as shown here:

Open		? X
Look in: ▭ Color Swatches ▾ 🔙 📁 📄 ▦▾		Preview
▭ Acme Industries Swatches.act		
▭ Mansell Photography Site.act		
▭ Osborne_McGraw-Hill Swatches.act		
		Format: Unknown
File name:	Osborne_McGraw-Hill Swatches.act	Open
		Size: 0.18K
Files of type:	Color table(*.act)	Cancel

3. Select the desired swatch set file, and click Open. The selected swatch set is added to the current set.

Replacing Swatches

In addition to adding swatches to a set, you can use the Options menu to replace a swatch set. This option is handy when you're creating a document for a particular client or application and you need to use a limited color palette that you've saved from a previous Fireworks session.

To replace the current swatch set:

1. Choose Replace Swatches from the Swatches panel Options menu. The Open dialog box (shown in the previous illustration) appears.

2. Navigate to the folder where your swatch files are stored.

3. Select the desired swatch set file and click Open. The current swatch set is replaced by the selected swatch set.

Clearing Swatches

Another task you can perform with a Swatches panel Options Menu command is clearing swatches. When you clear swatches, every color swatch is removed from the panel. This command is useful when you need to create a custom color swatch set using the colors in the document or you need to create a swatch set by sampling colors from selected graphics in the document.

To clear the Swatches panel: Choose Clear Swatches from the Swatches panel Options menu. After invoking the command, all color swatches are removed from the Swatches panel.

Sorting Swatches

After adding or deleting colors from a swatch set, you may have a hodge-podge arrangement of colors from all spectrums of the rainbow. When this happens, you can sort swatches by color, which makes it easier to find a particular swatch.

To sort swatches by color, choose Sort by Color from the Swatches panel Options menu.

Using the Current Color Palette

When you create a document for a Web page, you can replace all of the color swatches with only the colors used in the current document. When you work with a limited palette, it is easier to spot the exact color you need rather than browsing through the Web Safe 216 palette or a saved swatch set to select a color.

To use the current export palette (the colors used to create the document), you must build a color table. To build a color table, you use the Optimize panel. The Optimize panel will be discussed in detail in Chapter 21. A detailed discussion of the color table will be presented later in this chapter in the section "Working with the Color Table." Both topics will be presented here as they relate to replacing the current color swatches with the current export color set. You can only create a color table when you choose the GIF optimization method.

To replace the current swatch set with the colors used to create a document:

1. Open the Swatches panel.

2. In the panel window on the right side of the workspace, click the arrow to the left of the word Optimize. This opens the Optimize panel. If you don't have the Optimize panel docked in the panel window, choose Window | Optimize.

The Optimize panel is shown in the following illustration. The default optimization method is GIF WebSnap Adaptive with a maximum of 128 colors. This optimization method snaps all colors in the document to colors from the Web Safe palette.

3. Click the Rebuild button at the bottom of the Optimize panel. Fireworks creates a color swatch for every color that will be exported from the current document, as shown next.

4. Choose Current Export Palette from the Swatches panel Options menu. Fireworks creates a swatch set that matches the current export colors from the color table, as shown in Figure 8-2.

If you add other graphics to the document or create other graphics using colors other than those in the Swatches panel, you can add the new colors to the color table by opening the Optimize panel and then clicking the Rebuild button. After rebuilding the color table, choose Current Export Palette from the Swatches panel Options menu to update the swatch set.

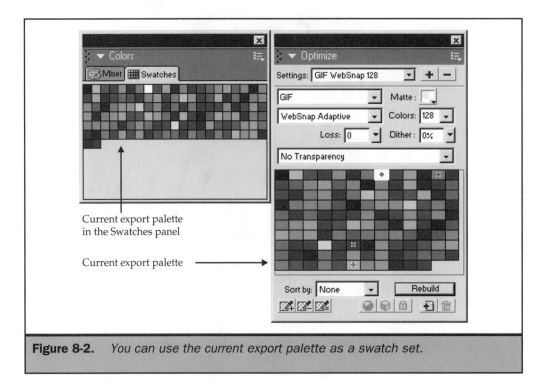

Figure 8-2.   *You can use the current export palette as a swatch set.*

After you populate the Swatches panel with the current color set, you can save the set for future use, as outlined in the next section.

Saving Swatches

When you begin a project and create a document with a color palette that you will use repeatedly on other documents, you can save the color palette as a swatch set. The ability to save swatches and load them when working on a document is a tremendous timesaver, especially when the palette is used for a client or an ongoing project. You have all of the colors you need for the project, thereby eliminating clutter in the Swatches panel.

To save the current color palette as a swatch set:

1. Open the Swatches panel.

2. If necessary, rebuild the color table as outlined previously.

3. Choose Current Export Palette from the Swatches panel Options menu. This loads the palette from the color table.

4. Choose Save Swatches from the Options menu. The Save As dialog box appears.

5. Navigate to the folder where you want to save the swatch set.

6. In the File Name field, enter a name for the swatch set. Choose a name that will make sense to you when you need to load the swatch set several months from now. Logical possibilities are the client's name, the project name, or a partial uniform resource locator (URL) for the Web site for which the swatch set will be used. It's also a good idea to save all of your swatch sets in the same folder for easy retrieval.

7. Click Save. Fireworks saves the swatch set with the .act extension.

Tip *To quickly create a Web Safe color palette set for a new client, create a new Fireworks document and import some artwork with the client's corporate colors. Open the Optimize panel and then click the Rebuild button. Save the color palette as a swatch set, and you can load it whenever you need to create a new document for the client.*

Loading Preset Fireworks Swatch Sets

Fireworks gives you a tremendous amount of latitude when it comes to choosing colors for your designs. If the project you are working on is not part of a Web design, you can load another swatch set to suit the intended destination of the document. You can easily switch from one swatch set to another by choosing one of the following from the Swatches panel Options menu: Color Cubes, Continuous Colors, Grayscale, Windows System, or Macintosh System. The following sections describe each swatch set.

Using Color Cubes

When you choose the Color Cubes swatch set, you load the Web Safe 216 color palette into the Swatches panel. The swatches are arranged with the darkest color (jet black, hexadecimal value #000000) in the upper-left corner of the panel and ending with the lightest color (white, hexadecimal value #FFFFFF) in the lower-right corner. The following illustration shows the Color Cubes swatch set.

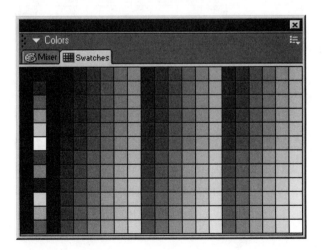

Using Continuous Tone

When you load the Continuous Tone swatch set into the Swatches panel, you are working with the Web Safe 216 palette in a slightly different arrangement. The colors in the Continuous Tone swatch set are arranged by tonal value, as shown here:

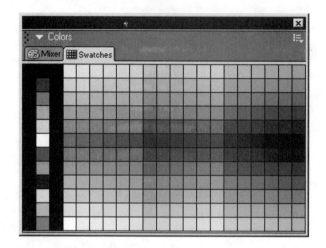

Using Grayscale

The Grayscale swatch set is 256 shades of gray ranging in value from jet black (hexadecimal value #000000) to white (hexadecimal value #FFFFFF). The following illustration shows the Grayscale swatch set in the Swatches panel.

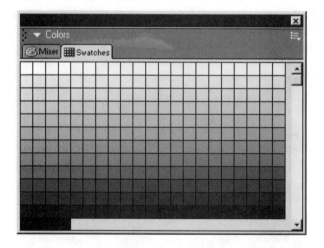

Using Windows System Colors

The Windows System Colors swatch set contains the colors used by the Windows operating system to display system software. The available colors in this palette are shown here:

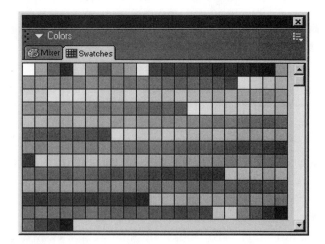

Using Macintosh System Colors

The Macintosh System Colors swatch set contains the colors used by the Macintosh operating system to display system software. The available colors in this palette are shown here:

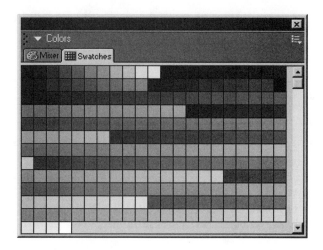

CREATING ARTWORK FOR YOUR DESIGNS

Loading a Different Color Swatch into the Fill and Stroke Color Wells

Working with the Swatches panel is very convenient for loading a swatch set, managing colors in a swatch set, and saving a swatch set. However, once you've attained the optimum color palette for the document or project you are working on, you can save yourself considerable time by loading the swatch set to the Fill or Stroke Color wells.

To load a swatch set into Fill or Stroke Color wells:

1. Click the color swatch in either the Fill or Stroke Color well. You can do this in either the toolbox or the Property inspector. After clicking one of the color swatches, the pop-up palette appears.

2. Click the arrow in the upper-right corner of the palette to open the pop-up palette Options menu, and choose one of the following:

   - **Swatches panel**   Loads the current swatch set into the pop-up palette. This option is handy if you've loaded the current export palette into the Swatches panel.

   - **Color Cubes**   Loads the Color Cubes swatch set into the pop-up palette.

   - **Continuous Colors**   Loads the Continuous Color swatch set into the pop-up palette.

   - **Windows System**   Loads the Windows System swatch set into the pop-up palette.

   - **Macintosh System**   Loads the Macintosh System swatch set into the pop-up palette.

   - **Grayscale**   Loads the Grayscale swatch set into the pop-up palette.

> **Tip**   *To snap any colors you mix in the System Color Mixer to the nearest Web Safe color, choose the Snap to Web Safe option from any color well Options menu. To access a color well Options menu, click the color well and then click the arrow in the upper-right corner of the pop-up palette.*

After you load a swatch set into a color well, as outlined in the previous steps, the swatch colors appear on a pop-up palette whenever you click a color swatch to modify a stroke or fill, and whenever you click a color pointer when modifying a linear or gradient fill.

> **Note**   *For more information on gradient fills, refer to Chapter 10.*

Using Color Models

When you create a document in Fireworks, you have wonderful diversity when it comes to color. In addition to using the default Web Safe 216 color palette, you can specify colors using several other color models. If the document you are creating requires you to match a known color value in the RGB color format, CMY color format, or grayscale color format, you can do so easily by using the Color Mixer. To specify a color model, you must first open the Color Mixer, shown in the following illustration, by choosing Window | Color Mixer.

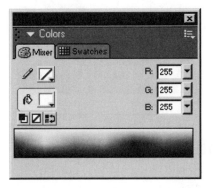

After you open the Color Mixer, you choose a color model by clicking the Options menu icon and then choosing a color model from the menu shown here:

Selecting Hexadecimal Colors

If you create a document and you need to match a color specified in the hexadecimal format, you can easily do so in the Color Mixer. When you specify a color in the Color Mixer for the hexadecimal color model or the RGB color model, you specify the red (R), green (G), and blue (B) color components by entering a value with the proper syntax for the selected color model. For example, to specify blue in hexadecimal format, the syntax is #0000FF.

To specify blue in the hexadecimal format:

1. Choose Window | Color Mixer.

2. Click the Options menu icon and choose Hexadecimal.

3. Enter the values shown in the following illustration to specify a bright blue color.

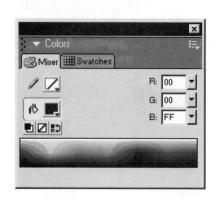

Choosing RGB Colors

When you specify a color in the RGB format, you enter a value for the red (R), green (G), and blue (B) color components. You enter a value between 0 (unsaturated) and 255 (totally saturated) for each color component. The following steps show you how to specify a bright blue color using the RGB color model.

To specify a bright blue color using the RGB color model:

1. Choose Window | Color Mixer.

2. Click the Options menu icon and choose RGB.

3. Enter the values shown in the following illustration to specify a bright blue color.

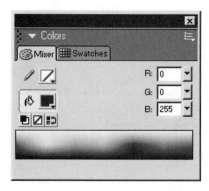

Using CMY Colors

The CMY color model uses values of cyan (C), magenta (M), and yellow (Y) to specify a color. Each color has a range of 0 to 255. The following steps show how to create the same bright blue color from the preceding sections using the CMY color format.

To specify a bright blue color using the CMY color model:

1. Choose Window | Color Mixer.

2. Click the Options menu icon and then choose CMY.

3. In the C, M, and Y fields, enter the values shown here:

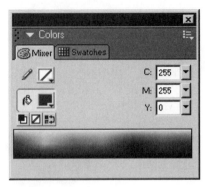

Using the HSB Color Model

Colors in the HSB color model are specified by entering values for hue (H), saturation (S), and brightness (B). You use a value between 0 and 255 for hue, and a percentage between 0 and 100 for saturation and brightness. The bright blue color used in the previous sections can be matched in the HSB color model by following the steps given next.

To create a bright blue color using the HSB color model:

1. Choose Window | Color Mixer.

2. Click the Options menu icon and then choose HSB.

3. In the H, S, and B fields, enter the values shown in the following illustration to mix a bright blue color.

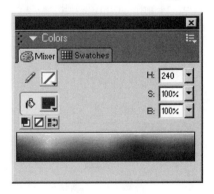

Specifying Grayscale Colors

When you use the Grayscale color model, you can create a shade of gray between pitch black and pure white. This color model uses only one parameter, K (black). You specify a value between 0 (white) and 100 (black).

To specify a grayscale color:

1. Choose Window | Color Mixer.

2. Click the Options menu icon and then choose Grayscale.

3. Enter a value between 0 and 100 in the K field. Alternatively, you can click inside the gradient bar, or click the triangle to the right of the K field and drag the slider to specify a color value. The following illustration shows a medium gray being mixed in the Color Mixer.

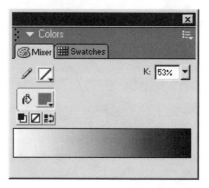

Adding Color with the Color Mixer

The Fireworks Color Mixer is a multifaceted tool that lets you specify or mix a color, or choose a color model. You use the Color Mixer, shown in the following illustration, to mix colors for objects in your design. You mix colors by dragging a slider for each color component. You can choose any of the color models previously discussed in this chapter.

Stroke Color well

Fill Color well

Set default stroke/
fill colors

No stroke or fill

Color component values

Swap stroke/fill colors

Color bar

To create a color with the Color Mixer:

1. Choose Window | Color Mixer.

2. Click the Options menu icon and choose a color model, as outlined previously.

3. Click either the Stroke or Fill Color well as the destination for the color you are mixing.

4. Enter a value for each color component by typing an applicable value in the field or by clicking the triangle to the right of the field and dragging the slider. After you mix the color, the destination color well updates to reflect the new color in the Color Mixer, the toolbox, and the Property inspector.

You can also use the Color Mixer color bar to mix a color. The color bar, shown in the previous illustration, can be used to access the full color range. If you have the Snap to Web Safe Colors option selected in the destination color well, the color you select will be snapped to a color from the Web Safe palette.

To mix a color using the color bar:

1. Choose Window | Color Mixer.

2. Click the Options menu icon and choose a color model.

3. Choose the destination color well.

4. Click inside the color bar, shown in the previous illustration. After clicking the color bar, your cursor becomes an eyedropper.

5. Drag inside the color bar to mix the color. As you move your cursor, the destination color well updates to reflect the currently selected color. The values for each color component change as well, as shown here:

6. Release your cursor to apply the color to the destination color well. The destination color well in the Color Mixer, the Colors section of the toolbox, and the Property inspector display the color you mixed. This color is applied to all new objects you create until you mix another color.

You can also mix a color for an object by selecting it, opening the Color Mixer, and then mixing a color as outlined in the preceding steps.

Tip   *If you're going to be using a color continuously on a project, add it to the Swatches panel as outlined previously.*

Another use of the Color Mixer is to match a known color value. To match a known color value:

1. Choose Window | Color Mixer.

2. Click the Options menu icon and choose the applicable color model.

3. Enter the value for each color component to create an exact match to the known color value.

Tip   *Fireworks does not recognize the CYMK color model. However, if you have other image-editing software that supports the CYMK model, enter the value in the program's color mixer, switch to the RGB color model, and record the values. Launch Fireworks, open the Color Mixer, choose the RGB model, and then enter the RGB values in the Color Mixer for a perfect match.*

Working with the Color Table

When you create a document and choose one of the GIF optimization methods, you can display a color table that contains every color in the document. As you edit a document and create new objects with different colors, you can rebuild the color table to display the current export palette. You can also perform various tasks using the color table such as editing or sorting colors in the palette, and more. Note that the color table is only available when the chosen optimization method uses no more than 8-bit (256 colors) color depth.

To view the colors in the current export palette:

1. In the panel window on the right side of the workspace, click the arrow to the left of the word Optimize. The Optimize panel opens. The default Fireworks optimization method is GIF WebSnap Adaptive. For more information on optimization methods, refer to Chapter 21.

2. Click the Rebuild button at the bottom of the Optimize panel. Fireworks rebuilds the color table to reflect all colors as they will be exported, as shown here:

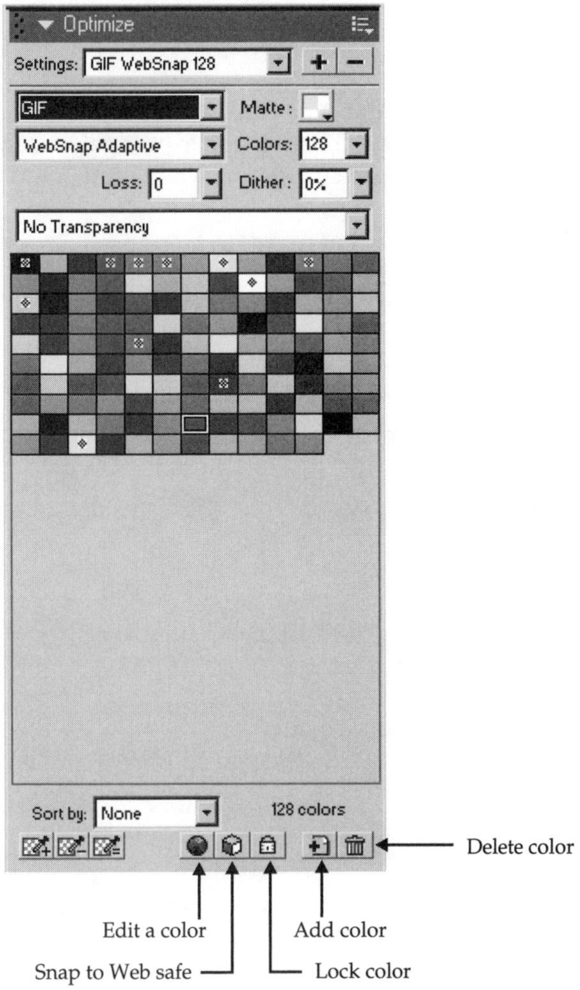

After you display the color table in the Optimize panel, you can perform a number of tasks. You can edit a color, snap a color to Web Safe, lock a color, and add or delete a color. After you rebuild a color table and edit the colors, a small symbol appears within the color swatch to indicate the characteristics of the color. A color with more than one characteristic is identified with more than one symbol. The following illustration shows an export palette containing several colors that have been modified.

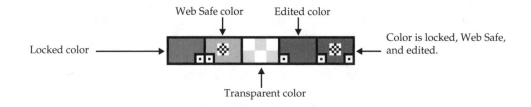

Editing a Color

After you rebuild a color table, you can edit individual colors within the export palette. When you edit a color, it is changed in the export palette, and all instances of the color in the exported document are changed as well. The color in the original image is unaffected.

To edit a color in the current export palette:

1. In the panel window on the right side of the workspace, click the arrow to the left of the word Optimize and rebuild the color table as outlined previously. If you don't have the Optimize panel docked in the panel window, choose Window | Optimize.

2. Either double-click the color you want to edit, or select the color and then click the Edit Color button at the bottom of the Optimize panel.

3. Edit the color in the system color picker, as illustrated next.

4. Click OK. The edits are applied to the color swatch in the color table, and all instances of the edited color are changed in the document as exported. You can preview the effects of the color change by clicking the Preview tab in the document window. The original document is unaffected.

Locking a Color

You can lock colors so that they cannot be removed from the export palette when you are reducing colors or importing another palette. If you load another palette, locked colors are added to the new palette.

To lock a selected color:

■ Click the Lock button at the bottom of the Optimize panel.

To unlock a color:

1. Select a locked color in the color table.

2. Click the Lock button at the bottom of the Optimize panel.

To unlock all colors, choose Unlock All Colors from the Optimize panel Options menu.

Snapping a Color to Web Safe

After you edit a color with the system color picker, chances are it will not be Web Safe. However, you can easily snap the color to the nearest Web Safe color.

To snap a color to Web Safe:

1. Select the color in the color table.

2. Click the Snap to Web Safe button at the bottom of the Optimize panel.

 You can select multiple colors to lock them or snap them to Web Safe colors. To select contiguous colors, select the first color, and then click additional colors while holding down the SHIFT *key. To select noncontiguous colors, select the first color and then click additional colors while holding down the* CTRL *key.*

Adding and Deleting Colors

While working with a color table, you may find it necessary to add or delete colors. You can easily add or delete a color by clicking the proper button at the bottom of the Optimize panel.

To add a color to the color table:

1. Click the Add Color button. The pop-up color palette appears, and your cursor icon changes to an eyedropper.

2. Click a color to add it to the color table.

To delete a color from the color table:

1. Select the color you want to delete.

2. Click the Delete Color button, which looks like a trash can.

To remove colors from the color table that are not used in the document, choose Remove Unused Colors from the Optimize panel Options menu.

Sorting Colors

When you work with a large color table or when you add, delete, or edit colors, you end up with a wide array of colors arranged in no particular fashion. You can sort the colors in a table to make it easier to select colors for the objects in your document.

To sort the colors in a color table:

1. In the panel window on the right side of the workspace, click the arrow to the left of the word Optimize.

2. If needed, rebuild the color table by clicking the Rebuild button at the bottom of the Optimize panel.

3. Right-click (Windows) or CTRL-click (Macintosh) to reveal the context menu shown here:

```
Rebuild Color Table
─────────────────────
Add Color...
Edit Color...
Delete Color
Replace Palette Entry...
─────────────────────
Snap to Web Safe
─────────────────────
Transparent
✓ Lock Color
Unlock All Colors
─────────────────────
Sort by Luminance
Sort by Popularity
✓ Unsorted
─────────────────────
✓ Show Swatch Feedback
─────────────────────
Remove Edit
Remove All Edits
─────────────────────
Load Palette...
Save Palette...
```

4. Choose Sort by Luminance to sort the table by color values, or choose Sort by Popularity to sort the colors by frequency of use in the document.

Exporting a Palette

If the current export palette is one you find useful, you can save the palette as an .act file for use in other documents. This feature is handy after you create the ideal palette for a project that involves multiple documents.

To save the current export color palette:

1. In the panel window on the right side of the workspace, click the arrow to the left of the word Optimize.

2. Click the Optimize panel Options menu icon and choose Save Palette from the menu. The Save As dialog box appears.

3. Navigate to the folder where you want to store the color palette. It's a good idea to store all of your color palettes and custom swatch sets in a designated folder.

4. Enter a filename for the palette and click Save. The palette is saved with the .act extension.

After you save a palette, you can load it into either the Optimize panel color table or into the Swatches panel, as outlined earlier in this chapter.

Loading a Palette

When you create a new document for a particular client or for a specific application, you can load a previously saved palette. Loading a previously saved palette ensures color continuity with previously created documents used for the same project or client. When you load a palette, you can load a previously saved .act palette, or you can select a .gif file. When you select a .gif file, Fireworks builds a color palette based on the colors used in the image.

To load a palette:

1. In the panel window on the right side of the workspace, click the arrow to the left of the word Optimize.

2. Click the Optimize panel Options menu icon and choose Load Palette.

3. The Open dialog box appears.

4. Locate the .act or .gif file you want to use as a palette.

5. Click Open. Fireworks builds the color palette.

Summary

In this chapter, you learned to work with color. You learned how to use the Swatches panel to work with a particular color palette and define stroke and fill colors. You learned how to use the Color Mixer to create a color. You also learned how to build a color table in the Optimize panel, edit the export palette, and save the export palette for future use. In Chapter 9, you'll put your knowledge of color to use as it pertains to strokes; in Chapter 10, you'll use color to create solid and gradient fills.

Chapter 9

Creating Stroke and Line Styles

When you create a path with one of the Fireworks drawing tools, you create a stroke. When you create an object with an outline, a stroke is also involved. The default stroke is a line one pixel wide. However, you can modify the style of the stroke to suit the design you are working on. You can choose from a preset stroke or create a custom stroke. You can mix and match stroke styles to achieve an artistic effect and create viewer interest in your design. In this chapter, you'll learn how to use the preset stroke styles as well as how to modify existing stroke styles to put your own stamp of originality on a project.

About Strokes

When you create an open or closed path, or a shape with an outline, the stroke style you choose defines the characteristic of the path or shape outline. When you accept the default stroke size and style, the path or outline is the Pencil stroke style, one pixel wide—the type of line you'd expect to draw using a mechanical pencil with a hard lead. If the default stroke style, width, and color don't suit your design, you can choose from a wide range of preset stroke styles or create your own. Figure 9-1 shows examples of the wide range of stroke styles you can choose from.

Modifying a Stroke

When you select a tool to draw a path or shape, you can modify the current stroke color to suit the path or shape you are creating. You can modify the stroke tip size and choose from a wide variety of styles before or after creating the path or shape outline. You can specify stroke color and other parameters by using the Property inspector or by clicking the Stroke color swatch in the Colors section of the toolbox. In the sections that follow, you'll learn to modify a stroke using both methods. Each stroke characteristic will be covered in a separate section.

The first step in modifying a stroke is to select a drawing tool or an object with a stroke, and then do one of the following:

- Open the Property inspector.
- Click the color swatch in the Stroke Color well.

When you select a drawing tool or path and choose to modify the stroke characteristics using the Property inspector, the panel is configured as shown in Figure 9-2.

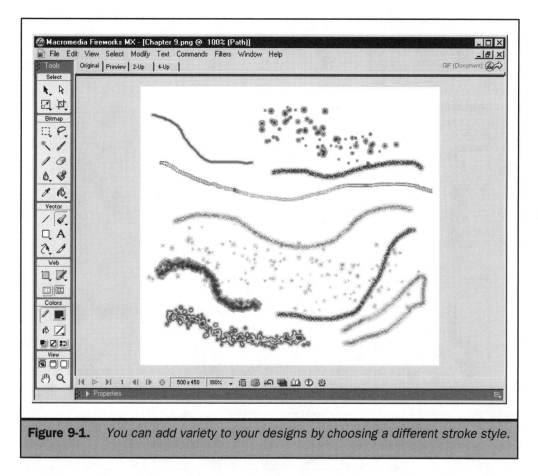

Figure 9-1. *You can add variety to your designs by choosing a different stroke style.*

You can also modify a stroke after it is created by selecting an object with a stroke, clicking the Stroke color swatch in the Colors section of the toolbox and then clicking the Stroke Options button shown here:

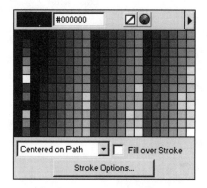

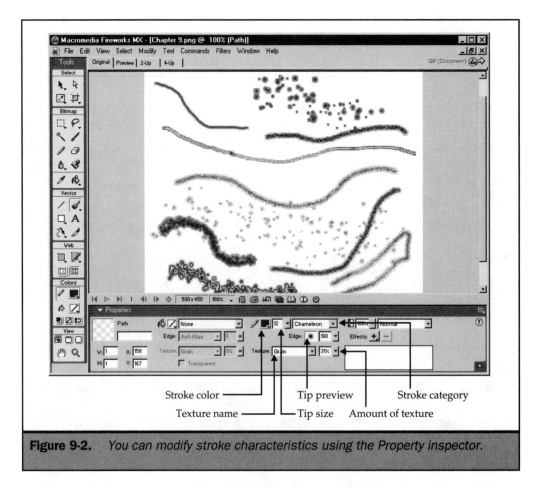

Stroke color

Tip preview

Stroke category

Texture name

Tip size

Amount of texture

Figure 9-2. *You can modify stroke characteristics using the Property inspector.*

After you click the Stroke Options button, the dialog box changes to the configuration shown here:

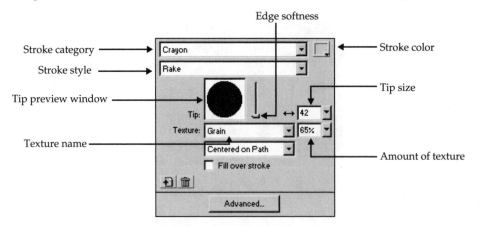

Edge softness

Stroke category

Stroke color

Stroke style

Tip preview window

Tip size

Texture name

Amount of texture

Changing Stroke Color

You can modify the color characteristic of a stroke to suit the path or object outline you are creating. You can use any color from the currently loaded palette or choose a stroke color from the system color picker.

To modify stroke color using the Property inspector:

1. Select the object whose stroke characteristics you want to modify, or select the tool you'll use to create a path or object with a stroke.

2. Open the Property inspector.

3. Click the color swatch to the right of the pencil icon and choose a color from the palette shown in the following illustration. Alternatively, you can click the System Color Picker button to choose a color from the system color picker.

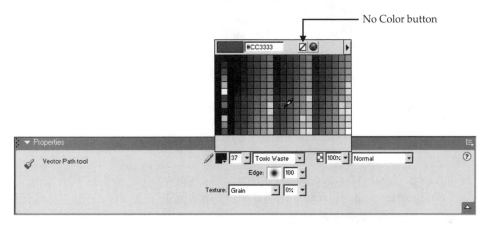

Note	*To create a shape with no stroke, click the No Color button shown in the previous illustration.*

To modify stroke color after it has been created using the Stroke Color well, do the following:

1. Select the object whose stroke characteristics you want to modify.

2. Click the color swatch in the Stroke Color well.

3. Choose a color from the pop-up palette shown in the following illustration. Alternatively, you can click the System Color Picker button and choose a color from the system color picker.

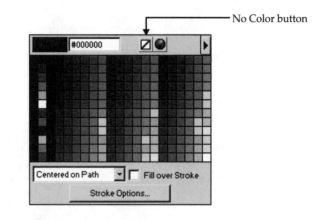

Specifying Stroke Tip Size
==========================

After you choose a stroke color, you can modify the stroke tip size (width) to suit your design. You can modify the stroke tip size using the versatile Property inspector or by specifying a tip size value from the Stroke Color well pop-up palette.

To modify the stroke tip size using the Property inspector:

1. Select the object whose stroke width you want to modify, or select the tool you'll use to create an object with a stroke or a path.

2. Open the Property inspector.

3. Click and drag the slider to the right of the Tip Size field to specify a value between 1 and 100. Alternatively, you can enter a value in the field.

You can use the Stroke Color well to modify a stroke after it has been created. To modify the stroke tip size from the Stroke Color well:

1. Select the path or shape whose stroke width you want to modify.

2. Click the color swatch in the Stroke Color well and then click the Stroke Options button from the pop-up color palette to reveal the Stroke Options dialog box.

3. Click and drag the Tip Size slider to specify a value, as shown in the following illustration. Alternatively, you can enter any reasonable value in the field.

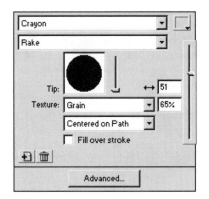

Selecting Stroke Style

The default stroke style looks very mechanical. The path you create with this stroke style is pencil thin. You can choose a different stroke style that makes a path or shape outline appear as though it were drawn with a felt tip marker, a paint brush, a crayon, and so on. You can also modify the edge softness to change the way a stroke looks. You can modify the stroke style either using the Property inspector or by clicking the Stroke Options button from the Stroke Color well pop-up palette.

To select a stroke style using the Property inspector:

1. Select the object whose stroke style you want to modify, or select the tool you'll use to create an object with a stroke or a path.

2. Open the Property inspector.

3. Click the triangle to the right of the Stroke Category field to reveal a menu of stroke categories.

4. Click the arrow to the right of any stroke category to select a style from the category, as shown in the following illustration. After you select a style, the stroke tip is displayed in the Tip preview window.

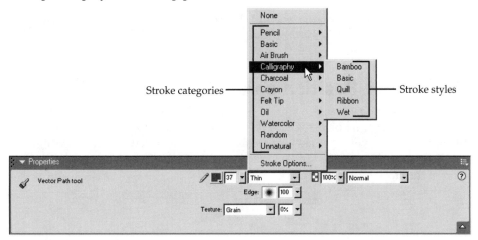

5. After you select a stroke style, accept the default edge softness (100) or drag the slider to the right of the Edge Softness field (shown in the preceding illustration) to change the way the stroke blends with the surrounding pixels of color. After you modify the edge softness, the window to the left of the field refreshes to preview the edge softness.

After you create an object with a stroke, you can modify the stroke style from within the Stroke Color well by doing the following:

1. Select the object whose stroke style you want to change.

2. Click the color swatch in the Stroke Color well and then click the Stroke Options button.

3. Click the triangle to the right of the Stroke Category field and choose an option from the drop-down menu.

4. Click the triangle to the right of the Stroke Name field and choose an option from the drop-down menu shown in the following illustration. After you choose a stroke style, it is displayed in the Tip preview window.

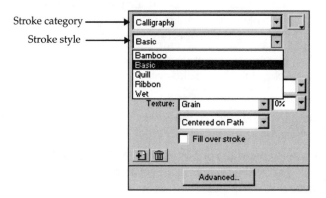

5. To modify edge softness, click and drag the slider to the right of the Tip preview window. After you choose a setting, the window refreshes to reveal the new tip shape.

Modifying Stroke Position on an Outline

When you create an object with a stroke, by default the stroke is centered on the path. When you create an object with a thin stroke, the position of the stroke isn't readily apparent. However, when you create an object with a wide stroke, you can modify the position of the stroke to achieve different effects. You modify the position of the stroke from the Stroke Color well.

To modify the position of the stroke on a path:

1. Select a solid object that has a stroke.
2. Click the color swatch in the Stroke Color well to open the pop-up palette.
3. Click the triangle to the right of the Location of Stroke field, and from the drop-down menu choose one of the following:

    ■ **Inside Path**   The stroke is rendered inside of the path.

    ■ **Centered on Path**   The stroke is rendered with the path in its center.

    ■ **Outside of Path**   The stroke is rendered outside of the path.

4. Click the Fill over Stroke checkbox to have the object fill rendered over the stroke. Figure 9-3 shows all of the stroke placement options.

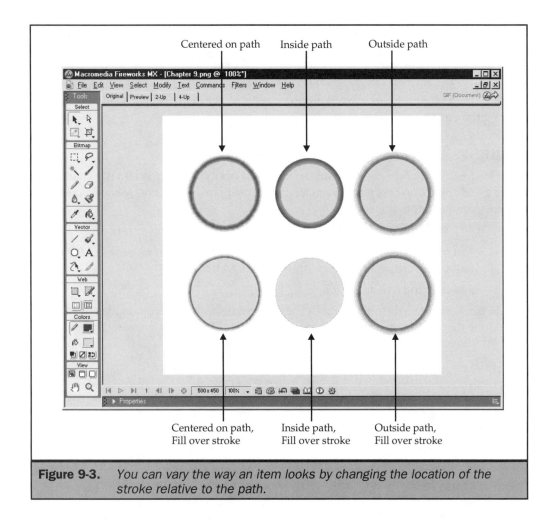

Figure 9-3.   *You can vary the way an item looks by changing the location of the stroke relative to the path.*

CREATING ARTWORK FOR YOUR DESIGNS

You can also use the versatile Property inspector to change the position of the fill relative to the stroke by doing the following:

1. Select a filled object with a stroke.

2. Click the arrow to the left of the word Properties. The Property inspector opens.

3. Click the color swatch in the Stroke Color well to reveal the pop-up palette. The dialog box is identical to the one that appears when you click the Stroke Color well in the Colors section of the toolbox.

4. Click the triangle to the right of the Location of Stroke field, and from the drop-down menu choose one of the options discussed in the previous steps.

5. Click the Fill over Stroke checkbox to position the fill over the stroke.

Applying Texture to a Stroke

By default, a stroke is a solid color with a default grain texture. The default value for amount of texture is 0 percent, so its effects are not visible. You can show the default texture by increasing the percentage of texture. You can also choose a texture from the Property inspector menu or by clicking the swatch in the Stroke Color well and then clicking the Stroke Options button.

Choosing a Texture

You can dress up an otherwise mundane stroke by applying a texture to it. When you apply a texture to a stroke, you can choose from the many presets or you can specify a texture stored in another location.

To assign a texture to a stroke using the Property inspector:

1. Select the object whose stroke you want to apply a texture to, or select the tool you'll use to create an object with a stroke or a path.

2. Open the Property inspector.

3. Click the triangle to the right of the Texture field and select a texture from the menu. As you move your cursor over the selections, a preview appears in the window to the right of the menu, as shown here:

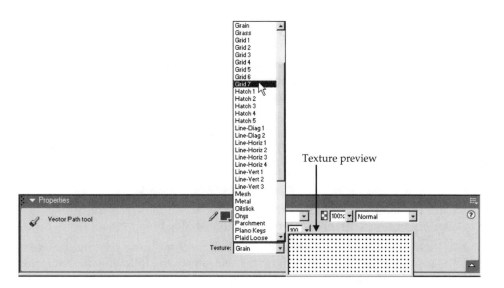

4. Click a texture to select it. The texture is applied to the stroke.

The default Fireworks textures are square grayscale images with a maximum dimension of 128 × 128 pixels. However, you can also use any image for a stroke texture. If you choose a color image, it is converted to grayscale. You achieve the best results when you choose a small grayscale image with sharp contrast. Choose a square image because images used for stroke textures are tiled.

To select a texture that is not a Fireworks preset:

1. Follow the steps given in the previous list, and then select Other to open the Locate File dialog box.

2. Click the triangle to the right of the Files of Type field and choose one of the following: Fireworks (.png), GIF (.gif), JPEG (.jpg, .jpe, .jpeg), BMP (.bmp, .dib, .rle), or TIFF (.tif, .tiff). These are the file types you can use as textures for a stroke. Alternatively, you can choose All Readable Files or All File Types. When you select a file, it is visible in the preview window, as shown here:

3. Select a file and click Open to use the file as a texture.

Note *You can also specify a directory where you store textures by modifying preferences. When you specify a directory of images, the images are added to the stroke texture menu for ready access. For more information, refer to the "Modifying Preferences" section in Chapter 3.*

You can also use the Stroke Color well to choose a texture after you've created an object with a stroke. To choose a texture using the Stroke Color well:

1. Select the object whose stroke you want to apply a texture to.

2. Click the color swatch in the Stroke Color well and then click the Stroke Options button to reveal the Stroke Options dialog box.

3. Click the triangle to the right of the Texture field and drag your mouse over the available presets. As you drag, the window in the following illustration appears, giving you a preview of the texture.

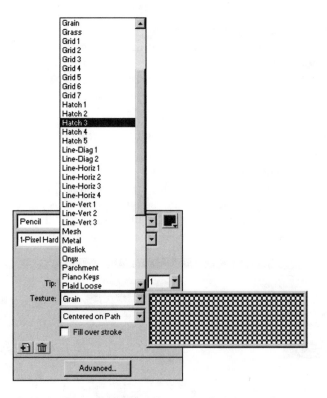

4. When you find the texture you want to use, click it to select it.

After you choose a texture, you have to modify the amount of texture percentage for the texture to show through the stroke color.

Changing the Amount of Texture

After you choose a texture, you make it visible by changing the Amount of Texture setting. You use this setting to modify the amount of texture that appears through the stroke. The default setting of 0 shows none of the texture through the stroke.

To modify the percentage of texture applied to a stroke:

1. Follow the steps in the previous section to select a texture.

2. If you selected the texture in the Property inspector, drag the slider to the right of the Amount of Texture field, as shown in the following illustration. As you drag up, more of the texture will show through the stroke.

3. Release the mouse button to select a value. Alternatively, you can enter a value from 0 to 100 in the field.

If you selected a texture using the Stroke Color well, steps 2 and 3 are the same; but the controls in the Stroke Options dialog box are slightly different, as shown here:

Creating a Custom Stroke Style

If none of the styles from the stroke categories suit the document you are working on, you can modify an existing stroke style to create a truly unique effect. You can even save a modified stroke style for future use. When you modify a stroke style, there are so many settings you can modify, the permutations are almost infinite. When you modify a stroke, you open the Edit Stroke dialog box, which is divided into sections for Options, Shape, and Sensitivity.

Modifying Stroke Options

The first set of stroke style parameters you can modify is located in the Options section of the Edit Stroke dialog box. In this section, you'll find settings for varying the number of tips used to create the stroke, ink amount, flow rate, and so on.

To modify stroke options:

1. Select the Vector Path tool. Note that you can also modify the stroke style of an object you've already created by selecting it and then following the next steps.

2. Click the arrow to the left of the word Properties. The Property inspector opens.

3. Click the triangle to the right of the Stroke styles field, and from the drop down menu choose Stroke Options.

4. In the Stroke Options dialog box, click the Advanced button to open the Edit Stroke dialog box. The options will vary depending on the stroke style you select. The following illustration shows the settings that are available when you select a stroke from the Airbrush stroke category.

5. Choose values for the ink amount and related flow settings if the stroke style you are modifying uses them.

6. Modify the Texture and Edge Texture settings. Choosing low values will cause the modified stroke to have little or no apparent texture; choosing high values will cause the stroke to appear as though it were drawn over textured paper.

7. Click the triangle to the right of the Edge Effect field and choose an option from the drop-down menu. These options can create effects similar to the hard edge of a paint stroke from a watercolor brush.

8. Click the triangle to the right of the Tips field, and drag the slider to increase the number of tips the modified stroke uses to create a path.

9. If you choose multiple tips, the Tip Spacing option becomes available. Click the triangle to the right of the Tip Spacing field, and drag the slider to increase the space between tips. When you increase tip spacing, it appears as though a multi-nozzle sprayer applied the stroke.

10. If you choose multiple tips, the Variation option becomes available as well. Click the triangle to the right of the Variation field and choose an option from the drop-down menu. The effect you achieve with this option will vary depending on your other settings. As you change settings, the preview window refreshes in real time to display the modified stroke with the current settings. The following illustration shows a modified stroke from the Air Brush category with multiple tips and the Complementary option selected for the type of variation.

11. Click OK to apply the settings to the stroke, or click the Shape tab to modify the tip shape. If you are modifying the style of an existing path on the canvas, click Apply to preview the modified style on the selected path. Clicking Apply only gives you a preview of the modified style on the path. Click OK to finish applying the changes, or click Cancel to void the operation and close the dialog box.

You can also use the Stroke Color well in the Colors section of the toolbox to modify the stroke style of a selected object by doing the following:

1. Select the object whose stroke style you want to modify.

2. In the Colors section of the toolbox, click the color swatch in the Stroke Color well to open the pop-up palette.

3. Click the Stroke Options button to open the Stroke Options dialog box.

4. Click the Advanced button to open the Edit Stroke dialog box shown previously and then follow the previous steps to edit the stroke style.

Modifying a Stroke Tip Shape

Each stroke style you choose has a distinct tip shape. The stroke styles from the Calligraphy category feature broad slanted tips, while the tips from the Pencil category are small, round, and have no slant. You can change the stroke tip shape to suit a specific need or to create an artistic path.

To modify a stroke tip shape:

1. Select the Vector Path tool, or select an existing object with a stroke on the canvas.

2. Follow the steps in the previous section to modify stroke style options and then click the Shape tab. The available tip shape settings are shown here:

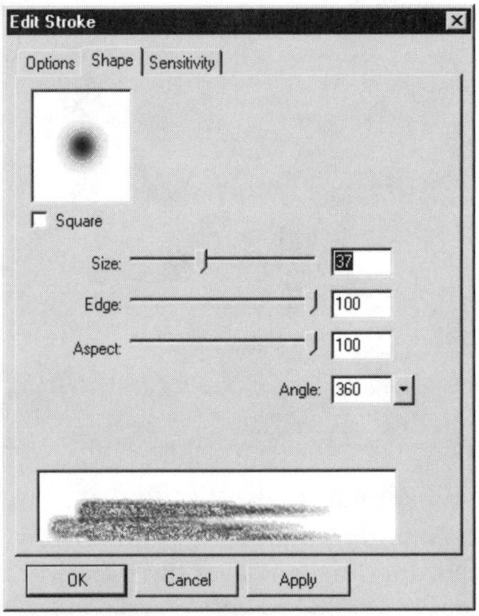

3. Select the Square checkbox to change a stroke tip shape from round to square. If this checkbox is already selected, deselect it if you want to change the tip from square to round.

4. Drag the Size slider to vary the width of the tip.

5. Drag the Edge slider to vary the softness of the edge. High settings produce edges that blend gently into the surrounding pixels of color; low settings produce abrupt transitions.

6. Drag the Aspect slider to further vary the look of the tip. The effects of this setting vary depending on whether you specify a round or a square tip. The angle of the tip also has a bearing on the effect you achieve when you modify this setting. For example, if you have a round tip with an angular setting of 0, dragging the slider toward a setting of 0 effectively flattens the tip.

7. Click the triangle to the right of the Angle field to reveal a round dial with a dot. Click the dot and drag it to change the tip angle of attack, as shown in the following illustration. Alternatively, you can enter a value between 0 and 360. As you modify the tip shape settings, the preview updates in real time.

8. Click OK to apply the settings to the Vector Path tool or a selected shape, or click the Sensitivity tab to modify sensitivity settings for the stroke. You can also click Apply to preview the new settings on a selected stroke and then click OK to finish applying the settings to the stroke.

Modifying Stroke Sensitivity Settings

If you use a digital tablet to create paths with the Vector Path tool, you can modify the sensitivity settings to change the way the stroke behaves when you modulate the amount of pressure you use to apply the pen to the tablet. These settings have limited effect on mouse-drawn strokes and, in fact, may render a mouse-drawn stroke invisible if you modify Pressure and Speed settings. You can modify one or several stroke properties such as size, ink flow, angle, scatter, and so on. After you select a stroke property, you can modify settings that affect the look of the stroke, such as the pressure, the speed, and the direction of the digital stylus on the tablet. To modify stroke sensitivity:

1. Select the Vector Path tool and then select a stroke style to modify. To modify an existing path in the document, select it.

2. Click the arrow to the left of the word Properties. The Property inspector opens.

3. Click the triangle to the right of the Stroke Category field and from the drop down menu choose Stroke Options to open the Stroke Options dialog box.

4. Click the Advanced button to open the Edit Stroke dialog box.

5. Click the Sensitivity tab to access the sensitivity settings shown here:

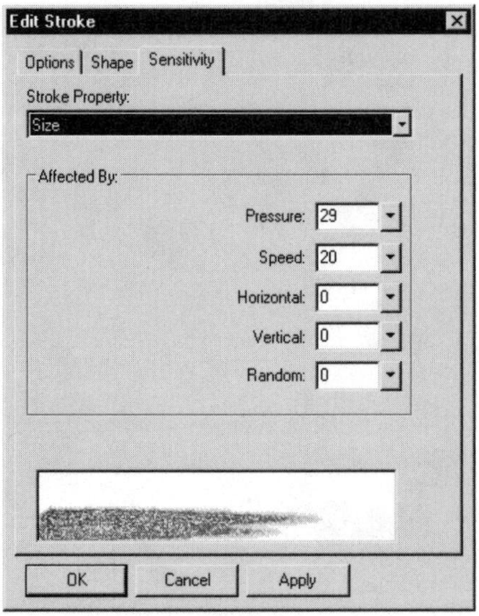

6. Click the triangle to the right of the Stroke Property field, and from the drop-down menu choose one of the following:

   ■ **Size**   Change the settings of this property to vary the size of the stroke.

   ■ **Ink Amount**   Modify this property to change the stroke ink flow.

- **Angle**   Modify the settings of this property to vary the angle based on the amount of pressure applied while creating the stroke.

- **Scatter**   Change these property settings to change the way color is distributed on the canvas.

- **Hue**   Modify this property to change the hue of the stroke as it is applied to the canvas.

- **Lightness**   Modify this property to vary the intensity of the stroke based on the pressure applied to the digital pen while creating the stroke.

- **Saturation**   Modify this property to change the saturation of the stroke color.

7. After choosing a stroke property to modify, change the settings of one or more of the following in the Affected By area:

- **Pressure**   Drag this slider to affect the look of the stroke based on the amount of pressure you exert with the digital stylus.

- **Speed**   Drag this slider to change how the selected stroke property is affected by the speed with which you draw the stroke.

- **Horizontal**   Modify this setting to determine how the stroke property is affected by horizontal movement of the digital stylus.

- **Vertical**   Modify this setting to determine how vertical movement of the stylus affects the selected stroke property.

- **Random**   Modify this setting to indicate how much randomness is applied to the selected stroke property.

8. Click OK to apply the settings and close the dialog box.

When you modify a stroke, it becomes the current stroke style and is applied to all paths or outlines you create until you select a different stroke style or until you modify the current stroke style again.

Saving a Custom Stroke Style

If after modifying a preset stroke, you decide you'd like to use it for other designs, you can save the stroke. When you save a stroke, you give it a unique name, which becomes available as a menu option in the same stroke category as the original stroke you modified.

To save the current stroke as a menu item:

1. Click the arrow to the left of the word Properties. The Property inspector opens.

2. Click the triangle to the right of the Stroke Category field and from the drop down menu choose Stroke Options. The Stroke Options dialog box appears as shown here:

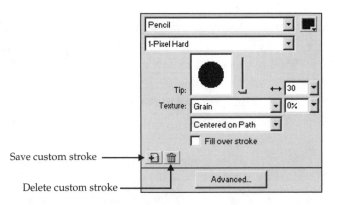

Save custom stroke ──────────▶

Delete custom stroke ─────────

3. Click the Save Custom Stroke button to open the Save Stroke dialog box shown here:

4. Enter a name for the stroke and click OK. The stroke is added as a style on the same menu as the stroke you modified.

Note *You can also open the Stroke Options dialog box from within the Colors section of the toolbox by selecting an object with a stroke, clicking the Stroke Color well color swatch and then clicking the Stroke Options button at the bottom of the pop-up palette.*

Deleting a Stroke Style

When a stroke style no longer suits your needs, you can delete it from the menu. If you've created many custom stroke styles for a particular project and no longer need them when the project is over, you can delete them to reduce clutter on the Stroke Style menu.

To delete a stroke:

1. Click the arrow to the left of the word Properties. The Property inspector opens.

2. Click the triangle to the right of the Stroke Category field and from the drop-down menu choose Stroke Options to access the Stroke Options dialog box.

3. Select the stroke style you want to delete.

4. Click the Delete Custom Stroke button, which looks like a trashcan. A warning dialog box appears, asking you to confirm the deletion.

5. Click OK to delete the selected stroke, or click Cancel to void the operation.

Creating Strokes with a Digital Tablet

If you use a digital tablet, you can achieve painterly effects when creating paths with a style from the Air Brush, Calligraphy, Charcoal, or Watercolor stroke categories. Choose the Vector Path tool. Specify a fairly wide tip size and choose a high edge softness setting. Vary the pressure as you drag the pen across the digital tablet to achieve strokes similar to those shown in Figure 9-4.

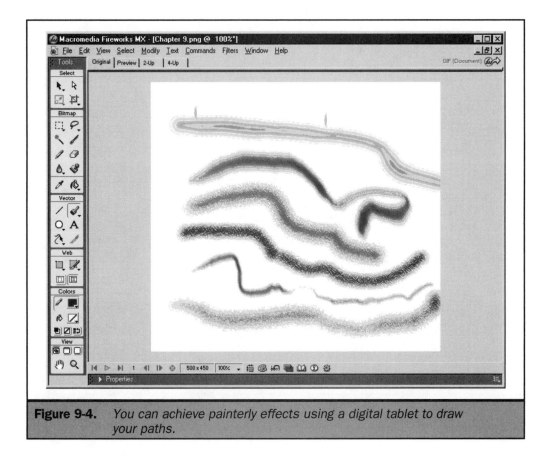

Figure 9-4.   *You can achieve painterly effects using a digital tablet to draw your paths.*

Summary

In this chapter, you learned how to modify the default stroke characteristics and choose a style to suit your work. You also saw how to edit a preset stroke style and then save it as a menu option. In addition, you learned how to create artistic paths using a digital tablet. In Chapter 10, you'll learn how to modify fills to add color to the objects in your designs. You'll also learn how to create custom textures and patterns to use in your work.

Chapter 10

Creating Colorful Fills, Textures, and Patterns

Color is the hallmark of any successful Web design. The effective use of color balances a design and can be used to accentuate points of interest such as banners, buttons, or text. Color can also be used to direct the viewer through the document. When you create a document in Fireworks, you can create objects with solid color fills and combine them with objects filled with a blend of two or more colors.

In addition to gradients, you can also use textures to accentuate the fills in your design. A texture is a grayscale image that appears underneath the fill. By default there is always a texture present, but you determine whether the texture shows through and, if so, by what percentage.

Another way to add color to your designs is to use a *pattern*. Patterns are small images that are tiled to fill an object. In this chapter, you will learn to liven up your designs by using patterns judiciously.

In previous chapters, you learned to work with the Web Safe color palette. In this chapter, you'll expand on your knowledge of color by creating Web dither fills. A Web dither fill blends colors from an existing palette to simulate a color that is not in the current palette.

Working with Color

If you are familiar with vector art, you may know that a blend of two or more colors is known as a *gradient*. You can create *linear* gradients, which are applied to objects such as rectangles and polygons, and *radial* gradients, which can be used to good effect with circular objects. In this chapter, you will learn to apply preset Fireworks gradients to objects in your documents. In this chapter, you will also learn to modify preset gradients to suit the designs you create and learn how to create seamless tiles for your Web pages. Figure 10-1 shows a few examples of fills applied to objects in a document.

Creating a Solid Fill

When you want an object to appear as though it is solid, you apply either a single color or one of the preset gradient fills. When you create a solid fill using a single color, you can choose a color from the preset palette or mix a custom color with the Color Mixer, as outlined in Chapter 8. You can create a solid fill using either the Fill Color well from the toolbox or the Property inspector.

Using the Fill Color Well

When you need to create a fill for objects yet to be created, you use the Fill Color well. In previous chapters, you used the Fill Color well to define a solid fill color. In addition to creating a solid fill, you can use the Fill Color well to choose a pattern fill, a Web dither fill, or a gradient fill.

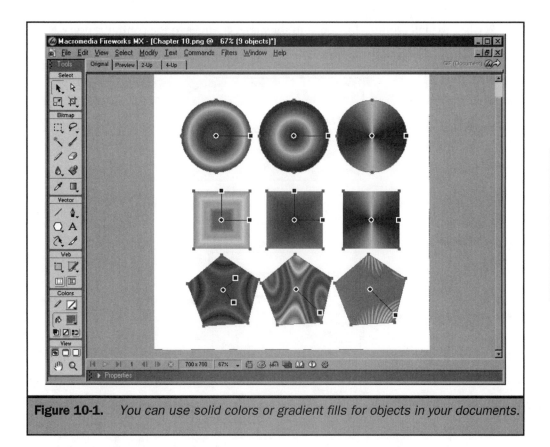

Figure 10-1.   *You can use solid colors or gradient fills for objects in your documents.*

To specify a fill:

1. Click the color swatch in the Fill Color well. The pop-up palette appears, as shown in the following illustration. The default fill type is solid.

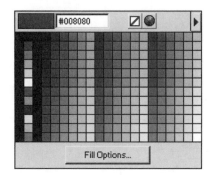

2. Click the Fill Options button, and the panel changes to the configuration shown here:

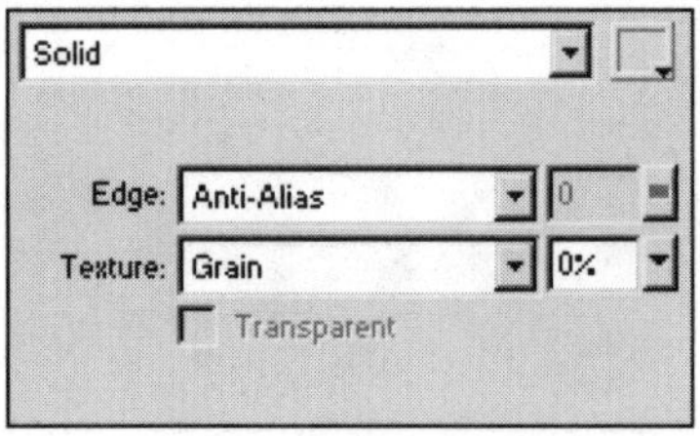

> | Solid |
> | Edge: Anti-Alias | 0 |
> | Texture: Grain | 0% |
> | Transparent |

3. Click the triangle to the right of the fill category to reveal the following menu:

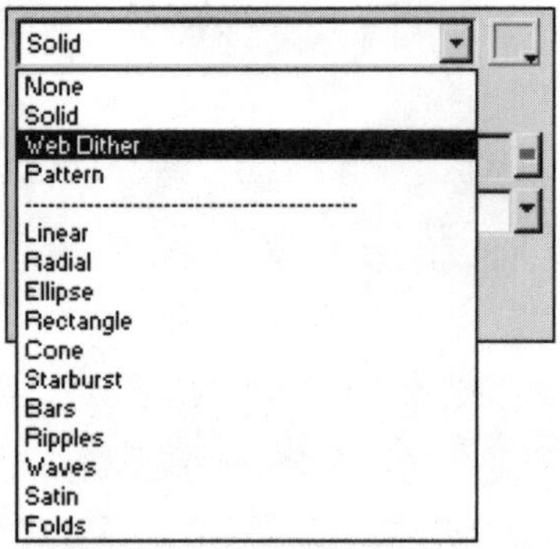

> | Solid |
> | None |
> | Solid |
> | Web Dither |
> | Pattern |
> | -------------------------------- |
> | Linear |
> | Radial |
> | Ellipse |
> | Rectangle |
> | Cone |
> | Starburst |
> | Bars |
> | Ripples |
> | Waves |
> | Satin |
> | Folds |

4. Choose a fill type category.

5. Click the triangle to the right of the Preset gradient color sets field and choose a preset gradient from the drop-down menu.

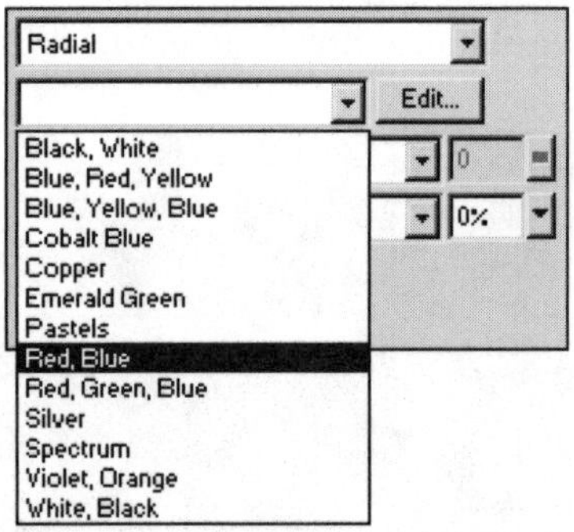

> | Radial |
> | | Edit... |
> | Black, White |
> | Blue, Red, Yellow |
> | Blue, Yellow, Blue |
> | Cobalt Blue |
> | Copper |
> | Emerald Green |
> | Pastels |
> | Red, Blue |
> | Red, Green, Blue |
> | Silver |
> | Spectrum |
> | Violet, Orange |
> | White, Black |

After you choose a preset, it becomes the current fill and is applied to all objects you create until you specify a different fill type or modify the existing fill type.

Using the Property Inspector

After you apply a fill to an object, you can select it and modify the fill within the Property inspector. When you select an object and open the Property inspector, the same options are available as for the Fill Color well; however, the setup is slightly different.

To modify a filled object from the Property inspector:

1. Select the object whose fill you want to modify.

2. Click the arrow to the left of the word Properties. The Property inspector opens.

3. Click the triangle to the right of the Fill category field. The drop-down menu in the following illustration appears.

4. Choose a fill type. After you choose a fill type, the default fill for that category is applied to the object, and it appears in the Fill Color well.

5. To choose a fill from the category, click the triangle to the right of the Fill category field and choose Fill Options from the drop-down menu. The Fill Options dialog box appears.

6. Click the triangle to the right of the Preset gradient color sets field, and a menu with preset gradients for the fill type appears. The following illustration shows the preset menu for the Starburst fill type.

7. Choose a preset, and it is applied to the selected object. It becomes the current fill until you choose a different one.

Modifying the Edge of a Filled Object

When you fill a vector object, by default Fireworks anti-aliases the fill. When a fill is anti-aliased, the color pixels from the fill are blended with the adjacent color pixels to produce a gentle transition from one object to the next. If you wish, you can modify the way a filled object blends with the surrounding objects.

To modify the way an object blends with surrounding objects:

1. Select a filled object whose edge characteristics you want to modify.

2. Click the arrow to the left of the word Properties. The Property inspector opens.

3. Click the triangle to the right of the Edge field and choose one of the following:

   ■ **Hard**   This option produces an abrupt transition between the filled object and neighboring color pixels.

   ■ **Anti Alias**   This option, the default, blends pixels at the edge of the object with surrounding pixels to produce a gentle transition between objects.

   ■ **Feather**   This option creates a halo-type effect in which Fireworks gently fades a given number of pixels (10, by default) at the edge of the object into the surrounding pixels of color.

4. If you choose Feather, the Amount of Feather field becomes active. Accept the default value of 10 or click and drag the slider to the right of the field to specify the amount of feathering. Alternatively, you can enter a value between 1 and 100 in the field. If you enter a value of 0 or drag the slider to 0, Fireworks reverts to the default Anti-Alias option.

Creating a Web Dither Fill

If you need to use a color that is not part of the Web Safe palette, you can choose a Web dither fill that mixes two colors from the Web Safe palette to render a reasonable facsimile of the original color. This fill type comes in handy when you have a client that needs a color reproduced exactly as it appears in other documents—for example, a logo with a unique color scheme.

To match a color with a Web dither fill:

1. Import the object containing a non-Web-safe color for which you want to create a Web dither fill.

2. Click the Fill Color well swatch. The pop-up palette appears.

3. Click the Fill Options button.

4. Click the triangle to the right of the fill category field and choose Web Dither. The Fill Options dialog box changes to Web Dither configuration, as shown here:

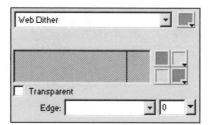

5. Click the color swatch in the upper-right corner. Your cursor becomes an eyedropper.

6. Click the non-Web-safe color to sample it.

7. The grid of four color swatches in the Fill Options dialog box changes to show Web-safe colors. The four swatches are a larger representation of the grid used to define the Web dither fill. The grid used to define the actual fill approximates the way pixels combine to create the illusion of a continuous image. The four squares are tiled within the object to which the Web dither fill is applied. Each grid is so small that when combined, the Web dither fill fools the eye into believing it is one continuous color.

You can also create custom colors using the System Color Mixer and then create a Web dither fill. However, when you create a custom color with the intention of creating a Web dither fill, disable the Snap to Web Safe Colors option; otherwise, Fireworks will snap your custom color to Web safe. When you create a Web dither fill from a custom color snapped to Web safe, all four color swatches are the same, effectively defeating the purpose of a Web dither fill.

Note   *A Web dither fill may increase the file size of the document when exported.*

Another way to create a Web dither fill is to select an object, use the Color Mixer to define the color, and then change the fill type to Web Dither. To create a Web dither fill in this manner, follow these steps:

1. Select an object on the canvas.

2. Choose Window | Color Mixer. Once you have the Color Mixer open, you can either match a known value or create a color by dragging your cursor inside the color bar.

3. To match a known value, select a color model from the Options menu, and then enter the values in the appropriate fields. Alternatively, to create a custom

color, drag your cursor inside the color bar. After using either method to create a color, the object updates to reveal the new fill.

4. Click the arrow to the left of the word Properties. The Property inspector opens.

5. Click the triangle to the right of the fill category field and choose Web Dither. Fireworks chooses two Web-safe colors to approximate the Web dither fill.

There is yet another method you can use to create a Web dither fill. This method involves mixing two colors from the Web Safe palette. To create a Web dither fill by mixing Web-safe colors, do the following:

1. Click the color swatch in the Fill Color well. The pop-up palette appears.

2. Click the Fill Options button shown previously.

3. Click the triangle to the right of the Fill category field and choose Web Dither. The Fill Options dialog box adopts the configuration shown here:

4. Click the color swatch near the upper-right corner of the panel and choose a color from the pop-up palette.

5. Click the color swatch near the lower-right corner of the panel and choose a color from the pop-up palette. The color grid in the Fill Options dialog box updates to reflect the new fill. The Source Color swatch and preview window display the Web dither fill. If the color is not acceptable, click either one of the color swatches on the right side of the window and choose a different color from the pop-up palette.

Creating a Pattern Fill

In addition to using solid colors and preset gradients to fill objects, you can fill objects with colorful patterns. Fireworks ships with a wide variety of interesting patterns that make your objects appear as though they are filled with splashes of color from an artist's paintbrush, carpet textures, and much more. Figure 10-2 shows a few of the colorful patterns available for your designs.

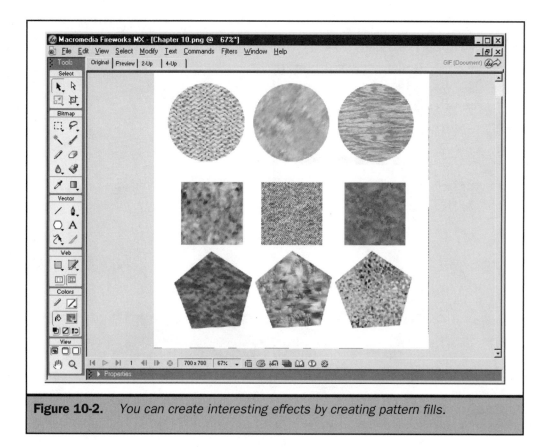

Figure 10-2.   *You can create interesting effects by creating pattern fills.*

You can define a pattern fill before creating an object or by selecting an object from the canvas and then modifying the fill. When you create a pattern fill to apply to objects yet to be created, you use the Fill Color well.

To create a pattern fill using the Fill Color well, follow these steps:

1. Click the color swatch in the Fill Color well. The pop-up palette appears.

2. Click the Fill Options button to open the Fill Options dialog box shown previously.

3. Click the triangle to the right of the Fill category field and choose Pattern.

4. Click the triangle to the right of the Pattern name field and choose a pattern from the drop-down menu. As you drag your cursor over the menu selections,

a window appears to the right of the dialog box showing a preview of the pattern, as you can see here:

After you create the pattern fill in this manner, it is applied to all future objects you create until you choose another pattern or until you specify a different fill type.

Applying a Pattern Fill to an Existing Object

If you already have objects on the canvas, you can change the existing fill to a pattern fill. You can do this within the toolbox's color section or within the Property inspector. In this section, you'll learn how to perform this task with the Property inspector.

To apply a pattern fill to an existing object:

1. Select the object whose fill you want to change.

2. Click the arrow to the left of the word Properties.

3. Click the triangle to the right of the Fill category field and choose Fill Options.

4. Click the triangle to the right of the Fill category field and choose Pattern from the drop-down menu.

5. Click the triangle to the right of the Pattern name field and move your cursor over the menu choices. As you move your cursor across the pattern names, a preview window opens to the right of the menu as shown in the following illustration. Notice the scroll bar, which you can use to view the additional menu choices.

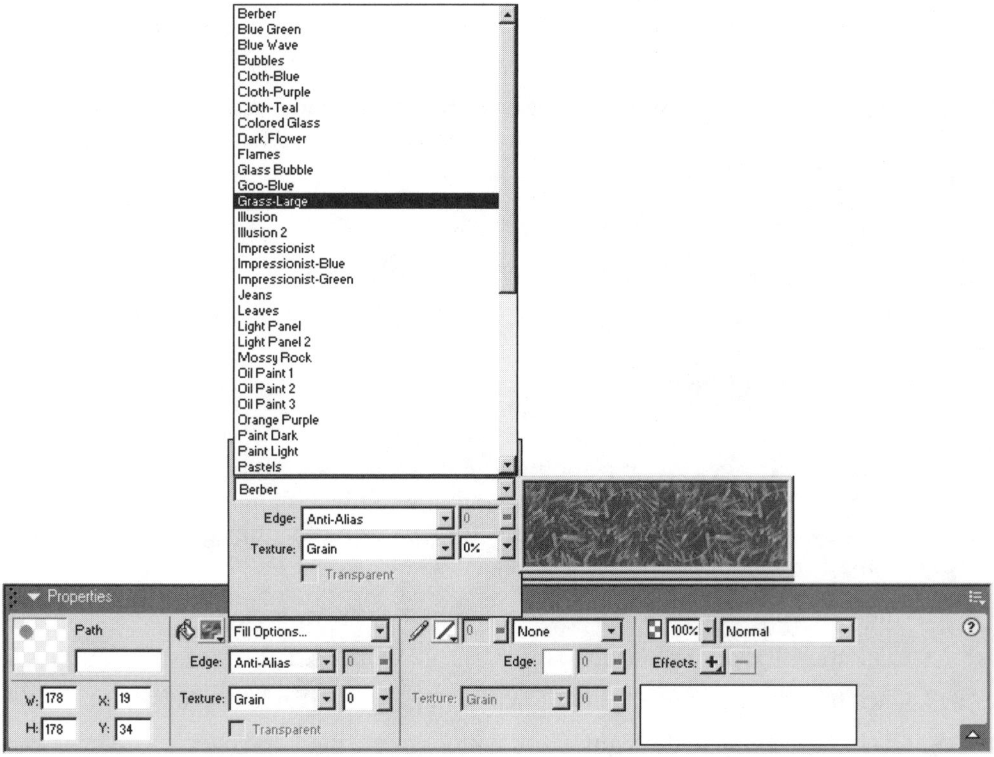

Berber
Blue Green
Blue Wave
Bubbles
Cloth-Blue
Cloth-Purple
Cloth-Teal
Colored Glass
Dark Flower
Flames
Glass Bubble
Goo-Blue
Grass-Large
Illusion
Illusion 2
Impressionist
Impressionist-Blue
Impressionist-Green
Jeans
Leaves
Light Panel
Light Panel 2
Mossy Rock
Oil Paint 1
Oil Paint 2
Oil Paint 3
Orange Purple
Paint Dark
Paint Light
Pastels

Berber

Edge: Anti-Alias   0

Texture: Grain   0%

☐ Transparent

Properties

Path   Fill Options...   None   100% Normal   ?

Edge: Anti-Alias   0   Edge: 0   Effects: + −

W: 178   X: 19   Texture: Grain   0   Texture: Grain   0

H: 178   Y: 34   ☐ Transparent

6. Click a pattern name to select it.

Editing a Pattern Fill

After you apply a pattern fill to an object, you can edit it at any time. You can replace
the fill with another pattern on the list or choose a pattern created with another
program and not stored in the Fireworks pattern directory.

To edit a pattern fill:

1. Select the object to which the pattern fill is applied.

2. Click the Fill Color well in the Colors section of the toolbox. The Fill Options
   dialog box opens, as shown in the following illustration. Notice that the current
   pattern is displayed.

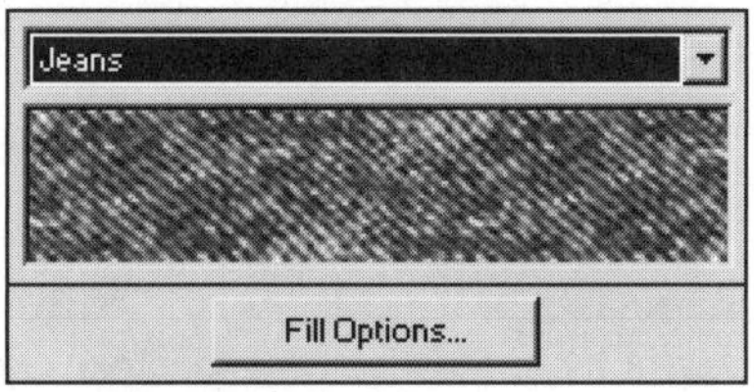

Jeans

Fill Options...

3. Click the triangle to the right of the fill type field and then choose a different pattern from the menu.

You can also edit a pattern fill from within the Property inspector. The technique is the same, but the dialog boxes are slightly different. To edit a pattern fill from the Property inspector:

1. Select the object whose pattern fill you want to edit.

2. Click the arrow to the left of the word Properties.

3. Click the triangle to the right of the fill category field and choose Fill Options from the menu.

4. Click the triangle to the right of the Pattern name field and choose a pattern from the menu.

You can use an image stored in another directory as a pattern fill. You can use any image; however, it's best to use a small image that will tile without showing a seam. You can use any of the following file formats for a pattern fill: .png, .gif, .jpg, and .bmp. To use an image for a pattern fill:

1. Click the Fill Color well in the Colors section of the toolbox.

2. Click the Fill Options button to open the Fill Options dialog box.

3. Click the triangle to the right of the fill category field and choose Pattern.

4. Click the triangle to the right of the pattern name field and choose Other. This is the last option in the list, so you'll have to use the scroll bar to find it. After you choose Other, the Locate File dialog box shown next opens.

5. Navigate to the directory where the image is stored, select it, and then click Open. The selected image is applied as a pattern fill to the next object you create.

You can also apply an image as a pattern fill while editing a fill. Edit the fill as outlined previously and choose Other for the new pattern. Follow the preceding steps to navigate to the image folder and apply it as a fill.

Creating a Seamless Tile

If you use tiled backgrounds for your Web pages, you can easily create an image to use as a seamless tile. When you use a tiled background for a Web page, it is a GIF image, which coincidentally is the default Fireworks export option. The Fireworks patterns are all seamless, which makes it relatively easy to create a seamless tile for a Web page.

To create a seamless tile, follow these steps:

1. Choose File | New. The New Document dialog box appears.

2. Enter a value of 200 in both the Width and Height fields. Accept the default canvas color of white and click OK.

3. Select the rectangle tool and while holding down the SHIFT key, create a square. Don't worry about getting the size just right; you can change the size in the Property inspector.

4. Click the arrow to the left of the word Properties. The Property inspector opens.

5. Enter 200 in the W and H fields, and enter 0 in the X and Y fields.

6. Click the triangle to the right of the Fill category field and choose Fill Options. The Fill Options dialog box appears.

7. Click the triangle to the right of the Fill category field and choose Pattern from the drop-down menu.

8. Click the triangle to the right of the Pattern name field and choose a pattern. The best backgrounds for Web pages are simple patterns that add a textured look to a page. Choose any of the patterns that look like carpet or fabric.

Click the triangle to the right of the Opacity field and drag the slider to fade the pattern. Your goal here is to apply the right opacity to create an interesting background that won't conflict with any text you have on the Web page. If you leave the opacity at 100 percent, viewers of the Web page will have a hard time reading the text. When you create an image for use as a seamless background tile, accept the default export option. After adjusting the opacity, you should have an image that looks similar to the following.

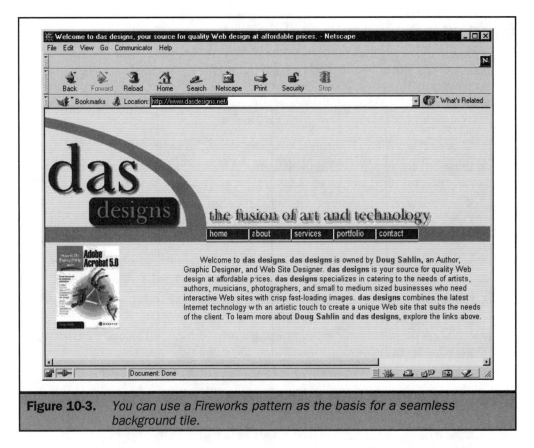

Figure 10-3. *You can use a Fireworks pattern as the basis for a seamless background tile.*

9. Optimize the image for export as a GIF file. For more information on optimizing your work, see Chapter 21.

10. Choose File | Export. The Export dialog box opens.

11. Choose a filename for the image, navigate to the folder where you store your Web site assets, and then click OK.

After you export the image, it's ready to use as a seamless background. Consult your HTML editor's software manual for information on applying the seamless tile as a background. Figure 10-3 shows an image created in Fireworks that is being used as a seamless tile on a Web page.

Creating Custom Textures

If you own an image-editing program that has the capability of creating a seamless tile, you have everything you need to create a custom pattern or texture. Most image-editing programs have a different way of creating a seamless tile. Refer to your software user's manual for specific instructions.

To create a custom texture:

1. Launch your image-editing software and create a new document 128 × 128 pixels.

2. Create a seamless tile. If your software has plug-ins that can generate fractal images, these are perfect for seamless tiles. If you own a version of the CorelDRAW suite, a utility called CorelTEXTURE is included. The utility has all manner of interesting textures that you can modify. The end result is a seamless tile.

3. To use the seamless tile as a pattern, convert it to the RGB color model with 24-bit or higher color depth. To use the seamless tile as a texture, convert it to 8-bit grayscale.

4. Save the image in one of the following file formats: .bmp, .gif, .jpg, .png, or .tif. If you're creating both textures and patterns, save these in separate folders so you will know which is which when you integrate them into Fireworks. Figure 10-4 shows several images created in a texture-generating program that are perfect candidates for Fireworks patterns or textures.

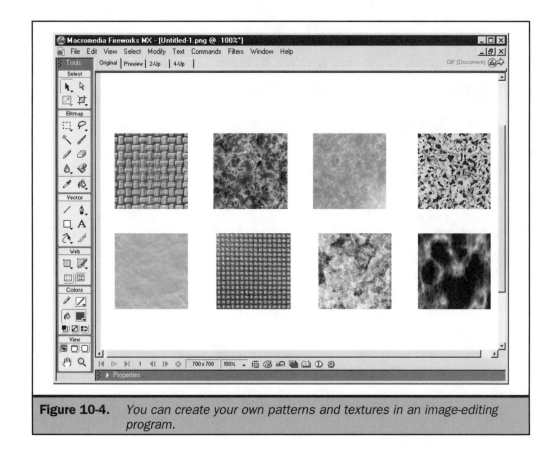

Figure 10-4. *You can create your own patterns and textures in an image-editing program.*

After you create several patterns and textures, you can integrate them into Fireworks in one of two ways. First, you can copy the files directly into the appropriate folder. For patterns, the path is Fireworks MX | Configuration | Patterns; for textures, the path is Fireworks MX | Configuration | Textures. Second, you can choose Edit | Preferences to open the Preferences dialog box. Click the Folders tab and follow the prompts to link your patterns and textures folders to Fireworks. Following either method will display the pattern or texture name on the applicable menu.

Adding Texture to Fills

Another way to add variety to your designs is to show a texture behind a fill. By default, a texture is always present when you create a fill; however the amount of texture is 0 by default. Using a texture can give a fill a more natural, organic look. When you vary the amount of texture, you can see it behind the texture. The following image shows the results of varying the amount of a texture behind a fill.

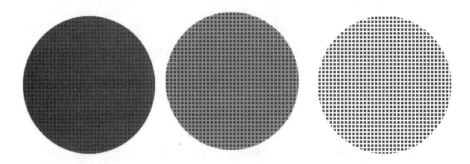

To show a texture behind a fill, follow these steps:

1. Click the Fill Color well in the Colors section of the toolbox.

2. Select a fill color or click the Fill Options button to select a preset gradient fill or a pattern fill.

3. Click the color swatch in the Fill Color well and click the Fill Options button.

4. Click the triangle to the right of the Texture name field and choose a texture from the menu shown here:

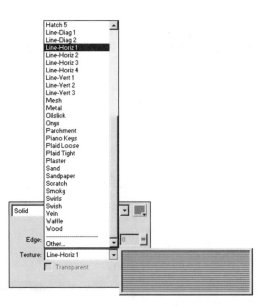

5. Click the triangle to the right of the Amount of texture field and drag the slider to vary the percentage of the texture that shows through the fill. Alternatively, you can enter a value between 0 (no texture shows through) and 100 (the texture is displayed at full opacity). The textured fill will be applied to all future objects you create until you modify the fill.

After you apply a texture to a fill, you can edit the amount of texture by clicking the color swatch in the Fill Color well. If you've applied the fill to an object, you can edit the way the fill appears by selecting the object, opening the Property inspector, and changing the value in the Amount of texture field.

Using Preset Gradient Fills

In the previous sections of this chapter, you've learned to work with solid fills, patterns, and textures. In this section, you'll learn how to use one of the many preset Fireworks gradient fills. A gradient fill is a blend of two or more colors. The Fireworks gradient presets are categorized so that you can choose a category that is appropriate for the shape to which the fill is applied. After you apply a preset gradient to an object, you can edit it to suit your document. Figure 10-5 shows several objects with preset gradient fills.

To use a preset gradient fill:

1. Click the color swatch in the Fill Color well. The pop-up palette appears.

2. Click the Fill Options button to open the Fill Options dialog box.

3. Click the triangle to the right of the Fill category field and choose a category from the menu shown here:

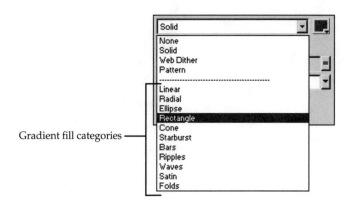

4. Click the triangle to the right of the Preset gradient color set field and choose a fill from the menu shown here:

5. Click anywhere in the workspace to close the Fill Options dialog box. The gradient preset is displayed in the Fill Color well color swatch and is applied to all future filled objects you create.

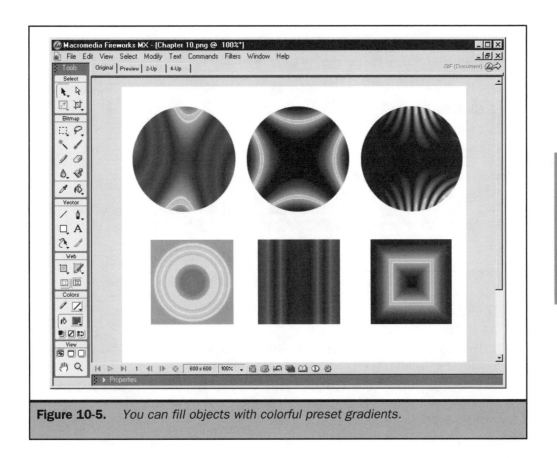

Figure 10-5. *You can fill objects with colorful preset gradients.*

After you apply a preset gradient to an object or choose a preset gradient for objects you are going to create, you can modify the gradient to suit your design, a technique you will learn in the next section.

Editing Preset Gradients

You can put your own stamp of originality on filled objects by editing one or more parameters of a preset fill. You can change the colors of a fill, vary the transparency of individual colors in a fill, and change the position where the color is blended in the gradient. You can edit a fill yet to be applied to an object by using the Fill Color well. You can also use the Fill Color well to modify a fill already applied to an object or use the Property inspector to achieve the same result. The steps that follow demonstrate how to use the Fill Color well to edit a gradient.

To edit a gradient fill:

1. Click the color swatch in the Fill Color well. The Fill Options dialog box appears, displaying a preview of the fill as shown here:

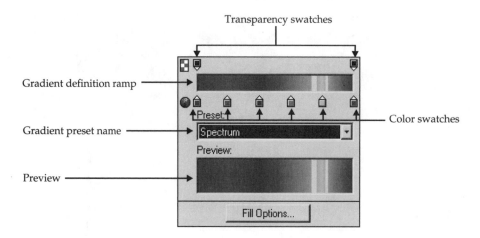

2. To choose a different preset, click the arrow to the right of the Gradient preset name field, and choose an option from the menu.

3. To change a color, click a color swatch. The pop-up palette appears and your cursor becomes an eyedropper. Choose a color by clicking a color swatch in the pop-up palette. Alternatively, you can click the System Color Picker button and use that palette to mix a color.

Tip *To match a color in a gradient to a color in the document, click the color swatch, move the cursor over the object whose color you want to match, and then click to sample the color.*

4. To add a color to the gradient, click below the gradient definition ramp where you want the new color to appear. After the new color swatch appears, click the pointer and choose the desired color, as outlined previously.

5. To change where a color appears in the gradient, click and drag a color swatch to a new position.

6. To modify the transparency of the beginning or ending color in the gradient, click a transparency swatch. The Opacity dialog box appears. Drag the slider to vary the transparency of the color or enter a value between 0 (transparent) and 100 (opaque).

7. To vary the transparency at another position in the gradient, click above the gradient definition ramp and a new transparency pointer appears. Click the pointer and then set the opacity as outlined in step 6.

8. Click anywhere in the workspace to finish editing the gradient and close the dialog box. The color swatch in the Fill Color well updates to reflect your changes, and the modified fill is applied to all future objects you create until you modify the fill again.

You can modify a fill already applied to a selected object in the Fill Color well as outlined previously, or you can edit the fill using the Property inspector. The method achieves the same end result, but you use slightly different dialog boxes, as you'll see in the following steps.

To edit a fill applied to an object using the Property inspector, follow these steps:

1. Select the object whose fill you want to modify.

2. Click the arrow to the left of the word Properties. The Property inspector opens.

3. Click the triangle to the right of the Fill category field and choose Fill Options from the menu. The Fill Options dialog box appears, as shown here:

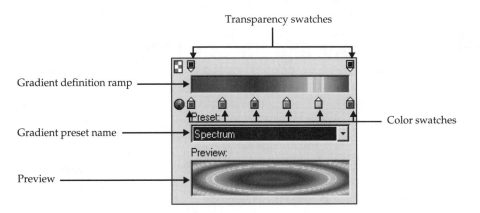

4. Click the Edit button. The Edit Gradient dialog box appears, as shown here:

Transparency swatches

Gradient definition ramp ⎯⎯⎯⎯⎯⎯⎯⎯⎯

Color swatches

Gradient preset name ⎯⎯⎯⎯⎯⎯⎯

Preview ⎯⎯⎯⎯⎯⎯⎯⎯⎯⎯⎯⎯⎯

5. Edit the gradient by adding color swatches, moving color swatches, or varying transparency, as outlined previously.

6. Click anywhere in the workspace to apply the changes.

When you create a custom fill you want to use on other documents, you can save it as a style. For more information on styles, refer to Chapter 15.

Creating a Transparent Fill

Even though you assign transparency to a fill color or an object, when you export the document for viewing in a Web browser, the background color of the Web page does not show through. If you want to create the illusion of transparency with a filled object, you can use a Web dither fill as a workaround.

To create a fill that appears transparent in a Web browser:

1. Select an object with a solid fill that you want to appear transparent in a Web browser.

2. Click the arrow to the left of the word Properties. The Property inspector opens.

3. Click the triangle to the right of the Fill category field and choose Fill Options to open the Fill Options dialog box.

4. Click the triangle to the right of the Fill category field and choose Web Dither.

5. Click the Transparent check box. The color swatches on the right side of the dialog box update to reflect the change. On the canvas, the object appears to be partially transparent.

6. Export the object as a .gif file or as an 8-bit .png file with Index Transparency or Alpha Transparency. When the exported object is viewed in a Web browser, every other pixel is transparent, which fools the eye into believing the background is actually showing through every pixel.

Modifying Gradient and Pattern Fills

In addition to modifying a fill's colors and transparency, you can also change how the fill is centered within an object, rotate the fill within the object, and change the scale of the fill as it appears in the object. You can achieve one or all of the above by selecting a filled object with the Pointer tool and then dragging handles to new locations.

To modify the appearance of a gradient or pattern fill within an object:

1. Select the object with the Pointer tool. If you select an object with a radial or linear fill, you have one handle to work with; select a rectangular or pattern fill, and two handles appear. A selected rectangular fill is shown here:

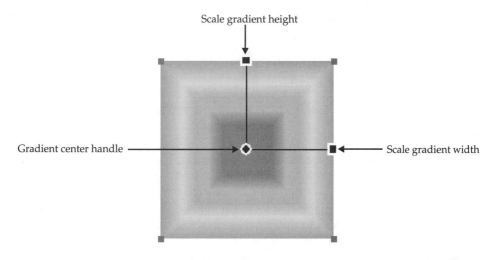

Scale gradient height

Gradient center handle ——————→ ◇ ■ ←—————— Scale gradient width

2. To rotate the fill, move your cursor toward a handle until it becomes a semicircle with an arrow at the end. Click and drag to rotate the fill within the object.

3. To move the center of the fill, click the center rectangle and drag to the desired position.

4. To scale the fill, click a handle and drag toward the fill center to decrease the fill's scale; drag away from the fill center to increase the fill's scale. If you're working with a rectangular or pattern fill, you can scale the width and height independently by dragging the appropriate handle.

Tip *To reset a fill to its default parameters, select the Paint Bucket tool and then while holding down the Shift key, double-click inside a filled object where you have modified the fill width, height, or rotation.*

Applying Solid Color with the Paint Bucket Tool

When you mix a solid color fill in the Fill Color well, you can apply the fill to other objects in your document with the Paint Bucket tool. The Paint Bucket tool provides a convenient way to change the fill of several objects in a document.

To color objects with the Paint Bucket tool:

1. Deselect all objects by clicking a blank spot on the canvas or by choosing Edit | Deselect All.

2. Click the color swatch in the Fill Color well and choose the desired color from the pop-up palette.

3. Select the Paint Bucket tool shown here:

4. Click an object with the tool to apply the fill. Click additional objects to apply the same fill.

If you click a bitmap object with the Paint Bucket tool, it will be filled with solid color; click it with the Gradient tool, and it will be filled with a gradient. However, you can use the Paint Bucket tool to recolor areas of a bitmap selected with either the Magic Wand tool or one of the Marquee selection tools. You can use the Gradient tool to create special effects on bitmap images by applying the tool to pixel selections.

Applying a Fill with the Gradient Tool

When you choose one of the preset gradient fills or edit a fill, you can apply the fill to other objects in the document with the Gradient tool. This is a handy way of making wholesale changes to many objects in the document or applying a special effect to a single object.

To apply a fill with the Gradient tool:

1. Click the color swatch in the Fill Color well.
2. Click the Fill Options button to open the Fill Options dialog box.
3. Click the triangle to the right of the Fill category field, and choose one of the gradient fill categories.
4. Click the triangle to the right of the Preset gradient color sets field and choose a preset from the menu.
5. Click a blank spot on the canvas to close the dialog box.
6. Select the Gradient tool, as shown in the following illustration. The Gradient tool and the Paint Bucket tool occupy the same space in the toolbox. If the Paint Bucket tool is displayed, click the tool and hold until the group flyout menu appears and then select the Gradient tool.

7. Click an object to fill it with the gradient. The Gradient tool retains the last gradient fill mixed, regardless of the current fill in the Fill Color well.

Summary

In this chapter, you learned to create fills to color objects in your designs. You learned to create solid color fills, gradient fills, Web dither fills, and pattern fills. You also learned to modify preset gradient fills to suit your document and to use textures to give the fills in your document a more natural or organic appearance. You received some tips on how to create your own patterns and textures. Finally, you discovered how to use the Paint Bucket tool and the Gradient tool to apply a fill to objects in your document. In Chapter 11, you'll learn how to modify the objects in your documents.

CREATING ARTWORK
FOR YOUR DESIGNS

The
Complete
Reference

Fireworks
MX

Part III

Modifying Artwork

Chapter 11

Modifying Objects

fter you create objects for a document using the vector object tools or the path tools, you can modify them to suit your design. In previous chapters, you learned to modify the color characteristics of an object by modifying its stroke and fill. In this chapter, you'll learn to modify the physical characteristics of an object. The characteristics you can modify are the object's position on the canvas, the object's size, and more. You can also modify an object's shape by manipulating the points that make up the object's path.

In this chapter, you'll learn to use Fireworks tools and menu commands to modify the objects in your documents. You'll transform objects with pinpoint accuracy using menu commands. You'll learn to select objects, create object groups, and transform every characteristic of an object. You'll also learn to modify object paths, combine object paths, and alter object paths using menu commands and tools.

Selecting Objects

Before you can edit an object, you must select it. If you've worked with other vector and image-editing programs, you know how difficult it can be to select an object that is under or adjacent to other objects. Fortunately, Fireworks gives you several different methods of selecting objects. You can select objects with menu commands or by using tools, which will be covered in this section. Fireworks gives you two powerful tools for object selection, the Pointer tool and the Select Behind tool.

Using the Pointer Tool

Before you perform any edits on an object, you must first select it. You can use the Pointer tool, shown next, to select individual objects or to create a selection of objects. Once you have created a selection, you can use the tool to move the selected objects or use another tool to modify the selection.

To select an object, select the Pointer tool and click the object. A bounding box of four filled squares (five when a polygon is selected) appears around the object, as shown here:

You also use the Pointer tool to select multiple objects. There are a two ways to handle this task. To select more than one object:

■ Select the Pointer tool and click an object. Hold down the SHIFT key and click additional objects to add them to the selection. Each selected object has a bounding box surrounded by filled squares, as shown here:

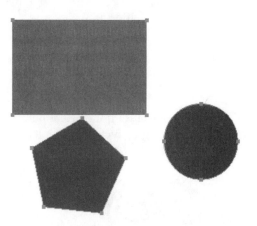

■ Select the Pointer tool, click a spot on the canvas beyond the area of the objects you want to select, and then drag down and across. As you drag, a bounding box appears and gives you an indication of the selection area, as shown in the following illustration. When the objects you want to select are within the bounding box, release the mouse button. The selected items are highlighted, as shown previously.

Using the Select Behind Tool

When you have multiple objects stacked on the canvas, it may be difficult to select an individual object for editing. If this is the case, you can use the Select Behind tool to select a hidden or partially obscured object. The Select Behind tool, shown next, occupies the same spot in the toolbox as Pointer tool. The toolbox display always defaults to the last tool used. If the Pointer tool is displayed, click and hold the tool's icon until the group flyout is displayed; then click the Select Behind tool.

To select an obscured or hidden object with the Select Behind tool, click the object at the top of the stack and continue clicking to cycle through the other objects in the stack until the desired item is highlighted, as shown here:

Once you have selected the desired object, you can move it to a new location, or modify it with another tool or menu command.

Deselecting Objects

After you have made an object selection and modified the selection, you need to deselect the objects before performing other tasks. You deselect an object when you select another one with the Pointer tool. When you have only a few objects in the document, this is a simple task. However, when you have multiple and overlapping objects on the canvas, you may have difficulty deselecting one object and selecting another. Fortunately, the Fireworks design team has given you a number of methods for deselecting objects.

To deselect an object or a selection of objects, do one of the following:

- ■ Click another object with the Pointer tool.
- ■ Click another object with the Select Behind tool.
- ■ Click a blank space on the canvas with either the Pointer or the Select Behind tool.
- ■ Choose Select | Deselect.

Note *When you have a document with multiple objects, you use a good bit of your CPU processing power. When you put a strain on your CPU resources, there may be times when you click another object or click the canvas, and your computer lags behind. Always make sure the object is deselected before performing the next task.*

Transforming Objects Manually

After selecting one or more objects, you can modify them. You can move objects, resize objects, and rotate, skew, and distort objects. You can accomplish these tasks with menu commands or by using tools. The sections that follow show you how to modify objects using tools.

Moving Objects

After selecting one or more objects, you can move the selection to a different spot on the canvas. You can reposition objects with either the Pointer tool or the Select Behind tool, or by using the arrow keys on your computer keyboard.

To manually move one or more objects, create the selection with either the Pointer or the Select Behind tool and do one of the following:

- Click and drag the selection to a new location.

- Press one of the arrow keys on your computer keyboard to nudge the selection in one-pixel increments to a different position. The selection continues to move as long as the key is pressed. Release the key when the selection is in the desired position.

- Press the SHIFT key while holding down one of the arrow keys. Holding the SHIFT key increases the nudge increment to 10 pixels. Release the key when the selection is in the desired position.

Resizing Objects

You can manually resize a selection using the Scale tool. With the Scale tool, you can change the object's width, height, or scale. You can resize an individual object or a selection of objects. When you use the tool on a selection of objects, the objects lose their individual identity and behave as a single unit. The Scale tool, shown next, shares a spot in the toolbox with the Skew and Distort tools.

To manually resize objects using the Scale tool:

1. Create a selection as outlined previously.

2. Select the Scale tool. Alternatively, you can choose Modify | Transform | Scale. After choosing the tool or menu command, eight handles appear around the object's perimeter, plus one handle in the center of the object. You resize the object by manipulating the handles as follows:

   ■ To change the object's width, click either the middle-left or the middle-right handle, and drag left or right.

   ■ To change the object's height, click either the top-center or bottom-center handle, and drag up or down.

   ■ To resize the object proportionately, click one of the corner handles and drag diagonally toward the center of the object to reduce the size or away from the center to increase the size. The handle in the opposite corner serves as the anchor for proportional scaling.

3. Double-click the object to apply the change. Alternatively, press ENTER or RETURN.

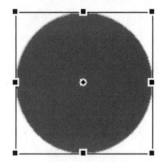

> **Tip**   *You can also move an object with the Scale tool. Move your cursor over the object; when it changes to a cross with four arrowheads, you can click and drag the object to a new location.*

Rotating Objects

You also use the Scale tool to rotate an object. You can rotate an object by its actual center point, or you can use the Scale tool to move the center handle to a different position. When you move the center handle (also known as the *registration point*) to a different position, the object rotates around that point rather than its physical center.

To rotate an object:

1. Select an object, or create a selection of objects as outlined previously.

2. Select the Scale tool. Alternatively, you can choose Modify | Transform | Scale. After choosing either method, eight handles appear around the object(s).

3. Move your cursor toward the selection. When the cursor changes to a semicircle with an arrow at the end, click and drag clockwise or counterclockwise.

4. Double-click the object to apply the change. Alternatively, press ENTER or RETURN.

To rotate the object from a different registration point:

1. Select one or more objects as outlined previously.

2. Select the Scale tool, and eight handles appear around the object's perimeter, in addition to one handle at its center.

3. Click the center handle and drag it to a different location.

4. Rotate the object(s) as outlined previously. Rotation takes place around the new reference point, as shown here:

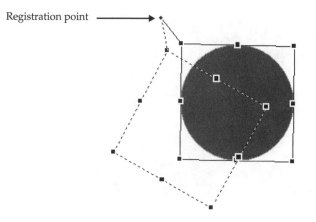

Registration point ————————→

5. Double-click the object to apply the change. Alternatively, press ENTER or RETURN.

Skewing Objects

You can also change the way an object looks by skewing it. Skewing an object is a good technique for animation. You can skew an object relative to its vertical or horizontal axis, or both. The Skew tool, shown next, resides on a flyout with the Scale and Distort tools. If the Skew tool is not displayed, click and hold the tool currently displayed until the tool group flyout appears, and then select the Skew tool.

To skew an object:

1. Select the object(s) you want to skew.

2. Select the Skew tool. Alternatively, you can choose Modify | Transform | Skew. Choose either method, and eight handles appear around the object(s).

3. To skew the object(s) vertically, move your cursor toward the center handle on either side. When your cursor becomes a vertical line with an arrow at each end, click and drag up or down to skew the object.

4. To skew the object(s) horizontally, move your cursor toward the center handle on the top or bottom of the selection. When your cursor becomes a horizontal line with an arrow at each end, click and drag left or right to skew the object.

5. To create the illusion of perspective, click one of the corner points and then drag in or out, or up or down, as shown here:

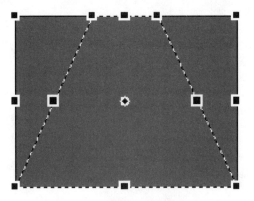

6. Double-click the object to apply the change. Alternatively, press ENTER or RETURN.

Tip *You can also rotate or move an object with the Skew tool. Click inside the object and drag to move it. To rotate an object with the Skew tool, move your cursor toward the object. When it becomes a semicircle with an arrow at one end, click and drag clockwise or counterclockwise.*

Distorting Objects

If you need to apply a freeform transformation to an object, the Distort tool is the answer. When you use the Distort tool on an object, you can mold the object into an interesting shape by dragging the handles. This tool combines skewing with individual point control. The Distort tool, shown next, resides in the same position in the toolbox as the Scale and Skew tools. If the tool is not displayed, click and hold your cursor on the displayed tool until the tool group flyout appears, and then select the tool.

To distort an object:

1. Select an object as outlined previously.

2. Select the Distort tool. Alternatively, you can choose Modify | Transform | Distort. After choosing either the tool or the menu command, eight handles appear around the object.

3. Click and drag the center handle on either side, or the top or bottom handle, to begin distorting the object. You can drag horizontally, vertically, or diagonally. Dragging a handle in two directions is the equivalent of scaling while skewing.

4. Click and drag any of the corner handles to further modify the shape, as shown in the following illustration. Again you can drag in any direction to distort the shape.

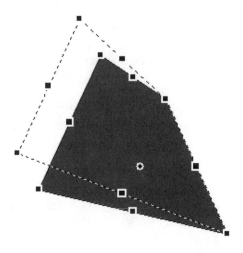

5. Double-click the object to apply the modifications. Alternatively, you can press ENTER or RETURN.

Tip *If after transforming an object, applying the changes, and editing other objects, you decide you need to return the object to its original state, select the object and choose Modify | Transform | Remove Transformations.*

Transforming Objects with Menu Commands

In addition to using the tools presented in the last section or their equivalent menu commands, you have additional menu commands at your disposal for modifying objects. As demonstrated in the following sections, you can use these menu commands to rotate an object, flip an object, and scale an object with numerical precision.

Rotating an Object with Menu Commands

You can rotate an object with the Scale, Skew, and Distort tools. However, when you use either of these tools to rotate an object, you do not have precise control over the number of degrees the object is rotated. You can rotate an object in 90-degree increments using menu commands as follows:

- To rotate a selected object 180 degrees, choose Modify | Transform | Rotate 180°.
- To rotate a selected object 90 degrees clockwise, choose Modify | Transform | Rotate 90° CW.
- To rotate a selected object 90 degrees counterclockwise, choose Modify | Transform | Rotate 90° CCW.

Flipping an Object with Menu Commands

Another transformation you can apply to objects with menu commands is flipping them. These commands come in handy when you duplicate an irregular object and want the duplicate to mirror the original either vertically or horizontally. You can flip an object as follows:

- To flip a selected object vertically, choose Modify | Transform | Flip Vertically.
- To flip a selected object horizontally, choose Modify | Transform | Flip Horizontally.

Tip *To duplicate an object, select it with the Pointer tool and while pressing the ALT key (Windows) or OPTION key (Macintosh), drag the selected object. A duplicate appears. To constrain the duplicated object, also press the SHIFT key and the duplicate is constrained horizontally, vertically, or 45 degrees diagonally depending on which way you drag the object.*

Scaling an Object Numerically

In previous sections of this chapter, you learned to scale an object using the Scale tool. You also learned to rotate an object manually using a tool and in 90-degree increments using a menu command. However, you have another menu command you can use to scale an object by percentage, or by a given measurement. You can use the same menu command to rotate an object by the number of degrees you specify.

To modify an object with mathematical precision:

1. Select an object as outlined previously.

2. Choose Modify | Transform | Numeric Transform. The Numeric Transform dialog box appears, as shown here:

3. Click the triangle to the right of the first field and choose one of the following:

   - **Scale**   Select this option to resize an object by a given percentage.

   - **Resize**   Select this option to scale the object to a hard pixel value. When you choose this option, the current size of the object is displayed in pixels.

   - **Rotate**   Select this option to rotate an object by a specific number of degrees.

4. If you choose Scale or Resize, the Constrain Proportions option is selected by default. With this option enabled, enter a value in either field, and the value in the other field is adjusted so that the object is resized proportionately. Deselect this option and you can enter a different value in each field to resize the object as desired.

5. Choose the Scale Attributes option (the default) and the stroke and fill, and any effects applied to the object are scaled with the object as well.

6. Enter a value in the appropriate field to resize the object. If you selected Rotate, click the triangle to the right of the field; a rotational dial slider appears, as shown here:

7. To rotate the object, click and drag the rotational slider. Alternatively, enter a value in the field.

8. Click OK to apply the transformation.

MODIFYING ARTWORK

There is another command you can use to modify an object. Choose Modify | Transform | Free Transform, and eight handles appear around the selected object. This command is a combination of the transformations you can apply with the Skew and Scale tools.

Using the View Tools

When you edit objects, you inevitably have to change the magnification of the document to get a better look at what you're doing, especially when you edit an object on a point-by-point basis. You can zoom in or out on the canvas by choosing a preset from the Set Magnification window at the bottom of the workspace. When you work at increased magnification, parts of the document are hidden from view. In this section, you will learn to interactively zoom in on an object with the Zoom tools and pan to a hidden part of the document with the Hand tool.

When you need to interactively zoom in or out on a document, you use the Zoom tool. The Zoom tool is in the View section of the toolbox. To use the Zoom tool:

1. Select the Zoom tool shown here:

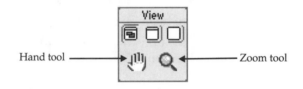

2. To zoom in, do one of the following:

   ■ Click the canvas to zoom to the next highest level of magnification. Each click zooms to the next level until the document is zoomed to 6400%.

   ■ Click the canvas and drag down and across to zoom in on a selected region. As you drag the tool, a bounding box appears, giving you a preview of the area the tool will zoom in on. Release the mouse button when the desired area is selected.

3. To zoom out, press and hold the ALT key (Windows) or OPTION key (Macintosh) and then click the canvas. Each click zooms out to the next lowest level of magnification. When you use the tool to zoom out, the tool icon is a magnifying glass with a minus sign (–) inside it. After you release the ALT key (Windows) or OPTION key (Macintosh), the tool returns to zoom in mode, as indicated by the plus sign (+) in the tool's icon.

When you change the magnification of a document, you can easily reveal hidden parts of the document by using the Hand tool. The Hand tool resides in the View section of the toolbox.

To pan to a different part of the document:

1. Select the Hand tool shown previously. As you move your cursor over the document window, it changes into a hand.

2. Click anywhere on the canvas and drag to pan to a different part of the document.

3. Release the mouse button when the desired part of the document is visible.

Tip   *To momentarily activate the Hand tool, press the* SPACEBAR *and then click and drag to pan to a different part of the document. After you release the* SPACEBAR, *the previously selected tool is once again active.*

There are three additional tools in the View section of the toolbox, as shown in the following illustration. You use these tools to change the way the document is displayed on your monitor. You have the following options:

- **Standard Screen mode**   The default viewing mode. When this mode is selected, the document you are working on appears in a window within the workspace. If any other documents are open, and you choose to view them as tiles or in cascading fashion, they are also visible.

- **Full Screen with Menus mode**   Maximizes Fireworks as well as the current document in the workspace. The document title bar is also hidden when you select this mode; however, all menus and any open panels are visible. This viewing mode is useful when you're working with a large document and need to view as much of the document as possible. Another use for this mode is if you're working with multiple programs and have scaled the Fireworks workspace to a smaller size than desktop resolution. Click the Full Screen with Menus button to size Fireworks to the screen.

- **Full Screen mode**   Sizes Fireworks to the desktop resolution and hides all menus. Panels and the toolbox are still visible when you choose this mode.

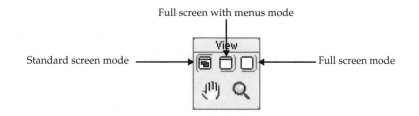

Full screen with menus mode

Standard screen mode ——————→   **View**   ←—————— Full screen mode

Positioning Objects

In previous sections of this chapter, you learned how to manually position objects with tools and how to use menu commands to transform and position objects. In the sections that follow, you will learn to position objects using the Info panel and Property inspector. You will also learn to align objects to the document, align objects to each other, and distribute, space, and size selected objects.

Using the Info Panel

The aptly named Info panel does as advertised and gives you information about an object. You can use the Info panel to change the position of an object on the canvas, as well as change the width and/or height of the object. The Info panel also gives you information about objects your cursor is over.

To modify an object with the Info panel:

1. Select an object.

2. Choose Window | Info. The Info panel, shown next, appears. When you initially open the Info panel, the fields at the bottom may not be visible. To display the fields, place your cursor over the panel's lower border and then click and drag until the fields are displayed.

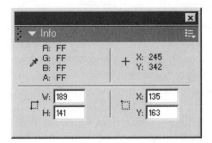

3. To modify an object's position on the canvas, enter a new value in the X and/ or Y field.

4. To modify the object's size, enter a new value in the W and/or H field. Note that when you enter a value in either field, the other field does not change; the object is not resized proportionately. To resize the object proportionately, it is suggested that you choose Modify | Transform | Numeric Transform and follow the steps previously discussed to scale the object by percentage or using a numeric value.

In addition to being able to modify an object's size or position, you can also use the Info panel to get information. When you open the Info panel and move your cursor about the canvas, the values in the upper part of the panel update in real time. The values in the left part of the panel display the color information for the object the cursor is currently over; the values in the right window reveal the current position of the cursor.

Using the Property Inspector

As you've seen throughout the course of this book, the Property inspector serves many functions. You can also use the Property inspector to size an object and position it on the canvas.

To modify an object's size and position with the Property inspector:

1. Select an object as outlined previously.

2. Click the arrow to the left of the word Properties. The Property inspector opens, as shown here:

3. Enter a value in the W and/or H field to resize an object. Be aware that this does not resize the object proportionately. To do that, you should choose Modify | Transform | Numeric Transform and scale the object by percentage or numeric value, as outlined previously in this chapter.

4. To change the object's position on the canvas, enter a value in the X and/or Y field.

Note *When you add objects to a document, they are stacked in the order that you create them; the first objects are at the bottom of the stack. You can change the stacking order by choosing Arrange and then choosing a command from the submenu. For complete information on how to use these commands, refer to Chapter 5.*

Aligning Objects

When you create objects, you can position them using the Pointer tool, the Info panel, or the Property inspector. However, when you need to align objects to other objects, you cannot get the exact alignment and spacing you need unless you use the commands from the Align menu. Using these commands, you can precisely align objects relative to each other.

To align objects in your document, follow these steps:

1. Select two or more objects.

2. Choose Modify | Align and then choose one of the following commands:

   ■ **Left** Aligns the selected objects to the left side of the object farthest left in the document

- **Center Vertical**   Aligns the selected objects to the vertical center between the farthest left and farthest right objects in the selection.
- **Right**   Aligns the selected objects to the right edge of the object farthest right in the document.
- **Top**   Aligns the selected objects to the top of the objects nearest the top border of the canvas.
- **Center Horizontal**   Aligns the selected objects to the horizontal center between the object nearest the top of the document and the object nearest the bottom of the document.
- **Bottom**   Aligns the selected objects to the bottom of the object nearest the bottom of the document.

When you work with more than two objects, spacing becomes a concern. To evenly space objects in a document, you could use the Info panel and do the math. Fortunately, there's an easier way to evenly distribute objects in the space that they occupy.

To distribute objects, do the following:

1. Select more than two objects.
2. Choose Modify | Align, and then choose one of the following:

- **Distribute Widths**   Spaces the objects evenly along the horizontal axis. When you choose this command, Fireworks then distributes the objects evenly along the horizontal axis according to the center of the object's width.
- **Distribute Heights**   Spaces the objects evenly along the vertical axis according to the center of each object's height.

Using the Align Panel

In previous versions of Fireworks, the only way to align objects relative to the actual document was to use the Center in Document command and work outward from there, or to use the Info panel and compute the actual positions of the objects based on the document's size and the object's size. Fortunately, in Fireworks MX there is a more automated method of accomplishing this task: the Align panel. The Align panel may be familiar to you if you've used Flash. It works in the same manner. And to give credit where credit is due, the Align panel is the brainchild of Fireworks beta tester Kleanthis Economou. You can use the Align panel to align objects relative to each other and to align objects relative to the canvas.

Aligning Objects to Each Other

When you have several objects that you need to align relative to each other, you can use the commands from the Align menu. If you need to perform a simple alignment, one command takes care of the task. However, if you need to perform more than one alignment task, this involves summoning another command. In lieu of applying multiple alignment commands to selected objects, you can use the Align panel and perform additional alignment tasks by clicking a different button.

To align objects to each other with the Align panel, follow these steps:

1. Select two or more objects.

2. Choose Window | Align. The Align panel appears, as shown here:

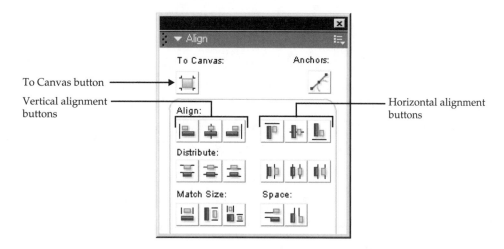

To Canvas button

Vertical alignment buttons

Horizontal alignment buttons

3. In the vertical alignment section, click a button to apply one of the following alignment options:

   ■ Vertically align selected objects along the top edge of the highest selected object.

   ■ Vertically align selected objects to the center point between the top and bottom objects.

   ■ Vertically align selected objects along the bottom edge of the lowest selected object.

4. In the horizontal alignment section, click a button to apply one of the following alignment options:

   ■ Horizontally align selected objects relative to the left edge of the object on the farthest left side of the canvas.

   ■ Horizontally align selected objects relative to the center point of the farthest left and farthest right objects.

   ■ Horizontally align selected objects relative to the right edge of the object on the farthest right side of the canvas.

5. To align objects both vertically and horizontally, click the desired alignment button from each section.

MODIFYING ARTWORK

Aligning Objects to the Canvas

In addition to giving you the capability of aligning objects to each other, you can also use the Align panel to align objects to the canvas. This comes in handy when you need to quickly align an object to a left border, center, right border or to the top or bottom of the canvas.

To align objects relative to the canvas:

1. Select two or more objects.
2. Choose Window | Align.
3. Click the To Canvas button.
4. In the horizontal alignment section, click a button to apply one of the following options:
   - Align selected objects to the left edge of the canvas.
   - Align selected objects to the horizontal center point of the canvas.
   - Align selected objects to the right edge of the canvas.
5. In the vertical alignment section, click a button to apply one of the following options:
   - Align selected objects to the top edge of the canvas.
   - Align selected objects to the vertical center point of the canvas.
   - Align selected objects to the bottom edge of the canvas.
6. To align objects both vertically and horizontally, click the appropriate buttons in each section.

Distributing Objects

The Align panel also has options that enable you to evenly distribute a selection of objects by their centers or edges. When you distribute objects, you can distribute two objects relative to the width or height of the canvas, or distribute a selection of three or more objects relative to each other.

To distribute objects:

1. Select the objects you want to distribute.
2. Choose Window | Align. The Align panel opens, as shown here:

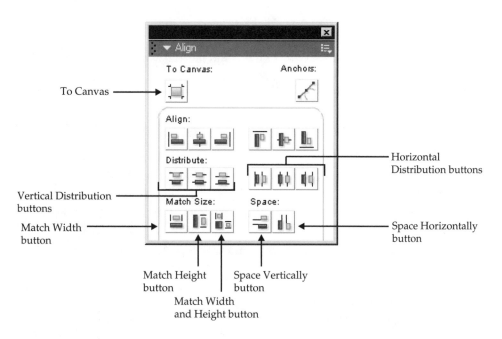

3. In the Vertical Distribution section, choose one of the following:

- Distribute selected objects vertically by their top edge.
- Distribute selected objects vertically by their center.
- Distribute selected objects vertically by their bottom edge.

4. In the Horizontal Distribution section, choose one of the following:

- Distribute selected objects horizontally by their left edge.
- Distribute selected objects horizontally by their center.
- Distribute selected objects horizontally by their right edge.

Spacing Objects

You can also use the versatile Align panel to space objects evenly by their centers. You can space objects relative to the canvas or relative to each other.

To space objects using the Align panel:

1. Select three or more objects.

2. Click the To Canvas button to space objects relative to the canvas.

3. Click the Space Vertically button to space objects vertically.

4. Click the Space Horizontally button to space objects horizontally.

MODIFYING ARTWORK

Matching the Size of Objects

Another manner in which you can utilize the Align panel is when you need to match the dimensions of objects. For example, you can use this option in conjunction with the other features of the Align panel to create a row of objects that are the same height.

To match the size of objects:

1. Select the objects whose dimensions you want to match.
2. Choose Window | Align.
3. Click the Match Height button to resize the objects' height to the tallest selected object.
4. Click the Match Width button to resize the objects' width to the widest selected object.
5. Click the Match Width and Height button to resize the objects' width and height to the tallest and widest dimension of the objects selected.

Grouping Objects

When you create an object for a document, you can modify it independently of other objects in the document. For the most part this is desirable, except when you have objects that perform a similar function, such as buttons for a navigation bar that you want to behave as a single object. To achieve this, you group objects. After grouping two or more objects, you can select the group and use any of the editing tools to edit the group as though it were a single object.

To create a group:

1. Select two or more objects.
2. Choose Modify | Group.

After you create a group, you may find it necessary to add an object to the group. To do this, you must ungroup the group, add the object, select the objects, and then invoke the Group command again.

To ungroup a group:

1. Select the group.
2. Choose Modify | Ungroup.

After you break apart a group, the individual objects regain their individual identity. However, there are times when all you need to do is edit one or more items in the group without breaking the group apart. You can achieve this result with a menu command, as shown in the next section.

Editing Items in a Group

When you need to edit individual items in a group, you can do so without breaking the group apart. To do this, you use the Subselect command.

To edit an individual item in a group:

1. Select the object group with the Pointer tool.

2. Choose Select | Subselect. After choosing the command, a square appears at each corner of the objects in the group. This indicates the objects can be individually selected and then edited.

3. Select the Subselection tool, shown here:

4. Click anywhere inside the group to deselect the objects.

5. Click the object you want to edit. After selecting an object, the squares that define the bounding box of the object are unfilled, indicating that the object is part of a group.

6. Use any of the tools to edit the object. You can also modify the object's fill and stroke characteristics.

7. After editing one or more objects in a group, choose Select | Superselect. After invoking this command, Fireworks reassembles the group.

Modifying Paths

As you learned previously, a path is comprised of straight and curved line segments. When you use the Pen tool to create an open or closed path, the transition from one segment to the next is defined by a point or node, as some illustrators refer to it. You can modify a path by editing one or more points, adding points, deleting points, and so on. In the sections that follow, you will learn to modify paths using tools and menu commands.

Using the Subselection Tool

When you need to edit individual points along a path, you use the Subselection tool. With this tool, you can select individual points along a path and move them. You can edit an individual point or a selection of points. You can also use the tool to convert a point from a straight point to a curve point. A curve point has Bezier handles, which can be manipulated to define the shape of the line segment the point belongs to. A curve point is designated by a circle, while a straight point is designated by a square.

To edit a path with the Subselection tool:

1. Select the Subselection tool shown previously.

2. Click the path you want to modify. The path points are indicated as hollow squares (straight points) or hollow circles (curve points). After selecting a path with the Subselection tool, you can do the following:

   - To select a point, click it. A selected point is displayed as a filled square (straight point) or a filled circle (curve point). You can add to the selection by holding down the SHIFT key and clicking additional points.

   - To marqee select points, select the Subselection tool, click outside of the boundary of the object whose points you want to select, and then drag down and across the object. Release the mouse button when the desired area is encompassed, and the selected points are shown as filled squares and/or circles. A marquee is a rectangular selection area.

   - To move a selection of points, click and drag. As you drag, the shape updates in real time, reflecting the current shape of the path. When you achieve the desired shape of the path, release the mouse button.

   - To nudge a point selection in one-pixel increments, press the arrow key on your computer keyboard that corresponds to the direction in which you want to nudge the points.

   - To nudge a point selection in ten-pixel increments, hold down the SHIFT key while pressing the arrow key that corresponds to the direction in which you want to move the selected points.

Modifying Rectangles

By default, the points of a shape created with the Rectangle or Rounded Rectangle tool are not editable. You can, however, edit the points of a shape created with either tool if they are first ungrouped.

To edit the points of a rectangle, do the following:

1. Using the Subselection tool, select the rectangle you want to edit. When you first select the shape, the points are displayed.

2. Click a point in order to modify it, and Fireworks displays the dialog box shown next.

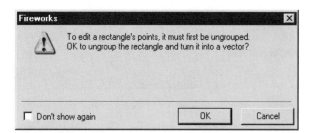

3. Click OK to ungroup the rectangle and convert it to an editable vector shape.

Alternatively, you can select the rectangular shape with the Subselection tool and then choose Modify | Ungroup, after which the rectangle becomes an editable vector shape.

Adding Points to a Path

After you create a path, you can add points at any time. When you add points to a path, you can further refine the path to suit the document you are working on. To add points to a path, you use the Pen tool. Note that adding points will increase the file size of the document.

To add a point to a path:

1. Using the Pointer tool, select the path you want to modify.

2. Select the Pen tool.

3. Move the tool toward the path location where you want to add the point. As you move close to the path, the tool's icon changes into a plus sign (+), as shown here:

4. Click to add the point. Add additional points as needed to further modify the path. If you add the point to a curved path segment, the point has Bezier handles, as shown here:

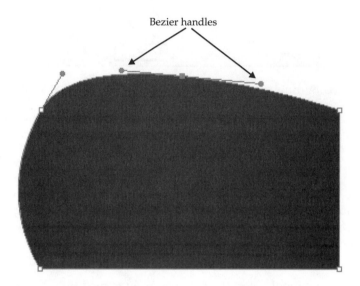

Bezier handles

Deleting Points from a Path

You can simplify a complex path by manually deleting unneeded points. There are menu commands to simplify paths, and these will be presented in future sections of this chapter; however, manually deleting points gives you more control over the process as you determine which points to delete. You can delete a point using the Subselection tool or the Pen tool.

To delete a point with the Subselection tool:

1. Use the Subselection tool to select the object whose path you want to modify. Each point on the path is designated by an unfilled square or circle.

2. Click a point to select it. The point is designated by a filled square (straight point) or filled circle (curve point).

3. Press the DELETE key. The point is removed, and Fireworks redraws the path.

You can remove multiple points by using the Subselection tool to create a selection of points, as outlined previously, and then pressing the DELETE key.

If you are modifying a path by using the Pen tool to add points to it, you do not have to switch tools should you decide to delete a point. The manner in which you delete a point differs depending on whether the point is a curve point or a straight point.

To delete a point with the Pen tool:

1. Move the Pen tool toward the point you want to delete.

2. If the point is a curve point, double-click the point. The first click converts the point to a straight point; the second click deletes the point.

3. If the point is a straight point, your cursor becomes a minus sign (–) as you near the point. Click the point to delete it.

Converting Points

While editing a path, you may find it necessary to convert a straight point to a curve point or vice versa. Again, you use two different tools depending on the desired outcome. If you need to convert a curve point to a straight point, you use the Pen tool; to convert a straight point to a curve point, you use the Subselection tool. A curve point will have one Bezier handle if it connects one straight and one curved line segment, and two Bezier handles if the point connects two curved line segments.

To convert a curve point to straight point:

1. Using the Subselection tool, click the point you want to convert to a straight point. The point becomes a filled circle, and the Bezier handle or handles that define the curve appear.

2. Select the Pen tool.

3. Click the point to convert it. The Bezier handle or handles disappear, and the segments connected to the point are redrawn.

To convert a straight point to a curve point, you use the Subselection tool to drag a Bezier handle from the point. If the point you are converting is an end point, you can only drag one Bezier handle from the point. If the point is in the middle of two straight line segments, you can drag one or two Bezier handles from the point.

To convert a straight point to a curve point:

1. Using the Subselection tool, click the path that contains the point you want to convert.

2. Click the point you want to convert and then, while holding down the ALT key (Windows) or OPTION key (Macintosh), drag away from the point. As you drag, a Bezier handle appears, as shown in the following illustration. As you drag the handle, the shape of the curve is defined. You can drag the handle in any direction

to achieve the desired result. Release the mouse button when the path is the desired shape.

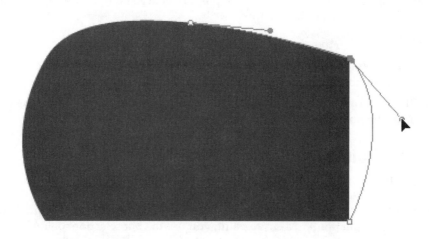

3. If the point is in the middle of two straight line segments, hold down the ALT key (Windows) or OPTION key (Macintosh) and drag away from the other side of the point. Drag the handle to define the shape of the curve segment, as shown in the following image. Release the mouse button when the curve is as desired.

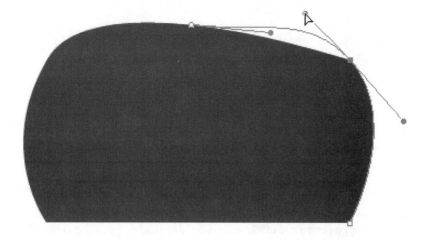

Using Bezier Handles

As you learned previously, a point that connects to a curved line segment has one or two Bezier handles. You use these handles to define the shape of a curved line segment. Each Bezier handle has a dot on the end and is angled from the curve point to which it is attached. By dragging the point at the end of the handle, you define the curved segment to which the point is connected.

To modify a curved segment:

1. Using the Subselection tool, click a curve point. One or more Bezier handles appear. The following illustration shows a point that connects two curved segments. Notice that the point has two Bezier handles.

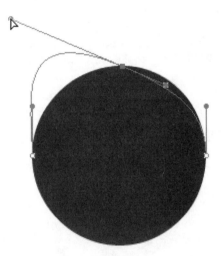

2. Click the point at the end of the handle and drag it to define the curve. You can drag the point in any direction. As you drag the point, Fireworks redraws the curve and displays the shape of the old curve in black, as shown in the preceding illustration. Release the mouse button when the curve is the desired shape.

3. If the point has two Bezier handles, you can modify the shape of the other curved segment by clicking the point and dragging. When the segment is the desired shape, release the mouse button.

Modifying Vector Objects with Tools

In addition to modifying vector objects by manipulating the vector path with modifications of individual points using the Subselection tool, you can also modify vector objects with tools in the Vector section of the toolbox. The tools presented in the upcoming sections allow you to modify a vector path by selecting a tool and then dragging the tool toward the path. The tool modifies the path and redraws the points for you.

Using the Redraw Path Tool

You can use the Redraw Path tool to interactively modify the shape of an open path or a closed path. You use this tool to reshape a path by clicking it and then dragging to define the path's new shape. You can also use the tool to extend a path. The Redraw Path tool occupies the same space in the toolbox as the Pen and the Vector Path tool. If the Redraw Path tool, shown next, is not displayed, click and hold your cursor over the tool currently displayed. When the tool group flyout appears, click the Redraw Path tool to select it.

To redraw a path:

1. Select the Redraw Path tool.

2. Move your cursor toward the path you want to modify. When the path is highlighted, it can be redrawn.

3. Click at the point along the path where you want to begin redrawing, and then drag. You can use the tool at any point in the path. As you drag the tool, Fireworks creates a preview of the section you are creating. It also previews the current shape of the path, as shown here:

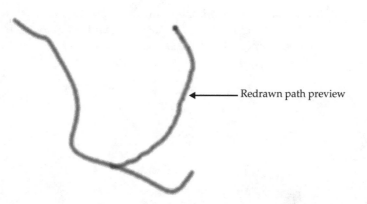

Redrawn path preview

4. When you achieve the desired shape of the path, release the mouse button. Fireworks creates the necessary points to redraw the path, as shown here:

Using the Path Scrubber Tool

You can use the Path Scrubber tool to alter the look of a path drawn with the Vector Path or Pen tool using one of the pressure-sensitive Stroke categories such as Air Brush, Calligraphy, or Charcoal. The Path Scrubber tool has two modes—Additive, which adds to the path, and Subtractive, which takes away from the path. You modify the amount added or subtracted from the path by varying the pressure and speed (using the tool with a digital tablet) or speed (using the tool with a mouse). The two modes of the Path Scrubber tool, shown next occupy the same space in the toolbox as the Freeform tool. If the tool you need is not displayed, click and hold your cursor over the currently displayed tool until the tool group flyout appears, and then select the desired mode of the Path Scrubber tool.

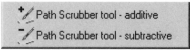

To modify a path with the Path Scrubber tool:

1. Select the desired Path Scrubber tool.

2. Click the arrow to the left of the word Properties. The Property inspector opens and displays the settings for the tool, as shown here:

![Property inspector showing Path Scrubber tool - additive, with Pressure and Speed checkboxes checked and Rate: 10]

3. Choose Pressure to vary the effect of the tool according to the amount of pressure you apply while using the tool with a digital stylus.

4. Choose Speed to vary the effect of the tool according to the speed with which you move the mouse or digital stylus.

5. Click the triangle to the right of the Rate field and drag the slider to vary the strength of the tool. Lower settings produce subtle changes, while higher settings produce more noticeable changes to the path. The slider limits you to a maximum value of 10; however, you can enter a higher value in the text field.

6. After finalizing settings, move the tool toward the path. When the path is highlighted and your cursor changes to a pen with a plus sign (additive mode) or minus sign (subtractive mode), drag across the path to modify it. The following illustration shows the tool being used in Subtractive mode to modify a path.

Using the Freeform Tool

You can reshape a vector object by pushing and pulling it as if it were virtual putty. To do this, you use the Freeform tool. You specify the strength and area of the tool in the Property inspector, and you can change it on the fly by using the arrow keys.

To push a path with the Freeform tool, follow these steps:

1. Select the Freeform tool shown here:

2. Click the arrow to the left of the word Properties. The Property inspector appears and displays the settings for the tool, as shown here:

3. Click the triangle to the right of the Size field and drag the slider to specify the tip size of the tool in pixels.

4. Select the Pressure checkbox, and you will be able to increase the size of the tip by exerting more pressure on your digital stylus.

5. Select the Preview checkbox, and Fireworks updates the shape in real time as you use the tool. If you disable this option, Fireworks displays an outline of the new shape and redraws it after you release the mouse button.

6. After choosing the settings for the tool, click anywhere on the canvas and your cursor becomes a circle. Push into the path to modify it, as shown here:

To pull a path with the Freeform tool:

1. Follow the previous steps (1–5) to choose the tool settings.

2. Move your cursor toward the path you want to modify until the cursor changes into the shape shown here:

3. Click and pull away from the path to modify it, as shown here:

Tip *To interactively resize the Freeform tool's tip, click the* UP *or* RIGHT ARROW *key to increase the size of the tip; and click the* DOWN *or* LEFT *arrow key to decrease the size of the tip. Release the mouse button when the tip is the desired size. Alternatively, you can press 2 on the numeric keypad to increase tip size, or press 1 to decrease tip size.*

Using the Reshape Area Tool

Another tool you can use to modify a path is the Reshape Area tool. The tool works slightly differently than the Freeform tool. Two concentric circles comprise the tool's tip. The tool modifies only points between the inner and outer circle. You can set the tool's strength within the Property inspector. The Reshape Area tool occupies the same position in the toolbox as the Freeform tool and the Scrubber tool. If the tool is not currently displayed, click and hold your cursor over the displayed tool until the tool group flyout appears; then select the Reshape Area tool shown here:

To modify a path with the Reshape Area tool:

1. Select the Reshape Area tool.

2. Click the arrow to the left of the word Properties. The Property inspector opens and displays the tool's settings, as shown here:

▼ Properties				
🖉 Reshape Area tool	Size: 40	Pressure: ☑ Size		⑦
	Strength: 80	☑ Strength		

3. Click the triangle to the right of the Size field and drag the slider to set the diameter in pixels of the tool's tip. Alternatively, you can enter a value in the text field.

4. Click the triangle to the right of the Strength field to set the tool's strength. Higher values produce more pronounced modifications to the path; lower values produce subtler effects.

5. Move your cursor toward the path, and then click and drag to alter the path's shape, as shown here:

Tip *You can interactively resize the Reshape Area tool's tip size. Press the* UP *or* RIGHT ARROW *key to increase tip size; press the* DOWN *or* LEFT ARROW *key to decrease tip size. Release the key when the tip is the desired size. Alternatively, you can press 2 on the numeric keypad to increase tip size or press 1 to decrease tip size.*

Using the Knife Tool

If you need to slice a path into sections, you can do so with the Knife tool. You can use the tool on open or closed paths. After using the tool, you have two separate paths. You can move the paths to different locations on the canvas or delete an unwanted section of a path. The tool is particularly effective on closed paths. For example, you can use the tool to slice an elliptical path and end up with a dome shape.

To slice a path with the Knife tool:

1. Select the Knife tool shown here:

2. Click and drag across the path you want to sever. As you drag the tool, Fireworks creates a preview of the tool's path. Release the mouse button when the tool's path extends beyond the path you want to sever. After you release the mouse button, Fireworks creates two additional points (closed path) or one additional point (open path), and this defines the boundary between the new paths.

3. Select the Pointer tool, and then select one of the new paths by clicking it. After selecting a path, you can move it to a new location, as shown in the following illustration; you can further modify it with another tool, or you can delete it.

Tip *To constrain the Knife tool horizontally, vertically, or diagonally 45 degrees, press the* SHIFT *key and drag the tool in the desired direction.*

Altering a Path with Menu Commands

As you can see, Fireworks gives you a lot of power when it comes to working with vector-based objects. In previous sections, you learned to modify vector objects using tools. Many of these tools add additional points to a path, which can bloat the file size of the document. In the following sections, you'll learn to simplify paths and more by using menu commands.

Simplifying a Path

When you perform extensive modifications on a path, it is possible to end up with more points than you actually need in order to define the path. You can use the Simplify command to quickly reduce the number of points in a path without adversely affecting the shape of the path.

To reduce the number of points in a path:

1. Using the Pointer tool, select the path.

2. Choose Modify | Alter Path | Simplify. The Simplify dialog box appears, as shown here:

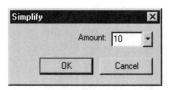

3. Click the triangle to the right of the Amount field, and drag to set the percentage amount by which you want the path simplified. Alternatively, you can enter a value in the text field. High values remove a greater number of points, but may adversely affect the shape of the path. Begin with the default value of 10 to be on the safe side. You can always invoke the command a second time to remove additional points. Alternatively, you can choose a higher setting and then undo the action if it drastically alters the path.

4. Click OK. Fireworks simplifies the path by the amount specified.

Expanding a Stroke

Another interesting vector effect you can add to your documents is to expand a stroke. When you expand the stroke of a filled object, say for example a circle, you end up with two concentric strokes. You can specify the width of the expanded stroke, the corner style, and the end cap style.

To expand a stroke, follow these steps:

1. Select the object whose stroke you want to expand.

2. Choose Modify | Alter Path | Expand Stroke. The Expand Stroke dialog box appears, as shown here:

3. Click the triangle to the right of the Width field and drag the slider to specify the width of the expanded stroke. Alternatively, you can enter a value in the text field.

4. In the Corners section, click the Miter, Round, or Beveled button to define the corner shape of the expanded stroke.

5. If you choose Miter for the corner type, enter a value in the Miter field. This determines the point when a mitered corner becomes beveled.

6. Choose an end cap style by clicking the Butt, Square, or Round button.

7. Click OK. Fireworks replaces the original path with a closed path the same shape as the original using the same stroke and fill attributes. In the following illustration, the original shape is on the left; and the shape as it appears after applying the Expand Stroke command is on the right.

Insetting a Path

If you need to expand or contract a path by given number of pixels, you can do so with the Inset Path command. When you choose this command, you specify the amount by which the path is expanded or contracted, as well as the corner type.

To expand or contract a path, follow these steps:

1. Select the object whose path you want to modify.

2. Choose Modify | Alter Path | Inset Path. The Inset Path dialog box appears, as shown here:

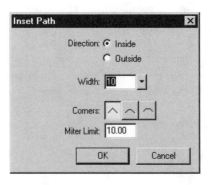

3. Choose an option in the Direction area. Inside contracts the path; Outside expands the path.

4. Click the triangle to the right of the Width field, and drag the slider to determine the number of pixels by which the path is offset. Alternatively, you can enter a value in the text field.

5. Click the Miter, Round, or Beveled button to specify the type of corner the inset path will have.

6. If you choose Miter for the corner option, click the triangle to the right of the Miter field and drag the slider to set the point at which the mitered corner is transformed into a beveled corner.

7. Click OK. Fireworks modifies the path according to your specifications.

Combining Vector Objects

You can combine vector objects in your documents to create different shapes. When you combine objects, you can often create a new object where the whole is much greater than the sum of its parts. You can join paths, join objects, subtract one object from another, and more, by arranging vector objects and then applying a menu command.

Joining Paths

When you have two or more paths in your document, you can join them to create a new path. You can align two paths end to end and then create a new path or combine multiple paths to create a composite path.

To join paths end-to-end:

1. Using the Pointer tool, align the paths end-to-end.

2. Select the Subselection tool.

3. Select the endpoints from each path.

4. Choose Modify | Combine Paths | Join. Fireworks combines the two paths, and they behave as a single object.

Note	*You can also join paths that are not aligned end-to-end by following the steps in the previous example. When you invoke the Combine Paths command, Fireworks fills the void between the selected points with a line segment.*

To create a composite path:

1. Select two or more paths with the Pointer tool. The paths can be open or closed.

2. Choose Modify | Combine Paths | Join.

To break apart joined paths:

1. Select a path to which you previously applied the Join command.

2. Choose Modify | Combine Paths | Split. Fireworks returns the paths to their original state, and they can be edited as individual objects.

Using the Union Command

When you have two or more closed paths, you can combine them to create a new shape. When you combine shapes using the Union command, the new shape inherits the stroke and fill attributes of the object that is lowest in the stack.

To create a shape using the Union command:

1. Using the Pointer tool, select the shapes you want to combine.

2. Choose Modify | Combine Paths | Union. Fireworks creates a new shape that encompasses the borders of the original shapes. The following illustration shows three shapes before and after the Union command is applied.

Using the Intersect Command

When you use the Intersect command to create a new shape, the new shape occupies the area where the selected shapes overlapped. You use this command on closed paths.
To create a new shape using the Intersect command:

1. Use the Pointer tool to overlap the shapes as desired.

2. Select the shapes with the Pointer tool.

3. Choose Modify | Combine Paths | Intersect. Fireworks creates a new shape using the common area of the selected objects. The following illustration shows three objects before and after the Intersect command was applied.

Using the Punch Command

You can also use a menu command to create a new shape by cutting one shape from another. The paths you use must be closed and must overlap.

To cut one shape from another:

1. Use the Pointer tool to arrange the objects to which you want to apply the Punch command. The object on top of the stack will cut from the other objects. If the object you want to use as the punch is lower in the stack, use the Select Behind tool to select it and then choose Modify | Arrange | Bring to Front.

2. Using the Pointer tool, select the objects.

3. Choose Modify | Combine Objects | Punch. The following illustration shows three shapes on the left, and on the right, the result after the Punch command was applied.

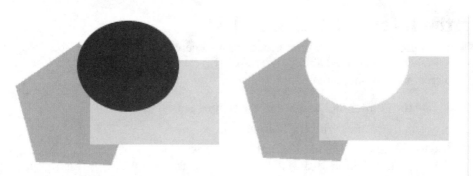

Using the Crop Command

You can use the Crop command to have the shape of a closed path crop other paths in your document. The path you are using to crop must be at the top of the stack.

To use a closed path to crop other paths:

1. Arrange two or more objects whose paths you want to crop.

2. Select the closed path whose shape you want to use to crop the other paths.

3. Choose Modify | Arrange | Bring to Front.

4. With the shape still selected, hold down the SHIFT key and click the other paths to add them to the selection.

5. Choose Modify | Combine Paths | Crop. Fireworks uses the top shape to crop the other paths. The following illustration shows three paths on the left, and on the right, the result after the Crop command was applied.

Summary

In this chapter, you learned about the variety of methods you can use to alter vector objects in your documents. You also learned how to use the selection tools to select individual objects and create selections of objects, as well as how to use menu commands to create a group of objects. You saw how to edit vector points on a point-by-point basis, how to convert points, and how to move selected points. You learned how to interactively reshape objects using tools and discovered how to combine paths to create new shapes. In Chapter 12, you'll learn to organize the objects in your document using layers.

MODIFYING ARTWORK

The
Complete
Reference

Fireworks
MX

Chapter 12

Organizing Your Artwork with Layers

When you create a document and begin to create objects, the objects appear on a layer. As previously discussed, each object has its own stacking order on the layer. You can rearrange the stacking order of objects in a layer using menu commands. However, when the complexity of a document gets to the point where it becomes difficult to work with all of the artwork on a single layer, you can create additional layers to organize the objects in your document.

In this chapter, you'll learn to use layers to organize your artwork. You'll learn to create new layers, organize the hierarchy of layers, transfer artwork between layers, and perform other tasks that will help you to better organize complex documents.

Exploring Layers

It may help to think of a layer as a thin plastic overlay. All of the objects in a layer are placed on top of the layer. When you create additional layers, the artwork you place on the layer is segregated from the content of other layers. When you select a layer, you can edit the artwork on that layer without affecting the content of other layers. This

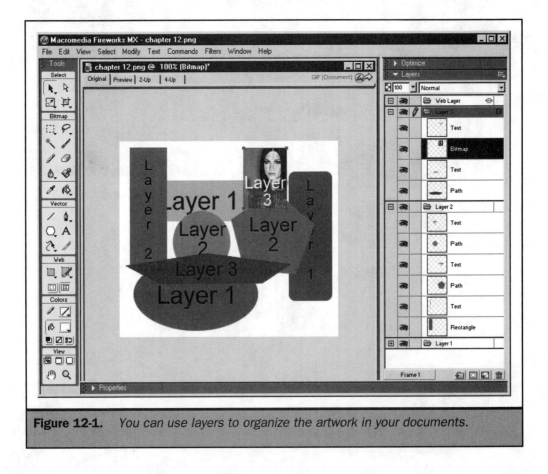

Figure 12-1.   *You can use layers to organize the artwork in your documents.*

feature is invaluable if you have several objects in your document that overlap. After you create artwork for a document and it's exactly the way you want it, you can create a new layer for additional objects you need to create. When you're working on the new layer, you won't be able to inadvertently select and move an object on a lower layer.

Figure 12-1 shows a document with several layers. Notice the objects on upper layers occlude the objects on lower layers where they overlap. The objects on each layer in this illustration are labeled to demonstrate the layer-stacking layer.

Using the Layers Panel

When you create a new document, you have two layers to work with: the Web layer and Layer 1. All of the objects you initially create reside on Layer 1. When you create additional layers in the document, you can use them to organize and separate the objects in your document. When you add objects to a layer, a thumbnail image of the object resides in the Layers panel, shown in the following illustration. Notice that each object in each thumbnail is positioned relative to where it appears on the canvas.

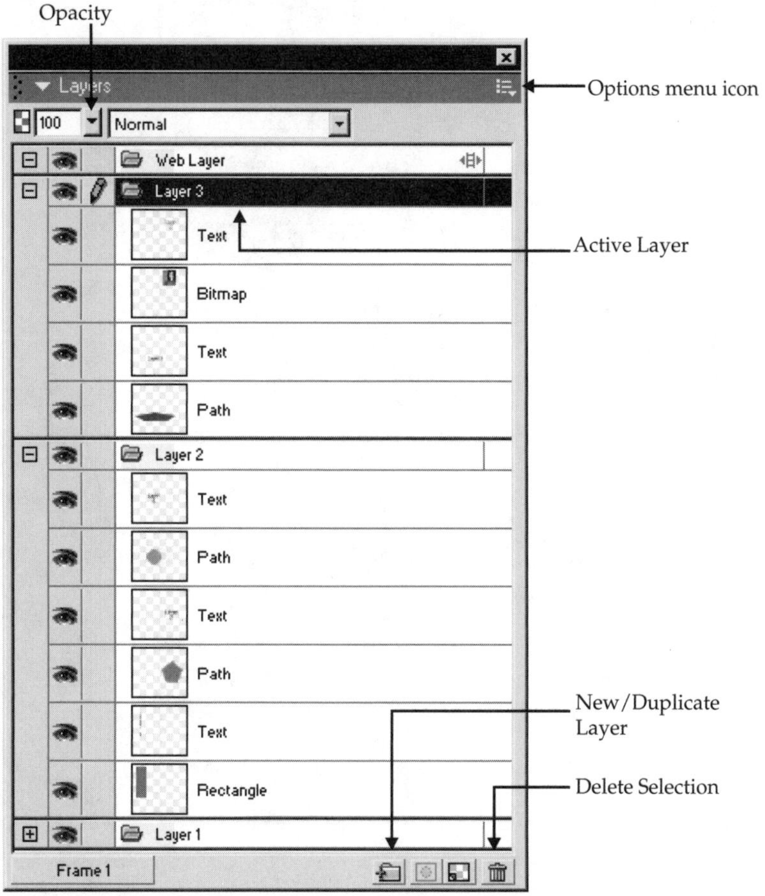

MODIFYING ARTWORK

By default, the Layers panel is part of the panel window on the right side of the workspace. You can open the Layers panel by clicking the arrow to the left of the word Layers or by clicking the word Layers. Alternatively, you can open the panel by choosing Window | Layers.

When you have multiple layers in a document and the objects on the highest layer overlap objects on lower layers, the objects on the lower layer are partially eclipsed. When you select a layer, it is the currently active layer and is highlighted in the Layers panel. When a layer is active, you can select and edit the objects on that layer. You can also use the Layers panel to hide layers or lock layers.

Using the Layers Panel Options Menu

Many of the commands and options that will be discussed in this chapter can be found on the Layers panel Options menu. The Layers panel Options menu, shown next, can be opened by clicking the icon in the upper-right corner of the Layers panel. To apply a command from the options menu, select it.

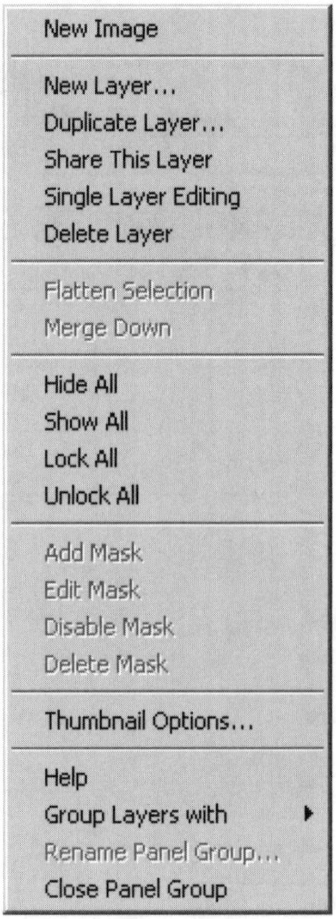

```
New Image

New Layer...
Duplicate Layer...
Share This Layer
Single Layer Editing
Delete Layer

Flatten Selection
Merge Down

Hide All
Show All
Lock All
Unlock All

Add Mask
Edit Mask
Disable Mask
Delete Mask

Thumbnail Options...

Help
Group Layers with        ▶
Rename Panel Group...
Close Panel Group
```

Using Thumbnails

Whether you work with one layer or multiple layers, all of the objects you create are displayed as thumbnails in the Layers panel, as shown previously. To edit an object or select it from within the Layers panel, you click its thumbnail.

The size of the Layers panel thumbnails is deemed optimum for a desktop resolution of 1024 × 768 or less. If you're working on a larger desktop size, the default thumbnail size may be too small. If this is the case, you can change the way thumbnails are displayed in the Layers panel.

To modify the appearance of thumbnails in the Layers panel:

1. Choose Thumbnail Options from the Layers panel Options menu to display the Thumbnail Options dialog box shown here:

2. Click a radio button to choose your preference. Note that if you choose None, only the object's name is displayed in the Layers panel. If you choose this option, you should give all objects a unique name.

About the Web Layer

The Web layer is the top layer in each document you create. The Web layer houses the slices and hotspots that are used for creating interactivity in your documents. You cannot disable sharing, nor can you delete, duplicate, or rename the Web layer. You cannot merge objects on the Web layer. Slices and hotspots are shared across all layers and are visible on all layers. You can, however, rename slices and hotspots by doing the following:

1. Click the arrow to the left of the word Layers.

2. Double-click the hotspot or slice you want to rename.

3. Enter a new name for the slice or hotspot.

4. Press ENTER or RETURN to apply the new name. Alternatively, you can click anywhere outside of the panel to apply the change.

MODIFYING ARTWORK

Adding a Layer

You can add a layer to the document any time you deem it necessary to organize the objects in your document. When you add a layer, it appears at the top of the stack and is the currently active layer.

To create a new layer, do one of the following:

- Choose Edit | Insert | Layer.
- Open the Layers panel, as outlined previously, and click the New/Duplicate Layer button.
- Click the Layers Options menu icon and choose Insert Layer from the menu.

After you insert a new layer using one of the previous methods, the new layer becomes the active layer and is given the default name of Layer, appended by the next available layer number. You can rename the layer, a practice that is highly recommended if you're creating a document that will have multiple layers.

Naming a Layer

You can rename any layer in the document except the Web layer. Giving a layer a unique name is advisable when you're creating a multilayer document or if you are working with other designers on a project. Give the layer a name that reflects what the objects on the layer contribute to the document. If your client approaches you three months after you've completed a project and asks you to revise a Web page you created with a Fireworks PNG document, you'll quickly remember why you created the layer and what it does when you read the layer name.

To rename a layer:

1. Double-click the layer's name.
2. In the Layer name dialog box, type a new name for the layer and then press ENTER or RETURN. Alternatively, you can click outside of the panel to apply the new name.

Tip *You can also rename an object in the Layers panel by double-clicking its current name, typing a new name, and then pressing* ENTER *or* RETURN *to apply the change. Naming objects is another advisable practice when you create complex documents or if you choose not to display thumbnails in the Layers panel.*

Distributing Artwork to Layers

You can quickly create several layers with a single menu command. This option comes in handy when you realize the sheer volume of objects in your document is getting to the point where editing the document will quickly become a logistical nightmare.

To distribute objects to layers:

1. Select the objects you want to distribute to individual layers.

2. Choose Commands | Documents | Distribute to Layers. After invoking this command, Fireworks creates a separate layer for each selected object, as shown next, using the default layer and object name. If desired, you can rename the objects and layers as outlined previously.

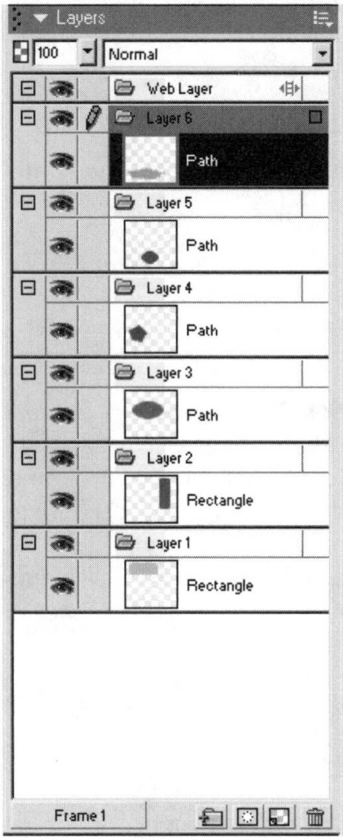

Flattening Layers

After you create a document with several layers, you can flatten the layers to a single layer at any time. The option to flatten layers comes in handy when a project reaches the point where you no longer need to segregate objects on their own layers, or the sheer volume of the current layers is more than you want to deal with. After you flatten layers to a single layer, you can create new layers as needed when you add additional artwork to the document.

MODIFYING ARTWORK

To flatten layers, choose Modify | Flatten Layers. After you invoke this command, Fireworks flattens all layers in the document, except the Web layer, to a single layer. The stacking order of the objects on the flattened layers is as it was when the objects were distributed among layers.

Flattening a Selection of Objects

When you have several objects on a layer perfectly arranged and edited to suit the document, you can alleviate clutter in the Layers panel by flattening the objects into a single object. When you flatten a selection of objects, they are converted to a bitmap.

To flatten a selection of objects:

1. Click the arrow to the left of the word Layers. The Layers panel opens.

2. Select the layer that contains the objects you want to flatten.

3. Click the objects to select them.

4. Choose Modify | Flatten Selection. The objects are flattened to a single bitmap.

Editing Layers

The ability to segregate artwork to layers gives you tremendous flexibility while creating a complex document. In addition to being able to separate artwork on layers, you can rearrange the order of individual objects on a layer. You can also rearrange the stacking order of layers within the document, copy objects between layers, specify an object's opacity from within the Layers panel, and more. In the following sections, you'll learn to edit layers and individual objects on a particular layer.

Selecting a Layer

Before you can work with a layer, it must be the currently active layer. To activate a layer, you select it.

To select a layer, do one of the following:

- In the Layers panel, click a layer's name.

- In the Layers panel, click an object's thumbnail that is in the layer you want to edit.

- On the canvas, click an object that is stored in the layer you want to work with.

Duplicating a Layer

In addition to creating new layers with no content, you can duplicate a layer. When you duplicate a layer, you create a new layer with a carbon copy of each object from the original layer.

To create a single duplicate of a layer:

1. Select a layer.

2. Drag it to the New/Duplicate Layer icon. A new layer is created, and all of the objects from the selected layer are duplicated as well.

If you need to create more than one duplicate of a layer, you can do so by using a command from the Layers panel Options menu.

To create multiple duplicates of a layer:

1. Select the layer you want to duplicate.

2. From the Layers panel Options menu, choose Duplicate Layer. The Duplicate Layer dialog box appears, as shown here:

3. Click the triangle to the right of the Number field and drag the slider to specify the number of layers to duplicate. Alternatively, you can enter a value in the text field. After choosing the number of layers, choose one of the following options:

- **At The Top**   Places the duplicate layers at the top of the layer stacking order.

- **Before Current Layer**   Places the number of duplicates specified before the current layer.

- **After Current Layer**   Places the duplicates above the current layer.

- **At The Bottom**   Places the duplicate layers at the bottom of the layer hierarchy.

4. Click OK. Fireworks duplicates the layers, and the dialog box closes.

Reordering Layers

Layers have their own hierarchy (stacking order), just as do objects you create on the canvas. Objects on upper layers occlude objects on lower layers where they overlap. You can change the way objects in your document are stacked by using the Arrange commands, or you can change the way all objects on a layer are ordered by changing the hierarchy of a layer.

To change the stacking order of a layer:

1. Open the Layers panel.
2. Select the layer you want to reorder, and then drag it up or down the list. Release the mouse button when the layer is at the desired position in the stack.

Deleting a Layer

You can delete a layer when it is no longer needed. When you delete a layer, you delete not only the layer, but also all of the objects on it. To delete a layer, do one of the following:

- Select a layer and then click the Delete Selection button, which looks like a trashcan.
- Select a layer and then drag it to the Delete Selection button.
- Select a layer, and then choose Delete Layer from the Layers panel Options menu.

| Note | *When you delete a layer, Fireworks does not warn you the objects will be deleted also. If you find that you delete a layer in error, choose Edit | Undo Delete Layer.* |

Hiding a Layer

One of the many benefits of organizing a document with layers is the ability to hide all objects on a layer. You can hide a layer any time you need to work with an unobstructed view of objects on a different layer. If you hide an upper layer, the objects on layers below it are no longer partially hidden, which makes it easier for you to edit those objects.

To hide a layer, click the eye icon to the left of a layer's name. The objects in the layer are hidden on the canvas, their thumbnail eye icons are dimmed in the Layers panel, and the eye icon for the layer disappears, as shown here:

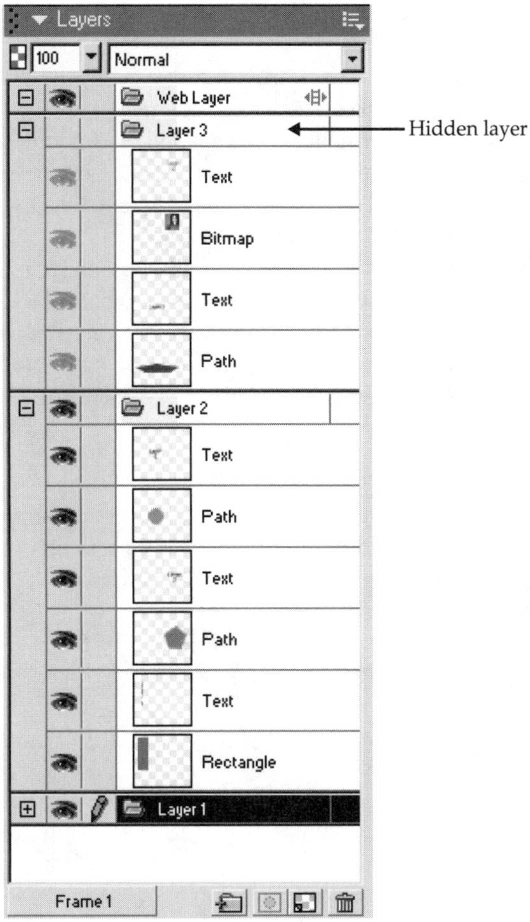

MODIFYING ARTWORK

To reveal a hidden layer, click the blank space to the left of the layer's name. The eyeball icon reappears, and the layer and its contents are once again visible.

If desired, you can also hide individual objects on a layer. To the left of each object's name is an eye icon. Click the icon to hide the object. The object's thumbnail is dimmed in the Layers panel, the eye icon disappears, and the object is no longer visible on the canvas.

To reveal a hidden object, click the blank space to the left of its name. The object is visible on the canvas, and the eye icon reappears.

You can also hide all layers other than a selected layer. This option is handy when you have multiple layers and want to edit objects on a specific layer without viewing the objects on other layers. To do this, select the layer you want to edit and then choose Commands | Document | Hide Other Layers.

Another layer-hiding option you have available is to hide all layers. Choose this option when the objects on other layers are edited to your satisfaction and you want to create a new layer and work with no visual distraction from objects on other layers. To hide all layers, click the Layers panel Options menu icon and choose Hide All from the menu.

To reveal all hidden layers, choose Show All from the Layers panel Options menu.

Locking a Layer

Creating a detailed graphic for use in a Web page is time-consuming work. To guard against inadvertently disturbing an object you have edited to perfection, you can lock the layer the object appears on. Objects on a locked layer cannot be selected or otherwise edited.

To lock a layer, click the pencil icon to the left of the layer's name. A lock icon replaces the pencil icon, as shown here:

Locked Layer ———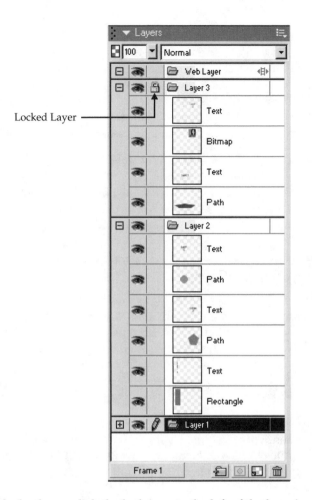

To unlock a layer, click the lock icon to the left of the layer's name. A pencil replaces the lock, and the layer is once again editable.

You also have the option to lock all layers other than a selected layer. Do this when you're on the home stretch and you only need to fine-tune a few objects on one layer.

To hide all layers other than a selected layer:

1. Select the layer you need to edit.

2. Choose Commands | Document | Lock Other Layers. After choosing this command, lock icons appear to the left of all layers except the selected layer.

If you need to lock all layers before creating a new layer, you can do so by choosing Lock All Layers from the Layers panel Options menu.

To unlock all locked layers, choose Unlock All from the Layers panel Options menu. After choosing this command, the lock icons in all locked layers disappear, and the layers can be edited.

Editing Objects on Layers

When you have a document filled with objects that span multiple layers, editing individual objects on the canvas can become an arduous task, especially when some of the objects are small and partially hidden on lower layers. In the sections that follow, you'll learn to work with objects by selecting them from the Layers panel. You'll also learn to copy an object from one layer to another and move an object from one layer to another.

Collapsing a Layer

When you work on a document with multiple layers and each layer has several objects, the Layers panel becomes quite cluttered. Fortunately, you can alleviate this problem by collapsing a layer. When you collapse a layer, it is displayed as a single icon and all of the object thumbnails are hidden.

To collapse a layer, click the minus sign (–) to the left of the Layer's name. When you collapse a layer, a plus sign (+) appears to the left of the layer's name, as shown in the following illustration, and the layer's thumbnails are hidden.

Collapsed Layer ———▶

Expanded Layer ———▶

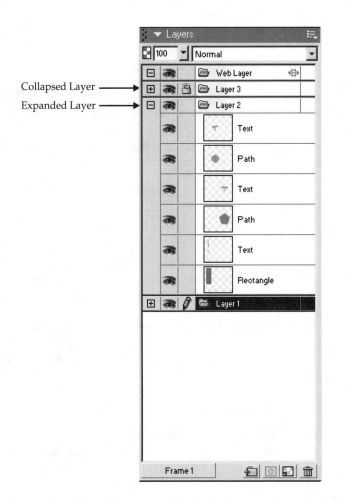

To reveal a collapsed layer, click the plus sign (+) to the left of the layer's name. When the layer is expanded, each object's thumbnail is visible and can be selected.

Selecting an Object on a Layer

When you have multiple objects in close proximity to one another, the task of selecting the proper object can become a little tricky. When you've been running Fireworks for a while and multitasking with other software, and you use the Pointer or Select Behind tool to select an object, Fireworks can get a mind of its own, selecting the wrong object or not selecting any object. This can be remedied by shutting down the computer and rebooting, but if you're pressed for time, you can select an object from within the Layer's panel and then use any tool to modify the selected object.

To select an object in the Layers panel:

1. Click the arrow to the left of the word Layers. The Layers panel opens.

2. If the layer on which the object appears is collapsed, click the minus sign (–) to the left of the layer's name.

3. Click the object to select it. After you click the object, a bounding box of four (five if the object is a polygon) filled squares appears around the object on canvas. You can now edit the object as needed.

> **Note** *If you notice objects are becoming harder to select, this can also be an indication that you are taxing your computer's processor. If you continue to work, the computer may crash and you'll lose your latest edits. It is advisable to save your document early and save it often to safeguard against a possible computer glitch.*

Copying an Object to Another Layer

You can copy an object or a selection of objects from one layer to the next. When you copy a selection of objects to another layer, they appear on the same place on the canvas and in front of the objects on the layer to which the objects are copied.

To copy one or more objects to another layer:

1. Select the Object(s).

2. Hold down the ALT key (Windows) or OPTION key (Macintosh) and drag the object(s) up or down. As you drag the object, an icon that looks like a document and a plus sign (+) appears in front of your cursor, as shown here:

3. Release the mouse button when the objects are over the desired layer.

Moving an Object to Another Layer

While editing a document, you may find it necessary to move one or more objects to another layer. When you move an object to a higher layer, it appears in front of objects on lower layers and other objects on the layer to which the object is moved.

To move an object to a different layer:

1. Choose Window | Layers. The Layers panel opens.

2. If necessary, expand the layer that contains the object you want to move.

3. Click the object's thumbnail and drag it toward another layer. As you drag, an icon that looks like a folder appears, as shown here:

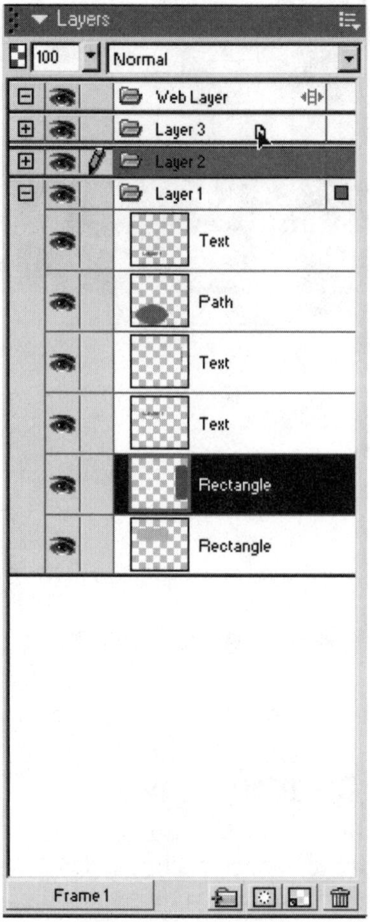

4. When the icon is over the desired folder, release the mouse button.

You can also move several items from one layer to another by doing the following:

1. Open the Layers panel.

2. If the layer from which you want to move items is collapsed, click the plus sign (+) to the left of the layer's title to expand it.

3. Select the objects you want to move. Click the first object's thumbnail to select it, and then while holding down the SHIFT key, click additional thumbnails to add them to the selection.

4. Click the blue icon to the right of the layer's name and drag it toward the desired layer. As you move toward another layer, an icon that looks like a document appears in front of your cursor.

5. Release the mouse button when the icon is over the desired layer. All selected items are moved to the layer.

Merging Objects

If your document has several bitmap objects, you can merge them with vector objects to reduce clutter in the Layers panel. You can merge bitmaps and vector objects into a single bitmap as long as the bottom object selected is above a bitmap. When you merge objects in the Layers panel, they are merged into the bitmap that is resident below the bottommost selected object. When you merge bitmaps and objects down to a bitmap, the vector objects lose their editable status.

To merge objects down to a bitmap:

1. Open the Layers panel and then select the object thumbnail(s) you want to merge down to a bitmap. Remember that the bottommost object must be directly above a bitmap. To select multiple thumbnails, select the first thumbnail and then, while holding down the SHIFT key, click additional thumbnails to add them to the selection.

2. To merge the objects to the bitmap, do one of the following:

   ■ Choose Modify | Merge Down.

   ■ Choose Merge Down from the Layers panel Options menu.

After choosing one of the above, the selected objects are merged down to the bitmap below the bottommost selected objects. The result is a single bitmap object that resides on the same layer as the bitmap on which the images and objects are merged down.

Changing an Object's Opacity

As you know, you can adjust an object's opacity within the Property inspector. You can also adjust an object's opacity while you are working in the Layers panel. You may find this is convenient when you are rearranging the order of objects in the Layers panel. After you move an object to a different location, adjust its opacity in the Layers panel and then view the results on the canvas.

To adjust an object's opacity in the Layers panel:

1. Click the object's thumbnail to select it.

2. Click the triangle to the right of the Opacity field and drag the slider shown in the following illustration. Alternatively, you can enter a value between 0 (transparent) and 100 (fully opaque).

Sharing Layers

When you use Fireworks to create an animation, you often need to edit an object's parameters across the entire animation. You can easily do this if you share a layer across all frames in the document. When you edit an object on a layer that is shared, the object is updated on all frames of the document.

To share a layer across all frames in a document:

- Double-click a layer's name and in the Layer Name dialog box and click the Share Across Layers checkbox.
- Choose Share This Layer from the Layers panel Options menu.

 When a layer is shared, an icon that looks like a film strip with an arrow on each side appears to the right of the layer's name. This is your clue that a layer is being shared across all frames of the document.

Summary

In this chapter you learned to simplify your editing tasks in Fireworks by distributing objects to layers. You learned to edit objects by selecting them on a layer, move objects from one layer to another, and copy objects from one layer to another. You also learned to rearrange the stacking order of layers and to duplicate and delete layers. In addition, you learned how to flatten objects into a single bitmap and how to merge objects into a single bitmap. In Chapter 13, you'll learn to create reusable artwork for your Fireworks documents.

Chapter 13

Creating
Reusable Artwork

When you create standalone artwork for a document, the graphic is used once. When you need a different graphic for your document, you create it from scratch. This is all well and good when you're dealing with different objects. However, when you use similar objects in your document, such as a button for a navigation menu, creating new artwork from scratch is a tedious and time-consuming task. You can, however, create one symbol and use it repeatedly in a document. After you create a symbol, it is stored in the document Library, which is part of the Assets panel. The ability to create reusable artwork streamlines your Fireworks workflow and frees your time for creating new artwork for the document.

What Are Symbols and Instances?

A *symbol* is a Fireworks object you can use repeatedly in a document. A symbol is stored in the document Library, which is part of the Assets panel. When you need to use artwork you've converted to a symbol, you open up the document Library and drag the symbol onto the canvas. When you use a symbol in the document, you are creating an *instance* of the symbol. The symbol is the original object, and instances are copies of the object. You can add as many instances of a symbol as needed to get the job done. Symbols are useful in animations across multiple frames.

Once you have an instance of a symbol in the document, you can modify it with the Scale, Skew, or Distort tool. You cannot, however, modify the instance's path with the Freeform, Reshape Area, or Path Scrubber tool. That would alter the basic shape of the symbol. Another way you can modify symbols is to apply a Live Effect or Style to the symbol. Figure 13-1 shows the diversity you can achieve by modifying instances of a symbol. All of the graphics in this figure are derived from one symbol.

Understanding Fireworks Symbol Behaviors

You have three symbol types in Fireworks: Animation, Button, and Graphic. Each symbol performs a different function. In the sections that follow, you'll receive a brief overview of what each symbol type does.

About Animation Symbols

Animation symbols are multiple frame animations in which one or several objects undergo a change from one frame to the next. When you create an animation symbol, it is designated in the document Library by the icon shown here:

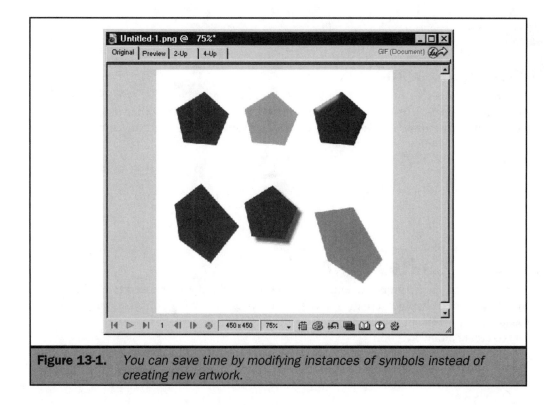

Figure 13-1. *You can save time by modifying instances of symbols instead of creating new artwork.*

> **Note**   *Animation will be covered in detail in Chapters 18 and 19.*

About Button Symbols

Buttons are navigation devices. When you create a button symbol, you have several states to work with. You can create a different graphic for each state or modify the graphic to achieve a different appearance when a user's mouse interacts with the button. A button symbol generally has a label that informs Web visitors what they can expect when the button is clicked. A button can also have a uniform resource locator (URL) assigned to it. When you create instances of buttons in your document, you can change the label and the URL for an individual instance without changing other instances in the document. When you create a button symbol, it is designated in the document Library by the icon shown here:

Note *Creating navigation buttons will be covered in Chapter 17.*

About Graphic Symbols

Graphic symbols are static objects or images. You can create a graphic symbol using one of the drawing tools, or you can import vector artwork created in other programs. You can also import bitmaps for use as symbols. A graphic symbol in the document Library is designated by the icon shown here:

Creating a New Symbol

You can create a new symbol whenever you know an object will be used more than once in a document. When you create a new symbol, you specify the behavior and either create or import the graphics.

To create a new symbol:

1. Choose Edit | Insert | New Symbol. Alternatively, you can press CTRL+F8. After choosing one of these methods, the Symbol Properties dialog box appears, as shown here:

Symbol Properties ☒

Name: Symbol

Type: ⦿ Graphic
   ○ Animation
   ○ Button

OK

Cancel

---

2. Accept the default name (the symbol appended by the next available number) or enter a unique name for the symbol. If you are creating a document with several symbols, it is advisable to enter a name for the symbol that describes what the symbol does.

3. Choose a symbol type and click OK. The Symbol window appears, and you are in symbol-editing mode.

Note   *If you specify the button symbol type, the Button Editor opens. The Button Editor is covered in detail in Chapter 17.*

4. Use the drawing tools to create the artwork for your symbol or import a graphic. The following illustration shows a bitmap that has been imported while in symbol-editing mode.

Figure 13-2.   *You can import bitmap graphics when in symbol-editing mode.*

5. After creating the graphic for the symbol, close the Symbol window. The symbol is added to the document Library and appears on the canvas. All symbol instances are designated by a small arrow at the instance's lower-left corner. The following illustration shows a symbol instance on the canvas, and the original symbol as it appears in the document Library.

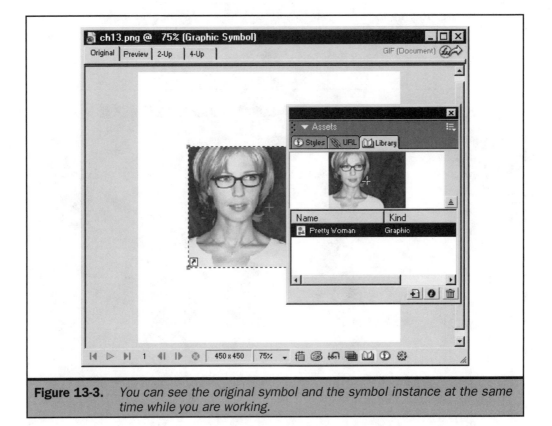

Figure 13-3. *You can see the original symbol and the symbol instance at the same time while you are working.*

Converting an Object to a Symbol

After you create an object for a document and decide that you'll need to use it repeatedly, you can convert the object to a symbol. When you convert an object to a symbol, it retains the appearance of the original graphic, except that it is now reusable.

To convert an object to a symbol:

1. Select the object you want to convert to a symbol.

2. Choose Modify | Symbol | Convert to Symbol. Alternatively, you can press F8. After choosing either method, the Symbol Properties dialog box shown previously appears.

3. Enter a name for the symbol and choose a symbol type.

4. Click OK. The symbol is added to the document Library, and the original object now has an arrow at its lower-left corner that signifies it is now a symbol instance.

Using the Library Panel

All of the symbols you use for a document are housed in the document Library. The document Library is docked in the panel window on the right side of the workspace and is part of the Assets panel group. You use the document Library to create additional instances of a symbol in your document, create new symbols, duplicate symbols, delete and edit symbols, and preview symbols.

To open the document Library, do one of the following:

■ Choose Window | Library.

■ Click the arrow to the left of the word "Assets" and click the Library tab.

The document Library, shown in the following illustration, consists of two windows. For the purpose of this illustration, the panel has been undocked from the panel window.

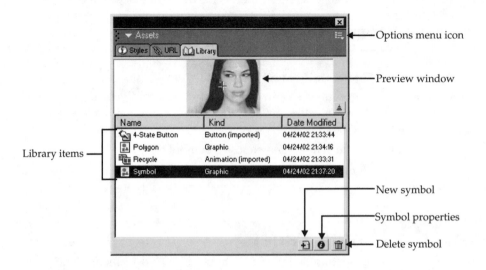

The upper window displays a preview of a selected symbol. If the symbol is an animation, a play button appears to the right of the window. You can preview the animation by clicking the button. The bottom window displays information about each symbol in the document Library, the symbol name, the type, and the date created. You can sort the items by name, type, or date created, by clicking the column title. After you click the column title, Fireworks sorts the symbols in ascending order. To reverse the sort order, click the Toggle Sorting button in the lower-right corner of the upper window.

Note   *When you open the document Library, you may not see all of the columns. You can reveal all of the columns by clicking the border between the panel window and the workspace and then dragging to the left.*

Creating Symbol Instances

After you add symbols to the document Library, you add them to the document as needed, rather than creating a new graphic. Adding a symbol instance to a document is a simple matter of dragging the symbol from the document Library onto the canvas.

To create a symbol instance:

1. Choose Window | Library. Alternatively, you can click the arrow to the left of the word Assets and then click the Library tab.

2. Click a symbol's name to select it. A preview of the symbol appears in the upper window of the panel. If the symbol is an animation or button, click the Play button to preview the symbol.

3. Click the symbol preview and drag it to the canvas. Alternatively, you can click the symbol name and drag it to the document. After choosing one of these methods, the symbol instance appears in the document.

Using the Library Panel Options Menu

You can do the majority of your document maintenance as pertains to symbols from within the document Library. The document Library Options menu contains the commands you will use to create, duplicate, edit, and remove unused symbols. There are also menu commands that enable you to import symbols directly into the Library and export symbols from the Library.

To open the Library panel Options menu, shown in the following illustration, click the Options menu icon shown previously.

Creating a New Symbol

You can create a new symbol from within the document Library. This option is useful when you're perusing the Library for a symbol and you don't see what you need. You can create a new symbol from within the Library by doing the following:

1. Click the New Symbol button at the bottom of the document Library. It looks like a plus sign (+) next to a document icon. Alternatively, you can choose New Symbol from the Library panel Options menu. After choosing either method, the Symbol Properties dialog box shown previously appears.

2. Enter a name for the symbol, choose a symbol type, and then click OK. The Symbol window opens, or if you specified the button type, the Button Editor opens.

3. Create or import the graphics you need for the symbol and close the Symbol window or Button Editor.

When you create a new symbol from within the Library, the symbol is added to the Library. However, an instance is not added to the document. To add an instance of the new symbol to the document, follow the steps outlined previously.

Duplicating a Symbol

If you have the need for a new symbol, but you already have a symbol that's nearly perfect, you can duplicate the symbol and then edit it to suit your needs. Duplicating and editing a symbol is much quicker than creating one from scratch.

To duplicate a symbol:

1. Open the document Library, as outlined previously.

2. Select the symbol you want to duplicate.

3. Choose Duplicate from the Options menu. A new symbol appears in the document Library. The duplicate symbol has the same name as the original appended by the next available number. You can rename the duplicate by following the steps in the next section.

Renaming a Symbol

When you duplicate a symbol or import a symbol into the Library, you can change its name to reflect the symbol's purpose in the document. Creating a unique name for a symbol is especially import when creating a document with multiple symbols. If you have to edit the document for a client three or four months down the road, you'll be glad you did name the symbol.

You can rename a symbol by doing one of the following:

■ Double-click the symbol's name.

■ Select the symbol and then click the Properties button that looks like the universal information icon.

■ Choose Properties from the Options menu.

After choosing one of these methods, the Symbol Properties dialog box shown previously opens. Enter a new name for the symbol, and then click OK. The symbol's name is updated in the document Library.

Deleting a Symbol

When a symbol has outlived its usefulness, you can delete it. When you delete a symbol from the document Library, all of the symbol's instances are deleted as well.
To delete a symbol from the document Library, do one of the following:

- Select the symbol you want to delete, and then click the Delete Symbol button, which looks like a trash can.

- Select the symbol you want to delete, and then drag it to the Delete Symbol button.

- Select the symbol you want to delete, and then choose Delete from the Options menu.

If you choose one of the above and the symbol is currently being used in the document, Fireworks displays a dialog box warning you that the symbol is in use. Click Delete to remove all instances of the symbol within the document, or click Cancel to void the operation.

Editing a Symbol

When necessary, you can edit a symbol from within the document Library. When you edit a symbol, all instances of it in the document are updated as well.
To edit a symbol from within the document Library, do one of the following:

- Double-click the symbol.

- Select the symbol and choose Edit from the Options menu.

After choosing either method, the symbol appears in the Symbol window (Animation or Graphic type) or the Button Editor (Button type). Edit the symbol as necessary and then close the window. All instances of the symbol are updated to reflect your edits.

Tip *You can also edit a symbol by selecting one of its instances on the canvas. After selecting the instance, right-click (Windows) or CTRL+click (Macintosh) and choose Symbol | Edit Symbol from the context menu. Edit the symbol as described previously, and all instances of the symbol are updated to reflect your changes. Alternatively, you can double-click the instance to edit the symbol from which the instance was spawned.*

Deleting Unused Symbols

If you do a lot of experimenting, you can end up with a document Library that's overflowing with symbols. When this happens, it's difficult to navigate the Library because of all the unused symbols. You can, however, clean house with a few quick clicks of the mouse button.

MODIFYING ARTWORK

To clear the document Library of all unused symbols:

1. Click the arrow to the left of the word Assets, and then click the Library tab.
2. From the Options menu, choose Select Unused Items. Fireworks highlights the unused symbols.
3. Click the Delete Symbol icon. Alternatively, you can drag the symbols to the Delete Symbol icon.

Importing Symbols

If the design you are creating requires graphics supplied by a client or graphics created in another program, you can import the graphics directly into the document Library. You can import any recognized file type into the document Library as a symbol.

To import a symbol into the document Library:

1. Open the document Library, as outlined previously.
2. Choose Import Symbols from the Library panel Options menu. The Open dialog box appears.
3. Navigate to the folder containing the file you want to import.
4. Select the file, and Fireworks generates a preview, as shown here:

5. Click Open. The file is imported into the Library. You can now create instances of the new symbol as needed. Note that you can only import one file at a time.

Tip *If you're using Fireworks to create several documents for a Web site, organize all the site assets in a folder. You can then easily import any of the graphics you will use as symbols by choosing the Import Symbol command and then navigating to the folder where you store the assets for the site.*

Updating Library Items

If you import graphics created in other programs into the Library and edit them outside of Fireworks, you can update the symbol without having to re-import it. When you import a symbol into Fireworks, a link is created with the original version of the file. When you update the file outside of Fireworks and then choose the Update command, if the original has changed, it is re-imported.

To update a symbol modified outside of Fireworks:

1. Click the arrow to the left of the word Assets, and then click the Library tab.

2. Select the symbol you modified outside of Fireworks.

3. Choose Update from the Library panel Options menu. Fireworks updates the graphic and displays a message that the file has been updated successfully.

Exporting Symbols

If you create a document with symbols that you can use in other documents, you can export any or all of the symbols in the document Library. This feature is handy when you do ongoing work for a client. Export the document Library as symbols, and Fireworks saves the symbols as a .png file. When you need to create a new document for the client, open the exported symbol file as previously outlined. Every symbol you exported appears on the canvas and in the document Library. Delete the symbols from the canvas—they still appear in the document Library—and you're ready to begin.

To export symbols:

1. Open the document Library, as outlined previously.

2. Choose Export Symbols from the Options menu, and the dialog box shown here appears.

3. Select the symbol you want to export. To select more than one symbol, hold down the CTRL key (Windows) or COMMAND key (Macintosh) and click additional symbols to add them to the selection. To export the entire document Library, choose Select All.

4. Choose Export. The Save As dialog box appears. You only have one choice for file type: Fireworks (.png).

5. Enter a filename for the symbols, and navigate to the folder where you want them saved.

6. Click Save. The symbols are saved for further use.

Modifying Symbol Instances

As previously mentioned, you can edit a symbol and update all instances of it in the document. You can also modify certain properties of a symbol instance to give it a unique look that while different than the original symbol, still retains the basic shape characteristic of the symbol.

To modify a symbol instance, select it and open the Property inspector; then modify any of the following:

- Blending mode
- Opacity
- Width (W) or Height (H)
- Application of one or more effects to the symbol instance
- X and Y coordinates (the instance position on the canvas)

You can also modify the appearance of the symbol instance using the Scale, Skew, and Distort tools. You can modify the instance to your heart's content with these tools, and the original symbol remains unaffected. If you attempt to use a tool such as the Path Scrubber or Freeform tool on the instance, a circle icon with a diagonal slash appears, indicating that the tool cannot be used on the instance.

If you want to change the fill characteristics of a symbol instance or alter the basic shape of the symbol instance, you must break the instance's link with the original symbol. After you break an instance's link, you can modify it using any of the transformation tools, and the original symbol is unaffected as the link has been broken. After modifying the unlinked instance, you can convert it to a new symbol by pressing F8.

To break an instance's link:

1. Select the symbol instance you want to unlink.

2. Choose | Modify | Symbol | Break Apart. After invoking the command, the object appears in the Layers panel as a group. If the object was formerly an instance of a button symbol or an animation symbol, it loses those characteristics.

Using the Fireworks Preset Libraries

Most Web designers prefer to create their own objects. By creating unique button styles and other original graphic symbols, designers put their own stamp of originality on a design. However, if you're new to graphic design or under the gun to get a project out quickly, you can use a symbol from one of the Fireworks preset libraries. The libraries contain various objects commonly used in a Web design such as buttons, bullets, horizontal dividers, and more.

To use an object from one of the preset libraries:

1. Choose Edit | Libraries and choose a library from the submenu. After choosing a library, the Import Symbols dialog box appears.

2. Choose one or more preset symbols by selecting them, as previously outlined.

3. Click Import or double-click to import the symbols into the document Library. An instance of each imported symbol is also stacked on the canvas. You can either delete the instances and insert them as needed from the document Library, or you can choose Commands | Document | Distribute To Layers to place each imported symbol instance on its own layer.

Once you have the preset symbol in your document, you can modify it as previously outlined.

Creating a Custom Library

In previous sections of this chapter, you learned to export symbols. If you create a group of symbols you feel you will use repeatedly in your designs, you can export the symbols and have them appear as a menu command. Doing this gives you almost instant access to your custom library as you bypass the Import Symbols command and don't have to search for the folder in which the exported symbols are stored.

To create a custom library:

1. Create a document and then create the symbols for your custom library. Alternatively, you can import symbols from other designs you have created.

2. After creating the symbols you want to save as a custom library, choose Window | Library.

3. From the Options menu choose Export Symbols. The Export Symbols dialog box shown previously appears.

4. To export all symbols in the library, click Select All, and then click Export. Alternatively, choose the symbols you want to export, and then click Export. The Save As dialog box appears, as shown previously.

5. Enter a name for the Library.

6. Click the triangle to the right of the Save In field, select the folder in which your programs are saved, and follow this path: Fireworks MX | Configuration | Libraries.

7. Click Save. When you next launch Fireworks, the custom library can be accessed by choosing Edit | Libraries and then choosing your custom library from the submenu.

Summary

In this chapter, you learned to create reusable artwork in the form of symbols. You learned to create instances of a symbol by dragging it to the canvas from the document Library. You also learned to edit symbols and create custom libraries. In Chapter 14, you'll learn to create special effects for your documents.

Chapter 14

Creating Special Effects

When you're creating a document for a Web design, you can change the look of the objects in your designs by applying one or more effects to them. With Fireworks, the number of effects you have to work with is staggering. You can apply multiple effects to objects to create unique items for your designs. With Fireworks, you have two types of effects you can work with: Live Effects and filters.

The beauty of Live Effects is that you can edit them at any time, even after you have saved the document. When you use filters, on the other hand, the effect is applied to the object and cannot be edited after the document is saved. In fact, if you need to edit an effect applied with an item from the Filters menu, you must undo all the steps you performed after applying the filter to an object. You can also link third-party, Photoshop-type filters to Fireworks. You can apply third-party filters as Live Effects or from the Filters menu.

In this chapter, you'll learn how to use Live Effects and filters to add variety and originality to the objects in your document. You'll also learn how to link Fireworks with any third-party, Photoshop-compatible plug-ins you may have on your system. You'll also learn how to use Fireworks' sophisticated color adjustment filters to modify a bitmap image, as well as how to use the Eye Candy and Splat filters to spice up bitmap images in your documents. Figure 14-1 shows some objects and bitmaps that have been modified with Live Effects and filters.

Exploring Live Effects and Filters

The special effects you can create with Fireworks will come from two sources: Live Effects and filters. You apply Live Effects to an object from within the Property inspector, and as previously mentioned, the effects can be modified or deleted any time after you apply

Figure 14-1.   *You can use Live Effects and filters to create a variety of special effects for your documents.*

them to an object. Filters have their own section on the menu bar. These filters are duplicated as Live Effects. Due to the enhanced ability to edit a Live Effect at any time, unless you are doing a one-off edit, it is usually in your best interest to use Live Effects.

Applying a Live Effect

You can apply a Live Effect to a bitmap or vector object. Certain Live Effects are designed for bitmaps; however, you can still use them to good effect on vector objects. You can create interesting effects like beveled buttons, embossed text, drop shadows, and glowing objects. You can use other effects to color-correct bitmap images, blur bitmap images, and more. When you apply a Live Effect to an object, the object updates in real time. You can then modify the effect by adjusting the effect's parameters until you get the desired result.

Each effect achieves different results and will be dealt with separately. In the sections that follow, you'll learn the basic steps involved in adding an effect, deleting an effect, and working with multiple effects.

Adding an Effect

When you decide to apply an effect to an object, you do so by using the Property inspector. When you add additional effects to an object, the new effects appear on a list. If you have several effects applied to an object, you can delete an effect that isn't to your liking, edit an effect, or change the order in which effects are applied to an object.

To add an effect to an object:

1. Select the object to which you want to apply the effect.

2. Click the arrow to the left of the word Properties. The Property inspector opens.

3. Click the Add Effects button, which looks like a plus sign (+), and choose an effect from the menu shown here:

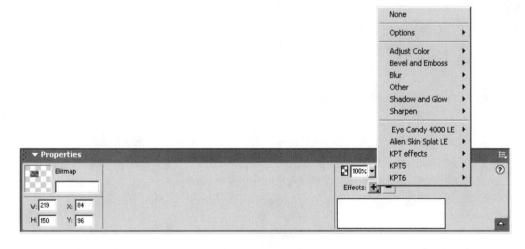

4. Adjust the settings for the effect. The following illustration shows the settings for the Inner Bevel effect.

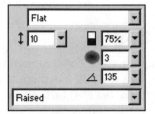

5. After adjusting the settings, click anywhere in the workspace to close the menu. Alternatively, you can press ENTER or RETURN.

6. Click the Add Effects button to add additional effects to the object.

Deleting an Effect

After you apply an effect, it appears on a list in the Property inspector. If after working with other objects in the document, you find an effect applied to another object is no longer needed, you can easily delete it.

To delete an effect from an object:

1. Select the object to which you've applied an effect that you want to delete.

2. Open the Property inspector.

3. Click the effect's name to select it.

4. Click the Delete Selected Effect button, which looks like a minus sign (–). The effect is removed from the object. If additional effects are applied to an object, they will remain in effect.

Tip   *To remove all effects from an object, click the Add Effects button and choose None from the menu.*

Editing an Effect

You can edit an effect at any time after applying it to an object. As you edit an effect, you see the results as soon as you modify one of the effect's parameters.

To edit an effect:

1. Select the object to which you have applied the effect that needs editing.

2. Open the Property inspector. After you open the Property inspector, you see all of the effects that have been applied to the object.

3. Double-click the effect you want to edit. The effect's dialog box opens.

4. Modify the settings to suit the document you are working on. As you change the settings, the object updates on the canvas.

5. After editing the object, click anywhere in the workspace to close the effect's dialog box.

Managing Multiple Effects

When you have more than one effect applied to an object, the order that they are applied to the object may have a bearing on the object's appearance. If an object to which you have applied multiple effects isn't to your liking, changing the order in which the effects are applied may give you the desired result.

To change the order in which effects are applied to an object:

1. Select the object to which you have applied multiple effects.

2. Open the Property inspector. The list of effects you've applied to the object is displayed in the Effects area.

3. Click an effect to select it and then drag it up or down the list.

4. Release the mouse button when the effect is in the order you want it applied. The following illustration shows the difference that changing the order of effects can have on an object. The object on the left has the Inner Bevel effect applied before the Glow effect; the object on the right shows the same effects with the order reversed.

> **Tip** When you have multiple effects applied to an object, you can toggle an individual effect on or off by clicking the checkmark to the left of the effect's name. After clicking the checkmark, a red x appears, and the effect is temporarily not applied to the object. Click the red x to toggle the effect on again.

Exploring the Filters Menu

If you are editing an individual bitmap image, you can choose effects from the Filters menu. All of the commands on the Filters menu are available as Live Effects from within the Property inspector. In this section, you'll receive a brief overview of the menu and available commands. The actual parameters that you modify will be covered in separate sections to follow. You can also link third-party plug-ins to this menu, which you'll learn to do by the end of the chapter.

MODIFYING ARTWORK

To use a command from the filters menu, choose Filters to open the menu shown in the following illustration. Note that many of the commands in the menu have submenus. Each item on the submenus will be covered in upcoming sections. In the upcoming sections, the commands from the Filters menu will be shown as Live Effects.

Note

Remember, when you apply a command from the Filters menu, you cannot modify or delete it except by choosing Edit | Undo immediately after applying the command. If you want the ability to remove a filter at any time after applying it, choose the filter from the Effects menu in the Property inspector. In addition, to being able to delete the effect at any time, you can also adjust any modifiable parameters at any time, even after saving the document.

Using Effects for Bitmap Images

You can perform sophisticated color manipulation on any bitmap image you import into Fireworks. If the image is a scan of an old, slightly faded photo, you can restore the image to a reasonable semblance of its former glory by following the steps in one or more of the upcoming sections.

Adjusting a Bitmap's Color Characteristics

You can modify the color characteristics of any bitmap you import into your document. You can adjust the brightness of the image and the tonal range, and you can also adjust the hue and saturation of a selected bitmap.

Applying a Live Effect to a Pixel Selection

You can also apply a Live Effect to a selected area of a bitmap. This comes in handy when only a certain area of an image needs color adjusting. You can use any of the color correction Live Effects presented in the following sections to modify a selected area of a bitmap.

To create a selection to which you can apply a Live Effect:

1. Create a selection of pixels using any of the following tools: Marquee, Lasso tool, or Magic Wand.

2. Choose Edit | Cut.

3. Choose Edit | Paste. The selection of pixels is pasted to the exact location from which they were cut.

4. Open the Layers panel and select the thumbnail for the pixel selection you just pasted.

5. Apply any Live Effect to modify the pixel selection.

If you're working with several objects in a document and you apply a live effect to a pixel selection, you should keep the bitmap and any selections you create on their own layer. After modifying the bitmap and any pixel selections you create, lock the layer to guard against inadvertently selecting and moving a pixel selection. If you create several pixel selections from a bitmap and modify them, you can use the Merge Down command to merge them into the bitmap from which they were cut. When you merge the selections into the bitmap, you will no longer be able to edit a Live Effect applied to the selection.

Adjusting a Bitmap's Tonal Range

If you've got an image that needs a bit of color balancing, you can let Fireworks handle the task for you. When you choose the Auto Levels effect, Fireworks adjusts the tonal range automatically.

To use the Auto Levels effect:

1. Select a bitmap or create a pixel selection, as outlined previously.

2. Open the Property inspector.

3. Click the Add Effects button, which looks like a plus sign (+), and choose Adjust Color | Auto Levels. The effect has no parameters. After applying the effect to a bitmap, it appears on the Effects list.

When you choose Auto Levels, Fireworks does a good job of adjusting the tonal range of an image that needs a little correction. However, if the bitmap you are working with requires extensive modification, you can modify the bitmap by applying the Levels or Curves effect. These effects enable you to manually adjust the bitmap's levels and tonal curves.

MODIFYING ARTWORK

Note *You can also apply Auto Levels by choosing Filters | Adjust Colors | Auto Levels.*

Adjusting a Bitmap's Brightness and Contrast

If you scan a bitmap into your document or import a bitmap that's a little anemic and washed out, you can give it a shot in the arm by adjusting the brightness and/or contrast of the image. When you choose this effect, you see the results of your editing in real time.

To change the brightness and/or contrast of an image:

1. Select a bitmap or make a bitmap selection, as outlined previously.
2. Open the Property inspector.
3. Click the Add Effects button and choose Adjust Color | Brightness/Contrast. The Brightness/Contrast dialog box appears.
4. Drag the Brightness slider right to lighten the image or left to darken it.
5. Drag the Contrast slider right to increase contrast or left to decrease contrast. The following illustration shows the effect being applied to a bitmap.

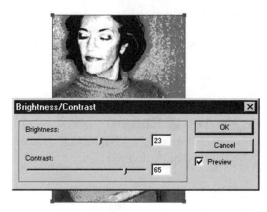

Note *To adjust an object's brightness and contrast from the Filters menu, choose Filters | Adjust Color | Brightness/Contrast.*

Using the Curves Live Effect

You can manually adjust a bitmap's colors by manually adjusting the color curve. When you adjust the color curve, you can manually adjust the colors for the entire color range or select a separate color component. You can change the color characteristics by manually adjusting a curve within the dialog box or by using eyedroppers to select the shadow, the midrange, and the highlight colors from within the bitmap.

To adjust the tonal range of an image using curves:

1. Select the bitmap whose tonal range you want to modify.

2. Open the Property inspector.

3. Click the Add Effects button, which looks like a plus sign (+), and choose Adjust Color | Curves. The dialog box shown in the following illustration appears.

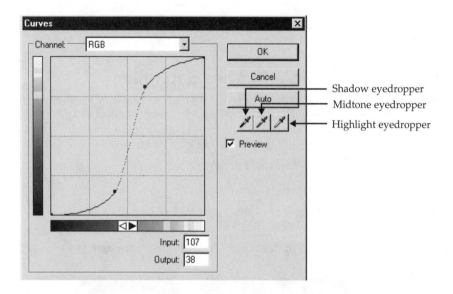

When the dialog box first opens, the diagonal line indicates that no changes have been made and that the color values for the input pixels (the original colors) and output pixels (modified color values) are the same.

4. Click the triangle to the right of the Channel field and choose RGB (modifies the entire color range), Red (affects only the red color channel), Green (affects only the green color channel), or Blue (affects only the blue color channel).

5. Click a point on the diagonal line and drag it to a new position to adjust the curve. The upper range of the curve represents the highlight colors, the middle part of the curve represents the midtone colors, and the lower part of the curve modifies the shadow colors.

6. Continue modifying points along the curve until the color balance of the image is as desired. If you want to delete a point, click it and drag it beyond the range of the grid.

7. Click OK to apply the changes.

In the previous illustration, notice the Auto button. You can click this button, and Fireworks will automatically set the levels for you. The three eyedroppers are used to manually select a color from the image that you want to be the basis for that color range. For example, click the Shadow eyedropper and then click a color in the image that you want to be the darkest color after the effect is applied. Click each of the other eyedroppers and choose a color from the image that you want to be the midtone and highlight value.

> **Note**   *You can adjust the color range of a bitmap by choosing Filter | Adjust Color | Curves.*

Adjusting a Bitmap's Hue and Saturation

Another method you can use to modify a bitmap's color is to change its hue and saturation. When you modify an image by adjusting hue and saturation, you modify the entire color range. You cannot modify a single color channel by adjusting hue and saturation as you can by adjusting a bitmap's color curve.

To adjust a bitmap's hue and saturation:

1. Select the bitmap you want to modify.

2. Open the Property inspector.

3. Click the Add Effects button, and choose Adjust Color | Hue/Saturation. The dialog box shown in the following illustration appears.

4. Drag the Hue slider to modify the color of the image. Alternatively, you can enter a value between –180 and 180.

5. Drag the Saturation slider to vary the purity of the colors in the images. Alternatively, you can enter a value between –100 and 100.

6. Drag the Lightness slider to change the lightness of the colors. Alternatively, you can enter a value between –100 and 100. Positive values lighten the image, negative values darken it.

7. Click OK to apply the changes. Figure 14-2 shows the original image and the image after increasing the color saturation.

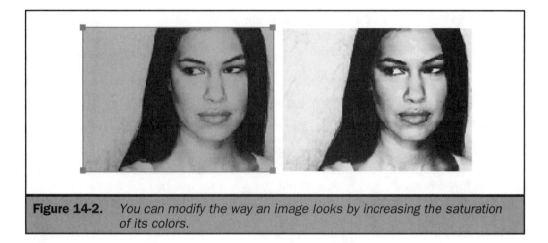

Figure 14-2.   *You can modify the way an image looks by increasing the saturation of its colors.*

Note   *To access the Hue/Saturation dialog box from the Filters menu, choose Filters | Adjust Colors | Hue/Saturation.*

Tip   *To add color to a grayscale image or to turn a color image into a two-tone image, choose Colorize in the Hue/Saturation dialog box.*

Inverting a Bitmap's Colors

Another interesting effect you can apply to a bitmap is to invert its colors. When you invert a bitmap's colors, the resulting image looks like a photographic negative.

To invert a bitmap's colors:

1. Select the bitmap whose colors you want to invert.

2. Open the Property inspector.

3. Click the Add Effects button, which looks like a plus sign (+), and choose Adjust Color | Invert. The effect has no parameters. The following illustration shows a bitmap before and after its colors were inverted.

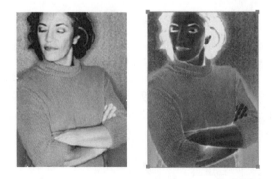

MODIFYING ARTWORK

Note   *To invert a bitmap's colors from the Filters menu, choose Filters | Adjust Color | Invert. Remember that when you choose a command from the Filters menu, the command cannot be edited after the fact and can only be undone immediately after it is applied.*

Adjusting a Bitmap's Color Levels

Another method you can use to adjust a bitmap's tonal range is to modify the levels of colors in the image. Choose this method of modifying a bitmap when the color range of an image is unbalanced and has pixels that are predominantly in the shadow, midtone, or highlight range. In other words, if an image has a dark cast, the pixels are predominantly in the shadow range; if it appears washed out, the pixels are weighed toward the midtone range; and if it is too bright, the pixels are on the high end or the highlight end of the tonal range.

To adjust the color levels in a bitmap image:

1. Select the bitmap whose colors you want to modify.

2. Open the Property inspector.

3. Click the Add Effects button and choose Adjust Color | Levels. The Levels dialog box appears, as shown here:

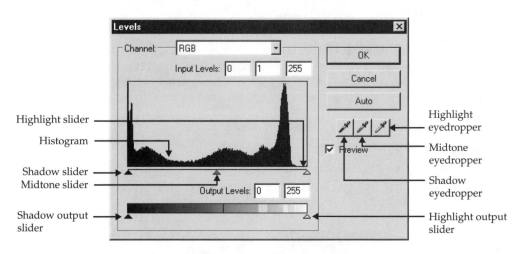

The graph in the previous image is called a histogram. This shows you how the color pixels are distributed across the tonal range. When you see a spike in the graph, that's an indication that there are a large number of pixels in a particular tonal range, a situation you can improve by modifying the levels.

4. Click the triangle to the left of the Channel field, and choose RGB (modifies the levels of every color channel), Red (modifies the levels of pixels in the red color

channel), Green (modifies the levels of pixels in the green color channel), or Blue (modifies the levels of pixels in the blue color channel).

5. Drag the Input level sliders underneath the histogram to redistribute the way the pixels are distributed.

- The left slider distributes the shadows in a range from 0 to 255.

- The middle slider distributes the midtones in a range from 0 to 10.

- The right slider distributes the highlights in a range from 255 to 0.

As you drag the sliders, the numerical values of the input boxes are automatically adjusted to reflect the new settings. If you drag either the shadow slider or the highlight slider, the midtone slider is automatically adjusted.

6. Drag the output sliders to affect the range of the shadow and highlight tones.

- Drag the left slider to adjust the shadows from 0 to 255. Dragging this slider to the right (higher values) washes out the shadows and lightens the image.

- Drag the right slider to adjust the highlights from 255 to 0. Dragging this slider to the left (lower values) washes out the highlights and darkens the image.

As you drag these sliders, the values in the output boxes update to reflect the new values.

You can have Fireworks automatically adjust the levels by clicking the Auto button shown in the previous illustration. You can also use the eyedroppers to select colors from the image by doing the following:

- Click the Shadows eyedropper and click a color in the image to set the shadow input level.

- Click the Midtone eyedropper and click a color in the image to set the midtone input level.

- Click the Highlight eyedropper and click a color in the image to set the highlight input level.

7. Click OK to apply the changes.

Note *To adjust a bitmap's levels from the Filters menu, choose Filters | Color Adjust | Levels. Note that filters applied in this manner cannot be edited.*

Using the Color Fill Effect

You can use the Color Fill effect to tint an image by filling the image with a color and then choosing a blend mode. When you choose this effect, you can choose the level of opacity for the fill and choose from any of the blending methods.

MODIFYING ARTWORK

To apply the Color Fill effect to an object:

1. Select the object you want to modify. The object can be a bitmap image or a vector object.

2. Open the Property inspector.

3. Click the Add Effects button, which looks like a plus sign (+), and choose Adjust Color | Color Fill. The dialog box shown in the following illustration appears. When the dialog box first appears, the default fill color replaces the object's fill color or the bitmap's colors.

Blending Mode:
Normal
100%

4. Click the color swatch and choose a fill color from the pop-up palette.

5. Click the triangle to the right of the Opacity field, and drag the slider to set the opacity of the color fill. Alternatively, you can enter a value between 0 and 100.

6. Click the triangle to the right of the Blending Mode field and choose a mode. If you accept the default Normal mode. The color fill effectively tints the image. Choose one of the other modes if a different effect is desired.

Note *For more information on blending modes, see Chapter 5.*

7. Click anywhere on the canvas to apply the color fill, or press ENTER or RETURN. The following illustration shows a bitmap in its original state on the left, and the same bitmap after a Color Fill is applied on the right.

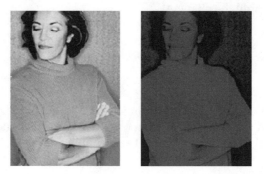

Using Effects for Bitmap and Vector Images

In addition to applying effects to bitmaps, there are effects that work on vector objects, as well as bitmaps. These effects include the ability to bevel, emboss, and create a drop shadow for an object. In the upcoming sections, you'll learn how to use these effects to modify objects in your documents. You can create an inner bevel, an outer bevel, or an embossed object, as you'll learn in the upcoming sections.

Beveling an Object

If you've surfed the Internet to any great degree, no doubt you've seen a profusion of buttons. Some buttons are flat with text-only messages, others are contoured to give them a 3D look. You can easily create this 3D effect and others in Fireworks by beveling an object. You can bevel both bitmaps and vector objects.

To bevel an object:

1. Select the object that you want to bevel.

2. Open the Property inspector.

3. Click the Add Effects button, which looks like a plus sign (+), and choose Bevel And Emboss | Inner Bevel. The dialog box shown in the following illustration appears.

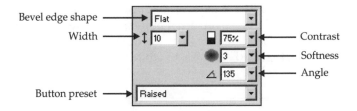

4. Click the triangle to the right of the Bevel Edge Shape field and from the drop-down menu, choose either Flat, Smooth, Sloped, Frame 1, Frame 2, Ring, or Ruffle.

5. Click the triangle to the right of the Width field and drag the slider to specify the width of the bevel. Alternatively, you can enter a value in the field.

6. Click the triangle to the right of the Contrast field and drag the slider to set a value. Alternatively, you can enter a value between 0 and 100. This setting determines the contrast between the lighting source and the bevel's shadow. Choose a higher value for a more pronounced bevel shape.

7. Click the triangle to the right of the Softness field and drag the slider to set a value. Lower values produce a more pronounced bevel effect.

8. Click the triangle to the right of the Angle field, and a circular dial pops up. Click and drag the dial to set the angle from which the light source is shining on the bevel. Alternatively, you can enter a value between 0 and 360.

9. Click the triangle to the right of the Button preset field, and from the drop-down menu choose one of the following: Raised, Highlighted, Inset, or Inverted.

10. Click anywhere in the workspace to apply the effect. Alternatively, you can press ENTER or RETURN.

You can also create an outer bevel. When you apply this effect to an object, the bevel appears outside of the object. An outer bevel is a good choice for a bitmap frame. To create an outer bevel:

1. Select the object to which you want to add the bevel.

2. Open the Property inspector.

3. Click the Add Effects button and choose Bevel And Emboss | Outer Bevel.

4. Follow steps 4 through 10 from the Inner Bevel instructions, as the dialog boxes are the same. Figure 14-3 shows two rows of objects. The objects on the top row have an inner bevel; the objects on the bottom row have an outer bevel.

Embossing an Object

You can also use the Emboss effect to make an object appear three dimensional. When you apply the Emboss effect to an object, it appears as though it is carved (Inset Emboss) or stamped (Raised Emboss) from the background. The effect works best when the document background color is something other than white.

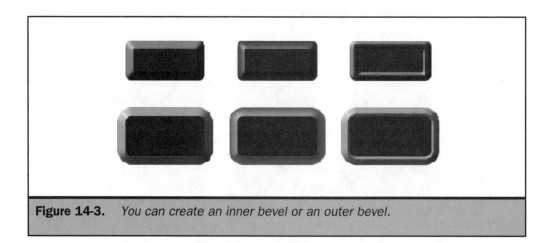

Figure 14-3. *You can create an inner bevel or an outer bevel.*

To emboss an object inward:

1. Select the object you want to emboss.

2. Open the Property inspector.

3. Click the Add Effects button, which looks like a plus sign (+), and choose Bevel And Emboss | Inset Emboss. The Inset dialog box appears, as shown here:

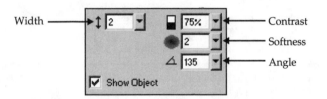

4. Click the triangle to the right of the Width field and drag the slider to select a value. Alternatively, you can enter a value in the field. This is the width of the emboss measured in pixels.

5. Click the triangle to the right of the Contrast field and drag the slider to set a value. Alternatively, you can enter a value between 0 and 100. Specify a high value for a more pronounced emboss effect.

6. Click the triangle to the right of the Softness field and drag the slider to select a value. Alternatively, you can enter a value between 0 and 10. Lower values produce a sharp definition between the background and the emboss; higher values produce a gentle transition between the background and the emboss.

7. Click the triangle to the right of the angle field and drag the dial slider to set the angle of the light source. Alternatively, you can enter a value between 0 and 360.

8. Click the Show Object checkbox (selected by default) to disable the option, and the original object is not shown. This makes it appear as though the background is embossed and not the object.

9. Click anywhere in the workspace to apply the effect. Alternatively, you can press ENTER or RETURN.

You can also emboss an object outward. This effect makes it appear as though the object (or the background, if you disable the Show Object checkbox) is stamped from the inside out.

To create an outer emboss:

1. Select the object you want to emboss.

2. Open the Property inspector.

MODIFYING ARTWORK

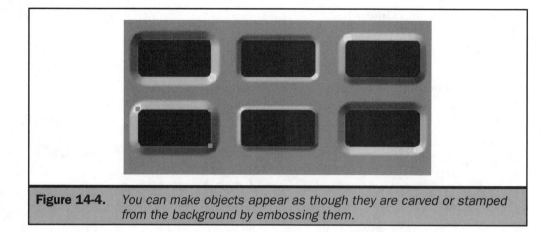

Figure 14-4. *You can make objects appear as though they are carved or stamped from the background by embossing them.*

3. Click the Add Effects button and choose Bevel And Emboss | Raised Emboss.

4. Follow steps 4 through 10 in the previous list of instructions to create an Inset Emboss effect, as the dialog boxes are the same. Figure 14-4 shows two rows of objects. The top row has had the Inset Emboss effect applied; the bottom row has had the Raised Emboss effect applied.

Creating a Drop Shadow

If you want to make an object or bitmap appear as though it's floating off the canvas, you can do so by applying a drop shadow to the object. Although the effect has been used at countless numbers of Web sites, the drop shadow still remains an effective way to accentuate an object on a Web page. When you create a drop shadow in Fireworks, you can specify several parameters such as shadow color, distance from the object, opacity, and more to fine-tune the effect to the document you are creating.

To create a drop shadow:

1. Select the object to which you want to apply the drop shadow. You can apply the effect to vector or bitmap objects.

2. Open the Property inspector.

3. Click the Add Effects button, which looks like a plus sign (+), and choose Shadow And Glow | Drop Shadow.

4. Click the triangle to the right of the Width field and drag the slider to set the width of the shadow. Alternatively, you can enter a value in the field.

5. Click the Shadow color swatch, and choose a color from the pop-up palette.

6. Click the triangle to the right of the Opacity field and drag the slider to set shadow opacity. Alternatively, you can enter a value between 0 and 100. Higher values produce a more pronounced shadow.

7. Click the triangle to the right of the Softness field and drag the slider to select a value. Alternatively, you can enter a value between 0 and 30. Lower values create a sharp definition between the object and the shadow, while higher values gently blend the shadow into the background and make it appear as though the object is being viewed in diffuse or soft lighting.

8. Click the triangle to the right of the Angle field to reveal a dial slider. Click the dial and drag it to set the angle from which the light source is shining on the object. Alternatively, you can enter a value between 0 and 360.

9. Deselect the Knock Out checkbox, and only the shadow will be visible.

10. Click anywhere in the workspace to apply the effect and close the dialog box. Alternatively, you can press ENTER or RETURN.

You can also make it appear as though the shadow is being cast on the object by creating an inner shadow. The Inner Shadow effect has the same parameters as the Drop Shadow effect.

To apply an Inner Shadow to an object:

1. Select the object to which you want to apply the effect.

2. Open the Property inspector.

3. Click the Add Effects button, and choose Shadow And Glow | Inner Shadow.

4. Follow steps 4 through 10 in the previous list of instructions to apply a Drop Shadow effect, as the dialog boxes are identical. The following illustration shows two bitmaps: the bitmap on the left has an inner shadow; the bitmap on the right has a drop shadow.

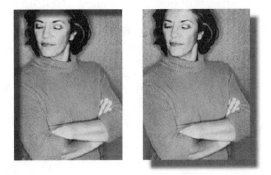

Creating a Glow

Another interesting effect you can apply to objects is a glow. When you add a glow effect to an object or bitmap image, it appears as though a colored halo surrounds the object (Glow) or appears inside the object (Inner Glow). You can choose the width, color, opacity, softness, and offset of the glow.

To create a halo effect:

1. Select the object to which you want to apply the effect.

2. Open the Property inspector.

3. Click the Add Effects button, which looks like a plus sign (+), and choose Shadow And Glow | Glow. The dialog box shown in the following illustration appears.

4. Click the triangle to the right of the Width field and drag the slider to set the glow width as measured in pixels. Alternatively, you can enter a value in the field.

5. Click the Glow color swatch and select a color from the pop-up palette. Alternatively, you can click the swatch, and when your cursor becomes an eyedropper, you can click any object in the document or workspace to sample the object's color. After selecting a color, the swatch refreshes to display the glow color.

6. Click the triangle to the right of the Opacity field and drag the slider to set a value. Higher values produce a more pronounced halo around the object.

7. Click the triangle to the right of the Softness field and drag the slider to specify the value. Alternatively, you can enter a value between 0 and 30. Lower values produce an abrupt transition between object and halo; higher values blend the halo into the background for a more ethereal effect.

8. Click the triangle to the right of the Offset field and drag the slider to set the offset between the halo and the object. Alternatively, you can enter a value in the field. Accept the default offset of 0, and the halo emanates from the border of the object; specify a value, and the halo appears that distance in pixels from the object.

9. Click anywhere in the workspace to apply the effect. Alternatively, you can press ENTER or RETURN.

You can also create a glow that appears inside an object. The settings for the Inner Glow effect are identical to those of the Glow effect.

To create an inner glow:

1. Select the object to which you want to apply the effect.

2. Open the Property inspector.

3. Click the Add Effects button, which looks like a plus sign (+), and choose Shadow And Glow | Inner Glow.

4. Follow steps 4 through 9 in the previous list of instructions to apply the Glow effect, as the dialog boxes are identical. The following illustration shows a bitmap with the Inner Glow effect on the left and the Glow effect on the right.

Note *There are also Blur and Sharpen effects that you can use on bitmaps and objects. Refer to Chapter 6 for instructions on applying the Blur and Sharpen effects.*

Exploring Eye Candy 4000 LE

Eye Candy 4000 (made by Alien Skin Software, www.alienskin.com) is an intoxicating set of filters that you can apply to objects to create special effects. Fireworks ships with Eye Candy 4000 LE, a stripped down version of the filter set, which can be accessed from the Filters menu or applied as a Live Effect. The sections that follow show you how to use the three Eye Candy filters that ship with Fireworks.

Note *If you like the Eye Candy filters that ship with Fireworks, you can purchase the full set by clicking the Buy Now button in any Eye Candy filter's dialog box.*

Using the Bevel Boss Filter

You can use the Eye Candy 4000 LE Bevel Boss filter to create interesting buttons or frames for bitmap images. The bevel effect is similar to the Inner and Outer Bevel effects, but you have more control over the final bevel shape with this filter.

To apply the Bevel Boss Filter to an object:

1. Select the object to which you want to apply the filter.

2. Open the Property inspector.

3. Click the Add Effects button, which looks like a plus sign (+), and choose Eye Candy 4000 LE | Bevel Boss. The dialog box shown in the following illustration appears.

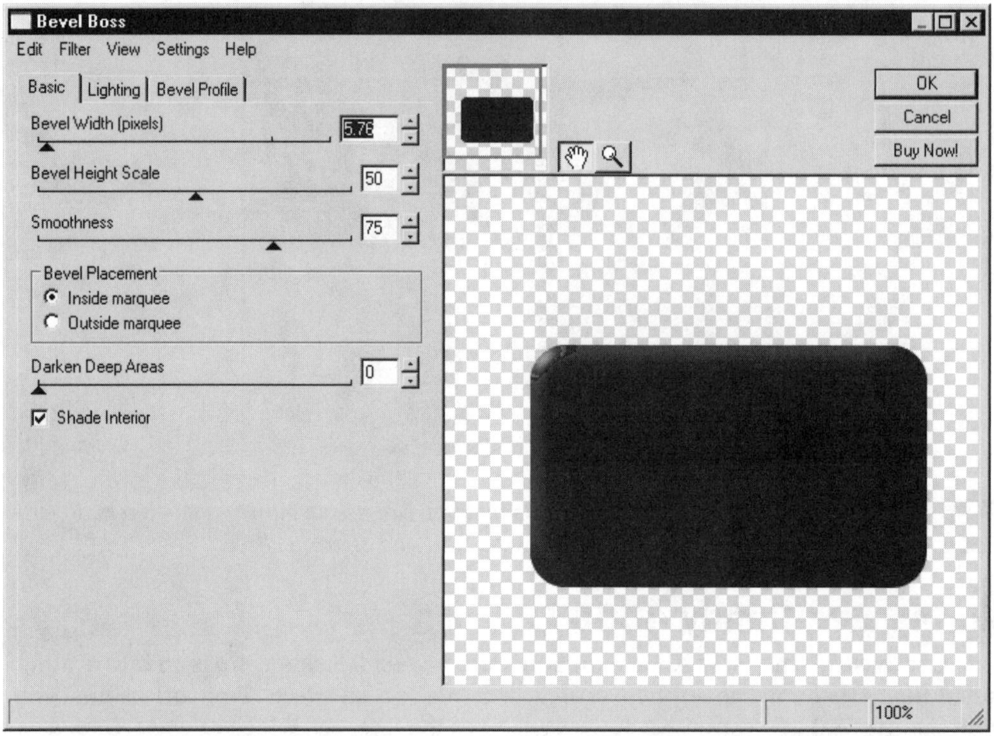

4. Drag the Bevel Width slider to specify the width in pixels of the bevel. Alternatively, you can enter a value in the text field.

5. Drag the Bevel Height Scale slider to set the height of the bevel. Alternatively, you can enter a value between 0 and 100 in the text field. This is a percentage of the value you chose for the width. In other words, if you choose a bevel width of 10 pixels and a bevel height scale of 50, the bevel appears to be 5 pixels high.

6. Drag the Smoothness slider to determine how the bevel blends with the object. Choose a low value, and the bevel will be sharp and angular; choose a high value, and the bevel will form a gentle curve between the background and the object.

7. In the Bevel Placement section, choose Inside Marquee (the default option, which places the bevel inside the object) or Outside Marquee (an option that creates the bevel outside of the object).

8. Drag the Darken Deep Areas slider to set a value. Select a value higher than 0 to create a dark area at the base of the bevel.

9. Deselect the Shade Interior checkbox, which shades the object inside the bevel, and the object will not be shaded.

10. Click the Lighting tab to open the dialog box shown here:

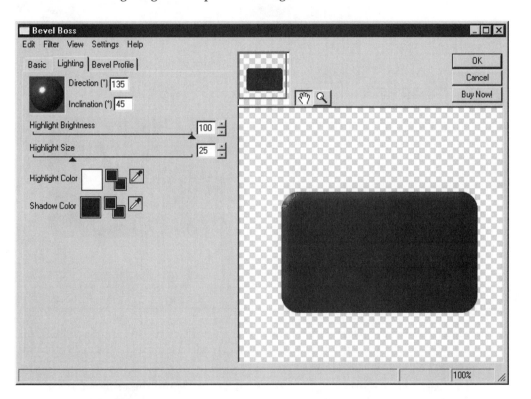

11. Click the white dot on the sphere and drag it to set the direction of the bevel's light source. As you drag, the preview window updates to show the effects of the lighting change.

12. Drag the Highlight Brightness slider to determine how bright the bevel highlight will be. Alternatively, you can enter a value between 0 and 100.

13. Drag the Highlight Size slider to determine the size of the bevel highlight.

14. Accept the default Highlight color and Shadow color or click a swatch to choose a color from the system color picker. Alternatively, you can click the eyedropper and sample a color from within the document by clicking an object.

15. Click the Bevel Profile tab to reveal the dialog box shown here:

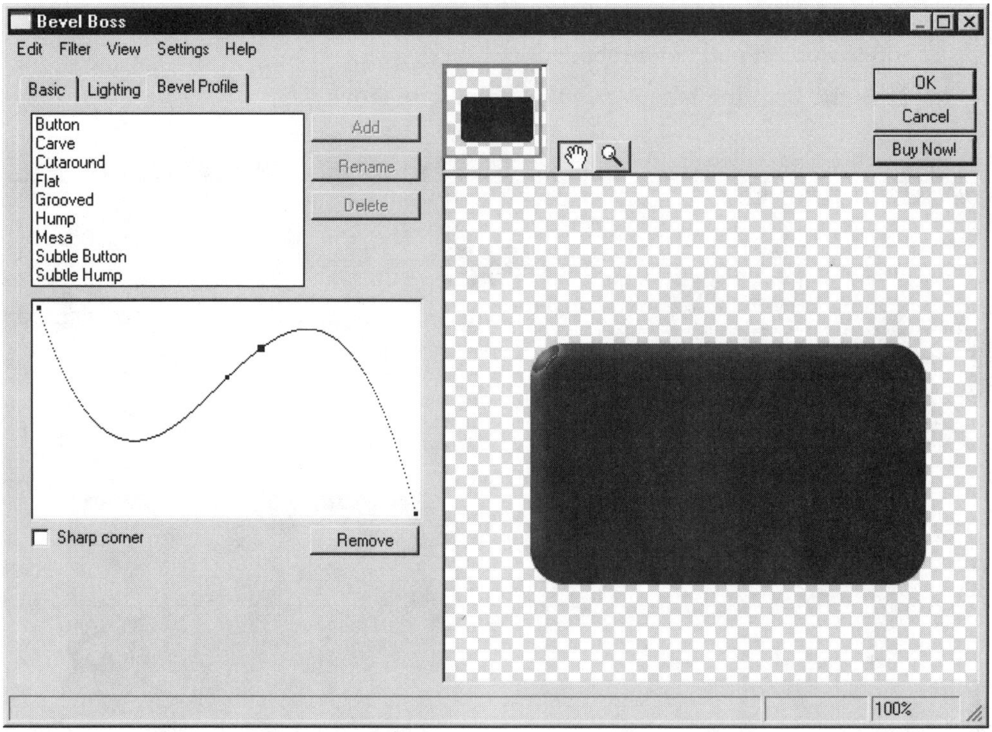

16. Choose one of the presets or click anywhere on the curve to create a point. Drag the point to change the bevel profile. You can add as many points as needed to define the profile of the bevel.

17. To create a sharp corner, select a point on the curve and then select the Sharp Corner checkbox. You can create as many or as few sharp corners as needed to define the profile of the bevel.

18. Click OK to apply the changes.

Tip *The Bevel Boss filter comes with a number of factory presets. After you open the Bevel Boss dialog box, choose Settings and then choose a preset from the drop-down menu.*

Creating a Marble Texture

Another interesting effect you can create with Eye Candy 4000 LE is a marble texture. If you've got an object in a document you want to dress up with a marble texture, you can do it easily with this filter. Apply the bevel boss filter first, add the marble texture, and you've got the basis for a marbleized button.

To apply a marble texture to an object:

1. Select the shape to which you want to apply the texture.

2. Open the Property inspector.

3. Click the Add Effects button, which looks like a plus sign (+), and then choose Eye Candy 4000 LE | Marble. The dialog box shown next appears.

4. Drag the Vein Size slider to set the vein size as measured in pixels. Alternatively, you can enter a value in the text field.

5. Drag the Vein Coverage slider to determine the percentage of the object that will be covered with marble veins. Alternatively, you can enter a value from 0 to 100. Specify a high value for a complex, tightly veined marble texture.

6. Drag the Vein Roughness slider to determine the appearance of the veins. Alternatively, you can enter a value from 0 to 100. Enter a high value for a tightly packed, fine-grained marble; enter a low value for a sparse, rough-grained marble texture.

7. Accept the default Bedrock color and Vein color or click a swatch to choose a different color from the system color picker. Alternatively, you can click the eyedropper and then click any object in the document to sample a color from it.

8. Select the Seamless Tile checkbox if you intend to export the object as a GIF file and use it for a seamless background on a Web page.

Note   *For more information on creating a seamless tile, see Chapter 10.*

9. Click the Random Seed button to generate a random vein pattern. Alternatively, enter a value between 0 and 9999 to generate a vein pattern.

10. Click OK to apply the effect.

Tip   *Alien Skin Software has a number of interesting presets that you can use as marble textures. Follow steps 1 through 3 to open the Marble dialog box, choose Settings, and then select an option from the drop-down menu.*

Adding a Motion Trail

If you want to simulate motion, you can add a motion trail to any vector object or bitmap in your document. The Eye Candy 4000 LE Motion Trail filter creates a blurry tail that emanates from the object to make it appear as though it was frozen in motion by a camera lens.

To add a motion trail to an object:

1. Select the object to which you want to apply the effect.

2. Open the Property inspector.

3. Click the Add Effects button, and choose Eye Candy 4000 LE | Motion Trail. The dialog box shown next appears.

4. Click the dot in the directional dial and drag it to set the angle at which the motion trail appears from the object. Alternatively, you can enter a value between 0 and 360 in the text field.

5. Drag the Length slider to determine the length in pixels of the motion trail.

6. Drag the Overall Opacity slider to determine how much of the background appears through the motion trail. Choose a high value for a noticeable motion trail effect; choose a low value for a subtle motion trail effect.

7. Deselect the Smear Color From Edges checkbox, and the motion trail will be created with only colors from the outside edge of the object.

MODIFYING ARTWORK

8. Deselect the Draw Only Outside Selection checkbox, and the motion trail will begin from inside the object.

9. Click OK to apply the effect. The following illustration shows the effect applied to a bitmap image.

Tip *You can choose from an interesting set of preset motion trails by following steps 1 through 4 above, choosing Settings, and then choosing a preset from the menu.*

Using Alien Skin Splat

Web designers are always trying to think of new and interesting ways to frame bitmaps. Included with Fireworks is another Alien Skin creation called Splat, a filter you can use to create an interesting border for a bitmap. Only one Splat filter is included, but there is a link within the dialog box you can use to purchase the full set of Splat filters.

To create an interesting border around a bitmap image:

1. Select the bitmap to which you want to apply the filter.

2. Click the Add Effects button and then choose Alien Skin Splat LE | Edges. The dialog box shown in the following illustration appears.

3. Drag the Edge Width slider to determine the width of the edge in pixels. Alternatively, you can enter a value in the text field.

4. Drag the Margin slider to determine the width of the margin in pixels. The margin is the area between the edge of the bitmap and the first occurrence of a visible edge.

5. Drag the Feature Size slider to determine the size of the edge features.

6. Click the triangle to the right of the Edge Mode field and choose an option from the drop-down menu. Your choices are Halftone Dots, Halftone Lines, Lumpy, Pixels, Rough, or Torn Paper. If you choose Halftone Dots, Halftone Lines, or Pixels, the directional dial becomes active.

7. If applicable, click and drag the dot in the directional dial to determine from which direction the features are coming. Alternatively, enter a value between 0 and 360.

8. Accept the default edge color of black or click the Color swatch and choose a color from the system color picker. Alternatively, you can click the eyedropper and then click an object in the document to sample its color.

9. Select the Transparent Fill checkbox, and the edge color will be transparent; the bitmap will appear as though it has torn edges.

10. Click the Random Seed button to randomly generate an edge. Alternatively, enter a value between 0 and 9999 in the text field.

11. Click OK to apply the filter. The following illustration shows the Edges filter applied to a bitmap.

Using Third-Party Plug-ins

If you own Photoshop-compatible plug-ins, you can create a link from the directory in which you store the plug-ins to Fireworks. After you create the link, the plug-ins appear on both the Filters menu and the Effects menu.

To link third-party plug-ins to Fireworks:

1. Select any object, and then open the Property inspector.

2. Click the Add Effects button and choose Options | Locate Plugins. The select Photoshop Plug Ins dialog box appears.

3. Click the triangle to the right of the Select field and navigate to the folder in which your plug-ins are stored.

4. After navigating to your plug-ins folder, the folder name appears on the Select button, as shown here:

5. Click the Select button. Fireworks displays a dialog box telling you that Fireworks must be restarted to load the plug-ins.

6. Click Open. The plug-ins will appear on the Filters menu and the Effects menu when you next launch Fireworks. If a filter cannot be edited as a Live Effect, it will only appear on the Filters menu.

Note *As of this writing, there is a compatibility issue with filters designed exclusively for Photoshop 7 and Fireworks MX. If you link Photoshop 7 plug-ins (or for that matter any plug-ins) to Fireworks and they do not work, you can unlink them by choosing Edit | Preferences. Click the Folders tab, and deselect the Photoshop filters option. When you launch Fireworks again, the filters will not be linked.*

Using the Paste Attributes Command

If you create several objects in your document that have a common stroke, fill, and effect applied, you may find that after further editing, you need to change one or more attributes. If the object is a symbol, this is no problem: change the attributes of the symbol, and all instances of the symbol are updated. If, however, the common attributes are not applied to a symbol, each and every object must be changed. Fortunately, when this event occurs, you can change the attributes of one object and then paste the attributes onto other objects in your document. The attributes you can paste are stroke, fill, effects, and text parameters.

To paste attributes to one or more objects in your document:

1. Select the object whose attributes you want to paste to others and choose Edit I Copy.

2. Deselect the object you copied and select one or more objects to which you want to paste the attributes. Remember that in order to add to a selection, you must hold down the SHIFT key while clicking additional objects.

3. Choose Edit I Paste Attributes. The attributes from the copied object are pasted to the selected object(s).

Summary

In this chapter, you learned to create special effects. You learned to work with commands from the Filters menu that modify an object but cannot be edited after the fact. You also learned to use Live Effects, which can be edited at any time after you apply them to an object. Working with effects for vector objects was another topic of discussion. The types of vector effects with which you learned to work are excellent choices for creating interesting button shapes. You learned to color correct bitmaps, as well as apply special effects to bitmaps with the Eye Candy 4000 LE and Alien Skin Splat filters. You also learned to link third-party Photoshop plug-in filters to Fireworks. In Chapter 15, you'll learn to modify objects using preset styles and commands from the Creative menu.

Chapter 15

Modifying Artwork with Styles

In previous chapters, you learned to create special effects by using filters, Live Effects, and by modifying paths with tools and menu commands. These techniques are terrific when you've got time on your hands. However, when you're under the gun to get a project out quickly, you don't have the luxury of time. That doesn't mean you have to create a second rate document. You can quickly create an artistic design for a client by using the Styles panel. Styles are a combination of strokes, fills, and effects that have been saved. When you need to quickly apply an effect to one or more objects in a document, you can choose a style from the Styles panel and then get on with the business of creating the rest of the document.

Just because styles are on a panel, that doesn't mean you're limited to the styles that ship with Fireworks. As you gain experience with the program and come up with an interesting effect, you can save it as a style. Once you save an effect as a style, it stays on the Styles panel until you decide to modify or delete it. Figure 15-1 shows the variety you can achieve by using the Styles panel.

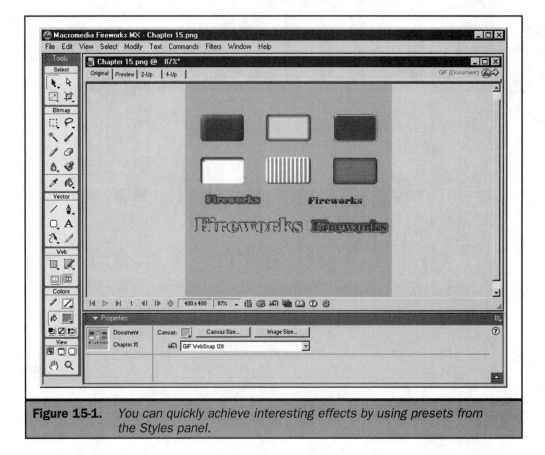

Figure 15-1. *You can quickly achieve interesting effects by using presets from the Styles panel.*

In this chapter, you'll learn to modify objects in your documents by applying styles to them. You'll also learn to create interesting effects by applying commands from the Command menu's Creative submenu.

Exploring Fireworks Styles

A Fireworks style is a preset style that you can use to change the appearance of an object. It has one or more of the following attributes: a fill style, a fill color, a stroke color, a stroke style, an effect, a text font, a text style, a text color, and other text attributes. When one or more attributes are saved as a style, the new style appears as part of the Styles panel. In the sections that follow, you'll learn to apply styles to objects, work with the Styles panel, maintain the Styles panel, import and export styles, and create your own styles.

Using the Styles Panel

Every style that ships with Fireworks is stored in the Styles panel. You use the Styles panel to apply styles to selected objects, as well as to edit, delete, and import styles. The Styles panel consists of several icons for the actual styles, as well as icons for adding and deleting styles. There is also an icon for opening the Styles panel Options menu.

To open the Styles shown in Figure 15-2, choose Window | Styles.

Applying Preset Styles

When you need to quickly apply a stroke, a fill, and an effect to an object, you can do so by selecting the object and then choosing a style from the Styles panel. You can apply the style to one object or to a selection of objects. Other styles are reserved for text objects. Each text object style is designated by the letters ABC on its icon.

To apply a preset style:

1. Select the object(s) or text block to which you want to apply the style.

2. Choose Window | Styles. The Styles panel opens.

3. Click a style icon to apply it to the object(s). The style attributes are applied to the selected object(s).

Using the Styles Panel Options Menu

When you need to edit items in the Styles panel, you can take advantage of the commands on the panel's Options menu. You use the commands on this menu to edit the panel's styles, create new styles, edit styles, and more.

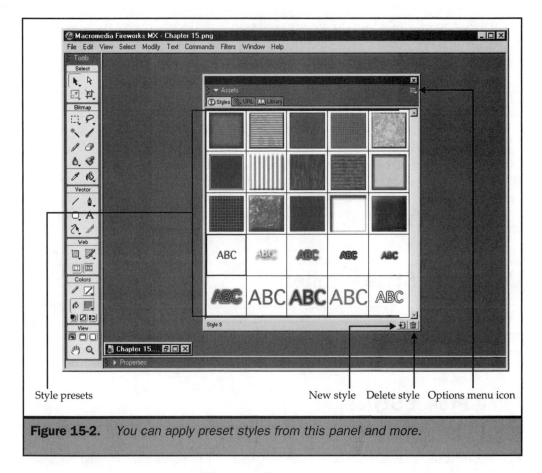

Style presets   New style   Delete style   Options menu icon

Figure 15-2.   *You can apply preset styles from this panel and more.*

To open the Styles panel's Options menu shown next, click the Options menu icon shown previously in Figure 15-2.

New Style...
Edit Style...
Delete Styles

Import Styles...
Export Styles...

Reset Styles

Large Icons

Help
Group Styles with   ▶
Rename Panel Group...
Close Panel Group

Editing Styles

You can edit the items in the Styles panel. When you edit a style, you decide which attributes of the style will be used. For example, if you decide that you like every attribute in a style except for the fill color, you can deselect the fill color attribute.

To edit a style:

1. Choose Window | Styles. The Styles panel opens.

2. Select the style you want to edit.

3. Choose Edit Style from the panel's Options menu. The Edit Style dialog box appears, as shown here:

4. To deselect an attribute, click its checkbox.

5. If desired, enter a different name in the Name field. A style's name appears at the bottom-left corner of the Styles panel when you hold your cursor over a style icon. If you're modifying an existing style to create a new style, give the modified style a unique name, otherwise you'll overwrite the existing style.

6. Click OK to apply the edits to the style and close the dialog box. The style's icon is updated to reflect your edits.

Creating New Styles

As you gain experience with Fireworks, you'll find yourself creating objects with fills, strokes, and effects that you'll want to use in other documents. You can create custom styles by experimenting with various elements, or you can create a new style by saving the attributes from an object you've created in a document.

To create a new style:

1. Create an object using one of the drawing tools or the text tool.

2. Open the Property inspector and choose a fill and stroke. Remember, you can use any of the fill categories and fill types, or you can create your own fill.

3. If the object is a text object, choose the font type, font style, font color, and any other attributes you want to include with the style.

4. Click the Add Effects button and add any desired effects to the object. You can add as many effects as needed for the desired style you are creating.

5. To save the attributes applied to the object as a style, click the Add Effects button and choose Options | Save As Style. The New Style dialog box appears, as shown here:

6. Enter a Name for the style.

7. Click the checkbox of each attribute you want included with the style. By default, any effect you've applied to the object is selected to be included with the style. For example, if the object whose attributes you are saving as a style is a text object, you can click the checkbox of one or more of the text attributes to save them with the style.

8. Click OK to save the style. The style is saved and appears in the Styles panel with the applicable icon.

Tip *If an existing style is perfect except for one attribute, apply the style to an object. Edit the object as needed to create the look you're after and then follow the previous steps to save the attributes as a custom style.*

You can also create a new style from within the Styles panel. This option is useful when you realize you have an object in the document with attributes you want to save as a style.

To create a new style from within the Styles panel:

1. Select the object whose attributes you want to save as a style.

2. Open the Styles panel, as outlined previously.

3. Click the New Style icon at the bottom of the Styles panel, as shown previously in Figure 5-2. The New Style dialog box shown previously opens.

4. Enter a name for the new style.

5. Accept the selected attributes, or deselect any attribute(s) you don't want saved with the style. By default, Fireworks selects every attribute applied to the object.

6. Click OK to save the attributes as a style. The new style's icon appears in the Styles panel.

Deleting Styles

After using Fireworks for a while, you may decide that there are some styles that you will never use. You can delete a style at any time. You cannot restore a custom style; however, you can restore the default Fireworks styles, a task you'll learn in an upcoming section.

To delete a style:

1. Open the Styles panel, as outlined previously.

2. Click the icon of the style you want to delete. If you want to delete more than one style, select one style and then hold down the SHIFT key and click contiguous styles to add them to the selection.

3. Click the Delete Style button, which looks like a trashcan. Alternatively, you can choose Delete Styles from the Options menu. After clicking the button or invoking the command, Fireworks displays a warning dialog asking if it's OK to delete the styles. Click OK to delete the styles, or click Cancel to void the action. After clicking OK, the selected styles are removed from the panel. This action cannot be undone; however, you can reset the panel to the default Fireworks style. You'll learn how to do this in an upcoming section.

Exporting Styles

If you continue to create new styles and add them to the Styles panel, you may find yourself awash in style icons, making it increasingly difficult to select a desired style. In order to keep the Styles panel manageable, you can select several styles and then export them. After you export several styles that you use, but use infrequently, you can delete the exported styles to avoid clutter in the Styles panel. After exporting styles, you can import them whenever needed. If you use Fireworks in different capacities, you can create custom styles for each and then export the custom styles.

To export styles:

1. Open the Styles panel, as outlined previously.

2. Select the styles you want to export.

3. Choose Export Styles from the Options menu. The Save As dialog box appears.

4. Enter a filename for the styles, and navigate to the folder where you want to store the styles. Give the group of styles a unique name that describes the type of styles stored in the file—Button Styles, for example, or perhaps a client's name.

5. Click Save. Fireworks exports the styles as a .stl (style) file.

After saving the styles, you can delete them from the Styles panel to avoid clutter. You can restore the exported styles by following the steps in the next section.

Importing Styles

If you've saved several styles as a .stl file, you can import them whenever you need them. When you import styles, Fireworks appends the styles you are importing to the styles currently contained in the panel.

To import previously saved styles:

1. Open the Styles panel.

2. Choose Import Styles from the Options menu. The Open dialog box appears.

3. Navigate to the folder where you've saved the styles and select it.

4. Click Open. The previously exported styles icons are added to the Styles panel.

If the styles file you are importing contains a large number of styles, you may find it beneficial to delete the default Fireworks styles from the panel before importing a styles file. Doing so will alleviate clutter in the panel and make it easier to select a desired style from the imported file. You can always restore the default styles to the panel by following the steps in the upcoming section.

Resetting Styles

After deleting several preset styles and replacing them with custom styles, you may find that you actually need one or more of the default styles you deleted. You can restore the Styles panel to its factory default. Doing so will result in the loss of any custom styles. However, before restoring the panel, you can save custom styles by exporting them, as outlined previously.

To restore the Styles panel to its default condition:

1. Open the Styles panel, as outlined previously.

2. Choose Reset Styles from the Options menu. Fireworks displays a warning dialog asking you if you want to restore the default styles.

3. Click OK to restore the styles, and the default icons reappear in the panel. Alternatively, you can choose Cancel to void the restore and save any custom styles before choosing the Reset Styles command again.

Changing Icon Size

The default icon size for the Styles panel works well for most Web designers. However, if you have a large monitor and use a desktop size greater than 1024 × 768, you may find the default icon size is a bit small. If this is the case, you can easily increase the icon size using a command from the Styles panel's Options menu.

To increase the size of the style icons:

1. Open the Styles panel.

2. Choose Large Icons. Fireworks increases the size of the icons in the Styles panel.

After increasing the icon size, you can restore the icons to their original size by invoking the command again.

Using Creative Commands

In addition to working with preset styles, you can also change the appearance of items in your documents by using commands from the Creative submenu of the Commands menu. The commands you find in this menu were created by other Fireworks users. The sections that follow show you how to use the preset Creative commands to modify objects in your documents. You'll learn to create your own custom commands in Chapter 20.

Adding Arrowheads to Lines

You can create straight lines with the Line tool and freeform lines with the Pen tool. However, there is no provision for adding an arrowhead to either end of a line you create. Thanks to the creative work of a Fireworks expert, you can add an arrowhead on either end of a line in your document. And you can choose from a wide variety of arrowhead types.

To create a line with an arrowhead:

1. Create a line with either the Pen or Line tool. Choose a stroke style from either the Pencil or Basic stroke category.

2. Choose Commands | Creative | Add Arrowheads. The Add Arrowheads dialog box appears, as shown here:

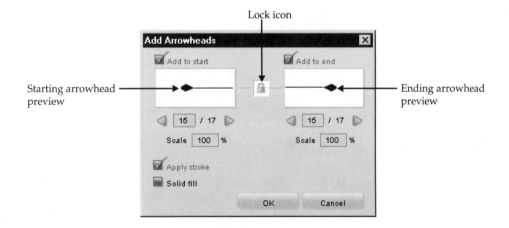

3. Click the Add To Start checkbox to add an arrowhead at the start of the line or the Add To End checkbox to add an arrowhead to the end of the line. Click both checkboxes to add arrowheads at the start and the end of the line. If you choose both sides, both previews are active; otherwise, the preview for the unselected arrowhead is grayed out.

4. If you choose to have an arrowhead on both ends of the line, you can choose different styles for each arrowhead by clicking the lock icon. By default, the starting and ending arrowhead styles are locked.

5. Click the arrows below the preview window to select an arrowhead style. As you click the arrow, the preview window displays the selected arrowhead. If you disable the lock option, you can click the arrows below the other preview window to choose an arrowhead style for the opposite end of the line.

6. To scale the arrowhead, enter a value in the Scale field.

7. To create a solid arrowhead, click the Solid Fill checkbox.

8. Click OK to add the arrowhead(s) to the line.

Adding a Picture Frame to a Document

You can add a creative touch to a Fireworks document by adding a picture frame. This technique works best if the document is a single bitmap image. You can add a frame to the bitmap, export it as a .jpg file, and then import it into another document where you need an image with a picture frame but don't want a frame around the entire document.

To add a picture frame to a document:

1. Choose Commands | Creative | Add Picture Frame. The Add Picture Frame dialog box appears, as shown here:

2. Click the triangle to the right of the Select A Pattern field and choose a pattern for the picture frame.

3. In the Frame Size field, enter a value. This is the width in pixels of the border.

4. Click OK to add the frame. The following illustration shows an example of a picture frame added to a document.

Converting a Bitmap to Grayscale or Sepia Tone

If you wish, you can convert a full-color image to grayscale, or give it an antique look by converting it to sepia tone. Both of these options are available as menu commands.

■ To convert a selected bitmap to grayscale, choose Commands | Creative | Convert To Grayscale.

■ To convert a selected bitmap to sepia tone choose Commands | Creative | Convert To Sepia Tone.

These commands have no parameters. These commands cannot be edited as Live Effects. If you are not happy with the result, choose Edit | Undo immediately after applying the command.

Fading an Image

You can create an artistic effect by fading a bitmap into the document background. You can do this by modifying the object's opacity in the Property inspector; however, this fades the entire image. If you want to fade a portion of the image into the background, you can do so with a menu command.

To fade an image, do the following:

1. Select the image you want to fade.

2. Choose Commands | Creative | Fade Image. The Fade Image dialog box appears, as shown here:

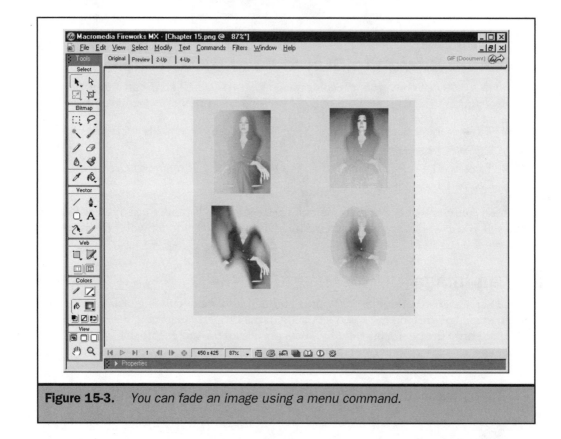

3. Click a preset. Fireworks applies the preset and fades the image. Figure 15-3 shows a few examples of the command at work.

Figure 15-3.   *You can fade an image using a menu command.*

Twisting and Fading an Image

When you apply the Twist and Fade command to an object, you create duplicates of the object, which are rotated, and each duplicate is faded by the amount you specify. You have the option to convert the end product to a symbol, create a random fade and twist, or fade the opacity. This command works on both bitmap and vector objects.

To twist and fade an object:

1. Select the object to which you want to apply the command.

2. Choose Commands | Creative | Twist and Fade. The Twist and Fade dialog box appears, as shown here:

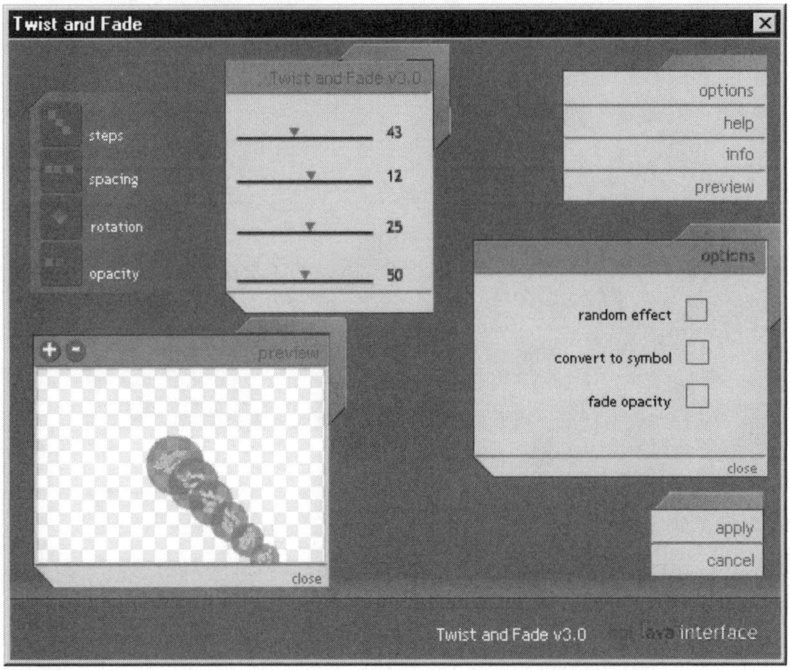

3. Drag the Steps slider to determine the number of duplicates the command creates.

4. Drag the Spacing slider to determine the spacing between each duplicate.

5. Drag the Rotation slider to determine the number of degrees each duplicate is rotated.

6. Drag the Opacity slider to determine the percentage by which the object is faded.

7. Click the Options tab, and you can choose from the following:

- **Random Effect**   Applies a random setting to each parameter.
- **Convert to Symbol**   Converts the end result into a symbol. After applying the command, an instance of the symbol appears on the canvas, and the original is stored in the document Library.
- **Fade Opacity**   Applies the specified opacity to each duplicate creating a cumulative fading effect.

8. Click Apply, and the object is twisted and faded. The following illustration shows an example of the end result after applying the command.

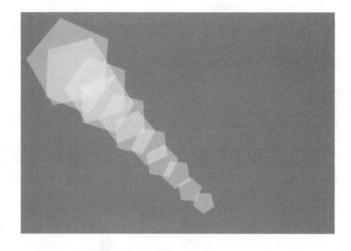

Summary

In this chapter, you learned to modify the appearance of objects in your documents by applying preset styles to them. You learned to apply these styles from the Styles panel. You also learned to create your own styles and maintain the Styles panel. In addition, you discovered how to create special effects by using commands from the Command menu's Creative submenu. In Chapter 16, you'll learn to add interactivity to your documents by creating hotspots and slices.

The
Complete
Reference

Fireworks
MX

Part IV

Creating Animations
and Interactive Web Pages

The
Complete
Reference

Fireworks
MX

Chapter 16

Creating Hotspots and Slices

When you need to add interactivity to a document, Fireworks provides you with the necessary tools to define a hotspot, an area that will be used for a behavior. A *behavior* is an interactive element such as an image swap. You can also slice a document to define areas of a document for a specific export method. For example, if you have bitmaps and vector objects in a document, you can specify the bitmap areas for export as .jpg files and the vector areas for export as .gif files. You can also define an area of the document to include another interactive element known as the pop-up menu.

In this chapter, you'll learn to use Fireworks to create hotspots and slices, and you'll learn to insert them using menu commands and tools. Topics of discussion include assigning uniform resource locators (URLs) to hotspots and slices. You'll learn to work with the URL library, where you can create and maintain URLs you frequently use in your documents. You'll also learn to create an image map.

Understanding Slices and Hotspots

In Fireworks, you have two elements you can use to create an area of interactivity: a hotspot and a slice. A *hotspot* is a specific region in a document. When you create a hotspot, you can assign a behavior to the hotspot. When a user's mouse interacts with the hotspot region, the behavior is executed. The types of behaviors you assign to a hotspot can range from a simple rollover to an image swap. You'll learn how to work with behaviors in Chapter 17.

A *slice* is used to specify an area of the document that will be exported using a different optimization method. For example, if you have bitmap images in a document, as well as vector and text objects, you have a potential conflict. Vector and text objects look best and export with significantly smaller file sizes when exported as .gif files. Bitmap images, on the other hand, look best and export with smaller file sizes when exported as .jpg files. The solution is to create separate slices for the vector, the text, and the bitmap objects, and then use the preferred method of optimization for each slice. You can also assign behaviors to slices; for example, you can have a pop-up menu sprout from a simple rollover button. Figure 16-1 shows a document with one hotspot and several slices.

Creating Hotspots

Like everything else in Fireworks, when you need to add a hotspot to a document, you have more than one method at your disposal to achieve the desired outcome. You can create a hotspot using one of the hotspot tools or by selecting an object and then choosing a menu command. A hotspot is designated by an aqua-colored overlay with a white dot (also known as a *behavior handle*) in the center, as shown in Figure 16-1.

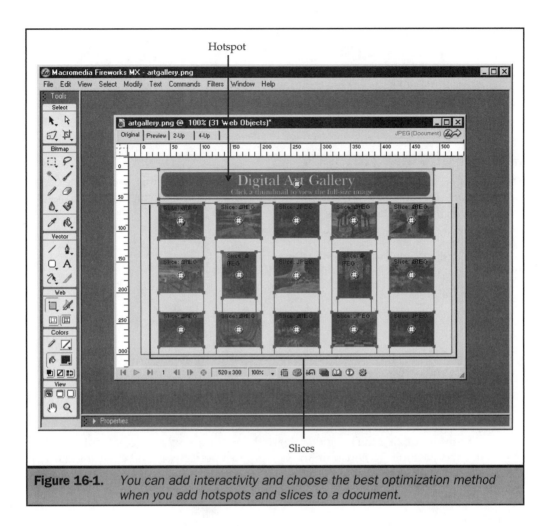

Hotspot

Slices

Figure 16-1.   *You can add interactivity and choose the best optimization method when you add hotspots and slices to a document.*

Creating a Rectangular Hotspot

If you have a rectangular area in a document, such as a block of text that is part of a bitmap, you can easily create a hotspot that encompasses the text block. You accomplish this task using the Rectangle Hotspot tool.

To create a rectangular hotspot, follow these steps:

1. Select the Rectangle Hotspot tool, shown here:

2. Click the spot on canvas where you want the hotspot to begin and then drag down and across. As you drag the tool, a bounding box appears, giving you a preview of the hotspot's size and shape. To move the hotspot as you're sizing it, press the SPACEBAR. To constrain the hotspot to a square, hold down the SHIFT key while using the Rectangle Hotspot tool.

3. Release the mouse button when the hotspot is the desired size.

Creating a Circular Hotspot

You can define a circular area of a document as a hotspot. To do this, you use the Circle Hotspot tool. You can create an elliptical hotspot with the tool or constrain the tool to create a perfectly round hotspot.

To create a circular hotspot, follow these steps:

1. Select the Circle Hotspot tool, shown here:

2. Click the spot on canvas where you want the hotspot to begin, and then drag down and across. As you drag the tool, a circular bounding box previews the size and position of the hotspot.

3. To move the hotspot to a different position as you're sizing it, press the SPACEBAR. As long as the SPACEBAR is pressed, the object moves instead of increasing in size. To continue sizing the hotspot, release the SPACEBAR when the hotspot is in the desired position. To constrain the hotspot to a perfectly round circle, hold down the SHIFT key while using the Circle Hotspot tool.

4. Release the mouse button when the hotspot is the desired size.

Note *If the hotspot is not in the correct position, you can move it with the Pointer tool, or you can specify a position by entering coordinates in the X and Y fields of the Property inspector.*

Creating a Polygonal Hotspot

If you have an oddly shaped area that you need to define as a hotspot, you can do so with the Polygon Hotspot tool. When you use the Polygon Hotspot tool, you define the individual points that the shape will comprise. For example, if you needed to create a hotspot the shape of a person's face in a bitmap, you can easily do so with this tool.

To create an irregularly shaped hotspot, follow these steps:

1. Select the Polygon Hotspot tool, shown here:

2. Click the spot on canvas where you want the hotspot to begin.

3. Click to define the second point of the irregularly shaped hotspot. A line joins the two points.

4. Click to define the other points of the hotspot. A line forms between the new point and the last point created. The shape is also represented by a light blue overlay. You can see the overlay in this illustration.

5. When the hotspot is the desired shape, click the first point to close the path and finish creating the hotspot.

If a point of a polygonal hotspot is not in the right position, select the Subselection tool, and then click and drag the point to a new position.

Note

You can neither add points to a polygonal hotspot nor convert a point to a curve point.

Converting an Object to a Hotspot

You can convert any object in your document to a hotspot. This is an ideal solution if you need to define a hotspot for a complex closed path created with the Pen tool. You also convert an object into a hotspot when you want to create interactivity for a bitmap.

To convert an object to a hotspot:

1. Select the object whose area you want to convert to a hotspot.

2. Choose Edit | Insert | Hotspot. A light blue overlay with a white dot in the center appears over the object.

You can also convert several objects into a hotspot. When you select more than one object and then choose the Insert Hotspot command, the warning dialog in the following illustration appears, asking you if you want to create one hotspot or multiple hotspots. Click Single, and Fireworks creates one hotspot that encompasses the area of the selected objects; click Multiple, and Fireworks creates a single hotspot for each selected object.

| Tip | *If you have an irregularly shaped area in a bitmap that you want to define as a hotspot, create a pixel selection using one of the Marquee tools, the Lasso tool, or the Magic Wand tool. Cut the selection, and then paste it. With the pixels still selected, choose Edit | Insert | Hotspot. A light blue overlay appears over the pixel selection.* |

Assigning a Link to a Hotspot

After you create a hotspot, you can create a hyperlink. This is one of the steps involved in creating an image map. You can also use a hotspot to create a hyperlink for a block of text.

To assign a link to a hotspot, do the following:

1. Select the hotspot to which you want to assign a link.

2. Open the Property inspector.

3. In the Link field, enter the URL to which you want the hotspot to link. If the URL is within the same Web site as the document, you need only enter the relative path (for example, portfolio.htm). If the URL is at an external Web site, you must enter the absolute path (for example, http://www.dasdesigns.net/portfolio.htm).

4. In the Alt field, enter any alternate text that you want to appear while the image associated with hotspot is downloading. Alternate text is also displayed if an image fails to download. On newer browsers, Alt Text appears as a tooltip when a user's mouse passes over the hotspot.

5. Click the triangle to the right of the Target field, and choose one of the following:

- ■ **Blank** Opens the link in a new Web browser window.
- ■ **Self** Opens the link in the same Web browser window.
- ■ **Parent** Opens the link in the parent frameset or in the frame associated with the link. If the specified URL is not in a nested frame, the link appears in a full browser window.
- ■ **Top** Loads the URL in a full browser window, removing any frames in which the exported document may be nested.

Editing a Hotspot

After you create a hotspot, you can modify it as needed to suit the document you are working on. You can move it to a new location using the Pointer tool. You can resize it using the Scale tool. You can also resize and reposition the hotspot using the Property inspector or the Info panel. You can distort a selected hotspot using the Skew or Distort tool.

You can also change a hotspot's basic shape using the Property inspector. To change a hotspot's shape, follow these steps:

1. Select the hotspot.

2. Open the Property inspector. When you select a hotspot and open the Property inspector, you can modify the parameters shown here:

3. Click the triangle to the right of the Shape menu and choose one of the following: Circle, Rectangle, or Polygon.

4. To change the overlay color of the hotspot, click the color swatch to the right of the Type field and choose a color from the pop-up palette.

Note *If you convert a rectangular or circular hotspot to a polygon, you can use the Subselection tool to edit individual points of the hotspot, whereas you cannot edit points of a circular or rectangular shaped hotspot.*

Naming a Hotspot

If you create a document with a lot of hotspots, you may find it beneficial to give each hotspot a unique name. This will help you ascertain exactly what the hotspot does. A hotspot's name is displayed in the Property inspector and next to the hotspot's thumbnail in the Web layer of the Layers panel.

To name a hotspot:

1. Create a hotspot, as outlined previously, or select a hotspot from within the document.

2. Open the Property inspector.

3. Enter a name for the hotspot in the blank text field below the word Hotspot, and then press ENTER or RETURN. The hotspot is now christened and can be easily identified in the Web Layer of the Layers panel.

If you prefer, you can name a hotspot in the Layers panel by double-clicking the hotspot's current name and entering a new one.

Creating an Image Map

When you import an image into Fireworks and you need to make one or more areas of it interactive, you create a hotspot for the areas, and then assign URLs to the hotspots. This is often an ideal way to link to URLs, especially if your intended audience is likely to be accessing your design using older browsers. Many older browsers cannot recognize the JavaScript associated with complex behaviors such as mouse rollovers and image swaps. By creating an image map, you can make an area of the document interactive, without taxing the resources of a user's computer or Web browser due to the additional HTML and JavaScript code that Fireworks generates when documents are exported with slices and complex behaviors. Create an image map when the document will be exported as a single image.

To create an image map:

1. Open the graphic you want to convert to an image map. Alternatively, you can create the graphics and import the bitmaps you will use with the image map.

2. Use the Hotspot tools to create a hotspot for each area of the document you want to be interactive.

3. Assign URLs to each hotspot, as outlined previously.

4. Optimize the document and then export it as a single image with HTML.

Note   *For information on optimizing and exporting a document, see Chapter 21.*

Slicing a Document

When you have a document that combines vector, text, and bitmaps, you have a potpourri of objects that respond differently depending on how you optimize them. For example, if you have a bitmap image with a text label, the bitmap requires JPEG optimization to look its best, but the text will not look good, especially if you use high levels of compression with the bitmap. On the other hand, the text will look quite lovely if you export it using Fireworks' default GIF optimization, but the bitmap will suffer. The solution is to slice the document and export the text objects as .gif files and the bitmap objects as .jpg files.

Creating a Slice

When you decide to slice a document, there are a couple of ways you can do it. You can use a tool or a menu command to create a slice. When you create a slice, it is indicated as a green overlay with a white dot in the center and red borders. The red borders are slice guides. The slice is exported from the document as a separate image file. After you create the slice, you choose an optimization method for the slice. In the following sections, you'll learn to create and edit slices.

Using the Slice Tool

You can use the Slice tool to create a rectangular slice. When you create a slice, you can snap the slice to the border of the canvas or to the border of other slices.

To create a slice:

1. Select the Slice tool, shown here:

2. Click the spot on the canvas where you want to begin the slice and then drag down and across. As you drag the tool, a bounding box appears, giving you a preview of the slice's size and position.

3. To move the slice while you're sizing it, hold down the SPACEBAR. When the slice is in the desired position, release the SPACEBAR to continue sizing the slice. To constrain the slice to a square, hold down the Shift key while dragging the tool on the canvas.

4. Release the mouse button when the slice is the desired size. The new slice is indicated by a green overlay with a white dot in the center. The slice also appears on the Web Layer in the Layers panel.

Using the Polygon Slice Tool

You can also create an irregularly shaped slice to follow the contours of an object such as an irregularly shaped logo. You use the Polygon Slice tool for this task. With this tool, you have pinpoint control over where you place each point that will make up the slice.

To create an irregularly shaped slice:

1. Select the Polygon Slice tool, shown here:

2. Click a spot on the canvas to begin creating the slice.

3. Click a second spot to begin defining the shape of the slice. Fireworks creates a straight line between the points.

4. Click to add additional points. As you create additional points, Fireworks joins points with a line segment, and the green overlay starts taking shape, giving you a preview of the slice's shape.

5. Continue adding points to further define the slice's shape.

6. To close the slice's path, click the first point. The following illustration shows a slice created with the Polygon Slice tool.

Inserting a Slice

If you have a rectangular-shaped object in your document such as a bitmap image and you want to create a slice for it, you can do so with a menu command. This is an ideal way to define a separate object for export.

To create a slice for an object in your document:

1. Select the object.

2. Choose Edit | Insert | Slice. Fireworks creates a rectangular slice to encompass the object. The slice appears in the Web layer of the Layers panel.

When you create a shape by inserting a slice, Fireworks creates a rectangular shape that conforms to the outer boundary of a shape. If you need to insert a slice that conforms to a nonrectangular object, follow these steps:

1. Select the irregularly shaped object for which you want to create a slice.

2. Choose Edit | Insert | Hotspot. Fireworks creates a hotspot that conforms to the object's shape.

3. Select the hotspot and choose Edit | Insert | Slice. Fireworks creates a slice that conforms to the shape of the hotspot.

You can choose more than one object and then create slices. When you do so, Fireworks gives you the option of creating a single slice that covers the border of all selected objects or multiple slices that conform to the size of each object.

To create slices for multiple objects:

1. Select the objects for which you want to create slices.

2. Choose Edit | Insert | Slice. Fireworks displays a dialog box asking if you want to create one slice or multiple slices for the selected objects. Click Single, and Fireworks creates a slice that includes the outermost border of all objects; click Multiple, and Fireworks creates a slice for each object.

Creating an HTML Slice

There will be times when you create a Fireworks document and want to use HTML text rather than create text in Fireworks and export the text object as a bitmap. You can easily create a slice for HTML text and then create and edit it within Fireworks. When you export the document, Fireworks creates the HTML to create the text in a Web browser. However, you cannot format the text in Fireworks because that is handled by the Web browser.

To create an HTML slice:

1. Select the Slice tool and create a slice, as outlined previously. If you have existing slices in the document, you can begin your HTML slice at the border (the red slice guide) of another slice, and Fireworks snaps the new slice to the border of the old.

2. Click the arrow to the left of the word Properties. The Property inspector opens.

3. Click the triangle to the right of the Type field and choose HTML from the menu. The Property inspector is reconfigured, as shown here:

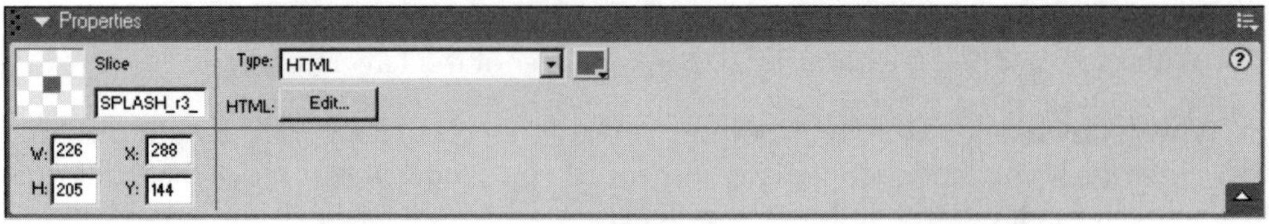

4. Click the Edit button. The Edit HTML Slice editor opens, as shown here:

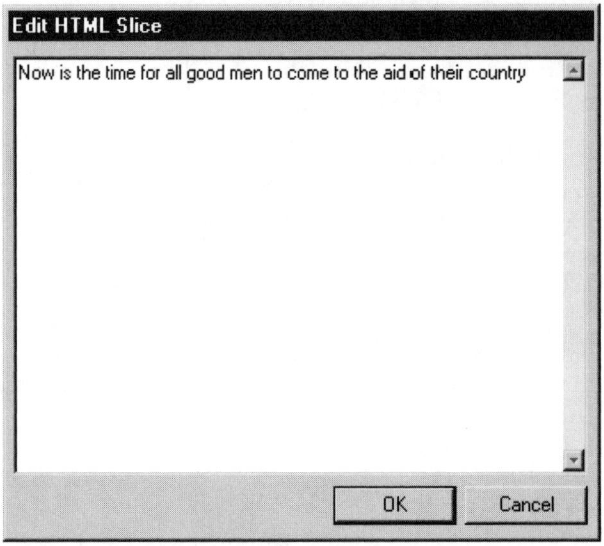

5. Enter the text you want to appear in the slice, and then click OK.

When you export the document, Fireworks creates the HTML text. Creating text in the Edit HTML Slice text editor is optional. If you export the document without creating text, Fireworks creates a table cell with no data. If you plan to further edit the document in an HTML editor, you can enter your text there.

Optimizing a Slice

After you create the slices for your document, you need to choose an optimization method. You can choose one of the preset optimization methods for a slice by opening the Property inspector and choosing a preset, as shown in the following illustration.

Alternatively, you can optimize a slice by opening the Optimize panel and modifying the export options to suit the slice.

Naming a Slice

When you slice a document and then export the document, an image is created for each slice. The default name of each slice corresponds to the row and column where the slice appears in the HTML table Fireworks creates. If you edit the HTML document in an HTML editor, the default name for a slice makes it difficult to understand what it does, especially when you're editing raw code. You can make your life as a Web designer a lot easier if you get in the habit of naming each slice.

To name a slice:

1. Create a slice, as outlined previously, or select a slice you've already created.

2. Open the Property inspector.

3. In the Text field below the word Slice, enter a name for the slice. Choose a descriptive name that will make sense to you when you're editing line after line of HTML code. As an example, choose a name such as About if you're naming a slice for a button that links to the About section of a Web site.

4. Press ENTER or RETURN. The slice's new name is displayed in the Property inspector beside its thumbnail in the Web layer of the Layers panel and at the upper-left border of the actual slice.

When you export the document, the image is exported with the same name as the slice that created it. For example, if you create a document and create a separate slice for the CEO's picture, label the slice CEO. When you export the document, the image associated with the slice is exported with the name CEO, followed by the file extension for the export format you select.

Tip   *You can also name a slice in the Layers panel. Double-click the slice's current name and then enter a new one.*

Editing Slices

After you create one or more slices in a document, you can edit them. You can edit a slice by dragging the red guides at a slice's border. When you drag the guides, adjacent slices are resized to reflect the new size of the slice you are editing. However, when you move the guides for an irregularly shaped slice, the guides for the other slices are not changed, and you may have overlapping slices. If you select multiple slices and drag a common guide, all slices are resized.

To resize a slice:

1. Select the Pointer or Subselection tool and move it over a slice guide.

2. When your cursor icon changes to the one shown here, click the guide and drag it to the desired position.

You can delete a slice guide when it is no longer needed by selecting it with the Pointer or Subselection tool and then dragging it beyond the boundary of the canvas.

You can also edit a slice by using the Pointer, Subselection, Scale, Skew, or Distort tool. You cannot distort or skew a rectangular slice; however, you can use these tools on a slice created with the Polygon Slice tool.

Changing Slice Properties

The default green overlay color and red slice guides are well suited for most documents. However, if you are working on a document where the overlay and guide colors make it difficult to spot slices and guides, you can easily change them.

To change a slice's overlay color:

1. Select the slice on the canvas or from within the Layers panel.

2. Open the Property inspector.

3. Click the color swatch to the right of the Type field and select a color from the pop-up palette.

You cannot globally change the colors of all slices in the document or alter the default color of the overlay created by the Slice tools and command; however, you can change the overlay color of all slices in a document by selecting them all from within the Web layer of the Layers panel. After selecting the slices, repeat steps 2 and 3 from the previous instructions.

To change the slice guide color:

1. Choose View | Guides | Edit Guides. The Guides dialog box appears, as shown here:

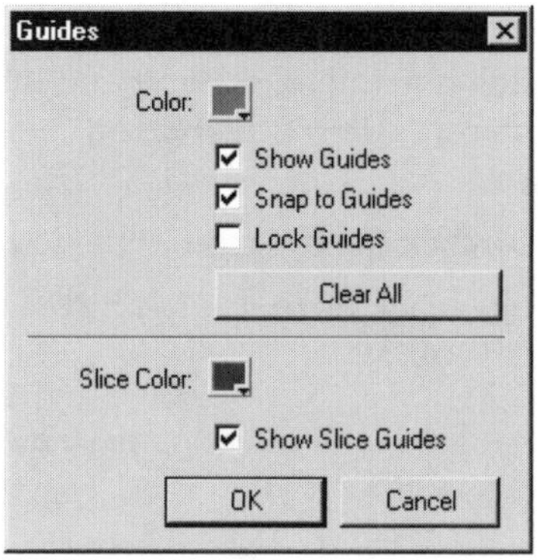

2. Click the Slice Color swatch, and then choose a color from the pop-up palette.

Editing Slices from the Layers Panel

When you have a document with several slices, selecting an individual slice can be troublesome. You can however, select slices from within the Layers panel. Every slice or hotspot that you create is stored in the Web Layer of the Layers panel. A typical Web Layer is shown here:

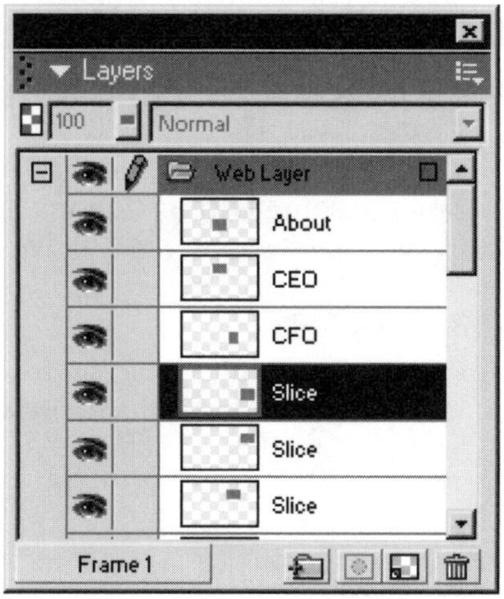

As you can see in the preceding illustration, the Web Layer has a thumbnail image of each slice in the document. There's another good reason for naming slices—it makes it easier to select them in the Layers panel. After opening the Layers panel, you can perform the following edits on a slice:

■ To select a slice, click its thumbnail.

■ To delete a slice from the document, select it and then click the Delete icon, which looks like a trash can. Alternatively, you can select the slice in the Layers panel and then press DELETE.

■ To hide a selected slide, click the eye icon to the left of the slice's title.

■ To rename a slice, double-click its title, enter a new name in the text field, and then press ENTER or RETURN.

You can also show or hide all slices in the document by clicking the toolbox icons shown here:

Hide slices and hotspots

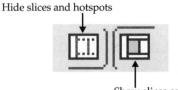

Show slices and hotspots

Managing Document Links with the URL Library

When you assign a URL for a hotspot or slice, you can enter it manually by typing it in the Link field in the Property inspector. This is fine if you're only using a URL once in a document. However, when you create several documents that have navigation links to the same URL, retyping the same URL is tedious, time consuming, and counterproductive. Fortunately, you have a tool to minimize this drudgery: the URL Library.

The URL Library is part of the Assets panel group and can be found with the Styles and Library panels. By default, the Assets panel group is docked in the panel window on the right side of the interface. When you first launch Fireworks, the URL Library is empty; you can populate it with frequently used URLs. When a URL appears in the URL Library, it is also listed on any drop-down menu in any Link field (for example, the Link field that appears in the Property inspector when you select a hotspot or slice). When a URL is listed on a Link menu, you simply select the URL instead of typing it. The following illustration shows the Fireworks URL Library containing a few URLs.

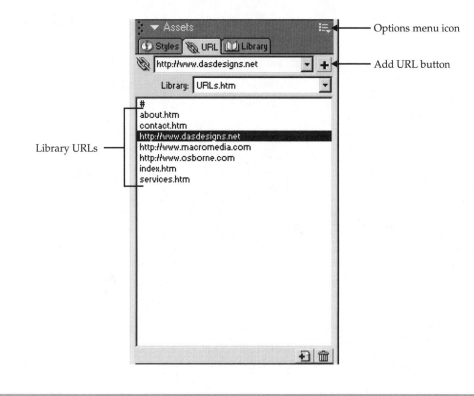

Creating a URL Library

You can store all of your frequently used URLs in a single library, or you can create multiple libraries. The default Fireworks URL Library is named URL.htm. It makes good sense to store your frequently used URLs in this library. If you do work for a specific client who has multiple sites with lots of URLs, you can create an additional library for that client.

Many of the commands needed to maintain a single URL library or multiple URL libraries are contained in the URL Library options menu. To open this menu, shown in the following illustration, click the Options menu icon shown in the previous illustration.

```
Add Used URLs to Library
Clear Unused URLs

Add URL...
Edit URL...
Delete URL

New URL Library...
Import URLs...
Export URLs...

Help
Group URL with            ▶
Rename Panel Group...
Close Panel Group
```

Adding URLs to a Library

Whether you work with the default Fireworks URL library or create one of your own, the first step is to add the frequently used URLs to the library. When you enter a URL in a library, you can enter either a relative path or an absolute path.

To add a URL to the URL Library:

1. In the panel window on the right side of the interface, click the arrow to the left of the word Assets and then click the URL tab.

2. Enter a URL in the Current URL field shown here:

Link field 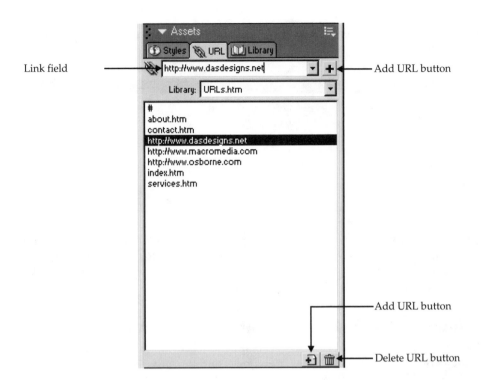 Add URL button

Add URL button

Delete URL button

3. Click the Add URL button, which looks like a plus sign (+). The URL is added
   to the library and then appears on the list.

You can also add a URL from the URL Library Options menu. To do so, choose
Add URL from the Options menu, and the New URL dialog box appears, as shown in the
following illustration. Notice that the dialog box has a much larger area for entering
the URL than does the Link field. Choosing this method to add a URL to the library

comes in handy when you need to enter a long URL. You can also open this dialog box by clicking the Add URL button at the bottom of the URL Library.

New URL	☒
URL:	
http://www.dasdesigns.net/portfolio.htm	
	OK Cancel

Tip   *You can quickly populate the URL Library by opening a previously saved .png document with URL links and then choosing Add Used URLs from the URL Library's Options menu. You can also use this command to add URLs you used for links in the current document but did not add to the URL Library.*

Assigning a URL to a Web Object and the Library

When you create the first Web objects (hotspots or slices) in your documents, you can simultaneously assign a URL to the Web object and the URL Library. Using this option for adding a URL to the Library is time efficient because you handle two tasks in one fell swoop.

To assign a URL to a Web object and the URL Library at the same time:

1. Select the object to which you want to assign the URL.

2. In the panel window on the left side of the workspace, click the arrow to the left of the word Assets and then click the URL tab.

3. To enter the URL, do one of the following:

   ■ Enter the URL in the Current URL field.

   ■ Choose Add URL from the URL Library's Options menu and enter either the relative or the absolute URL in the New URL dialog box shown previously.

   ■ Click the Add URL button at the bottom of the URL Library and enter the URL in the New URL dialog box.

After choosing one of these methods, the URL is assigned to the Web object and is also added to the URL Library.

Deleting URLs

When you no longer have a need for a URL, you can delete it from the Library. Deleting unused URLs makes it easier for you to find a URL in the library.

To delete a URL from the URL Library:

1. In the panel window on the right side of the workspace, click the arrow to the left of the word Assets and then click the URL tab.

2. Select the URL you want to delete, and then click the Delete URL button, which looks like a trashcan. Alternatively, you can choose Delete URL from the URL Library Options menu.

Clearing Unused URLs

Another maintenance task you can perform is ridding the URL Library of unused URLs. You do this by choosing a command from the URL Library's Options menu.

To clear all unused URLs from the URL Library, choose Clear Unused URLs from the Options menu.

Saving a URL Library

When you add a group of URLs for a specific project or client to the URL Library, you can export them as a separate Library. When you export the URLs in the Library, you create an HTML document.

To export all URLs in the URL Library:

1. In the panel window on the right side of the interface, click the arrow to the left of the word Assets and then click the URL tab.

2. From the URL Library Options menu, choose Export URLs. The Save As dialog box appears.

3. Enter a filename for the URLs you're exporting. Choose a logical name, such as the client's name or the type of project for which you'll use the URLs.

4. Navigate to the folder where you store your Web site assets, and then click Save. The exported URLs are saved as an HTML file.

Importing URLs

You can import URLs that you have previously exported. You can also import URLs from a previously created HTML document. When you import URLs from a previously created HTML document, Fireworks scans the entire document for URLs and adds them to the library. This is a quick and easy method for building a URL Library when you first use Fireworks.

To import URLs from a previously saved file:

1. In the panel window on the right side of the interface, click the arrow to the left of the word Assets and then click the URL tab.

2. Choose Import URLs from the Options menu. The Open dialog box appears.

3. Navigate to the folder that contains the HTML file with the URLs you want to import.

4. Select the file and click Open. The imported URLs append to the URLs currently in the library.

Creating a New URL Library

You can create a new URL Library when you want to store URLs for a particular project or client. When you create a new URL Library, you start with a blank slate. You can populate the URL Library by importing URLs from previously saved HTML documents or by using any of the methods previously discussed in this chapter for adding a URL to the new library.

To create a new URL Library, do the following:

1. In the panel window on the right side of the interface, click the arrow to the left of the word Assets and then click the URL tab.

2. From the Options menu, choose New URL Library. The New URL Library dialog box appears.

3. Enter a name for the URL Library and then click OK. The new URL Library is added to the Library menu in the URL Library. You can now populate the library with URLs.

Loading an Existing URL Library

You can load a saved URL Library at any time. When you load a URL Library, the URLs from the previous library are replaced.

To load a different URL Library:

1. In the panel window on the right side of the interface, click the arrow to the left of the word Assets and then click the URL tab.

2. Click the triangle to the right of the Current URL Library field and choose a library from the drop-down menu shown in the following illustration.

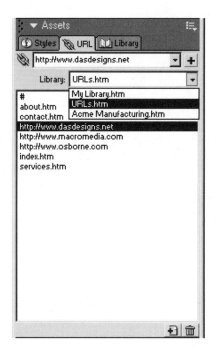

CREATING ANIMATIONS
AND INTERACTIVE
WEB PAGES

Note *All URL Libraries you create are stored in the Fireworks MX URL Libraries folder. The exact location of the folder varies depending on the operating system you use. You can remove a URL Library from the URL Library list by deleting it from the URL Libraries folder.*

Summary

In this chapter, you learned to create areas of interactivity in your documents by creating hotspots. You learned to create rectangular, round, and polygonal hotspots, as well as to create a hotspot that encompasses the area of an object in the document. You also learned to create slices. When you slice a document, you create an area that is exported as a separate image. You can choose the export option best suited to the slice's contents. Finally, you learned how to work with the URL library. You can store frequently used URLs in the URL Library to streamline your workflow and spare yourself the drudgery of entering the same URL over and over when creating multiple documents for a Web site. In Chapter 17 you'll learn to create buttons, pop-up menus and other interactive elements to add interest to your designs.

Chapter 17

Creating Interactive Graphics for the Web

When you create a Fireworks document for the Web, you can add much more than just pretty graphics and anti-aliased text. When you create a design for the Web, you need navigation devices such as buttons and navigation bars. To make your site stand out from the hundreds of thousands of HTML pages already on the Web, you need to add other touches, such as image rollovers, pop-up menus, messages on the status bar, and more. Although these effects are already commonplace, with a bit of imagination and artistic talent you can use them to create an effective design that has your own personal touch.

In this chapter, you'll learn to add interactive elements to your designs. You'll learn to use the Fireworks button editor to quickly create an interesting button. You'll also learn to create an entire navigation bar by creating a single button and then changing duplicates of the button to display a different text message and link to a different URL. And if a standard navigation bar doesn't give you enough room for all your menu choices, you can add a pop-up menu to any button.

Creating Buttons

Integral to every Web site is the time-honored button. You use buttons to navigate to other Web sites or to other pages within the site for which you are creating a document. When you create a button, you can let your imagination run rampant and use bitmaps, vector objects you create in Fireworks, imported vector objects, text objects, and more to create the graphics for a button. You can create a simple rollover button that displays a different graphic when the user's mouse rolls over the button target area, or you can create a sophisticated multi-state rollover button that displays a different graphic when the user's mouse is off the button, over the button, and clicking the button. If the button graphic is small, you can define the target area to give the user a bigger target.

When you create a button, you are creating a symbol. You can create instances of the button symbol and change the text and URL to suit the page that loads when the button is clicked. A button is defined as a slice area. When you export the document, the button is exported as a minimum of two images, one for the Up state and one for the Over state. To make editing after the fact easier, you can name the button in the Property inspector. When you name the button, the exported images reflect the name you selected, making it easier to identify each button when you edit the document in an HTML editor.

Creating a Button Symbol

When you create a button in Fireworks, it is a rollover button; you use a minimum of two button states: Up and Over. The button states determine what graphic users see when their mouse interacts with a button. When you create a simple button with two states, users see two different graphics, one in the button's default state as it first loads into a browser, and a second graphic when users roll their mouse over a button. In all you can use up to four button states. The available button states are

- **Up** The default state of the button when the page first loads into a user's browser.
- **Over** When a user's mouse passes over the button. You can create a different graphic for this state to alert users that something will happen when the button is clicked.
- **Down** When users click their mouse over a button. The graphic in this state signifies that the button has successfully been clicked. When used on a multi-state navigation bar, this state is displayed when the linked page loads, alerting users that the button is the link to the page they are currently viewing.
- **Over While Down** The graphic that is displayed when a user's mouse rolls over a button in the Down state. This is used on a multi-state navigation bar to alert users that the button is for the page they are currently viewing.

You create the graphics for each of these states using the Button Editor, as outlined in the next section.

Using the Button Editor

You manipulate the graphics for your button using the Button Editor. The editor has a tab for each button state mentioned in the previous section, as well as a tab called Active Area. The active area designates the target area of the button. The result of your work in the Button Editor is revealed when you export the document; Fireworks creates a graphic for each button state you choose, as well as the JavaScript to display the proper button state when users interact with the button.

The simplest button you can create is a two-state button. When you create this button, you use a graphic for the Up and Over states. To create a two-state rollover button:

1. Choose Edit | Insert | New Button. The Button Editor appears, as shown here:

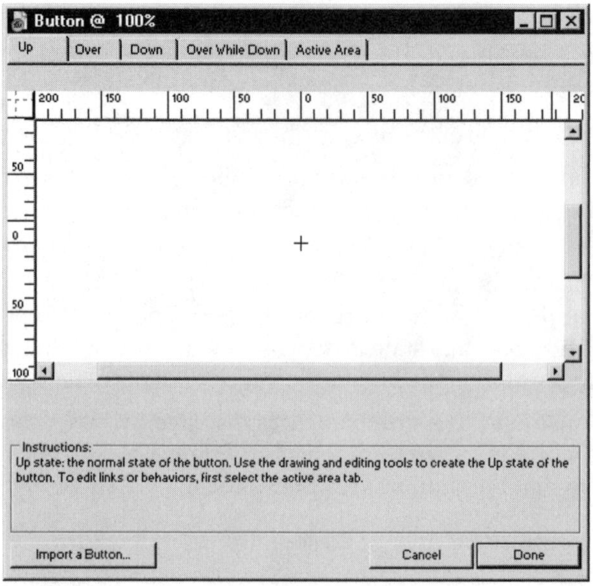

2. Create or import a graphic for the Up state. If desired, you can add text that describes what the button does. You can also apply an Effect to the button shape. For example, if you begin with a short, wide, rounded rectangle and then use

the Inner Bevel effect, you can create your own facsimile of the pill button shape, as shown here:

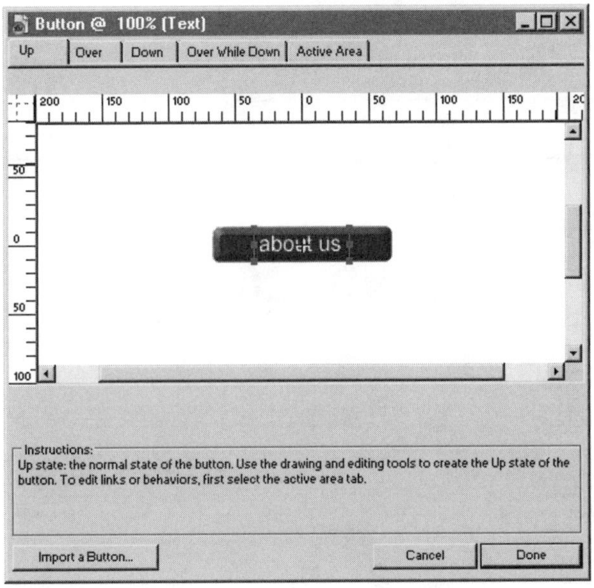

3. Click the Over tab. The Over tab is blank. You can import a graphic, create a new graphic, or copy the other graphic. When you copy the graphic from the Up state, you can modify the graphic.

4. Click the Copy Up Graphic button and edit the shape from the Up state. The following illustration shows the edited button graphic from the Up state in

the Over tab. In this case, the graphics from the Up state were copied and their colors were changed, one of the many variations possible for differentiating the button from its previous state.

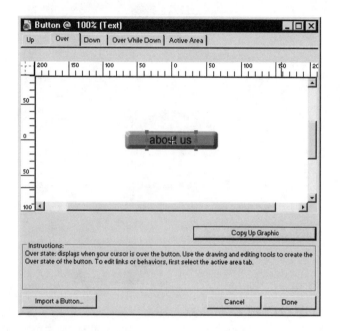

Creating a Multi-State Button

To create additional interaction for the visitors to your Web design, you can include two states in addition to the Up and Over states. Adding states gives your viewers additional visual clues and creates additional interest in the pages they are viewing.

To create a three- or four-state button:

1. Create a two-state button as outlined in the last section.

2. Click the Down tab.

3. To create the graphic for the Down state, do one of the following:

   ■ Click the Copy Up Graphic button and edit the graphic to give it a different appearance. You can change the fill characteristics of the graphic or apply an Effect to the graphic.

   ■ Import or create a graphic.

4. Click the Down While Over tab.

5. To create a graphic for the Down While Over state, do one of the following:

■ Click the Copy Up Graphic button and edit the graphic to give it a different appearance. You can change the fill characteristics of the graphic or apply an Effect to the graphic.

■ Import or create a graphic.

6. Click the Active Area tab to modify the button's target area. The Button Editor's Active Area tab is shown here:

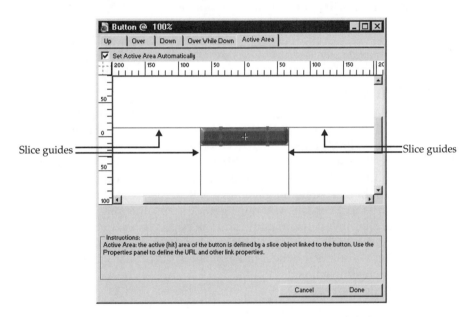

Slice guides ────────────────→ ←────────── Slice guides

7. Click a slice guide and drag it to change the button's active area.

8. Click Done to close the Button Editor. The button symbol appears on the canvas and is added to the document Library.

Adding the Finishing Touches to a Button

After you create a button in the button editor, you still have a few tasks ahead of you. If the button is used for navigation, you assign a URL to the button. You also need to optimize the button for export. Additionally, you can modify other aspects of the button, such as the target window in which the button's link opens in, and you can add an Alt tag. In the upcoming sections, you'll learn to make your buttons fully functional by applying these finishing touches.

Optimizing a Button

When you add buttons to a document, they are exported as individual images. You have one image for each button state you use in the Button Editor. When you create a button, you generally have a fairly limited color palette—that is, of course, unless you decide to use bitmaps for your button graphics. If you've used vector objects for your buttons, select the buttons and choose the same optimization setting for all. You can probably get by with exporting fewer than 16 colors for the buttons, which means each button graphic will have a smaller file size and will load quicker into the user's browser.

Note	*For more information on optimizing, refer to Chapter 21.*

Creating Button Links

Another item you need to create to make the button fully functional is its link. A link is a path to another Web page. There are two types of link paths you can create for a button: relative and absolute. A link's path is relative when the link is at the same Web site. For example, if you need to create a link to an HTML page with the filename about.htm, the relative link is about.htm. If a relative link occurs in a different directory at the same Web site, the link might look something like this: /client/clientList.htm.

If the link is at another Web site, you must enter the absolute path to the Web site page. This includes the site's domain name and the page. An example of an absolute link is http://www.dasdesigns.net/portfolio.htm. Note that some designers use the .htm extension, whereas others use the .html extension. Make sure you enter the proper file extension when creating a link.

To create a link for a button:

1. Select the button.

2. Open the Property inspector. When you select a button and open the Property inspector, it is configured as follows.

Link field   Alt field

Target field

3. Enter the URL in the Link field. Alternatively, you can enter a link by opening the URL Library and selecting a link. You can also click the triangle to the right of the Link field and choose a URL from the drop-down menu.

Specifying the Target Window

Another button option you can specify from the Property inspector is the target window in which the link opens. By default, the link will open in the same window from which it was called. However, you can change the default behavior so that the linked page opens in a different window.

To specify the link's target window:

1. Select the button from either the document Library or from the canvas. When you select the button from the library, the changes are applied to the symbol and all instances of it. When you select a button instance, the changes are applied only to the selected button.

2. Open the Property inspector shown previously.

3. Click the triangle to the right of the Target field and choose one of the following:

   ■ **Blank**   Opens the link in a new Web browser window.

   ■ **Self**   Opens the link in the same Web browser window.

   ■ **Parent**   Opens the link in the parent frameset or the frame associated with the link. If the specified URL is not in a nested frame, the link appears in a full browser window.

   ■ **Top**   Loads the URL in a full browser window, removing any frames in which the exported document may be nested.

Adding an Alt Tag

You can add an Alt tag to a button. An Alt tag is a text tag that is displayed while the page is loading. With certain browsers, the Alt tag is displayed as a tooltip when users roll their mouse over a button.

To add an Alt tag to a button:

1. Select the button. Select the button symbol in the document Library to apply changes to the actual symbol and all instances of the symbol. Alternatively, you can select a button instance on the canvas, and the tag will apply only to the selected instance.

2. Open the Property inspector shown previously.

3. Enter the desired text in the Alt field. Keep the text to a minimum. If you enter an excessive amount of text, it will be truncated.

Editing Buttons

When you create a button in Fireworks, you create a symbol. The Button symbol is unique in the fact that you can edit certain properties of the original symbol, and it will have a global effect on all instances of the symbol used in the document. Other properties can be edited on a per-instance basis, without affecting the original symbol or other instances of the symbol. In the upcoming sections, you'll learn how to globally edit all instances of a symbol and edit properties that affect only a single instance.

Globally Editing a Button Symbol

When you need to change a characteristic of a button such as its shape, color, or size, you can edit the original symbol and update all instances of the symbol in your document. This feature comes in quite handy when you or your client suddenly decide to change the color scheme of the Web site.

To edit all instances of a symbol in a document:

1. Choose Window | Library. The document Library opens.

2. To open the button in the Button Editor, do one of the following:

   ■ In the document Library, double-click the icon to the left of the button symbol's name.

   ■ In the document Library, select the button symbol, and then choose Edit Symbol from the Library Options menu.

   ■ In the document Library, double-click the button symbol's name to open the Symbol Properties dialog box. From the Symbol Properties dialog box, choose Edit.

3. Edit the button by changing one of the following:

   ■ Fill and/or stroke color, size, shape, or images

   ■ Effects, opacity, or blend mode

   ■ URL link

   ■ Optimization settings

   ■ Target window

4. After editing the button, click Done. The button symbol and all instances of it are updated to reflect your edits.

Modifying a Button Instance

When you have multiple instances of the same button in a document, you can perform edits to an instance without affecting the original button symbol or other instances. This is a benefit to you as a designer. You only need to create one button symbol to create the basic shape and specify the text font, color, and other parameters. You can edit each instance of a button to change the button instance's text, URL, Alt text, and target window. You can also modify an instance of a button symbol by varying its opacity and blend mode or by adding effects to the instance.

To edit an instance of a button symbol:

1. On the canvas, select the button instance you want to modify.

2. Open the Property inspector. When you open the Property inspector after selecting an instance of a button symbol, it is configured as follows.

3. To edit the button text, select the current text in the Text field and enter the desired text.

4. To edit the link, enter a new link in the Link field or select a link from the URL Library.

5. To edit the Alt text, select the current text in the Alt field and enter new text.

6. To change the target window, click the triangle to the right of the Target field and choose an option from the drop-down menu. The target options were discussed previously.

7. To edit the instance's effects, click the Edit Effects button and either edit a currently applied effect or add a new one. For more information on effects, refer to Chapter 14.

8. To change the button instance's opacity, click the triangle to the right of the Opacity field and drag the slider to set a value. Alternatively, you can enter a value between 0 and 100 in the field.

9. To change the instance's blend mode, click the triangle to the right of the Blend field and choose an option from the drop-down menu. For more information on blend modes, refer to Chapter 5.

After you modify an instance, you can change it as needed by opening the Property inspector again and repeating the previous steps. The ability to edit individual instances of a button comes in handy if you do work for a client that frequently changes the content of a site you've designed. Rather than creating a document from scratch, you can open the original document, change the content of the page, update the button instances, export the document again, and you're good to go. You don't need to tell your client you received a helping hand from Fireworks.

Creating Beveled Buttons

Beveled buttons are a mainstay on the Web. You see them at just about every site you visit. You can apply an effect to a button to give it a unique look. You can use the Inner Bevel effect and Bevel Boss effect to create some good-looking beveled buttons. You can apply different effects to each button state to make it appear as though an actual button is being clicked and not a 2D Web graphic. For example, you can create a rectangular shape and apply the Inner Bevel effect to it in the Up state. Click the Over tab, click the Copy Up Graphic button, and change the Inner Bevel effect from a raised inner bevel to an inverted inner bevel. The following illustration shows an example of a beveled button with different effects in the Up and Over state.

Creating a Navigation Bar

When you create a document that will be used for navigation throughout a Web site, you can create a single document that contains the common elements in the site, such as the banner or the header and a navigation bar. When you create the navigation bar, you create a single button symbol, duplicate the symbol for the number of buttons needed, and then change the text and URLs. When you plan the initial document that contains the navigation bar, choose a size that will enable you to evenly space the buttons across the design.

To create a navigation bar:

1. Create a four-state button, as outlined previously. Be sure to add the text that describes the page to which the button will link. For the purposes of this demonstration, the button text will be Home. After you create the button, it is added to the document Library, and an instance of the button appears on the canvas.

2. Align the button symbol to the leftmost corner of your navigation bar. The actual position will vary depending on your design. As a rule, you can position a navigation bar below the banner that displays the site name and logo. Another popular position for a navigation bar is below a splash image.

3. Select the button, and then open the Property inspector.

4. In the Links field, enter the URL for the button. Alternatively, you can select a link from the URL Library.

5. With the button still selected, hold down the ALT key (Windows) or OPTION key (Macintosh) and drag the button to the right. Fireworks creates a duplicate of the button.

6. Choose Edit | Repeat Duplicate to create another instance of the button. Repeat this action for the rest of the buttons on your navigation bar.

7. Select the second button.

8. Open the Property inspector.

9. In the Text field, enter the text that describes the page to which this button links. Fireworks updates the button text without changing the original symbol or other instances.

10. To show the Down state of the button when the page the button links to loads, click the Show Down State On Load checkbox. When you enable this option, viewers of your design receive a visual clue that the button links to the page they are viewing.

11. In the Links field, enter a URL. Alternatively, you can choose a URL from the URL Library.

12. Continue editing the remaining buttons for your navigation bar as outlined in steps 8–11. The following illustration shows a typical navigation bar.

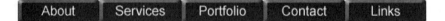

 While you're in the Property inspector, give the button instance a name by filling in the blank field below the word Button. When you export the document, the images for each state of the button will bear the name you entered.

If you use Fireworks in conjunction with Dreamweaver to create your Web pages, you can size the document to the navigation bar. Alternatively, you can lay out the navigation buttons first, and then choose Modify | Canvas | Trim Canvas. Optimize the navigation bar, and then export it as HTML and images. When you launch Dreamweaver, you can insert the navigation bar in a table row by choosing Edit | Insert Interactive Images | Fireworks HTML. Follow the prompts in Dreamweaver, and your navigation bar is good to go.

Creating Bitmap Buttons

You can use any type of graphic for a button's state. If you create a site for a photographer, a thumbnail-sized bitmap button is an ideal way to visually display the photographer's talent. You can use a bitmap image in the Up frame, text in the Over frame, or a combination of a bitmap and text to display what viewers will see when the button is clicked. For an interesting effect, you can place an unmodified bitmap in the Up state, copy up the image into the Over state, and then apply the Invert effect to the bitmap. When users roll their mouse over the button, they'll see what looks like a negative of the image you used in the Up state.

Importing a Button

If you're under a tight deadline and don't have time to create a button symbol, you can import a button preset. After you import the button preset, you can modify it by changing the fill color or applying an effect to it.

To import a button preset:

1. Choose Edit | Insert Button. The Button Editor shown previously opens.

2. Click the Import A Button button. The Import Button Symbols dialog box appears, as shown here:

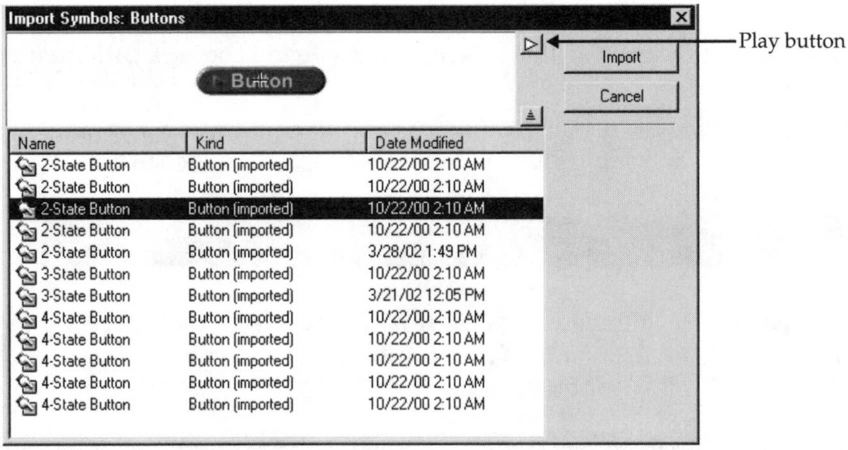

3. Click a button to select it. The button is displayed in the Preview window.

4. Click the Play button to preview a multi-state rollover button.

5. Click Import to import the button. The button appears in the Button Editor.

6. Edit the button as needed. For example, you can change the default text to something more apropos in the Property inspector.

7. Click Done. The button is added to the document Library, and an instance of the button appears on the canvas.

Adding Interactivity with Behaviors

When you add a hotspot or a slice to a document, a white dot known as a behavior handle appears in the middle of the hotspot or the slice's overlay. Whenever you have a behavior handle, you can add interactivity to the object. The interactivity you add can be anything from a simple rollover to complex effects like a pop-up menu. When you add a behavior to an object, Fireworks creates all the necessary JavaScript to pull off the effect in a user's browser when you export the document.

When you move your cursor over a behavior handle, the cursor icon becomes a pointing finger. When your cursor changes, click the behavior handle to reveal the Behaviors menu shown here:

Behavior handle

Behaviors menu

Adding a Behavior

You can add a behavior to any object in your document. Before you add a behavior to an object, you must first insert a hotspot using one of the Hotspot tools or the Insert Hotspot menu command, or create a slice using one of the Slice tools or the Insert Slice menu command. Creating hotspots and slices is covered in detail in Chapter 16. After creating a hotspot or slice, click the behavior handle and choose a behavior from the drop-down menu shown previously. The individual behaviors are covered in detail in upcoming sections.

You can add more than one behavior to an object. For example, you can create a simple rollover behavior for an object and have a pop-up menu appear in conjunction with a user's mouse rolling over the object. When you have more than one behavior applied to an object, you can manage behaviors using the Behaviors panel.

Using the Behaviors Panel

You can use the Behaviors panel to manage behaviors that are applied to an object in your document. You can also use the panel to add behaviors, delete behaviors, get information about applied behaviors, and modify parameters of selected behaviors. The actual parameters you can modify depend on the behavior you apply to an object. For example, if you use the Set Text Of Status Bar behavior, you can specify whether the text is displayed on mouseover, on mouseout, when the object is clicked, or when the page loads. You can also use the Behaviors panel to modify the text displayed in the Status bar.

To open the Behaviors panel shown next, choose Window | Behaviors.

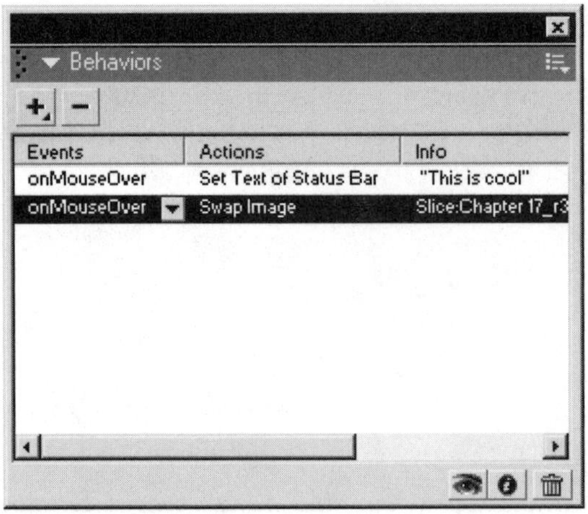

After you open the Behaviors panel, you can do the following:

■ To add a behavior, click the Add Behavior button to display the menu shown in the following illustration. Click a behavior to add it to the object.

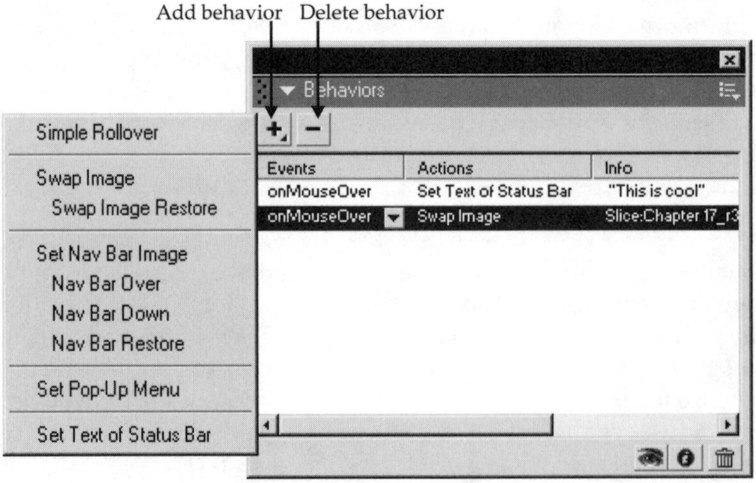

- To delete a behavior from an object, select it and then click the Delete Behavior button, which looks like a minus sign (–). Alternatively, you can click the Delete Behavior button, which looks like a trashcan.

- To modify the event that triggers a behavior, select the behavior, click the downward-pointing triangle between the Events and Actions columns, and choose an event from the menu shown here:

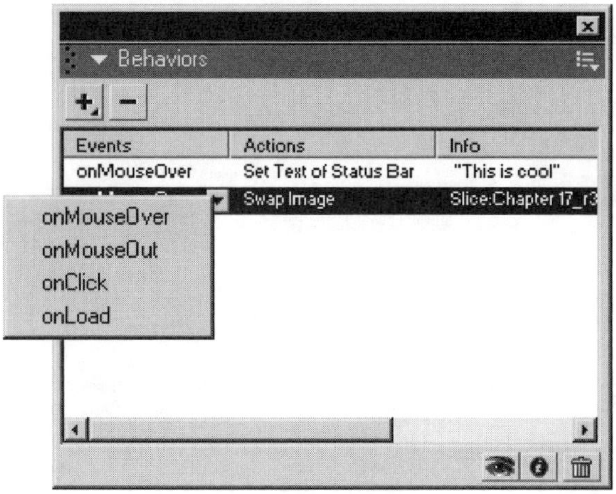

Creating a Pop-Up Menu

When you create a design for a client that requires an extensive Web site with multiple menu choices, you find yourself running out of room when creating a conventional navigation bar; your client's number of choices would force you into creating a navigation bar with print so tiny it would be rendered illegible on most browsers. When faced with this problem, you can use pop-up menus to display additional menu options. When you create a pop-up menu in Fireworks, all of the JavaScript needed to create the pop-up menu is exported with the accompanying HTML document. Figure 17-1 shows a pop-up menu sprouting from a navigation bar's button as seen in a Web browser.

The most logical choice for creating a pop-up menu is to use it in conjunction with a button, although you can create a pop-up menu from any slice or hotspot in the document.

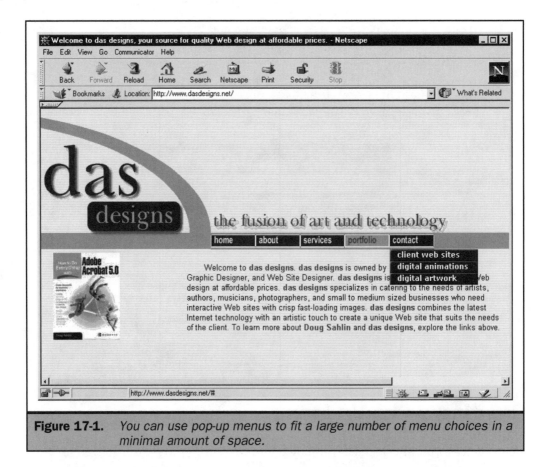

Figure 17-1.   *You can use pop-up menus to fit a large number of menu choices in a minimal amount of space.*

To create a pop-up menu:

1. Select the desired hotspot, slice, or button in your document.

2. Click the white dot (behavior handle) of any button, hotspot, or slice in the document, and choose Add Pop-Up Menu from the Behaviors menu shown previously. The Pop-Up Menu Editor shown next appears.

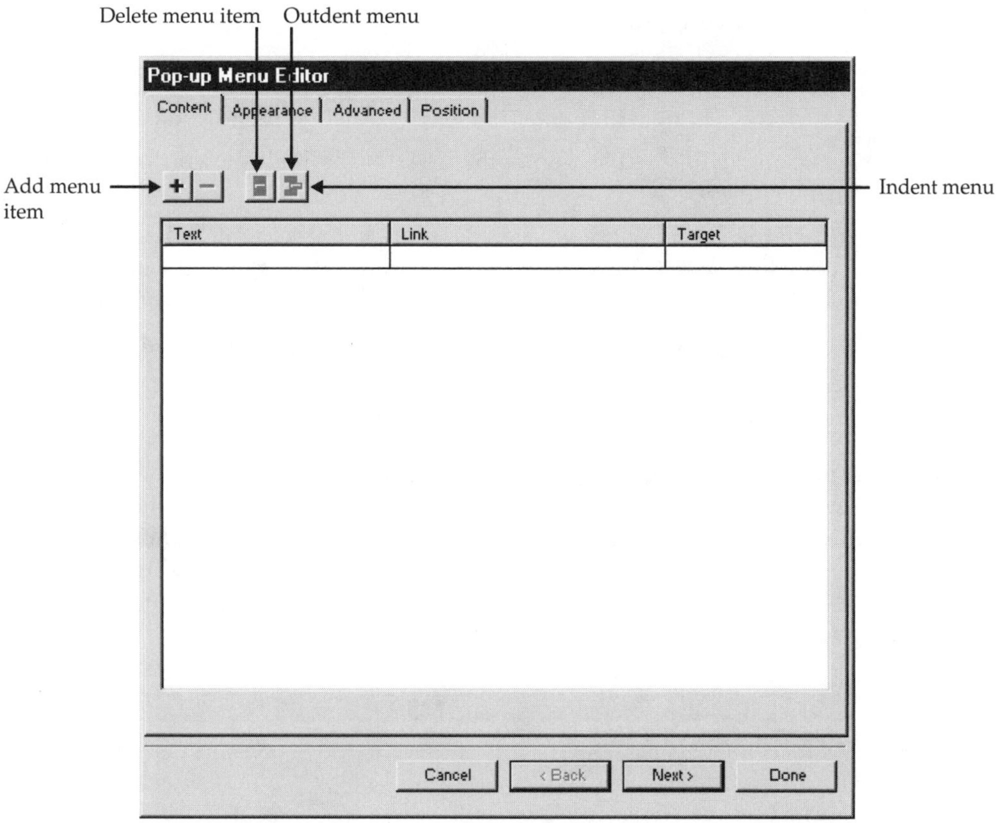

Delete menu item   Outdent menu

Add menu → item

Indent menu

As you can see, the editor consists of four tabs. The choices within each tab enable you to specify the menu items, URLs, menu appearance, and more. The tabs will be covered in detail in upcoming sections.

Creating Content for Your Pop-Up Menu

After you open the Pop-Up Menu Editor, you can begin creating the content for your menu. A completed pop-up menu consists of text items and associated URLs. You can specify the target window for the associated links as well as create submenus. When you create a submenu, you can really pack a lot of content into a pop-up menu.

To create content for your pop-up menu:

1. Open the Pop-Up Menu Editor, as outlined previously.

2. Double-click the text field and enter the text for the first menu choice.

3. Double-click the URL field and enter the URL for the Web site you want linked to the menu choice.

4. Double-click the Target window, click the triangle to the right of the field and choose one of the following: _blank, _self, _parent, or _top. If you want the link to open in the same window, you do not have to choose an option from this field.

5. To add another choice to the menu, click the plus sign (+) and repeat the previous steps.

6. Continue adding menu choices to flesh out your menu.

After you create several menu choices, you can create a submenu that branches out from another menu choice. To create a submenu, click the Indent Menu button shown previously. After you indent a menu, you can create submenu items by clicking the plus sign (+) and then specifying the menu item text, URL, and Target window. The following illustration shows the Content tab of the Pop-up Menu Editor being used to create a pop-up menu with several items and a submenu.

Pop-up Menu Editor

Content | Appearance | Advanced | Position

Text	Link	Target
About	about.htm	_self
Services	services.htm	_self
Flash Web Design	flash.htm	_self
HTML Web Design	htmldesign.htm	_self
Web Makeovers	makeover.htm	_self
Portfolio	portfolio.htm	_self
Client Web Sites	client.htm	_self
Digital Animations	animations.htm	_self
Digital Artwork	gallery.htm	_self
Contact	contact.htm	_self

Cancel | < Back | Next > | Done

After you populate your pop-up menu, you specify the appearance of the menu items. You can choose between HTML style or display items as images by following the steps in the next section.

Setting Menu Item Appearance

You have a tremendous amount of latitude in the appearance of your pop-up menu. You can specify whether the pop-up menu is vertical or horizontal, specify the font type, font size, font color, and more.

To set the menu appearance of the items in your pop-up menu using the HTML formatting:

1. Create the choices for your pop-up menu as outlined previously.

2. Click the Pop-Up Menu Editor's Appearance tab. The Pop-Up Menu Editor is reconfigured, as shown in the following illustration. The default appearance choice is HTML. The Preview window at the bottom of the editor displays the menu choices as currently configured.

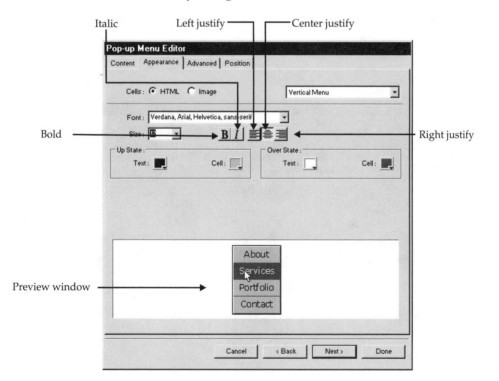

3. Click the Horizontal radio button to create a horizontal pop-up menu.

4. Click the triangle to the right of the font menu, and choose one of the five options. These are standard HTML text choices. Each set has multiple choices. If the user doesn't have the first font installed, the menu defaults to the second choice. The

final choice in all sets creates the menu text by using a serif, sans-serif, or Courier font from the user's system.

5. Click the triangle to the right of the Size field and choose a font size from the drop-down menu.

6. To boldface and/or italicize the menu choices, click the appropriate buttons.

7. To justify the text within the cell, click the desired button. By default, the text is aligned to the left side of the cell.

8. In the Up State section, click each color swatch and choose a color from the pop-up palette to specify the text color and cell color when the pop-up menu is loaded.

9. In the Over State section, click each color swatch and choose a color from the pop-up palette to specify the text color and cell color when the user's mouse is over a menu choice.

To display the menu choices as images:

1. Complete steps 1 and 2 from the instructions to display menu choices with HTML formatting.

2. Click the Image radio button. The Pop-Up Menu Editor is configured as shown here:

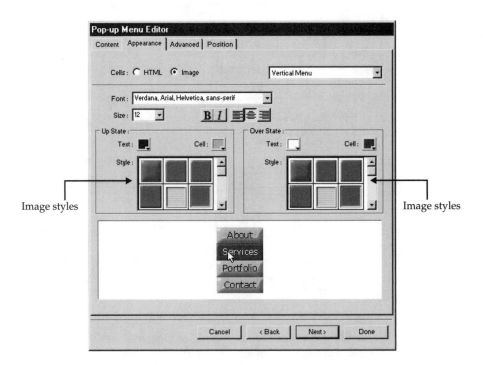

3. Follow steps 2 through 7 of the HTML formatting section to set the font attributes.

4. In the Up State section, click the Text and Cell color swatches to specify the text and cell color when the menu first loads.

5. In the Up State Style section, click a button to specify the style when the menu first loads. There are many choices in this and the Over State Style window. Click the scrollbar and drag to see the rest of the available styles. In fact, these are the same styles you see on the Styles menu, with the exception of the text styles.

6. In the Over State section, click the Text and Cell color swatches to specify text and cell colors when users pass their mouse over a menu choice.

7. In the Over State Style section, click a button to select the image style that will be displayed when users roll their mouse over a menu choice.

As you make your choices for the appearance of menu items, the preview window updates in real time. You can either accept the menu items as they are by clicking the Done button, or you can further modify the parameters of the menu by following the steps in the next section.

Tip *You can create your own custom styles for a pop-up menu. Create an object and apply the desired Live Effects to the object. Save it as a style and then export it from the Styles menu as outlined in Chapter 15. Export the style to the Nav Menu folder on your hard drive. The actual location of this folder varies depending on your operating system. The next time you open the Pop-Up Menu Editor, the exported style appears as a choice when you choose Image for the cell type.*

Modifying Menu Item Parameters

Fireworks 4 made it possible for designers to easily add a pop-up menu to their designs, without knowing a single thing about JavaScript. However, if any of the parameters, such as cell width, cell padding, and menu delay needed to be modified, the JavaScript needed to be modified in an HTML editor. In Fireworks MX, two new tabs are available: Advanced and Position. The Advanced tab, covered in this section, enables you to change the physical characteristics of each menu cell and specify the amount of time the menu is displayed after the user's mouse rolls off the menu.

To modify the menu item cells:

1. Create a pop-up menu and specify the content and appearance as outlined previously.

2. Click the Advanced tab. The Pop-Up Menu Editor is reconfigured as shown here:

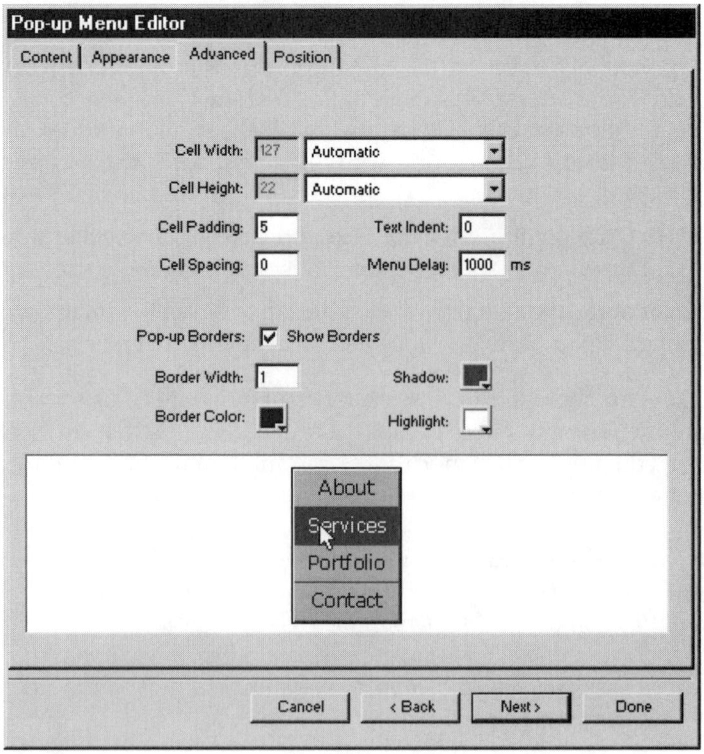

3. Accept the default Automatic cell sizing, or click the triangle to the right of the Cell Width and/or Cell Height fields and choose Pixels from the drop-down menu.

4. If you chose the Pixels option in step 3, enter a value for the Cell Width and/ or Height.

5. Accept the default Cell Padding value, or enter a different value. Cell Padding is the area in pixels that borders all sides of the menu text.

6. Accept the default Text Indent value of 0 pixels, or enter a value in the field to specify the distance the text is indented within the cell. Note that if the indent and width of the cell text exceed the width of the cell, the menu text is truncated.

7. Accept the default Cell Spacing value of 0 pixels, or enter a value in the field. This value determines the distance between each cell.

8. Accept the default menu delay of 1000ms (1 second) or enter a different value to display the menu for a longer or shorter time after a user's mouse rolls off the menu.

9. Click the Pop-up Menu Show Borders checkbox (selected by default) to create a pop-up menu with no cell borders. If you disable cell borders, the rest of the options in this tab are unavailable. If you chose Image for the cell appearance in the previous tab, the remaining options are unavailable as well.

10. If your pop-up menu displays borders, accept the default value of 1 pixel. Alternatively, you can enter a different value in the field to create a wider border.

11. To change the cell shadow color, click the Shadow color swatch and select a color from the pop-up palette.

12. To change the cell border color, click the Border color swatch and select a color from the pop-up palette.

13. To change the cell highlight color, click the Highlight color swatch and select a color from the pop-up palette.

After you finish specifying parameters in the Advanced tab, you can click Done to close the dialog box; or you can modify the position of the menu as outlined in the next section.

Note *To preview the functionality of your pop-up menu, press* F12 *to display the text in your system's default browser.*

Changing Menu Position

When you create a pop-up menu, the default position for the menu is directly below the hotspot or slice from which the menu will be spawned when the document is published. A submenu appears 5 pixels to the right of the menu item from which it appears and 7 pixels below it. You can modify the position of either item by choosing a different preset or specifying a value in pixels to offset the pop-up menu or submenu.

To change the position of a pop-up menu:

1. Create a pop-up menu and specify the content, appearance, and (if needed) advanced parameters of the menu.

2. Click the Menu Position tab. The Pop-Up Menu Editor is reconfigured as shown here:

Pop-up Menu Editor

Content | Appearance | Advanced | Position

Menu position:

X: 0   Y: 0

Submenu position:

X: -5   Y: 28

☑ Place in Same Position

Cancel | < Back | Next > | Done

3. In the Menu Position section, click a button to specify the position of the menu relative to the slice that will create the menu. Each button has a blue rectangle that indicates the position of the menu relative to the slice as shown in the previous illustration. Alternatively, you can enter values in the X and Y fields. These values specify the offset from the slice itself, not the coordinates of the menu within the document. If you have a submenu in your pop-up menu, the options in the submenu section are available, as shown in the preceding illustration.

4. In the submenu section, click a button to define the position of the submenu. Each button has an icon that shows the position of the submenu relative to the slice from which it appears. Alternatively, you can enter a value to offset the submenu in pixels.

5. Click the Place In Same Position checkbox to position the submenu relative to its parent menu item.

6. Click Done to exit the Pop-Up Menu Editor and apply the changes.

Note *When you export a document with a pop-up menu and then upload the document to a Web site, be sure to upload the mm_menu.js file. This file contains the JavaScript that makes the menu functional. If your pop-up menu has a submenu, you will also have to upload a file called arrows.gif, which is exported along with the document. This file contains the image that creates the arrow for each submenu.*

Editing a Pop-Up Menu

One of the major advantages of Fireworks PNG format is the ability to edit the document at any time. If you create a document for a client with a pop-up menu and the client needs to add or delete items from the pop-up menu, you can easily make the changes at any time.

To edit a pop-up menu:

1. Click the white behavior handle of the slice that generates the pop-up menu. The Behaviors menu appears, as shown previously.

2. Choose Edit Pop-Up Menu. The Pop-Up Menu Editor shown previously appears.

3. In the Content section of the editor, you can perform the following edits:

   ■ To add a menu item, click the Add Menu button, which looks like a plus sign (+).

   ■ To delete a menu item, select it and then click the Delete Menu button, which looks like a minus sign (–).

   ■ To rearrange the position of a menu item, select it and then drag it up or down the list. Release the mouse button when the menu item is in the desired position.

   ■ To outdent a submenu item, select it and then click the Outdent Menu button. Note that if there is more than one item on the submenu, only the selected item is affected.

4. To edit other menu parameters, click the applicable tab and follow the instructions from previous sections to make the desired changes.

5. Click Done to apply the edits and exit the Pop-Up Menu Editor.

Creating an Image Swap

Another effect you can easily include in a Fireworks design is an image swap. When you create an image swap, you replace a slice in the document with another image. You can create an image swap that occurs in the same area as the slice that generates it, or you can create a disjoint rollover, whereupon an image is swapped with another image that resides in a different area of the document. A disjoint rollover can also be used on a button; the button acts as the trigger to display an image hidden on another frame of the document. To create an image swap as outlined, you will create additional frames in the document. Frames will be discussed in detail in Chapter 18. Alternatively, you can specify an image file to swap with an image in the document.

To swap one image for another:

1. Select the image in the document you want to swap and then choose Edit | Insert Slice.

2. Choose Window | Frames. The Frames panel shown here opens.

New/Duplicate Frame

3. Click the New/Duplicate Frame button at the bottom of the Frames panel.

4. Choose File | Import. Navigate to the image you want to be swapped with the image on the first frame, and click Open to import it.

5. Align your cursor with the upper-left corner of the slice, and click to position the image.

6. In the Frames panel, click Frame 1 to select it.

7. Select the slice and then click the white behavior handle. The Behaviors menu appears, as shown previously. If the slice is difficult to select, open the Layers panel and in the Web layer, click the slice's thumbnail to select it.

8. Choose Swap Image from the Behaviors menu. The Swap Image dialog box appears, as shown in the following illustration. Each slice in the document is indicated by a rectangle.

9. Select the slice by clicking the appropriate rectangle, and then select the frame in which the image to be swapped is located. Click OK.

10. Click the Preview tab, roll your mouse over the image, and the image in the second frame appears. When you export the document, Fireworks creates the JavaScript for the rollover and exports the image in the second frame with the same name as the document. It also exports the image with the row and column number of the table it will appear in, appended by _f2, which is how this image is referred to in the JavaScript for the Image Swap behavior.

The following steps will show you how to use a button as a trigger for a disjoint rollover. When you use a rollover of this type on a document, you can swap a different image for each navigation button in your document. Rollovers of this type work best when the images being swapped are the same size.

To create a disjoint rollover:

1. Select the image that you want swapped for another when a navigation button is rolled over.

2. Choose Edit | Insert Slice. A slice appears over the image.

3. Choose Window | Frames. The Frames panel opens.

4. Click the New/Duplicate Frame button, as outlined previously.

5. Import the image you want to appear when the button is rolled over and align it with the upper-left corner of the slice.

6. In the Frames panel, click Frame 1 to select it.

7. Select the button you want to trigger the image swap, and then click the white behavior handle. The Behaviors menu appears.

8. Choose Image Swap. The Swap Image dialog box appears, as shown in the following illustration. When the Swap Image dialog box opens, all slices in your document appear as blue rectangles.

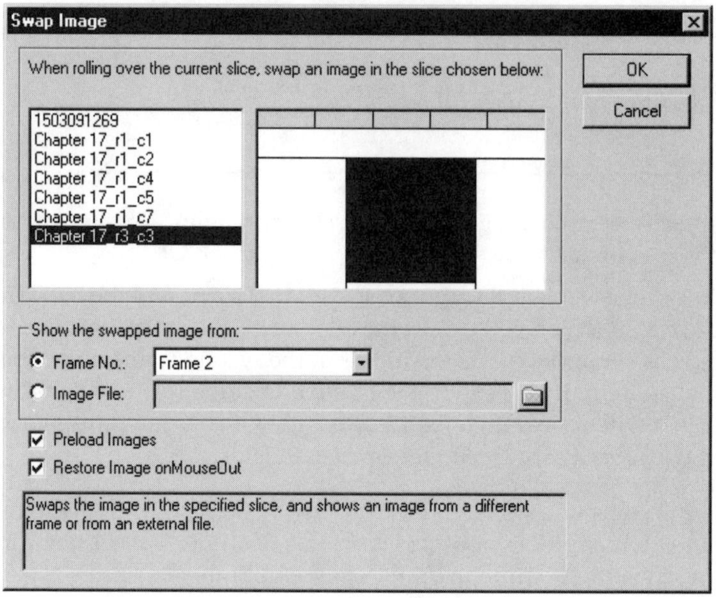

9. Click the rectangle that corresponds to the slice where the image swap will occur.

10. Click OK. A blue behavior line appears from the button to the target slice, as shown here:

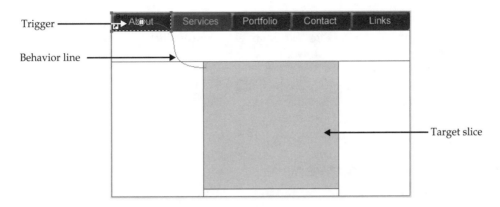

You can also click the behavior handle on the triggering object's slice, and drag it to the target object's slice. The trigger and the target can be the same object. When you create an image swap in this manner, you get an abbreviated dialog box that shows only the number of frames in the document, as shown in the following illustration. Click the More Options button to reveal the full dialog box shown in the preceding illustration.

11. Click the Preview tab, roll your mouse over the button, and the image on the second frame appears.

When you want to create an image swap for each button in a navigation menu, create enough additional frames for every button. Individually select each frame, import the image that you want to appear when the button is rolled over, and align the image with the slice as previously outlined. When you add the image swap behavior to the button, choose the corresponding frame where the image you want swapped is located.

In the Swap Image dialog box, shown in the previous illustration, notice that there is also a radio button for Image File. Alternatively, you can click the Image File radio button and then select the image you want to appear when the effect behavior is triggered. Note that the image will be resized to the slice. If you're going to use this option, it's best to work with same-size images. Also note that when you choose this option, Fireworks will insert the relative path to the image when creating the JavaScript in order to pull off the image swap. Therefore, it is imperative that the image file has the same relative path when you select the file as it will when the image is uploaded to the host Web site.

Creating a Simple Rollover

When you want to add a little smoke and mirrors to a Web design, one of the easiest effects to apply is a simple rollover. When a Web page with a simple rollover is viewed, one image replaces another in the same location. The images are on different frames but share a common slice.

To create a simple rollover:

1. Select the image that will be the trigger for the behavior, and choose Edit | Insert | Slice.

2. Choose Window | Frames. The Frames panel opens, as shown previously.

3. Click the New/Duplicate Frame button.

4. Choose File | Import. After the Import dialog box opens, locate the desired image file and click Open.

5. Click the upper-left corner of the slice to position the image.

6. In the Frames panel, select Frame 1.

7. Select the slice, and then click the white behavior handle.

8. From the Behavior menu, choose Simple Rollover.

9. Click the Preview tab and roll your mouse over the image to trigger the rollover.

Note *When you preview behaviors using the Preview section of the document window, areas with slices or hotspots have a slightly opaque overlay. To display the document as it will appear when published, in the Web section of the toolbox click the Hide Slices and Hotspots button.*

Creating a Browser Status Bar Message

At the bottom of most modern Web browsers is a status bar, which displays information about the status of an operation being performed by the browser (for example, the number of bytes being loaded or the Web host being contacted). You can use the status bar to display information (for example, what viewers can expect to see when they click a button).

To display a message in a browser status bar:

1. Select the button, hotspot, or slice you want to trigger the behavior.
2. Click the white behavior handle. The behaviors menu opens.
3. Choose Add Status Bar Message from the Behaviors menu. The Set Text Of Status Bar dialog box, shown here, opens.

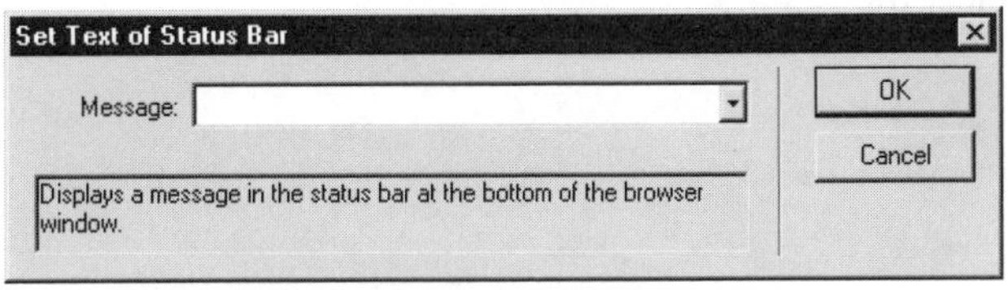

4. Enter the text you want displayed when users roll their mouse over the trigger, and then Click OK.
5. To test the behavior, press F12. Fireworks opens the document in your default Web browser. Take the appropriate action such as pausing your cursor over a button, to display the status bar message.

Summary

In this chapter you learned to create navigation buttons as links from the document you are creating to other Web pages. You also learned to create navigation bars, and you learned to create pop-up menus as an adjunct when a navigation bar is not enough to display all the necessary menu choices. You also learned to associate interactive behaviors that are associated with hotspots and slices in your document, such as swapping one image for another and displaying a message in the user's browser status bar. In Chapter 18, you'll learn to create animations in Fireworks.

CREATING ANIMATIONS
AND INTERACTIVE
WEB PAGES

Chapter 18

Creating Animations

Animation seems to be everywhere on the Internet. When surfing the Net, you can find everything from a full-fledged Flash site to an animated logo in the corner of a site banner. If your design calls for motion, you can use Fireworks to create it. When you add animation to a Web design, you catch the viewer's attention. Motion is always more exciting to watch than a still image. When you create an animation with Fireworks, it can be a standalone animation that you plug into a Web page, such as an animated banner, or it can be incorporated in a Fireworks design.

In Fireworks, you have two different types of animation. You can let Fireworks do the grunt work and create a frame-by-frame animation, or you can create the illusion of motion by duplicating a symbol by *tweening* instances. When you create an animation using tweening, you supply the starting and ending images and Fireworks creates the images in between. If you want the ultimate control over an animation, you can create the frames needed, and then change one or more properties of the objects in the document to create motion.

In this chapter, you'll learn to create animations by letting Fireworks take the reins, and you'll also learn to create your own animations. When you create your own animations, you can control the pace of the action and much more.

Understanding Animated GIFs

When you create an animation in Fireworks for use on the Web, you create an animated GIF. If you've ever taken a pad of paper, scribbled a stick figure on one page, created different variations of the figure on other pages, and then flipped the pages to simulate motion, you've created a rudimentary animation. An animation is nothing more than a sequence of frames. On each frame, something is different. You control how quickly the animation takes place by varying the time delay between frames. When the frames are compiled and played back, the illusion of motion is achieved. After you create an animated GIF, it is exported as a single file. When the file is opened in a Web browser, the frames play in order and viewers see motion.

Planning the Animation

After you decide to spice up a design with an animation, a little planning is in order. The document you are creating eventually will be displayed on the Internet, so file size is an important consideration, especially if some of your viewers access the Internet at slow connection speeds. When you create additional frames, you add to the size of the finished file. Therefore, it's in your best interest to pack the most action into the least amount of frames.

The best way to begin your planning is to conceptualize what you want to achieve with the animation. Are you showcasing a client's product? Creating a teaser ad for a product with a link to another Web page? Creating a text animation to display a message? Once you have a firm grasp of the goal of your animation, you can begin to put pen or pencil to paper.

Creating a Storyboard

The easiest way to plan an animation is to create a storyboard. The storyboard need not be a piece of artwork, it can be as rudimentary as rough sketches you create on paper napkins while discussing the project with your client over lunch. When you create the storyboard, be sparse. Don't create any more sketches than you need to portray the idea. If you do a good job, the number of sketches you create will translate into the number of frames in your animation.

One all time favorite for creating a storyboard is the legal pad. Create a rectangle for each frame of the production and sketch out the action change in each rectangle. Remember, you can use a combination of text objects, vector objects you create in Fireworks, and imported graphics to get the job done. As you create the storyboard, jot down in the margins the assets you'll need to get the job done. For example, do you need a copy of your client's logo, a picture of your client's CEO? When you create the storyboard, take the Zen approach to animation: less is more. After you create your storyboard, you'll have a good idea of how many frames you'll need to get the job done.

Choosing a Color Set

When you choose a color set for an animation, use as sparse a palette as possible. If you're using text and vector objects created in Fireworks, try to create a color palette with less than 16 colors and at most 32. Remember, you can create a color table as outlined in Chapter 8 and then delete colors, snap colors to Web safe, and more to limit the number of colors in the document.

If you use bitmaps in your animation, they will be converted to the GIF format. You can generally get by with an optimized palette of 128 colors, possibly 64, if the images are small. The motion of the images will offset the lack of colors. Optimizing documents for export will be covered in detail in Chapter 21.

Creating an Animation Symbol

As you learned in Chapter 13, symbols are reusable artwork. When you create a symbol, you can use it as needed throughout the document. The easiest way to create an animation symbol is to let Fireworks handle it for you.

To create an animation symbol:

1. Create or import an object.

2. Choose Modify | Animation | Animate Selection. The Animate dialog box appears, as shown here:

```
┌─────────────────────────────────────┐
│ Animate                          [X] │
│                                      │
│         Frames: [5    ▾]              │
│  ─────────────────────────────────   │
│                                      │
│          Move: [72   ▾]              │
│     Direction: [0    ▾]              │
│      Scale to: [100  ▾]              │
│       Opacity: [100  ▾]  to [100  ▾] │
│        Rotate: [0    ▾]  ⊙ CW  ○ CCW │
│  ─────────────────────────────────   │
│                                      │
│              [ Cancel ]  [   OK   ]  │
└─────────────────────────────────────┘
```

3. Accept the default number of frames (5) or click the triangle to the right of the Frames field and drag the slider to specify the number of frames you will use to animate the object. Alternatively, you can enter the desired value in the field.

4. Click the triangle to the right of the Move field and drag the slider to specify the distance in pixels that the object will move.

5. Click the triangle to the right of the Direction field to reveal a dial type slider. Click the dot and drag to specify the angle that the object will move away from its current position. The default setting of 0 moves the object horizontally from left to right. Specify 180 to move from right to left, 90 to move toward the top of the document, and 270 to move the object toward the bottom of the document. Select any value in between for diagonal movement.

6. Click the triangle to the right of the Scale To field, and drag the slider to select a percentage value to which you want to scale the object. The default setting of 100 does not change the size of the object. Select a smaller value to decrease the size of the object or a higher value to increase the size of the object.

7. In the Opacity field you have two settings: the window on the left determines the object's opacity as the animation begins; the window on the right determines the object's opacity when the animation ends. Click the triangle to the right of each field and drag the slider to select an opacity setting. Alternatively, you can enter a value in the field.

8. Click the triangle to the right of the Rotate field and drag the slider to specify the number of degrees the object rotates during the animation. Alternatively, you can enter a value between 0 and 360 in the field.

9. Click the CW (clockwise) or CCW (counterclockwise) radio button to specify the direction of rotation.

10. Click OK. If there are not enough frames in the document to create the animation, Fireworks displays a dialog box to that effect. Click OK to add the frames. Fireworks adds the animation symbol to the document Library and displays an instance of it on the canvas, as shown here:

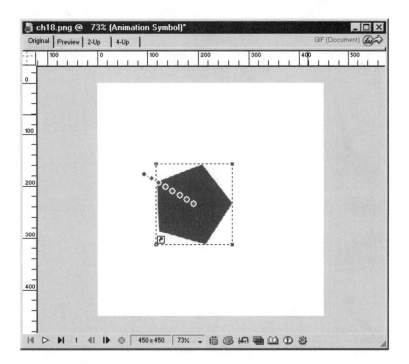

Previewing the Animation Symbol

After you create an animation symbol, Fireworks creates the number of frames you specified. In each frame, the object is changed according to the settings you chose in the Animate dialog box. You can get a good idea of the type of animation the symbol will provide by previewing it in the document window. After you create an animation, controls appear at the bottom of the document window. These controls, shown in Figure 18-1, are used to play, stop, and advance the animation from one frame to the next.

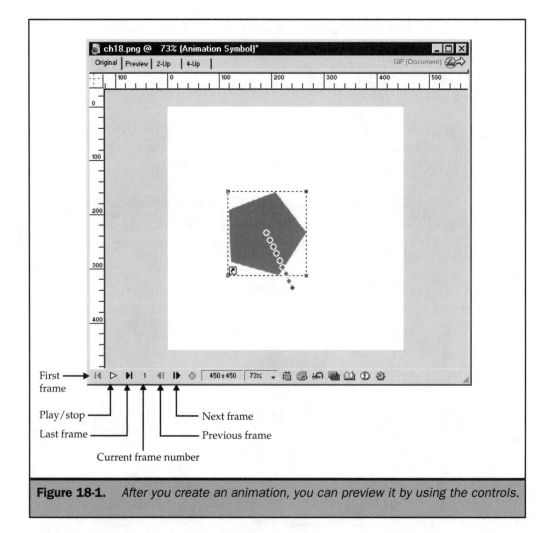

Figure 18-1.   *After you create an animation, you can preview it by using the controls.*

Manually Editing an Animation Symbol

After you preview an animation, you may need to edit it to suit your design. When you create an animation symbol, Fireworks creates a handle on each instance of the object that represents the object as it appears in each frame of the animation. You cannot edit the frames in between the start and the end of the animation; however, you can select the beginning or ending handle and drag it to a new location to modify the animation. The handle for the object as it appears in the first frame of the animation symbol is green in color; the handle for the object as it appears in the last frame is red. It may help you to think of a traffic signal: green is for go, and red is for stop.

You can make the following modification to the animation by dragging the handles:

■ To begin the animation in a different position, click the green handle and drag it to the desired location.

■ To end the animation in a different position, click the red handle and drag it to the desired location.

■ To change the distance the object moves each frame, click either the red or green handle and drag it away from the next handle to increase the distance; drag it toward the next handle to decrease the distance.

■ To change the direction the object moves during the animation, click either the starting or ending handle and drag diagonally to the desired direction. Hold down the SHIFT key while dragging to constrain motion to 45-degree angles.

Editing the Object's Shape

When you create an animation object, you create a symbol. As such, you can edit the basic shape of the symbol as needed. When you edit a symbol's shape, you also modify all instances of it in the document. You have three ways to edit the shape used in your animation symbol.

To edit an object in an animation symbol, do one of the following:

■ Double-click an instance of the animation symbol on the canvas.

■ Choose Window | Library, select the animation symbol you want to edit and then choose Edit Symbol from the Library Options menu. Alternatively, you can select the symbol and then double-click it in the Library preview window.

■ Select the animation symbol on the canvas, choose Modify | Animation | Settings to open the Animate dialog box and then click the Edit button.

After choosing one of these methods, the object appears in the Symbol dialog box. Use any tool or menu command to modify the shape, and then close the window. All instances of the object are updated to reflect your edits.

Editing the Animation Settings

In addition to manually editing the shape and manually changing the direction of the animation by dragging the handles, you can also edit the animation settings after the fact.

To modify an animation's settings:

1. Select the animation symbol on the canvas or from within the document Library and choose Modify | Animation Settings. This command opens the Animate dialog box shown previously.

2. Modify the settings as desired.

3. Click OK to close the dialog box.

Fireworks applies the changes to the animation symbol and all instances of it used in the document.

Alternatively, you can edit the parameters of an animation symbol using the Property inspector. To edit an animation symbol in the Property inspector:

1. Select the animation symbol by clicking an instance of it with the Pointer tool or by selecting it from the document Library.

2. Click the arrow to the left of the word Properties. The Property inspector opens and is configured as shown here:

3. Modify the parameters as needed and close the Property inspector.

Tip *To remove animation from an object, select the first frame of the animation, select the object, and then choose Modify | Animation | Remove Animation. Fireworks removes the animation from the object; however, the frames created to support the animation still remain.*

Animating with Frames

When you create a document with the sole purpose of creating an animation, you generally create a storyboard, as outlined previously. Armed with your storyboard, you're ready to begin work on the animation. Your first step is to allocate the number of frames needed to create the animation. You accomplish this task with the Frames panel.

Using the Frames Panel

You use the Frames panel to add, duplicate, and delete frames from a document. You can also use the Frames panel to copy objects to frames and rearrange the sequence of frames.

To open the Frames panel, shown next, choose Window | Frames.

Onion skin column ——

Frame name ——

Onion skinning ——

Options menu icon

Time delay

Distribute to frames

New/Duplicate frame

Delete frame

Adding Frames

When you decide to create an animation, you can create the frames immediately after you create the document. Alternatively, you can create a frame when needed. You can create frames from within the Frames panel or by using a menu command.

To create a new frame from within the Frames panel:

1. Choose Window | Frames. The Frames panel shown previously opens.

2. Select the frame before the location where you want the new frame to appear.

3. Click the New/Duplicate Frame button at the bottom of the Frames panel.

You can also create a new frame by using a menu command. This method is useful when you're previewing an animation and decide you need to add a frame for additional content.

To add a frame using a menu command:

1. In the main document window, use the Next Frame or Previous Frame controls to navigate to the frame before the new frame you're going to create.

2. Choose Edit | Insert | Frame. A new frame appears after the frame you selected before invoking the command.

CREATING ANIMATIONS
AND INTERACTIVE
WEB PAGES

If you need to add more than one frame to a document, you can do so by using a command from the Frames panel's Options menu. When you create multiple frames using this command, you can specify where the frames appear in the animation.

To create multiple frames:

1. Choose Window | Frames. The Frames panel shown previously opens. When you open the panel, the currently selected frame is highlighted.

2. From the Options menu, choose Add Frames. The Add Frames dialog box appears, as shown here:

3. Click the triangle to the right of the Number field and drag the slider to specify the number of frames to add. Alternatively, you can enter a value in the text field.

4. In the Insert New Frames section, choose one of the following options:

   - **At The Beginning** Adds the new frames at the beginning of the animation, before the current first frame

   - **Before Current Frame** Adds the new frames before the currently selected frame

   - **After Current Frame** Adds the new frames after the currently selected frame

   - **At The End** Adds the new frames at the end of the animation, after the last frame

5. Click OK. Fireworks adds the number of frames specified at the location you chose.

Naming Frames

When you create a frame for an animation, Fireworks assigns the default frame name of Frame, appended by the next available frame number. The default frame names are fine if you're creating a simple two- or three-frame animation. However, when you work with multiple frames, add frames, delete frames, and rearrange the order of frames, a descriptive frame name will make your editing tasks easier to handle.

To name a frame:

1. Choose Window | Frames. The Frames panel opens.

2. Double-click the frame you want to name. A text box appears over the frame's location.

3. Type a name and then press ENTER or RETURN.

Specifying Frame Delay

When you create an animation, the frame delay determines the amount of time each individual frame is displayed. The default frame delay of 7/100 of a second has the frames whizzing past so fast, you can barely see them. You can change the frame delay of one frame or all of the frames. You can choose a different frame delay for each frame. For example, if you want to display a manufacturer's logo or a Web site's URL for a longer amount of time, you can easily do so.

To specify the frame rate for an individual frame:

1. Choose Window | Frames.

2. Double-click the frame delay column of the frame whose delay you want to modify. The Frame Delay dialog box appears, as shown here:

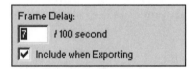

3. Enter a value in the text field. By default, the Include When Exporting option is selected. This option exports the delay rate with the file. Click to deselect the checkbox if you don't want to export a time delay with the file.

4. Press ENTER or RETURN. The new frame delay is displayed to the right of the frame's name.

You can also set the frame delay for several or all frames in the animation. When you choose this option, you specify the same rate for all selected frames.

To set the frame rate for multiple frames:

1. Choose Window | Frames. The Frames panel shown previously appears.

2. Click a frame to select it and then, while holding down the SHIFT key, click contiguous frames to add them to the selection.

3. Double-click any frame delay value to open the Frame Delay dialog box shown previously.

4. Enter a value and then press ENTER or RETURN. The new frame delay is applied to the selected frames.

Duplicating Frames

Many of the animations you create will have the same object in several frames. To create the animation, you change one or more characteristics of the object in succeeding frames. When you create an animation where the same objects are used repeatedly, you can save yourself time by creating a frame with the object(s) that will be used throughout the animation and then duplicating the frame.

To create a duplicate of a single frame and its contents:

1. Choose Window | Frames. The Frames panel appears.

2. Click the frame you want to duplicate and then drag and drop it on the New/ Duplicate Frame icon. After you release the mouse button, Fireworks creates a carbon copy of the frame and positions it after the frame that was duplicated.

Note *You can also duplicate a selected frame by choosing Duplicate Frame from the Frames panel's Options menu.*

Deleting Frames

After you create an animation and preview it, you may decide to delete a frame or two to cut down on the file size of the finished animation. If, when you preview the animation, you notice little or no difference between consecutive frames, chances are your viewers won't miss the frames but will appreciate the fact that the animation loaded quickly.

To delete a frame:

1. Choose Window | Frames. The Frames panel appears.

2. Select the frame(s) you want to delete and do one of the following:

   ■ Click the Delete Frame button, which looks like a trash can.

   ■ Drag and drop the selected frame(s) on the Delete Frame button.

   ■ Choose Delete Frames from the Options menu.

Moving Objects from Frame to Frame

As you fine-tune an animation, you find yourself adding objects to frames. After you preview the animation, you may decide that one or more objects in one frame should actually be in a different frame. Or perhaps one or more objects in a frame need to be copied into another frame. You can easily move and copy objects between frames by selecting them in the document window and then using the Frames panel to transfer or copy the objects.

To move objects from one frame to another:

1. Choose Window | Frames. The Frames panel opens.

2. Select the frame that contains the object(s) you want to move. The document window opens to the selected frame.

3. In the document window, select the object(s) you want to move. After you select the objects, a blue square appears in the Frames panel to the right of the frame's delay rate.

4. Click the blue square and drag it toward the frame to which you want to move the objects. As you drag toward another frame, an icon that looks like a document appears above your cursor. When your cursor is over a frame, a black square appears to the right of the frame delay rate.

5. Release the mouse button when the black square is over the frame to which you want to move the objects. Fireworks moves the selected object(s) to the frame.

Copying Objects to Frames

In addition to moving objects to another frame, you can copy them. You can copy objects to a single frame or to multiple frames.

To copy objects to another frame:

1. Choose Window | Frames. The Frames panel opens.

2. Select the frame that contains the object(s) you want to copy. The selected frame is displayed in the document window.

3. In the document window, select the object(s) you want to copy to another frame. In the Frames panel, a blue square appears to the right of the frame's delay rate.

4. In the Frames panel, click the blue square; and then, while holding down the ALT key (Windows) or OPTION key (Macintosh), move your cursor toward the frame to which you want to copy the object(s). An icon that looks like a document appears above your cursor, and to the right of your cursor a plus sign (+) appears.

5. When your cursor is over the frame to which you want to copy the object(s), release the mouse button. Fireworks copies the selected objects into the frame.

You can copy a selection of objects to multiple frames by using a command from the Frames panel's Options menu. When you copy an object selection in this manner, you can specify the location of the frame to which to copy the object(s), you can copy the object(s) to all frames, or you can copy the selection to a range of frames.

To copy an object selection using the Options menu's Copy to Frames command:

1. Choose Window | Frames. The Frames panel opens.

2. Select the frame that contains the objects you want to copy.

3. In the document window, select the objects you want to copy.

4. From the Frames panel's Options menu, choose Copy To Frames.
The Copy To Frames dialog box appears, as shown here:

5. Choose one of the following:

- **All Frames**   Copies the selection to all frames in the document.

- **Previous Frame**   Copies the objects to the frame previous to the one from which the objects were selected.

- **Next Frame**   Copies the selected objects to the next frame in the document.

- **Range**   Copies the objects to a range of frames. When you choose this selection, two fields below the radio button become active and display the starting and ending frames in the document. In the first field, enter the number of the first frame to which you want the objects copied; and in the second, enter the ending frame to which you want the objects copied.

6. Click OK. Fireworks copies the selected objects to the specified frames.

Arranging Frames

When you create an animation, the frames play in the order in which they were created. When reviewing the animation, if you decide you need to rearrange the order in which the frames play, you can do so from within the Frames panel.

To change the order in which a frame plays:

1. Choose Window | Frames. The Frames panel appears.

2. Select the frame you want to reposition.

3. Drag the frame up or down in the list. As you drag the frame, an icon that looks like a small document appears above your cursor. As you approach the border between two frames, a dark line appears on either side of the boundary.

4. Release the mouse button to reposition the frame. When you rearrange the order of frames with the default naming system, Fireworks renumbers the repositioned frame to reflect its new position. If you've given the frame a unique name, it is unaffected when you move the frame.

Distributing Objects to Frames

Another useful option you have when creating an animation is distributing a selection of objects to frames. If you are creating an animation where bitmap images are displayed one after another, you can quickly create the animation by importing the images and then distributing each image to a frame.

To distribute objects to frames:

1. In the document window, select the objects you want to distribute to frames.

2. Choose Window I Frames. The Frames panel appears, as shown here:

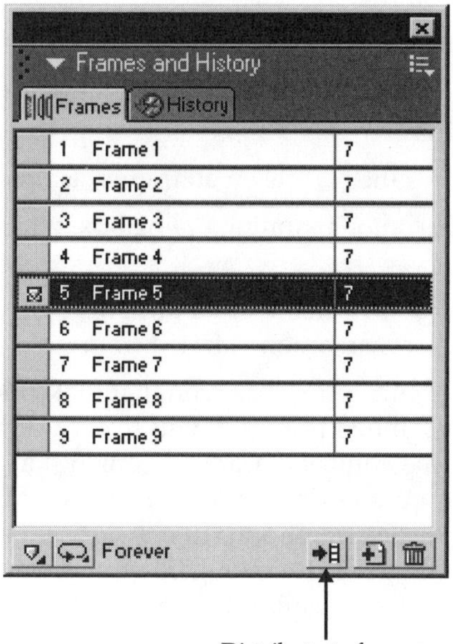

Distribute to frames

3. Click the Distribute To Frames button. Fireworks creates a single frame for each object selected.

Previewing Multiple Frames of an Animation

When creating an animation with multiple frames where you are animating several objects, it is often desirable to view more than one frame. The ability to view objects on the frames prior to and after the frame on which you are working makes it easier to position the object(s) relative to the contents of other frames in the animation. You can do this by viewing frames as onion skins. When you view frames as onion skins, the contents of the onion-skinned frames are displayed as dimmed images.

To preview multiple frames as onion skins:

1. Choose Window | Frames. The Frames panel opens.

2. Click the Onion Skin button at the lower-left corner of the panel, and choose one of the following options:

   ■ **Next Frame**   Displays the objects on the next frame as onion skins.

   ■ **Before And After**   Displays the objects on the preceding and following frames as onion skins.

   ■ **All Frames**   Displays the objects on all frames as onion skins.

   ■ **Custom**   Opens the Onion Skinning dialog box, which will be discussed in the next set of steps.

   ■ **Multi-Frame Editing**   Selected by default. This option gives you the ability to select and edit objects on onion-skinned frames.

After you select onion-skinning options, an icon that looks like an onion appears in the starting and ending onion-skinned frames. If you select a different frame, the icons move with it and display the same number of frames as onion skins. To modify the number of frames that are displayed as onion skins, click the blank spot to the left of a frame's name. The icon moves to the specified frame and either increases or decreases the number of frames displayed as onion skins. The following illustration shows the Frames panel as it appears when several frames are displayed as onion skins.

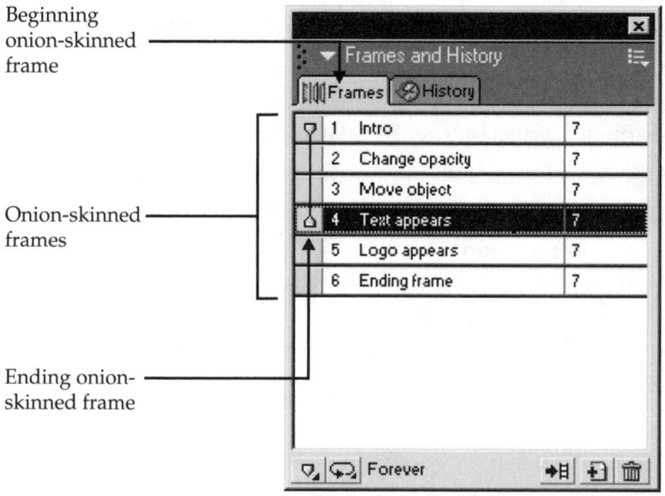

Beginning
onion-skinned
frame

Onion-skinned
frames

Ending onion-
skinned frame

If the default onion-skinning options are not to your liking, you can modify the number of frames shown before and after the selected frame, as well as vary the opacity of the objects on onion-skinned frames.

To modify the standard onion-skinning options:

1. Choose Window | Frames. The Frames panel opens.

2. Click the Onion Skin button, and from the drop-down menu choose Custom. The Onion Skinning dialog box appears, as shown here:

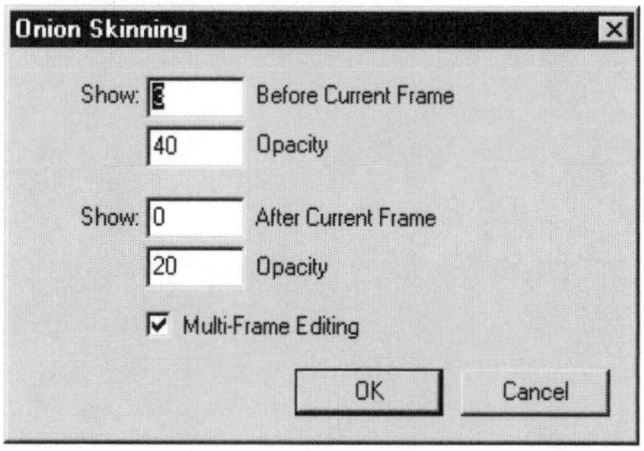

3. In the Show [ ] Before Current Frame field, enter a value for the number of frames you want displayed before the selected frame.

4. In the first Opacity field, enter a value. This is the opacity at which objects are displayed in onion-skinned frames before the selected frame.

5. In the Show [ ] After Current Frame field, enter the value for the number of frames you want displayed as onion skins after the currently selected frame.

6. In the last Opacity field, enter a value. This is the opacity at which objects are displayed in onion-skinned frames after the currently selected frame.

7. If you don't want the ability to edit objects in onion-skinned frames, deselect the Multi-Frame Editing option.

8. Click OK. Fireworks displays the number of frames selected as onion skins at the opacity you specified.

Looping an Animation

When you create an animation, by default it plays once. If desired, you can modify the number of times the animation plays. You can choose a set number of times to play the animation or loop it forever.

To change the number of times an animation plays:

1. Choose Window | Frames. The Frames panel opens.

2. Click the GIF Animation Looping button to display the drop-down menu shown here:

3. Choose the number of times you want the animation to play and then press ENTER or RETURN. Fireworks displays the number of times the animation will loop to the right of the GIF Animation Looping button. When you export the document as an Animated GIF file, the file will play for the selected number of loops when displayed in a Web browser.

Animating Objects

When you create an animation, you can let your imagination wander. There are so many different ways to animate objects, the subject warrants a book of its own. However, you can begin by modifying certain properties of an object from one frame to the next. The following list is by no means all inclusive, but will give you a good jumping off point. To animate an object from one frame to another you can:

- Move it to a new position.
- Change its dimensions.
- Change its opacity.
- Change its blend mode.
- Change its color.
- Rotate, skew, or otherwise distort the object.
- Display a text object, one letter at a time in consecutive frames. This makes it look as though the text is being typed.
- Display a phrase one word at a time in consecutive frames.
- Modify the kerning, baseline shift, and other parameters of a text object to simulate moving text.

The best way to become an animator is to create a document, create or import some objects, and then experiment. Follow the instructions in the previous sections to create frames and copy objects to frames, and then use your knowledge of the other Fireworks tools to modify the objects in your document.

Tweening Symbol Instances

If you've created a graphic symbol, you have the starting point for an animation. To animate a symbol, you create two instances of it on the canvas, change one or more properties of an instance, and then have Fireworks tween the instances. You specify the number of steps, and Fireworks creates the animation by modifying the shapes in the number of steps specified in between the selected instances.

To create an animation by tweening instances:

1. Create a graphic symbol. The symbol can be one you create with the Fireworks tools or a vector object that you import.

2. Create two instances of the symbol on the canvas.

3. Modify one of the instances. You can rotate, skew, or distort an instance of the symbol. Alternatively, you can change the instance's blend mode or opacity.

4. Select the two instances.

5. Choose Modify | Symbol | Tween Instances. The Tween Instances dialog box appears, as shown here:

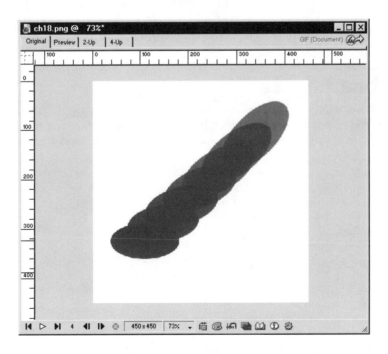

6. Enter a value in the Steps field. This value is the number of shapes Fireworks will create between the instances.

7. Click the Distribute To Frames checkbox, and Fireworks will create a separate frame for each step. If you don't select this option, Fireworks creates the in-between objects on a single frame.

8. Click OK. Fireworks tweens the instances. The following illustration shows tweened instances that have not been distributed to frames.

Animating Bitmaps

In addition to creating animations of objects, you can also create animations that display bitmaps. For example, if your client represents several product lines, you can create an animated GIF that displays the logos of selected product lines. If you create such an animation, resample the bitmaps to a size where they are recognizable, yet not so large as to create a large file. As a rule, you'll be using an animation of this sort in conjunction with other elements in a Web page; therefore, you should optimize the file to as small a size as possible. Remember that each bitmap will be displayed with a maximum of 256 colors. This is fine for logos, but if your client represents fashion models and wants you to create an animation showing each model's face, do not use an animated GIF. The end result will not be flattering to the model or to your client. A program like Flash is better suited to creating animations of this sort.

Creating an Image Sequence

When you create an animation that displays several images, you can simulate a movie by creating an image sequence. For example, you can display several thumbnail images of a person in different poses. When you string them together in frames to create an animation, it appears as though the person is moving. If you use this technique, keep the number of frames to a minimum—no more than eight. If your client coerces you into using close-up shots, you'll have no choice but to export the document with 256 colors. However, if such an animation is used on a Web page without too many other elements, the download time probably will still be acceptable.

Animating Effects

In a previous section, you learned to tween instances of a symbol. You can achieve some interesting effects by applying an effect to a symbol, duplicating the symbol, and then moving it to another position. Edit the effect on the duplicated symbol, and then choose Modify | Symbol | Tween Instances. The following illustration shows two instances of an oval symbol with different settings of the Inner Bevel effect. The instances simulate the effect that the bevel is growing.

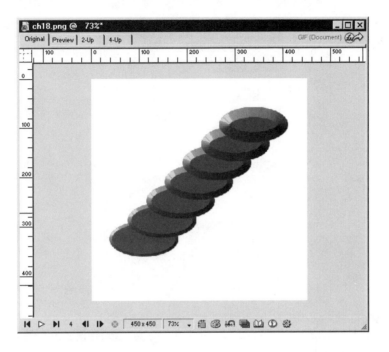

Optimizing the Animation

Before you can export a multi-frame file as an animation, you must choose the proper optimization method. If you export a multi-frame document as a GIF file, it will not play in a Web browser. Before you export the file, you must choose the Animated GIF format.

To export the file as an Animated GIF:

1. Choose Window | Optimize. The Optimize panel opens, as shown here:

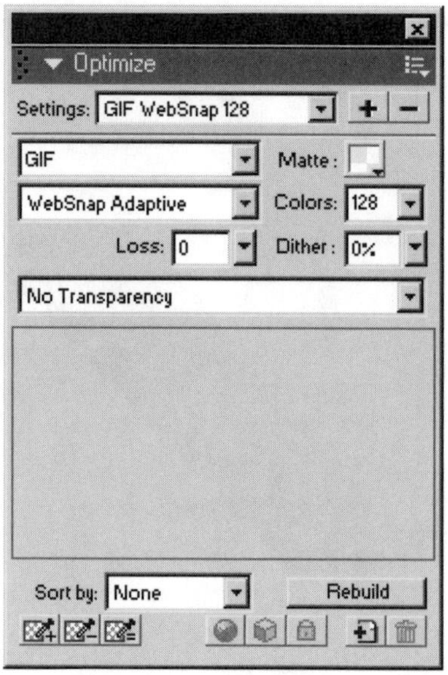

2. Click the triangle to the right of the Settings field and choose Animated GIF Web 128. You should always use this setting as a starting point for optimizing an animated GIF.

> **Note** *There are several other settings you can change to create the smallest possible file while still preserving good image quality. For more information on optimization, see Chapter 21.*

Previewing an Animation in a Web Browser

When you create an animated GIF, the best way to preview it is in a Web browser. When you preview an animation in a Web browser, you see it exactly as your viewers will. To preview an animation in a browser, press F12.

Fine-Tuning an Animation

If you preview the animation and it looks wonderful, you're almost home. In the document window, click the 2-Up tab and note the file size and projected download time. If you are going to display the animation with other objects in a Web page, you may have to preview it with the other elements in your HTML editor. If the file size and animation are acceptable, export the document. However, if the animation doesn't play as you'd like or the file size is unwieldy, you can fine-tune the animation by doing one or more of the following:

- Increase the time delay between frames to slow down an animation sequence.
- Decrease the time delay between frames to speed up an animation sequence.
- To accentuate a particular frame in your animation, increase its time delay so it is displayed longer.
- Delete frames to create a smaller file.
- Add frames if an animation sequence appears choppy.

Summary

In this chapter, you learned how to create animations using the Animate command, and you learned how to use the Frames panel to create frame-by-frame animations. In addition, you learned how to create animations by tweening symbol instances, as well as how to animate bitmaps and create image sequences. In Chapter 19, you'll take your knowledge of animation one step further and learn how to create animated banners.

Chapter 19

Creating Animated Banners

nother effective use for animation is the time-honored banner. Banners can be annoying when you're viewing a Web site, but they can be lucrative from a design standpoint because many clients require an animated banner of some sort. When you create an animated banner for a Web page, there are certain industry-accepted standards such as size and placement of the banner. If you think these standards fly in the face of logic, feel free to create your own take on banner size and placement. However, if your client is a stickler for conforming to standards, stick to the sizes and placements you'll learn about in this chapter. Another thing to be concerned with when creating a banner is bandwidth. When you create a banner, it's generally larger in physical size than an animated logo, and that equates to a larger file size. However, with the judicious use of frames and colors, you can create an effective banner ad that downloads quickly.

In this chapter, you'll build on the animation techniques you learned in the last chapter. You'll learn the standard sizes and placements for animated banners, as well as how to create an effective banner that doesn't break the user's bandwidth.

Creating Web Site Banners

When you create an animated banner for a Web page, you must take several factors into consideration. First and foremost is the file size of the exported animation. When you add the overhead of an animated banner to the other elements on a Web page, you run the risk of creating a document that will take a long time to download. Visitors to a Web site expect things to happen instantaneously, and they may not wait for your banner to download.

There are several factors that determine the file size of the exported animation. The file size of your animation increases when you add frames, colors, and objects to the document. Another factor that determines the file size is the physical size of the animation itself. Like any other project you create for fun or profit, a little bit of forethought is in order before you rush blindly into creating what may be a dismal failure.

Controlling Bandwidth

Bandwidth is the maximum amount of data in Kbps (kilobytes per second) that can be downloaded at a given connection speed. As you create a document, you can click the Preview tab to display the document as it is currently optimized. In the Preview tab, Fireworks also displays the size of the file in kilobytes and the projected download time. This is an invaluable tool when you are creating an animation; however, if you've created two frames of a projected six-frame animation and the projected download time is 15 seconds, you've got a problem on your hands.

Before you begin creating the animation, create a storyboard as outlined in previous chapters. Gather the assets you'll need for the banner, such as corporate logos and bitmap images. Use Fireworks to resize the bitmaps and other assets to an appropriate size for the banner. Then you can combine all of the assets in a single frame document the same size as your banner and note the file size. If the assets will be used throughout the animation, multiply the size by the projected number of frames, and you'll have a good idea of how large the exported animation will be. If it's excessive, the first step is to reduce the number of objects in the animation and perhaps the number of frames. You can blur objects to simulate motion rather than create a large number of frames to simulate motion. Remember that when you exceed a user's bandwidth, the animation will halt while enough additional data downloads to play the next frame.

After you determine the number of objects you can safely use without exceeding a user's bandwidth, your next consideration is the number of colors with which to export the document.

Choosing Colors

If you're creating an animation with only vector objects, you have total control over the number of colors you use. If you've saved color palettes from other projects, you can import them by using the Load Palette command from the Optimize panel Options menu or by using the Add Swatches command from the Swatches panel Options menu. As you create the animation, you can click the Preview tab in the document window to preview the document and the file size. If you're judicious in your use of color and the effects you apply, you can generally export an animated banner with 16 colors or 32 at the most.

Note *When you preview an animation, remember to choose Window | Optimize to open the Optimize panel. Click the triangle to the right of the Settings field and choose Animated GIF Websnap 128 as the optimization method. Otherwise, the Preview window will show the file size and download time for only the selected frame and not the entire animation.*

When you add bitmaps to the equation, the degree of difficulty jumps up a notch or two. As you know, most bitmaps are .jpg files with millions of colors. When you export a bitmap in GIF format, the file size may end up being larger than the original .jpg file, especially if you use 256 colors. When a bitmap with millions of colors is exported as a .gif file, Fireworks dithers colors from the Web Safe palette or from the selected palette simulate a color not present in the palette.

You also increase the number of colors in the export palette when adding effects to vector or bitmap objects. When you add a drop shadow or glow to an object, Fireworks creates the additional colors needed to blend the vector or text object with the drop shadow or glow. For example, adding a drop shadow to a gray rectangle changes the number of colors in the export color table from 10 to 32.

There are a couple of methods you can use to reduce the file size of an animation when your client requests that you use bitmaps:

- Import the bitmap into the document and choose Commands | Creative | Convert To Grayscale. After converting the original bitmap to grayscale, copy it to additional frames as needed.

- Import the bitmap into the document and choose Commands | Creative | Convert To Sepia.

- Import the bitmap into the document, open the Property inspector, and add the Hue/Saturation effect to the bitmap. The Hue/Saturation effect is used to achieve the commands used in the Creative commands listed in the prior color reduction methods. However, when you choose the actual effect, you can tweak the settings to add a bit of color to the image while still keeping the number of colors in the palette at a manageable level.

Remember that after you use any of the above methods to reduce the number of colors in the document, you can further modify the export palette by snapping colors to Web safe or deleting them from within the Optimize panel. After you modify the color palette, click the Preview tab to see the results of your color reduction. If you've gone too far and the bitmap quality is degraded to a point where it is not pleasing, you can remove the effects you've applied to the bitmaps, choose a different optimization method, and then rebuild the color table. Remember that after you rebuild the color table, you'll have to choose the Animated GIF optimization method again and then adjust the number of color exported to the number of colors in the color table, or choose a color palette with more colors than the color palette that degraded the image.

Planning the Banner

When you add a Web banner to a site, you're generally telling a story on behalf of your client. Like any story, it has a beginning, a middle, and an end. At the beginning of the animation, you tease the viewers or plant a hook to catch their attention. The hook can be an image, the first word of a phrase or product, or you can use a brilliant splash of color to attract the viewer's attention to the banner instead of the rest of the objects that are loading into the page. If you do a good job of creating a limited color palette, the animation will load quickly, and you will be able to use the first frame to grab the viewer.

The meat of the banner is in the middle of the production. Here's where you tell the story. You can tell the story by revealing more text or by adding an object or image to the animation. If you use a combination of the two, you can trail the image in from the right to left and trail the text from left to right.

Most banners are commercial in nature. Therefore, the final frame of the animation should be designed to make the viewer take action. You can do this by revealing the price of a product or service or by displaying the uniform resource locator (URL) where the product or service can be procured. Figure 19-1 shows how a four-frame animation can be effectively used to create an ad banner.

Choosing Banner Size

Banners come in many flavors. Banners that are Web site fixtures are generally long and short or tall and narrow. Another type of banner is the pop-up banner. These appear in conjunction with a page that is loading or a button click. Pop-up banners are usually square. Table 19-1 lists some popular banner sizes.

Setting the Frame Delay

After you decide how many frames the animation will be and create the content for the banner, you set the frame delay. As mentioned in Chapter 18, the default frame delay of $7/100^{th}$ of a second is too fast to see any detail. You can decide what frame delay to use when you preview the animation in a Web browser. Fine-tune the frame rate until you get the desired effect. As you preview the animation, keep the overall goal or storyline of the animation in mind. Does the story require frenetic action, or do you want the viewer to look at each individual frame and absorb the message you are portraying with the animation. In that regard, you can also draw viewers' attention to

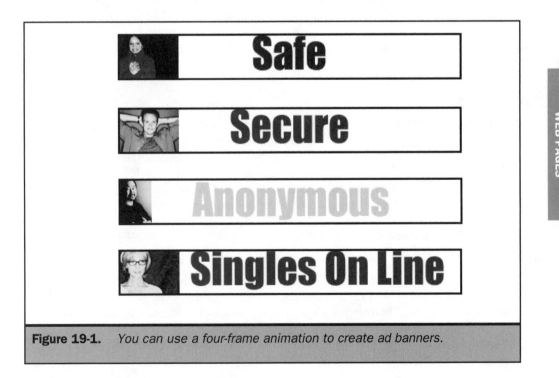

Figure 19-1. *You can use a four-frame animation to create ad banners.*

Banner Location	Banner Size in Pixels
Top of browser window	468 × 60
Right or left side of page content	120 × 600
Right or left side of page content	160 × 600
Small ad on side of page content	160 × 120
Small ad on side of page content	120 × 160
Mini ad on side of page content	148 × 60
Pop-up window ad	250 × 250
Pop-up window ad	180 × 150

Table 19-1.   *Popular Banner Ad Sizes*

specific frames by increasing the frame delay and thereby giving the viewers additional time to reflect on the contents of a given frame. You should always consider a longer frame delay for the final frame when you call the viewer to action.

Note   *For specific information on creating the frame delay for your animation, refer to Chapter 18.*

Looping the Animation

Another method you can use to accentuate an ad banner and draw a viewer's attention to a particular frame is by controlling the number of times the animation loops. As you learned in Chapter 18, you can specify the number of times an animation plays. If you create an effective ad banner with a call to action, let the animation loop two or three times. The motion attracts the attention of viewers and draws them to the banner ad. When the animation stops looping, it stops on the last frame; and if you've done your job correctly, it calls the viewer to action.

Animating Text

There are so many ways to attract a viewers attention when you have unlimited bandwidth or you are creating a multimedia production for a CD-ROM. However, when you create an ad banner for a Web page, you are constricted by your viewer's available bandwidth. Therefore, you've got to be creative and come up with ways to attract viewers to the banner, while at the same time creating a relatively small file.

One of the techniques you can use is animating text. Some techniques for animating text were presented in the last chapter. Remember, you can also animate text by applying an effect to it and then vary the effect from one frame to another. Other techniques you can use are changing text color from one frame to another or changing the baseline shift of a word or letter between frames. If you change text colors, make sure you don't exceed the original number of colors you planned to use for the animation. As always, preview the animation to keep tabs on the file size and the projected download time.

Linking the Banner

If the banner you are creating needs to be linked to an external site, you can do so by creating a hotspot and then assigning the desired URL to the hotspot. You can create a hotspot that encompasses the entire document; or you can create a button on the last frame, select the button, and then choose Edit | Insert | Hotpsot. Even though logic may dictate that the hotspot will only be active on the frame to which you added it, a hotspot is a Web object on the Web layer. Therefore, it is shared on all frames. If a user rolls a mouse over the hotspot area, the familiar pointing finger icon appears. To take control of the animation and direct the viewer to the link when desired, it is suggested you create a button symbol and place it on the last frame. Adjust the frame delay so the animation stays on this frame longer than the others. Viewers will recognize the button and click it out of curiosity. When you create the link for the button, choose _blank for the target, and the link opens in another browser window.

Creating a Transparent Background

If you create an ad banner that will be used on different sites, the banner may be displayed on different color backgrounds. If you create the banner on a different color canvas than the Web page background, the colors may clash. Therefore, you should create the banner with a transparent background.

To create a transparent background:

1. Choose Modify | Canvas | Canvas Color.

2. Choose Transparent.

3. Click OK. When you export the document as an Animated GIF file and display the file in a Web browser, the background of the Web page will appear wherever there is a blank spot on the canvas.

Blurring to Simulate Motion

When you create an animation for display on a Web page, file size is an important consideration. If you're displaying the animation in conjunction with several other elements on a Web page, you may not be able to pack as much action into the presentation as you'd like. To create action with smooth-flowing motion requires the use of several frames; otherwise, the animation appears choppy, as if it was filmed on an old-fashioned motion picture camera from the turn of the last century. You can simulate smooth motion and cut down on the number of frames in the document by blurring objects. You can blur individual objects in the document. For example, if you have a bitmap image of a car and you want to move it from one side of the document to another, you can apply a Gaussian Blur to the car. In subsequent frames, you can move the bitmap a considerable distance. The blur tricks the viewer's eye into believing that the car is moving at a fast rate of speed.

> **Tip** *To simulate motion with a vector image, skew it. In the first frame of the animation, do not skew the image. In subsequent frames, skew the image horizontally to simulate an object that is accelerating or braking.*

Using the Data Driven Graphics Wizard

One of the many new features of Fireworks MX is the Data Driven Graphics Wizard. With the Data Driven Graphics Wizard, it is possible to generate multiple files from a single template. With this wizard, you are able to specify areas of a document as placeholders for graphic images and text. You specify individual areas with variable names. The Data Driven Graphics Wizard links these variable names with information or data records in an Extensible Markup Language (XML) file. After you put the wizard through its paces, individual files are generated for each record in the XML file. If you've ever spent hours creating multiple files where the only things that change are one or two central images, a line or two of text, or a URL, you'll appreciate the amount of time you can save using the Data Driven Graphics Wizard.

Creating XML Files for the Wizard

You can create XML files for the Data Driven Graphics Wizard in any database program, such as Microsoft Access 2002, which has the capability of generating version 1.0 XML files. You can also create the files manually in a text editor or in your favorite HTML editor. When you create the XML file, you create the data for each document with a beginning record tag (<record>) followed by the data that will change within each document, followed by an ending record tag (</record>). The information in each record consists of the variable names from the document. As shown in the following illustration, you can have more than one variable name in each record.

```
C:\Documents and Settings\Doug Sahlin\Desktop\Acme Computers\Acme_Computers...

File   Edit   View   Favorites   Tools   Help

    <?xml version="1.0" encoding="iso-8859-1" ?>
  - <records>
    - <record>
        <varModel>StarDust</varModel>
        <listPrice>$899</listPrice>
        <varBitmap>StarDust.png</varBitmap>
        <url>http://www.acmecomputers.net/Stardust.html</url>
        <varTag>High Speed Modem.</varTag>
      </record>
    - <record>
        <varModel>StarTrek</varModel>
        <listPrice>$1099</listPrice>
        <varBitmap>StarTrek.png</varBitmap>
        <url>http://www.acmecomputers.net/Startrek.html</url>
        <varTag>512 MB DDR RAM</varTag>
      </record>
    - <record>
        <varModel>Voyager</varModel>
        <listPrice>$1299</listPrice>
        <varBitmap>Voyager.png</varBitmap>
        <url>http://www.acmecomputers.net/Voyager.html</url>
        <varTag>CD/CDR DVD</varTag>
      </record>
    - <record>
        <varModel>Enterprise</varModel>
        <listPrice>$1499</listPrice>
        <varBitmap>Enterprise.png</varBitmap>
        <url>http://www.acmecomputers.net/Enterprise.html</url>
        <varTag>Tape Backup</varTag>
      </record>
    </records>
```

Creating the Template in Fireworks

You can use the Data Driven Graphics Wizard to create animated banners. In fact, you can use the wizard anytime you need to create multiple files where the only difference from one banner to the next is an image, a text tagline, or a URL. To turn a Fireworks document into a template for the Data Driven Graphics Wizard, you embed variables that correspond to data names in the XML document. The Data Driven Graphics Wizard recognizes Fireworks text as a variable when you encompass the text in curly braces (for example, {varURL}). When you create a variable name, use a meaningful name that can be easily identified by other designers who may use the file. Do not use any spaces when creating the variable name. If you need to differentiate between two words in a variable name, capitalize the second word ({lastName}), or separate the first and last name with an underscore ({last_name}). When you create a text variable, all of the text formatting you apply to the variable name is applied to the data read from the XML file.

In addition to being able to change text and URL data, you can also change an image by giving it a variable name. When you create the images that appear in other documents created by the Data Driven Graphics Wizard, make sure they are the same size as the image in the template. You can use Fireworks batch processing to resample multiple images to the same size.

To convert a bitmap image into a variable:

1. Select the bitmap in the document.

2. Click the arrow to the left of the word Properties. The Property inspector opens.

3. In the Object Name field, enter the variable name for the image. Remember, the variable name cannot have spaces and must be surrounded by curly braces (for example, {varBitmap}). The following illustration shows a bitmap that has been converted to a variable name.

Another data type that you can convert into a variable is a URL link. You do this by creating a hotspot or slice and converting its name into a variable.

To convert a hotspot or slice into a variable:

1. Select the hotspot or slice.

2. Click the arrow to the left of the word Properties. The Property inspector opens.

3. In the Links field, enter a variable name. For example: {URL}.

When you create variable names in Fireworks, use the same names as you used in the XML document from which the Data Driven Graphics Wizard will read the information. You can use the wizard to manually map the information from the records to the variables in the document. However, if you use the same names, the wizard automatically links the document variable to the XML data.

Before you put the wizard to work, store all of your data in a folder for easy retrieval. Store the template and XML file within this folder. In a subfolder, store all of the images the wizard will use to create the documents. After you organize your assets, you're ready to put the wizard to work.

Using the Data Driven Graphics Wizard

After you create an XML document and a template in Fireworks, you're ready to put the Data Driven Graphics Wizard through its paces. The wizard guides you through the process in six steps.

To create multiple files using the Data Driven Graphics Wizard, follow these steps:

1. Open the document template in Fireworks.

2. Choose Commands | Data Driven Graphics Wizard. The first Data Driven Graphics Wizard dialog box opens, as shown here:

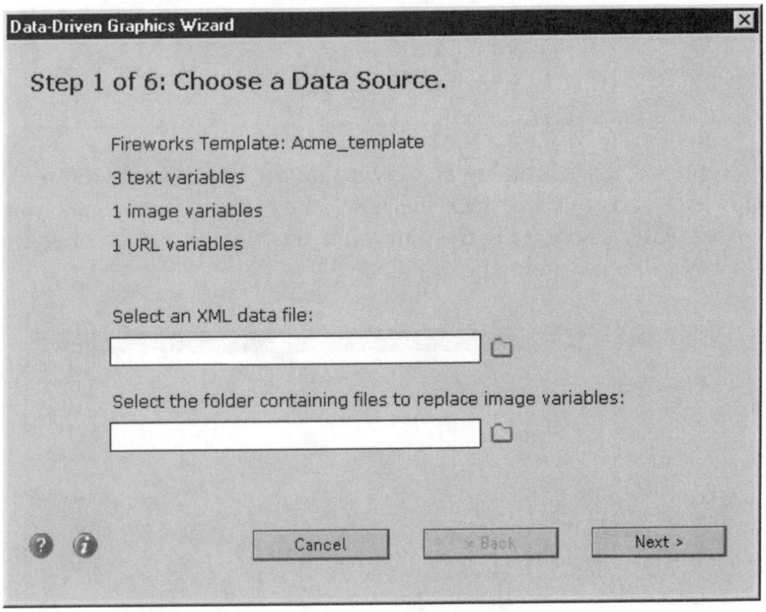

3. Click the file folder icon to the right of the Select An XML Data File field, navigate to the folder in which your XML file is stored, and click Open.

4. Click the file folder icon to the right of the Select The Folder field containing files to replace image variables. Navigate to the folder in which the files are stored and select the folder.

5. Click the Next button to open the second dialog box shown here:

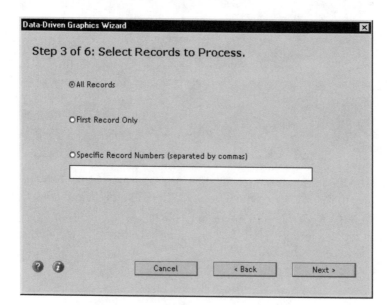

6. The Preview The Data dialog box gives you the opportunity to preview the data in each record of the XML file. Click the buttons to advance from record to record. After previewing the data, click the Next button to open the Select Records To Process dialog box.

7. Accept the default All Records option, and then choose First Record Only or Specific Record Numbers. If you choose Specific Record Numbers, list each record number you want to use, separating them with commas. For example, enter **1,3,7**, and Fireworks will use the first, third, and seventh records from the XML document to generate the files. After selecting the files to process, click the Next button to open the Map Variables To Fields dialog box, shown here:

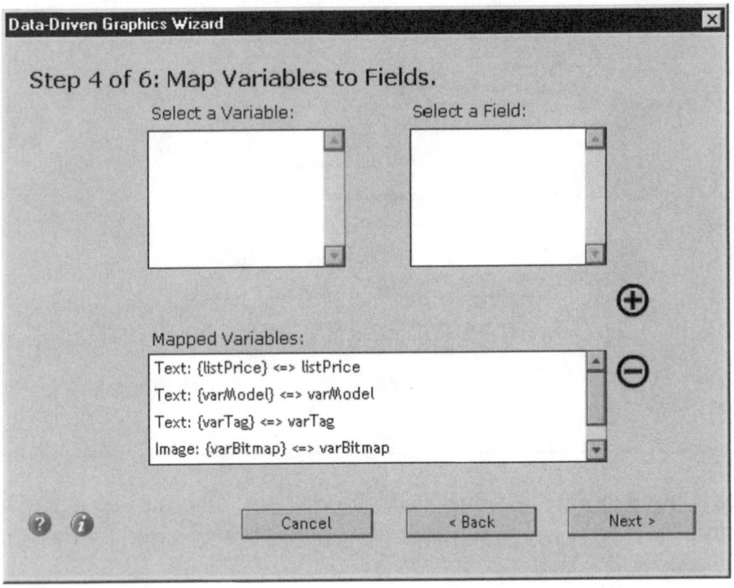

8. Any unmapped variables in your Fireworks document appear in the Select A Variable field. Any unused fields in the XML document appear in the Select A Field field.

9. To link an unmapped variable with an XML field, click the variable, click the field that contains the matching data for the variable, and then click the plus sign (+) to map the variable. By default, the wizard maps all variables to matching field names in the XML document, an important reason to use the same name.

10. To delete a mapped variable from processing, select it in the Mapped Variables section of the dialog box, and then click the minus sign (–). After mapping the

variables, click the Next button to open the Export Settings dialog box, shown here:

11. Enter a name in the Filename field. This is the name that the Data Driven Graphics Wizard assigns to the processed files, appended by the numbering preference you select.

12. Click the triangle to the right of the File Numbering field and choose a preference from the drop-down menu.

13. Accept the default starting value of 1, or enter a different value in the field. Enter a different value if you've already created several files using the same template. This alleviates overwriting files you've already created with the wizard.

14. Accept the default Export Images file, and the Wizard generates an image file for each record using the optimization method you choose.

15. Click the triangle to the right of the Template Export field and choose one of the default options from the drop-down menu. These are the same options that are available in the Property inspector. If you've already optimized the document using another method, accept the default Template Export Settings.

16. Click the file folder to the right of the Select A Folder For Exported Graphics field and choose the folder in which you want to store the processed files.

17. Click the Save Source PNG Files checkbox, and the wizard generates a PNG file for each exported image file. If you choose this option, click the file folder to the

right of the Select A Folder For Source PNG Files and choose a folder in which you want to store the files. Click the Next button to open the Review Settings dialog box, shown here:

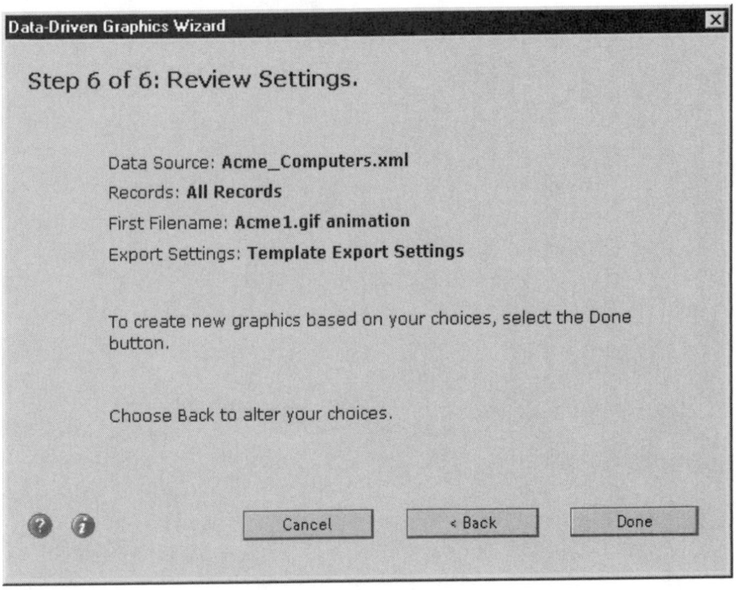

18. If everything is in order, click Done, and the wizard generates the files and stores them in the specified folders. If any of the settings are incorrect, click the Back button to navigate to the appropriate dialog box, where you can change the settings.

If you do a lot of work for clients that use the same general format for ad banners and other documents, the Data Driven Graphics Wizard makes child's play out of updating files. As long as you save the template, all you need to do to update all of the files is to update the XML document, changing records where needed. In the worst case scenario, you'll have to batch process new image files. After updating the XML file and accompanying image files, open the template in Fireworks and run the wizard again.

■ Summary

In this chapter, you learned to plan and create animated banners for the Web. You learned how to choose an optimal color palette for the animation, loop the animation, and create a transparent background. In the last part of the chapter, you learned to use the Data Driven Graphics Wizard to quickly create multiple files from a template with variables, an XML file, and accompanying images. In Chapter 20, you'll learn additional methods for automating Fireworks.

The Complete Reference

Fireworks MX

Part V

Optimizing and Exporting Documents

Chapter 20

Automating Fireworks

As you use a program like Fireworks to create new documents for animations and Web pages, you'll find that your creative energy flows and time flies by. However, when working on the more routine tasks—such as resampling a large number of bitmaps into thumbnail-sized images for a client's Web page—time seems to stand still as you perform the same task over and over. Fortunately, you don't have to suffer the drudgery of repetitive operations when using Fireworks. As you've learned in earlier chapters, you can create reusable artwork in the form of symbols, create animations on the fly with menu commands, and perform complex tasks such as creating several banners with similar content by using a wizard. And you'll be glad to know that you can use other Fireworks features to streamline your workflow.

If you need to perform the same command or series of commands on several image files, instead of opening several documents and then performing the individual menu commands on each document, you can use Fireworks batch processing to select the documents and commands, and then with one button click, Fireworks will process and save all the files. This single feature will save you from the boredom of manually performing repetitive tasks. If your work involves performing a set of tasks and menu commands in a given sequence, you can save the steps as a menu command. If you need to find and replace objects in a document, you can easily do so with the Find and Replace panel.

In this chapter, you'll learn to streamline your work through the use of Fireworks commands and features. These features don't automate Fireworks, but they come close. The features offer a way to speed up your production and spend your time where it counts—in creating new content for fun and profit.

Finding and Replacing Elements

You've probably used find and replace commands in your favorite word processing program. If you're a Dreamweaver veteran, you may have used this program's find and replace commands to fine tune your HTML code. In Fireworks you can find and replace text, URLs, fonts, and more. You perform these tasks quickly and easily using the Find and Replace panel.

Using the Find and Replace Panel

When you need to find and replace elements in a single document, or in multiple documents, you use the Find and Replace panel. This multiple-purpose workhorse can be used to find fonts, colors, text, and URLs. You can limit a search to a single document or search multiple documents.

To open the Find and Replace panel shown in the following illustration, choose Window | Find And Replace. Alternatively, you can choose Edit | Find And Replace, or press CTRL+F (Windows) or COMMAND+F (Macintosh) to open the panel.

Defining a Search

Using the Find and Replace panel, you can fine-tune a search to a specific document, a specific selection, or a series of files. When you define the search, you tell Fireworks the source file(s) to search.

To define a search with the Find and Replace panel:

1. Open the document in which you want to search. (This step is not needed if you are searching multiple files.)

2. Choose Window | Find And Replace. The Find and Replace panel opens.

3. Click the triangle to the right of the Search field, and from the drop-down menu, choose one of the following:

   ■ **Search Selection** Confines the search to the currently selected text or objects.

   ■ **Search Frame** Confines the search to the currently selected frame.

   ■ **Search Document** Confines the search to the currently active document. If multiple documents are open, select the document you want to search and then open the panel. If you want to search multiple files, choose the Search Files option.

   ■ **Search Project Log** Confines the search to files listed in the Project Log. The Project Log will be covered in detail later in the section "Managing Multiple Files with the Project Log."

- **Search Files** Confines the search to a selection of files. When you choose this option, the Open dialog box appears. Navigate to the files you want to search, select them, and then click Done. When you replace objects in multiple files, you can choose whether to replace a single instance of the object for which you are searching or replace them all.

4. Click the triangle to the right of the Find What field, and from the drop-down menu, select one of the following: Find Text, Find Font, Find Color, Find URL, or Find Non-Web216. The available options vary depending on the object you are searching for and will be covered in upcoming sections.

5. Click the Find button to begin your search. Fireworks finds the first instance of your search query and highlights it.

6. Click Replace to replace a single instance of the item. To continue searching for other instances of your search query, click the Find button.

7. To replace all instances of your search query, click Replace All. Fireworks replaces all occurrences of your search item.

Using the Find and Replace Panel with Multiple Files

When you use the Find and Replace panel to search multiple files, you can specify how Fireworks replaces objects. You can choose to archive the original files, perform incremental backups, or simply save the files after replacing the desired objects.

To set options for finding and replacing objects in multiple files:

1. Choose Window | Find And Replace. The Find and Replace panel opens.

2. Define a search as outlined in the previous section.

3. Click the Options menu icon in the upper-right corner of the panel (which looks like a mini-bulleted list icon), and choose Replace Options to open the Replace Options dialog box, shown here:

4. Deselect the Save And Close Files option (selected by default), and the file(s) you searched remain open after the search is completed and are saved with the same filename in the same directory when the find and replace operation is completed. If you deselect this option, the Backup Original Files options are grayed out.

5. Or, if you choose the Save And Close Files option, click the triangle to the right of the Backup Original Files field and choose one of the following options:

   ■ **No Backups**   The default option. When you choose this option, Fireworks overwrites the original files and saves them with the same filename.

   ■ **Overwrite Existing Backups**   Makes it possible for you to create one backup of the original file. If you choose to find and replace items at a later date using the same filename, the original file is overwritten and the backup is archived. When you choose this option, backup files are stored in a subfolder called Original Files.

   ■ **Incremental Backup Files**   Makes it possible for you to create additional backups of a file when performing the find and replace operation more than once. When you choose this option, the original file is unaffected. Incremental backups are appended by numbers—for example myfile.png, myfile-1.png, myfile-2.png, and so on.

6. Click OK to apply the options and close the dialog box.

Finding and Replacing Text

If you've created several documents for a client and the client asks you to change a text item in all documents, you can perform the task quickly using the Find and Replace panel's Find Text option. When you choose this option, you can fine-tune the search to find only whole words, match case when finding a word, or find the search word if it's part of a regular expression.

To find and replace text objects:

1. Choose Window | Find And Replace.

2. Define your search parameters as outlined previously. Remember that you can search a section of a document, the entire document, or a selection of files.

3. Click the triangle to the right of the Find What field, and from the drop-down menu choose Find Text. The Find and Replace panel is reconfigured, as shown next.

4. In the Find field, enter the text for which you want Fireworks to search.

5. In the Change To field, enter the replacement text.

6. To further refine the search, choose one or more of the following options:

   ■ **Whole Word**   Returns only instances of the entire word or phrase you entered in the Find field. For example, if you enter the word *text*, Fireworks finds only instances of the whole word and not words such as *context*.

   ■ **Match Case**   Returns only instances of a word when the case matches.

   ■ **Regular Expressions**   Returns instances of the word you enter in the Find field when the searched word is part of a word in the file(s) being searched. When you choose this option and enter the word *text*, Fireworks will find instances of *text* and also words such as *context*.

7. Click Find to begin the search. Fireworks locates the first instance of the word.

8. Click Replace to replace the word. Alternatively, you can click Replace All to replace all instances of the searched word or click Find to find the next instance of your query.

Finding and Replacing Fonts

You can find and replace fonts in one or more documents as well. This option comes in handy when you or your client decide that a different font would be better suited to one or more documents you've created.

To replace fonts:

1. Choose Window | Find And Replace. The Find and Replace panel opens.

2. Define your search as outlined earlier in this chapter.

3. Click the triangle to the right of the Find What field, and from the drop-down menu choose Find Font. The Find and Replace panel is reconfigured to search for fonts, as shown here:

4. Click the triangle to the right of the Find Font field, and from the drop-down menu, choose the font you want Fireworks to find.

5. Click the triangle to the right of the Find Style field, and from the drop-down menu, choose an option. The default option (Any Style) returns all instances of the font type specified in step 4. You can fine-tune the search by choosing to find only fonts that are boldfaced, italicized, underlined, and so on.

6. In the Min field, enter the minimum font size you want Fireworks to search for. This value is in points.

7. In the Max field, enter the maximum font size you want Fireworks to search for.

8. In the Change To section, click the triangle to the right of the Font Type field and from the drop-down menu choose a font type. Choose the default option (Same Font) when you don't want Fireworks to change the font type but you want other parameters changed, such as font style or size.

9. Click the triangle to the right of the Font Style field, and from the drop-down menu choose the font style you want used as a replacement. Choose the default option (Same Style) when you don't want to change the style of the font but you want other parameters changed.

10. Click the triangle to the right of the Font Size field and drag the slider to specify the new font size. Alternatively, you can enter a value in the field.

11. Click Find, and Fireworks returns the first instance of the font you specified.

12. Click Replace to replace the found instance of the font. Alternatively, click Replace All to replace all instances of the font, or click Find to find the next instance of the specified font.

Finding and Replacing Colors

Another item you can quickly find and replace is a color. You can use this option to replace a specific color in one or more documents. The ability to find and replace a color quickly is valuable if you need to make extensive modifications to several documents.
    To find and replace a color:

1. Choose Window | Find And Replace. The Find and Replace panel opens.

2. Click the triangle to the right of the Find What field, and from the drop-down menu choose Find Color. The Find and Replace panel is reconfigured for a color search, as shown here:

3. In the Find field, click the color swatch to open the pop-up palette that contains the colors of the currently loaded swatch set. Click a color to select it. Alternatively, in the text field, you can enter the hexadecimal value of the color you want to replace.

4. In the Change To field, click the color swatch and choose a color from the pop-up palette.

5. Click the triangle to the right of the Apply To field, and choose one of the following options:

   - **Fills And Strokes**   Returns all instances of the specified color when used for an object's stroke and/or fill.

   - **All Properties**   Returns all instances of the color when used for an object's stroke, fill, or as part of an effect applied to an object.

   - **Fills**   Returns only instances of the specified color when used for an object's fill.

   - **Strokes**   Returns only instances of the specified color when used to define an object's stroke.

   - **Effects**   Returns only instances of the color when used as part of an effect applied to an object, such as the color of a drop shadow.

6. Click Find, and Fireworks returns the first instance of the color when used as specified. Click Replace to replace the found instance of the color. Alternatively, you can click Replace All to replace all instances of the specified color, or you can click Find to search for the next instance of the color.

Finding and Replacing URLs

If you've ever had to search manually through several documents to update links because of a changed URL, you'll appreciate the speed with which you can change a URL in several documents using the Find and Replace panel. You can find and replace URLs assigned to buttons, hot spots, or slices.

To find and replace a URL:

1. Choose Window | Find And Replace. The Find and Replace panel opens.

2. Define the parameters of your search, as outlined previously.

3. Click the triangle to the right of the Find What field, and from the drop-down menu choose Find URL. The Find and Replace panel is reconfigured as shown next.

4. In the Find field, enter the URL for which you want to search.

5. In the Change To field, enter the replacement URL.

6. To further refine your search, choose any or all of the following options:

   ■ **Whole Word**   Searches for the URL exactly as you have entered it in the Find field.

   ■ **Match Case**   Searches for the URL, matching the case of each word you enter in the Find field.

   ■ **Regular Expressions**   Searches for URLs that contain the word you enter in the Find field.

7. Click Find to begin your search. Fireworks returns the first instance of the URL that matches your search parameters. Click Replace to replace this instance of the URL. Alternatively, click Replace All to replace all instances of URLs that match your search parameters, or click Find to find the next match.

Finding and Replacing Non-Web-Safe Colors

As you learned in earlier chapters, if you use a non-Web-safe color, you run the risk of the document appearing differently in a viewer's browser than you intended. You can use the Find and Replace panel to safeguard against this by finding and replacing all colors that are not part of the Web Safe 216 palette. When you use this feature, you can specify exactly which items are snapped to the Web Safe palette.

To find and replace all non-Web-safe colors:

1. Choose Window | Find And Replace. The Find and Replace panel opens.

2. Select the documents you want to search, as outlined previously.

3. Click the triangle to the right of the Find What field, and from the drop-down menu choose Find Non-Web216.

4. Click the triangle to the right of the Apply To field, and choose one of the following:

   ■ **Fills And Strokes**   Returns all instances of non-Web-safe color used for an object's stroke and/or fill.

   ■ **All Properties**   Returns all instances of non-Web-safe color when used for an object's stroke, fill, or as part of an effect applied to an object.

   ■ **Fills**   Returns only instances of non-Web-safe color when used for an object's fill.

   ■ **Strokes**   Returns only instances of non-Web-safe color when used to define an object's stroke.

   ■ **Effects**   Returns only instances of non-Web-safe color when used as part of an effect applied to an object.

5. Click Find to begin the search. Fireworks finds the first instance of a non-Web-safe color that has been applied according to the option you selected in step 4.

6. Click Replace to snap the color to the nearest Web-safe color. Alternatively, click Replace All to snap all instances of non-Web-safe color to Web safe, or click Find to locate the next instance of non-Web-safe color.

Using the History Panel

When you perform a task or invoke a menu command, it is stored in the History panel. The History panel stores the number of steps up to the number of undo levels you specified when you set Fireworks Preferences. You can use the History panel to perform the following tasks:

- Undo recent actions.
- Select and repeat recently performed actions from the History panel.
- Copy selected commands or actions to the clipboard as JavaScript text.
- Save a selected set of commands and actions as a custom command. When you save a set of actions as a command, your custom command appears as a menu item in the Commands menu list.

To open the History panel, choose Window | History. If your workspace is set up with the Fireworks default panel layout, or you have the History panel grouped with another panel and docked in the panel window, click the arrow to the left of the panel group's name and then click the History tab, as shown here:

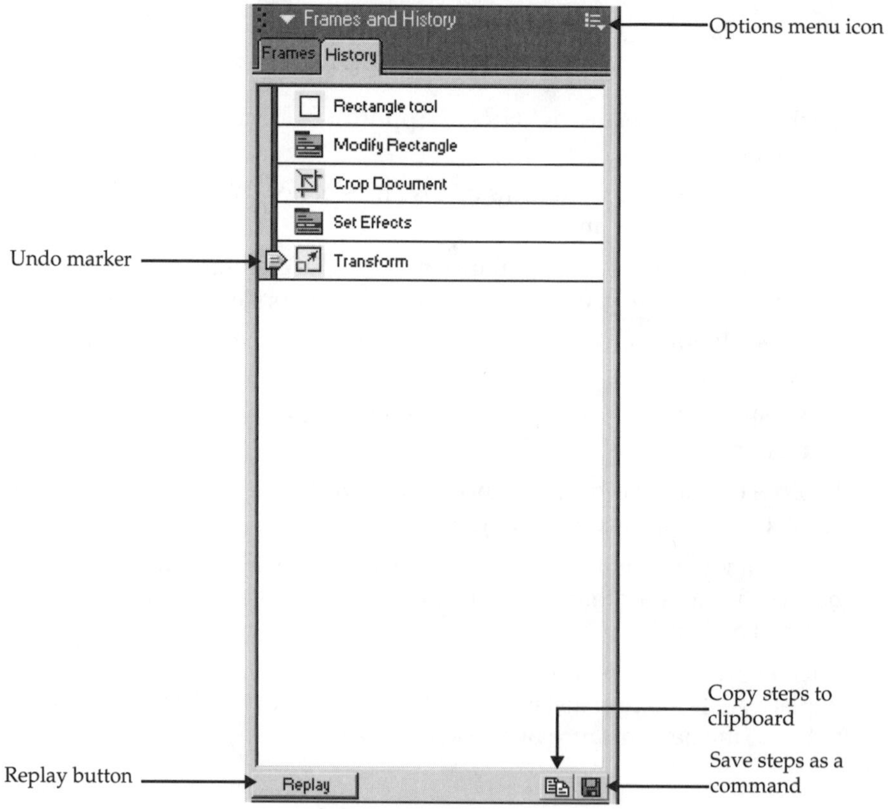

Undoing Recent Actions

From the History panel, you can quickly undo recent actions. When you use the panel in this manner, you can undo a single step or multiple steps.

To undo recent actions:

1. Choose Window | History. The History panel opens.

2. Drag the Undo marker up to select the steps you want to undo. As you move the marker, the selected steps are highlighted. If you accidentally select too many steps, drag the marker toward the bottom of the panel.

3. After selecting the steps you want to undo, perform a new action. The highlighted steps are replaced by the new action you performed. When you undo steps in this manner, the action cannot be undone.

When you choose Edit | Undo, the Undo marker backs up one step; however, the step is still recorded in the History panel until you perform the next action. If you undo multiple steps using the Undo command, before performing a new command you can open the History panel and drag the Undo marker toward the bottom of the panel to redo the steps.

Replaying Selected Steps

You can use the History panel to replay contiguous steps or noncontiguous steps. This is a quick way to apply one or more commands to a number of objects in your document. For example, if you scale an object in the document and want to scale other objects in the document by the same percentage, select the command in the History panel, select the objects, and then replay the step.

To replay a selection of steps:

1. Choose Window | History. The History panel opens.

2. Do one of the following to select the actions you want to repeat:

   ■ Click a single action to select it. When you select an action, it is highlighted.

   ■ Click a single action to select it, and while holding down the SHIFT key, click contiguous actions to add them to the selection. The selected actions are highlighted.

   ■ To select several contiguous steps quickly, click a single action to select it, and then, while holding down the SHIFT key, click the last action you want repeated. The range of actions is highlighted.

   ■ Click an action to select it, and then while holding down the CTRL key (Windows) or COMMAND key (Macintosh), click noncontiguous actions to add them to the selection.

3. Select the objects you want to perform the selected actions on and then click the Replay button. The selected actions are repeated. When you repeat a group of actions, it is shown in the History panel as a single action called Play Steps, as shown next.

Clearing the History Panel

While you are working on a document, each step is saved in the History panel. However, saving steps uses system resources. When you have created and formatted a document to your satisfaction, you can clear the History panel to free up system resources.

To clear the History panel:

1. Click the History panel Options menu icon. The Options menu appears.

2. Choose Clear History. Fireworks displays a warning dialog telling you the command will free up system resources, and that it cannot be undone.

3. Click OK to clear the History panel. After you clear the History panel, you will not be able to undo any actions or commands performed prior to clearing the panel.

Creating New Commands

If you perform a group of actions repeatedly in your work, you can save the steps as a menu command. The commands will then be included on the Commands menu. When you invoke a command, the steps are replayed in the same order you originally performed them.

Saving Steps as a Command

You can create a custom command by saving steps from within the History panel. You can create the command by selecting contiguous or noncontiguous steps.

To save steps as a command:

1. Choose Window | History. The History panel opens.

2. Perform the steps you want to save as a command.

3. Select the steps as outlined previously.

4. Click the Save Steps as a Command icon that looks like a computer floppy disk. The Save Command dialog box appears, as shown here:

5. Enter a name for the command, and click OK. Fireworks saves the steps as a menu command.

When you know exactly which actions you need to use to create a new command, you can create the command using the previous steps. However, sometimes it becomes apparent that a given set of actions you've just performed would be useful as a single command.

Here's how to save a set of actions you've just performed:

1. Choose Window | History. The History panel opens.

2. Select the actions you want to save as a menu command. Remember that you can select contiguous or noncontiguous actions.

3. Click the Save Steps As A Command button located at the lower-right corner of the History panel. The Save Command dialog box appears.

4. Enter a name for the command. Choose a name that accurately reflects the results of the action. If desired, you can enter a lengthy name, as the menu expands to show commands with long names.

5. Click OK to save the steps as a command and close the dialog box.

Copying Steps

If you're adept with JavaScript, you can create a custom command by modifying the JavaScript used to perform one or more actions. You can also copy a selection of steps to the clipboard and apply them to objects in other open documents.

To copy a selection of steps:

1. Choose Window | History. The History panel opens.

2. Select the steps you want to copy to the clipboard.

3. Click the Copy Steps button near the bottom of the panel. Fireworks copies the steps to the clipboard.

After you copy steps to the clipboard, you can use them to modify objects in other open documents. To apply a set of steps to objects in other documents:

1. Copy a set of steps to the clipboard, as outlined previously.

2. Select the document that contains the item(s) to which you want to apply the steps.

3. Select the object(s) to which you want to apply the copied steps.

4. Choose Edit | Paste. Fireworks applies the steps to the selected object. The copied steps are condensed to a single step in the document's History panel and entitled Command Script. To run the script again, select an object and then choose Edit | Repeat Command Script.

After you copy a series of steps to the clipboard, you can paste them into a text editor. If you're proficient with JavaScript, you can modify the copied steps to suit other actions you perform frequently in Fireworks. As you may remember, JavaScript is a scripting language that is used to create numerous effects such as image rollovers and pop-up menus. The illustration shown next shows several steps pasted into a text editor.

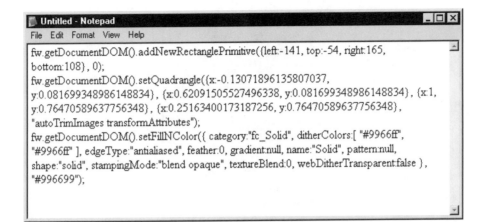

```
Untitled - Notepad                                          _ □ X
File  Edit  Format  View  Help
fw.getDocumentDOM().addNewRectanglePrimitive({left:-141, top:-54, right:165,
bottom:108}, 0);
fw.getDocumentDOM().setQuadrangle({x:-0.13071896135807037,
y:0.081699348986148834}, {x:0.62091505527496338, y:0.081699348986148834}, {x:1,
y:0.76470589637756348}, {x:0.25163400173187256, y:0.76470589637756348},
"autoTrimImages transformAttributes");
fw.getDocumentDOM().setFillNColor({ category:"fc_Solid", ditherColors:[ "#9966ff",
"#9966ff" ], edgeType:"antialiased", feather:0, gradient:null, name:"Solid", pattern:null,
shape:"solid", stampingMode:"blend opaque", textureBlend:0, webDitherTransparent:false },
"#996699");
```

Note *Creating custom JavaScript commands is beyond the scope of this book. For more information on creating custom commands using JavaScript, refer to the "Extending Fireworks MX PDF" file on the Fireworks MX program installation CD-ROM. For more information on JavaScript, check out the selection of titles available at www.Osborne.com.*

Using a Custom Command

A saved command appears on the Commands menu list. The manner in which you use a saved command depends on the steps you used to create it. Remember that you can save a set of steps and use them to create or modify an object.

To use a saved command:

1. Select the object to which you want to apply the command. If the command is used to create new objects, deselect any selected objects.

2. Choose Command, and then select a custom command from the menu list. Commands that you have created appear at the bottom of the Commands menu, as shown next.

```
Commands
    Manage Saved Commands...
    Manage Extensions...
    Run Script...

    Creative                      ▶
    Data-Driven Graphics Wizard
    Document                      ▶
    Panel Layout Sets             ▶
    Reset Warning Dialogs
    Resize Selected Objects
    Web                           ▶

    Create 150 x 113 thumbnail
    Create Skewed Rectangle
    Resample
```
}—— Custom commands

Managing the Commands Menu

Commands that you create and custom panel sets are stored as .jsf files. When a custom command or a panel set has outlived its usefulness, you can delete it to free up room on the Commands menu. You can also rename panel sets or commands.

To delete a saved command or saved panel set:

1. Choose Commands | Manage Saved Commands. The Manage Saved Commands dialog box, shown here, appears.

```
Manage Saved Commands
┌──────────────────────────────────┐   ┌──────────┐
│ Create 150 x 113 thumbnail       │   │    OK    │
│ Create Skewed Rectangle          │   └──────────┘
│ Panel Layout Sets / Doug's panel set │
│ Resample                         │   ┌──────────┐
│                                  │   │ Rename...│
│                                  │   └──────────┘
│                                  │   ┌──────────┐
│                                  │   │  Delete  │
│                                  │   └──────────┘
└──────────────────────────────────┘
```

2. Select the command or panel set you want to delete.

3. Click the Delete button. Fireworks displays a warning dialog telling you the action cannot be undone.

4. Click OK to delete the selected command or panel set. Alternatively, click Cancel to void the action and close the dialog box.

5. Click OK to close the Manage Saved Commands dialog box. Alternatively, select another saved command or panel set you want to edit.

You can also rename a menu command or panel set. To rename a saved command or panel set:

1. Choose Commands | Manage Saved Commands. The Manage Saved Commands dialog box appears.

2. Select the command or panel set you want to rename.

3. Click the Rename button. The Save Command dialog box appears.

4. Enter a new name for the command or panel set, and click OK. Fireworks renames the command and the Manage Saved Commands dialog box displays the new name.

5. Click OK to close the Manage Saved Commands dialog box.

Batch Processing Files

In this chapter, you learned to create custom commands using the History panel, and you learned to copy steps to the clipboard and then apply them to other open documents. You can also apply several steps to a large number of files and Fireworks will process the files for you. This feature is known as *batch processing*. When you batch process a selection of files, you can overwrite the original files, back up the original files, or save the processed files in a different folder.

When you batch process, you can perform the following operations to selected files:

- Convert selected files to another format.

- Change the optimization settings of selected files.

- Scale a selection of image files to a given size.

- Find and replace objects in selected files. The options are identical to those on the Find and Replace panel discussed earlier in this chapter.

- Change the filename of selected files by adding a suffix or a prefix.

- Modify selected files by performing one or more commands from the Commands menu.

Using the Batch Processor

When you need to perform the same actions or commands on several—or several hundred—files, you can quickly do so with the batch processor. When you launch the batch processor, you specify the commands or actions to be performed as well as whether to overwrite the existing files, back up the existing files, or save the processed files in another folder.

To batch process several files:

1. Choose File | Batch Process. The Batch dialog box opens, as shown here:

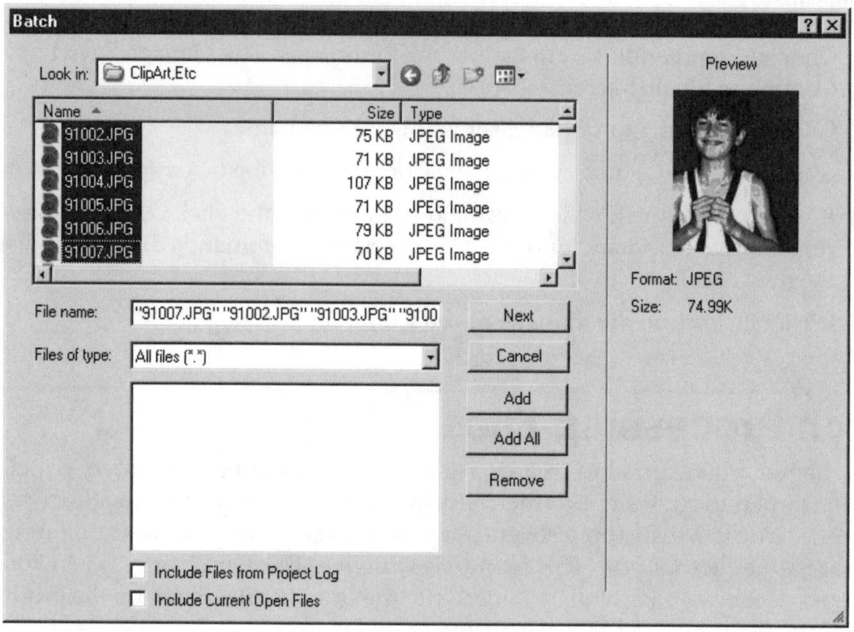

2. Navigate to the folder that contains the files you want to process, and then select the files. You can manually select the files by clicking the first file and then, while holding down the SHIFT key, clicking additional files to add them to the selection.

3. Click the Add button to include the files in the batch process. Alternatively, you can click Add All to add all files in the folder. You can add to the selection by navigating to another folder and selecting additional files.

4. Click the Include Files From Project Log checkbox to add files in the Project Log to the selection. The Project Log will be covered in detail in "Managing Multiple Files with the Project Log" later in this chapter.

5. Click the Include Current Open Files option to add all files currently open in Fireworks to the selection.

6. Click the Next button to open the Batch Process dialog box, shown here:

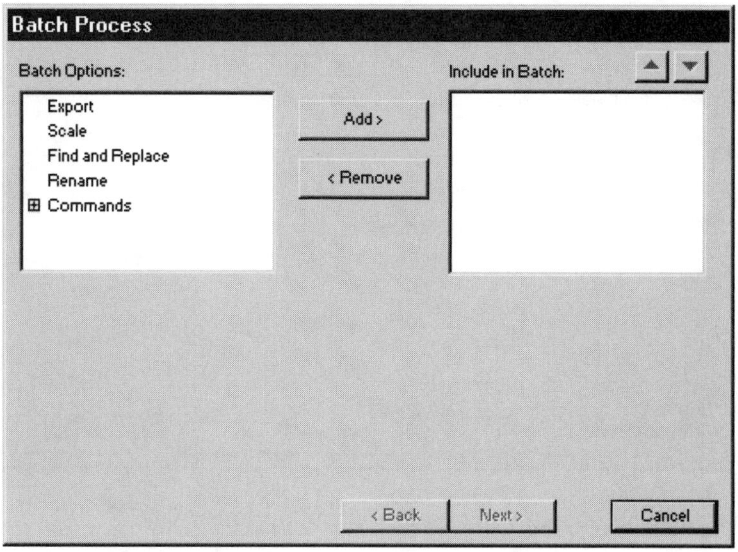

7. In the Batch Options window, click a command to add it to the Include In Batch
   list. Select a menu command, and then click the Add button to add it to the batch
   list. If you select a command with options—for example, the Scale command—
   the available parameters for the command appear at the bottom of the dialog
   box. The popular batch processing options will be discussed in detail in upcoming
   sections. To select one of the commands from the Commands menu, click the
   plus sign (Windows) or the triangle (Macintosh) to the left of the Commands
   item to expand the list. The commands on this list are JavaScript-based and
   therefore have no parameters and cannot be edited.

8. To add commands to the batch list, select them and click the Add button. To
   remove a command from the batch list, select it from the Include In Batch list
   and then click the Remove button.

9. To change the order in which a command is applied, select the command from
   the Include In Batch list and then click the Up or Down arrow to change the
   command's position in the list.

10. Click the Next button to open the Batch Process dialog box shown in the
    following illustration. This dialog box is used to specify a location for
    the processed files and apply any backup options.

Batch Process

Saving Files

Batch Output: ◉ Same Location as Original File
○ Custom Location   Browse

☐ Backups: ◉ Overwrite Existing Backups
○ Incremental Backups

Save Script

< Back   Batch   Cancel

11. Choose one of the following Batch Output options:

- **Same Location As Original File**   Saves the processed files in the folder from which you selected them.

- **Custom Location**   Allows you to specify the location in which the processed files will be saved. When you choose this option, the Browse button becomes active. Click the button to open the Select Images dialog box, navigate to the folder in which you want the processed files saved, and then click Open.

12. Click the Backups checkbox to back up the original files. When you choose to backup files, choose one of the following options:

- **Overwrite Existing Files**   Creates one backup of the original file. If you apply batch processing to the same file again, the original file is overwritten when Fireworks creates a backup of the previously processed file.

- **Incremental Backups**   Creates a backup each time you batch process the file. Each processed file is appended by a number. For example, if the original file is entitled home.jpg, each processed file is saved as home-1.jpg, home-2.jpg, and so on.

13. Click the Save Script button to save the selected commands as a script for future use.

14. Click the Batch button and Fireworks processes the files using the selected commands and saves the files to the specified folder.

Using Batch Processing to Change Export Settings

Batch processing can save you a lot of time when you need to perform redundant tasks. For example, if a client sends you a CD-ROM with high-resolution image files for use at a Web site, you can quickly optimize them and rescale them using batch processing.

To change optimization settings for several files:

1. Choose File | Batch Process. The Batch dialog box opens.

2. Select the files to optimize, and then click Next. The Batch Process dialog box opens.

3. In the Batch Options list, click Export and then click the Add button to add the command to the Include In Batch list. When you select this option, the Settings field appears at the bottom of the dialog box.

4. Click the triangle to the right of the Settings field and choose one of the optimization methods from the menu shown here:

- ■ Choose Use Settings From Each File to preserve the optimization method originally used for the file. This option is useful if you are batch processing files with different formats—for example GIF and JPEG.

- Click the Custom or Edit button to open the Export Preview dialog box. Choose this option when you need to fine-tune the selected optimization method. The Export Preview dialog box will be discussed in detail in Chapter 22.

- Choose one of the presets to convert all selected files to the same format.

Note *If you are processing files with mixed formats and want to retain the original format, click Edit to open the Export Preview dialog box, click the Optimize to Size Wizard button and enter the file size to which you want the files optimized.*

5. Click the Next button and follow the steps outlined previously to process and save the files.

Using Batch Processing to Scale Image Files

If your work requires that you scale multiple images to a specific size, you can accomplish the task with relatively little effort using batch processing. A common use for scaling multiple images is creating thumbnail images for Web site buttons or hotspot areas.

To resample images using batch processing:

1. Choose File | Batch Process. The Batch dialog box opens.

2. Select the files to resize, and then click Next. The Batch Process dialog box opens.

3. In the Batch Options window, click Scale; then click the Add button to add the command to the Include In Batch list. When you choose this option, the Scale section opens at the bottom of the dialog box.

Tip *You can also double-click a command in the Batch Options window to add it to the Include In Batch list.*

4. In the Scale section of the dialog box, click the triangle to the right of the text field; from the drop-down menu, choose one of the following options:

- **No Scaling**   Exports the images without resizing them.

- **Scale To Size**   Resizes the image files to the width and height you specify. When you choose this option, two text fields appear: one for height and one for width. You can choose one of the preset values or enter your own value. Each field also contains a Variable option. When you choose Variable, Fireworks sizes the image proportionately based on the value you enter in the other field. For example, you can specify a width, choose Variable for the height, and Fireworks will resize each image proportionately based on the value you enter for the width.

- **Scale To Fit Area** Resizes the images proportionately so that they fit within the area for which you specify the width and height. This is a great way to create thumbnail images for buttons or hotspots.

- **Scale To Percentage** Resizes the images proportionately to the percentage you specify. When you choose this option, you enter the value in the percentage (%) text field. Alternatively, you can click the triangle to the right of the field and drag a slider to set the desired percentage value.

5. Click the Next button and then follow the steps previously outlined to complete the batch process.

Finding and Replacing Items During a Batch Process

The find and replace items option finds and replaces the same objects as the Find and Replace panel. However, when batch processing, you can find and replace items while performing other tasks.

To find and replace items during a batch process:

1. Choose File | Batch Process. The Batch dialog opens.

2. Select the files to process, and then click Next. The Batch Process dialog box opens.

3. From the Batch Options window, choose Find And Replace; then click the Add button to add the command to the Include In Batch list.

4. Click the Edit button to specify the parameters for the find and replace operation. The Batch Replace dialog box, shown here, appears.

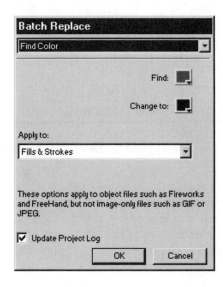

5. Click the triangle to the right of the Find What field and choose an option. The available options are the same as those discussed earlier in the chapter in the "Using the Find and Replace Panel" section.

6. The available options for the Find and Replace fields differ depending on the option you choose. Refer to the earlier sections on finding and replacing objects for specific instructions. For example, finding and replacing text is covered in the "Finding and Replacing Text" section and so on.

7. Click the Update Project Log checkbox (the default option), and the results of the batch processing operation are recorded if the files are listed in the Project Log.

8. Click OK to close the Batch Replace dialog box. Then click the Next button and follow the steps presented earlier to complete the batch processing operation.

Renaming Files During a Batch Process

When you process files during a batch process, you have the option of backing up the files. When you back up the files, Fireworks appends the filename with a number. However, you can also modify the filename of any file by adding a prefix or a suffix. This option comes in handy if you need to tag files for identification at a certain phase of the Web design process—for example, at the alpha or beta testing phase of a Web site.

To rename files while batch processing them:

1. Choose File | Batch Process. The Batch dialog box opens.

2. Select the files to process, and then click Next. The Batch Process dialog box opens.

3. In the Batch Options window, select Rename and then click the Add button to add the command to the Include In Batch list.

4. Click the triangle to the right of the Rename field, and from the drop-down menu choose one of the following options:

   ■ **Original Name** Leaves the filename unaltered.

   ■ **Add Prefix** Allows you to add text to the beginning of the current filename of each file in the batch.

   ■ **Add Suffix** Lets you add text to the end of the current filename of each file in the batch.

5. If you choose either Add Suffix or Add Prefix, a text field becomes available to the right of the Rename field. Enter the desired suffix or prefix. For example, if you chose Add Prefix and enter the text **beta_**, an image file currently named *CEO.jpg* would be renamed *beta_CEO.jpg*.

6. Click the Next button and follow the steps outlined previously to complete the batch processing operation.

Creating a Script

If you frequently use the same commands in a batch process operation, you can save all the commands as a script to re-create the sequence of commands. When you create a script, you won't need to go through the batch process dialog boxes again; you simply apply the script to selected files.

To create a script:

1. Choose File | Batch Process. The Batch dialog box opens.

2. Select the files to process, and then click Next. The Batch Process dialog box opens.

3. Choose the commands for the batch processing operation as outlined previously.

4. In the final Batch Process dialog box, click the Save Script button.

5. The Save As dialog box appears. Navigate to the folder where you want to store the script, enter a filename for the script, and then click Save.

When you save a batch process as a script, it is saved with the .jsf (JavaScript file) extension. If you save a script in the Fireworks MX Commands folder, it becomes available as a menu command. The location of this folder varies depending upon the operating system you use. Refer to the Macromedia Fireworks MX documentation for the exact location of this folder for your operating system.

Running a Script

After you save a script, you can run it at any time. How you run the script depends on the folder in which you saved the script. If you saved the script in the Commands folder, you can run the script as a menu command.

To run a script:

1. If you saved the script to the Fireworks MX Commands folder, choose Commands and then choose the script from the menu. Or, if you did not save the script to the Commands folder, do one of the following:

   ■ From within Fireworks, choose Commands | Run Script to access the Open dialog box. Navigate to the script you want to run and then click Open.

   ■ From outside Fireworks, navigate to the file folder in which you stored the script and double-click the filename. Remember all scripts are saved with the .jsf extension. If you give your scripts an appropriate name, you'll have no problem locating the proper script.

2. After choosing one of the above options, the Files To Process dialog box appears.

3. Click the triangle to the right of the Files To Process field and choose one of the following:

   ■ **Currently Open Files**   Applies the script to all files currently open in Fireworks.

   ■ **Project Log (All Files)**   Applies the script commands to all files in the Project Log.

   ■ **Project Log (Selected Files)**   Applies the script commands to all files currently selected in the Project Log.

   ■ **Custom**   Enables you to select the files to process. When you choose this option, click the button with ellipses (...) to the right of the Files To Process field, choose the files from within the Open dialog box, and then click Open.

4. Click OK to run the script on the selected files.

<blockquote>

Tip   *If you use a script frequently, you can save it and then create a shortcut to the script on your desktop. Double-click the shortcut icon to launch Fireworks and run the script. You can also run the script by dragging and dropping the script shortcut icon onto an open file in Fireworks.*

</blockquote>

Using Web Commands

You can use commands from the Web Commands menu to streamline your Fireworks projects. For example, you can quickly create a shared color palette by choosing a folder with images. You can also scan the current document for blank ALT tags and set ALT tags for a document. If you ever need to create a Fireworks document from a Web page, you can do so with a single menu command.

Creating a Shared Palette

You can create a palette of colors that are common to a folder of images. When you create a shared palette, you can specify the number of colors in the palette. The results are saved as an .act file, which you can load into the Swatches panel or into the Optimize panel Color Table.

To create a shared palette:

1. Choose Commands | Web | Create Shared Palette. The Create Shared Palette dialog box appears, as shown here:

Create Shared Palette

Maximum number of colors:

128

Select a folder of images:

Browse...

OK   Cancel

2. Enter a value in the Maximum Number Of Colors field.

3. Click the Browse button to the right of the Select A Folder Of Images field.

4. Navigate to the folder that contains the images from which you want to create a shared palette; select the folder, and then click Open.

5. Click OK. Fireworks samples the images in the folder, creates a palette, and then prompts you for a filename and location.

6. Navigate to the folder in which you want to store the shared palette, enter a filename for the palette, and then click Save.

Creating a Document by Importing HTML

You can quickly create a Fireworks document by importing HTML. When you do this, you create a document complete with hotspots and slices. Extra frames will be created for objects such as rollover buttons and image swaps. Text will not be editable.

You can create a document by re-creating all tables in an HTML file. You use the Reconstitute Table command to perform this task.

To create Fireworks documents by reconstituting all tables within an HTML document:

1. Choose File | Reconstitute Table. The Open dialog box appears.

2. Navigate to the folder that contains the HTML file from which you want to reconstitute tables, and then click Open. Fireworks creates an individual document for each table in the HTML file.

You can also create a Fireworks document by importing HTML. When you import HTML, Fireworks imports the first table it finds in the current document.

To create a Fireworks document by importing HTML:

1. Create a new document. Alternatively, you can import the HTML into an existing document.

2. Choose File | Import. The Import dialog box appears.

3. Navigate to the folder that contains the HTML file from which you want to import a table; select the file, and then click Open. A right angle pointer replaces your cursor.

4. Click the spot in the document where you want the table to appear. Fireworks reassembles the images from the table and creates the necessary slices.

You can also create a Fireworks document by opening the first table in an HTML file. This method is useful when you need to reconstruct a navigation menu that you know to be in the first table of an HTML file.

To re-create the first table in an HTML document:

1. Choose File | Open. The Open dialog box appears.

2. Navigate to the folder that contains the HTML file from which you want to create a Fireworks document. Select the file, and then click Open. Fireworks creates a new document that comprises the images in the first table of the HTML file.

Setting ALT Tags for the Document

You can streamline your workflow in Fireworks by setting all the ALT tags in a document with one menu command. When you choose this command, all the ALT tags are given the same name. However, you can still edit the tags in the Property inspector. Setting ALT tags comes in handy when all of the ALT tags in a document will have similar text—for example, a company named followed by a description.

To set ALT tags for a document:

1. Choose Commands | Web | Set ALT Tags. If no blank ALT tags appear in the document, Fireworks displays a warning to that effect. Otherwise, the JavaScript dialog box appears.

2. Enter a name for the ALT tags in the text field and click OK. Fireworks creates ALT tags for any hotspot or slice with a blank ALT tag.

Note *You can also scan the document for any blank ALT tags by choosing Commands | Web | Select Blank ALT Tags. After invoking the command, Fireworks highlights all hotspots and slices that do not have ALT tags.*

Managing Multiple Files with the Project Log

When you use the Find and Replace command or batch processing on files you've added to the Project Log, the results of these actions are stored in the Project Log. The Project Log enables you to keep track of frequently used files as well as record other information, such as the time and date the file was last modified. The Project Log, as shown next, has an Options menu that you use to add files to the panel.

Adding Files

Before you can use the Project Log, you must add the files that you want to track. After you have added several files to the Project Log, you can open files and export files from within the panel. You can also include Project Log files in a batch process or when you use the Find and Replace panel.

To add files to the Project Log:

1. Choose Window | Project Log. The Project Log opens.

2. Click the Options menu icon, and choose Add Files To Log. The Open dialog box appears.

3. Navigate to the folder that contains the files you want to add to the Project Log, select the files, and then click Open. Fireworks adds the files to the Project Log.

Opening Files

After you add several files to the Project Log, you can open them from within the panel. This option is handy when you have stored assets in several different folders. Instead of navigating to each folder, selecting the files, and then opening them, you can select the files from within the Project Log and open them all at once, regardless of the location of the files.

To open files with the Project Log:

1. Choose Window | Project Log. The Project Log opens.

2. Select the files you want to open.

3. Click the Open button. Fireworks opens each file in its own window.

Note *You can also open a single file from the Project Log by selecting it and then clicking the Open button. Alternatively, you can open a file from the Project Log by double-clicking its filename.*

Removing Files from the Project Log

When you are finished with a project, you can remove the associated files to avoid clutter in the Project Log. You can remove selected files, or all files.

To remove files from the Project Log:

1. Choose Window | Project Log.

2. Select the files you want to remove from the Project Log.

3. From the Project Log Options menu choose Clear Selection.

Note *To remove all files from the Project Log, open the Project Log and click the Options menu icon and choose Clear All.*

Exporting Files

If you've previously exported files listed in the Project Log using specific optimization settings, you can export the files again using the previous export settings. You can export a single file or multiple files.

To export files from within the Project Log:

1. Choose Window | Project Log.

2. Select the files you want to export.

3. From the Project Log Options menu, choose Export Again. The first file opens in Fireworks and an Export dialog box appears.

4. Navigate to the file folder to which you want to export the image(s).

5. Accept the current filename, or enter a different filename; then click Save. The file is exported using the previous export settings. If you've selected more than one file to export, the next file appears, and so on.

Summary

In this chapter, you learned to use Fireworks features to streamline your productivity. You were shown how to find and replace elements in multiple files using the Find and Replace panel. You also learned to use the History panel to undo multiple steps and create your own commands. You learned to use batch processing to perform the same tasks on multiple files. In addition you learned to create scripts from the tasks performed in a batch process. You were also shown how to manage multiple files using the Project Log. In Chapter 21, you'll learn how to optimize your documents for export.

Chapter 21

Optimizing
Fireworks Documents

W hen you create a document in Fireworks, you go through a series of steps to add elements, create objects, and add interactivity to the objects through the use of hotspots and slices. You assign URLs to hotspots and links that will open other documents from the same Web site or from external Web sites. After you have the document just the way you want it, you preview the document and start fine-tuning it for its intended destination. This fine-tuning is known as *optimizing* the document. When you optimize a document, you choose an export setting for the document. The export setting is the image file format. When you optimize a document with slices, you can choose the same export setting for the entire document or optimize each slice with the optimal export setting.

During the optimization process, you preview the document to see exactly what your intended audience will see when the document is opened in a Web browser or as part of a multimedia presentation. You can preview the document in a Web browser or within the document window.

When optimizing a document, your job is to choose the best export setting for the document's intended destination. In this chapter, you'll learn to use the various Fireworks tools for optimizing a document. You'll learn to use the Optimize panel to fine-tune the optimization for an entire document or an individual slice of the document. You'll also learn to use the various features of the document window to compare the document as currently optimized to the original document.

Choosing the Proper Format

When you create a Fireworks document, you generally create a document that will be displayed on a Web site. However, you might create a Fireworks document that will end up in a multimedia presentation or in a printed document. You can also optimize documents for viewing in portable computing devices such as handheld devices. When you optimize a document or slice, you can choose from the formats shown in Table 21-1.

Using the Optimize Panel

Whether you're optimizing a slice or the entire document, the most efficient way of handling the task is to use the Optimize panel. Although you can choose one of the default optimization methods from within the Property inspector, you can have much better control over the process when you use the Optimize panel because you can modify individual parameters of one of the presets to suit the document and intended destination.

Format	Color Depth	Features
GIF	Maximum of 256 colors	Best suited for documents or slices with large areas of similar color. Transparent colors can be specified.
Animated GIF	Maximum of 256 colors	Used for a multi-frame document. When displayed in a Web browser, the frames play to simulate action. Transparent colors can be specified.
JPEG	Millions of colors	Best suited for photographic images. Image compression can be adjusted to create optimal file size and image quality for the intended destination.
PNG 8	Maximum of 256 colors	Can be used for Web pages; however, this format is not supported by all browsers. Transparent colors can be specified.
PNG 24	Millions of colors (24-bit)	Best suited for print or multimedia applications. Documents exported in this format are not compressed. Transparency is not available.
PNG 32	24-bit color and 8-bit alpha transparency	Best suited for multimedia applications. You can also use this format when creating a document that will be edited in other photo imaging programs that support alpha transparency.
WBMP	1-bit color (black-and-white)	Best suited for wireless devices such as PDAs and cellular phones.
TIFF 8	Maximum of 256 colors	Well suited for print. Transparent colors are not available.
TIFF 24	24-bit color	An excellent choice for printed documents and some multimedia applications.
TIFF 32	24-bit color and 8-bit alpha transparency	Well suited for print. This format can also be used in image editing software that supports alpha transparency.

Table 21-1. *Fireworks Export Formats*

Format	Color Depth	Features
BMP 8	Maximum of 256 colors	Can be used for images that will be displayed on the Windows operating system.
BMP 24	Millions of colors (24-bit)	Best suited for full color images that will be displayed on the Windows operating system.
PICT (Macintosh only)	Millions of colors	Supported by many popular image-editing programs.

Table 21-1. *Fireworks Export Formats* (continued)

To open the Optimize panel, shown next, choose Window | Optimize. If the panel is docked in the panel window, you can also open the panel by clicking the arrow to the left of the word Optimize. For the purpose of the illustrations in this chapter, the panel will be shown undocked.

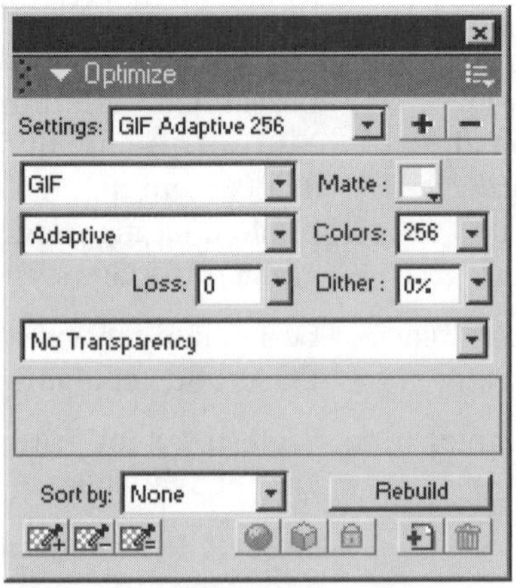

Note *You can also use the Export Wizard and Export Preview to set export settings. These menu commands are covered in Chapter 22.*

Optimizing for the Web

When you optimize a document for the Web, you generally begin with one of the GIF export settings and then fine-tune the setting to suit the objects in your document. If your document includes a combination of vector objects, text objects, and bitmaps, you can use different export settings for different objects by creating slices, as outlined in Chapter 16. You then choose the optimal export settings for each slice.

You can also use the PNG 8 format for images you create for the Web. The PNG 8 format has a color depth of 256 colors and supports transparency. However, this format is not supported by all Web browsers.

Another popular file format for the Web is JPEG, which is best suited for images with millions of colors. The format compresses the image. JPEG is not particularly well suited for text objects, as artifacts appear around the text when it's compressed to a large degree.

Using GIF Optimization

When you specify export settings for a document with a combination of bitmaps, vector objects, and text objects, you choose one of the GIF export methods for the entire document. You can then optimize the bitmaps in your document using the JPEG format or by dithering the entire document to create facsimiles of colors not found in the palette. Dithering can significantly increase the file size of the document. It's always best to create a slice for each bitmap in your document and then choose JPEG export settings for the slice.

Choosing a Preset

The quickest way to optimize a document or a selected slice is to use one of the presets. You can use the preset as the final export setting for the document or selected slice(s), or you can use it as a starting point and then fine-tune the setting.

To choose an export preset:

1. Select one or more slices to optimize. To choose an optimization method for the entire document, deselect all objects.

2. Open the Optimize panel.

3. Click the triangle to the right of the Settings field and choose one of the following:

   - **GIF Web 216**   Snaps all colors in the document to colors in the Web Safe 216 palette. This option dithers (mixes colors from the Web Safe palette) to create reasonable facsimiles of colors in the document that are not present in the Web Safe palette.

   - **GIF Web Snap 256**   Snaps all non-Web-safe colors in the document to their Web-safe equivalents using a maximum of 256 colors.

   - **GIF Web Snap 128**   Snaps all non-Web-safe colors in the document to the closest Web-safe colors using a maximum of 128 colors.

   - **GIF Adaptive 256**   Creates a palette with a maximum of 256 colors using the colors present in the document.

- **JPEG - Better Quality** Compresses the image to a setting of 80 with no smoothing. This method yields a high quality image at the expense of a larger file size.

- **JPEG - Smaller File** Compresses the image to a setting of 60 with a Smoothing setting of 2. This method gives you a smaller file size while sacrificing image quality.

- **Animated GIF Websnap 128** Optimizes a multiple-frame document for export as an animation. Colors in the document are snapped to the nearest Web-safe equivalent and the export palette is limited to 128 colors.

You can also specify one of the preset optimization settings for the document or a slice from within the Property inspector. This is a good choice when you need to set baseline optimization for a slice or the document. If after previewing the document you are not satisfied with the image quality or file size, you can fine-tune the export settings with the Optimize panel.

To choose a preset export setting for one or more slices:

1. Select the slices you want to optimize.

2. Click the arrow to the left of the word Properties. The Property inspector opens and is configured as shown here:

Slice Export Settings field

3. Click the triangle to the right of the Slice Export Settings field and from the drop-down menu, choose a preset. The presets are identical to the export settings in the Optimize panel.

To use the Property inspector to choose an export preset for the entire document:

1. Deselect all objects in the document.

2. Click the arrow to the left of the word Properties to access the Property inspector as shown here:

Default Export Options field

3. Click the triangle to the right of the Default Export Options field and from the drop-down menu, choose one of the preset export settings.

Previewing the Document

An important part of the optimization process is previewing the document as it will appear with the current export settings applied. With Fireworks, you can preview a document with current export settings in a single window or in a multiple-pane window, where you can compare the document with one or more optimization settings applied to the original document. You can also preview the document in a Web browser.

Previewing in the Document Window

In the document window, you can preview the document in a single window with current optimization methods applied, or you can preview the original document with one or more optimized versions in a multiple-pane window. When you compare the document to optimized versions, you can do so in a two-pane or four-pane window.

To preview the document with current optimization methods in a single pane window, click the Preview tab in the document pane. Figure 12-1 shows a document in the Preview tab of the document window.

When you preview a document in the Preview window, you see an unobscured view of the entire document. In the upper-right corner of the Preview window, the file size of the document and projected download time are displayed. Compare this information to the image quality you see in the window and you'll have a good idea of how effective the current optimization settings are.

You can also compare the original document to the document with current optimization applied by clicking the 2-Up tab in the document window. The following illustration shows an optimized version of the document being compared to the original. Notice the small window below each document. This window shows the file size of each document. The window below the optimized version of the document displays the projected download time as well. By comparing the two versions of the document side by side, as in Figure 21-2, you can easily judge how the image quality is affected by the export settings.

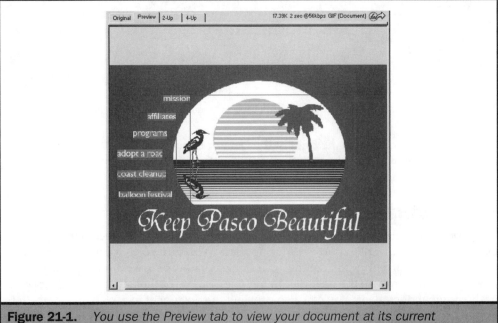

Figure 21-1.   You use the Preview tab to view your document at its current optimization.

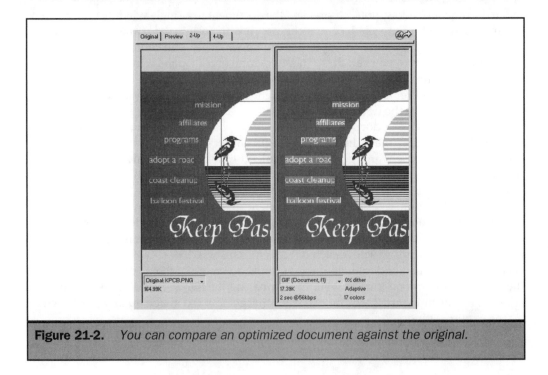

Figure 21-2.   You can compare an optimized document against the original.

If you prefer, you can compare the original document with three optimized versions. When you preview a document in this manner, you can choose the optimization method that yields the smallest file size while still providing acceptable image quality. To preview the original to three optimized versions, click the 4-Up tab, and the document window is configured as in Figure 21-3.

When you initially choose the 4-Up preview mode, the original image appears in the upper-left pane. The other three panes reflect the current export settings. When you preview a document in 4-Up mode, you can click a pane and then choose an optimization setting from the Optimize panel. Choose a different export setting for three panes and compare the difference in image quality against the original document. The export settings are displayed in each pane, as well as the file size and projected download time.

If the Optimize panel is open while you're previewing the document, you can change the export settings and the optimized version updates in real time. You can continue to change the export settings until you arrive at the optimal file size while preserving reasonable image quality.

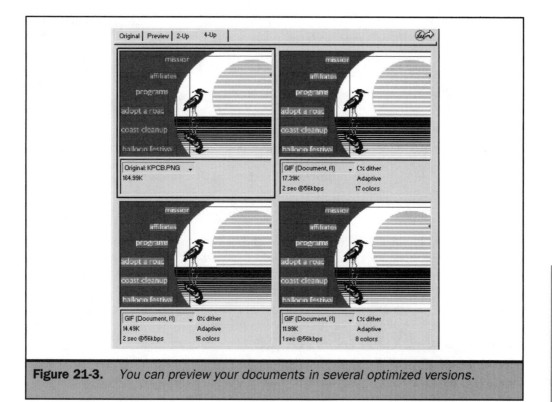

Figure 21-3.   *You can preview your documents in several optimized versions.*

> **Tip** *When previewing a large document, you may not be able to see everything. To view a hidden part of the document, press the SPACEBAR to momentarily activate the Hand tool, and then drag to pan to a different viewpoint.*

Previewing in a Web Browser

When you've arrived at what you feel is the best export setting for the document, you can preview the document as viewers will see it in a Web browser. This is often the ultimate litmus test—as you'll preview the document without the visual clutter of the Fireworks workspace.

To preview the document in a Web browser, choose File | Preview In Browser and then select a browser from the submenu.

When you install Fireworks, the install utility detects your system's default browser and creates a menu item for it. This browser is designated as your primary browser.

When you design Web pages, however, it's a good idea to have a copy of the two most popular browsers installed on your system. You can then preview the document in each browser and detect any anomalies that may prevent your document from displaying properly.

When more than one Web browser is installed on your system, you can change the primary browser by following these steps:

1. Choose File | Preview In Browser | Set Primary Browser. The Locate Browser dialog box appears.

2. Navigate to the .exe file of the browser you want to designated as your primary browser. select it and then click Open.

To set your secondary browser, follow these steps:

1. Choose File | Preview In Browser | Set Secondary Browser to access the Locate Browser dialog box.

2. Navigate to the .exe file of your secondary browser, select it, and then click Open.

When you have linked a secondary browser to the menu, you can preview a document using the browser by choosing File | Preview and selecting the name of your secondary browser from the submenu. Alternatively, you can press CTRL+F12 (Windows) or COMMAND+F12 (Macintosh).

Modifying Export Settings

After you choose one of the preset export settings, you can fine-tune the setting to suit your document. If, for example, you've created a document with nothing more than a navigation bar that you'll insert into an HTML document, you are probably dealing with only a few colors in the document. You can create a significantly smaller file size for each slice by exporting the file with the exact number of colors used to create the navigation bar. You can also modify settings by choosing a different file format, choosing a different palette, or importing a palette. Modifying export settings for a specific destination will be covered in future sections of this chapter.

Choosing a File Format

When you choose to export a document for a specific file format, you can choose a preset for your baseline settings or you can start with the export format and then modify the settings.

To choose an export file format:

1. Choose Window | Optimize. The Optimize panel opens.

2. Click the triangle to the right of the Export File Format field, as shown in the following illustration, and from the drop-down menu choose an option.

Choosing a Color Palette

If you choose an export file format with format limited to an 8-bit (256 colors) color depth, you must choose a color palette. If you choose one of the presets, a color palette is selected for you. If you decide to modify the settings, you can choose a different color palette or import a previously saved color palette.

To modify the color palette:

1. Open the Optimize panel, as outlined previously.
2. Click the triangle to the right of the Indexed Palette field and from the drop-down menu, choose one of the following:
   - **Adaptive**   Uses the colors from the document to create a palette that yields the highest image quality. However, the colors are not snapped to the Web Safe palette.
   - **Websnap Adaptive**   Chooses colors from the document and snaps them to the nearest color in the Web Safe 216 palette.
   - **Web 216**   Uses the default Fireworks Web Safe 216 palette.
   - **Exact**   Uses the exact colors from the document. If you choose this color palette and images in the document contain more than 256 colors, the palette defaults to Adaptive.
   - **Macintosh**   Uses the 256 colors used to display software icons and interfaces on the Macintosh operating system.
   - **Windows**   Uses the 256 colors used to display software icons and interface elements on the Windows operating system.
   - **Grayscale**   Converts all colors in the document to the 256 or fewer shades of gray.
   - **Black And White**   Converts all colors in the document to either black or white.
   - **Uniform**   Transforms the colors in the document to the RGB color scale.
   - **Custom**   Allows you to load a previously saved color palette and use it as the export pallet.

When you choose the Custom palette option, the Open dialog box appears, and you can navigate to the folder where you've saved a color palette, or you can select a GIF image and have Fireworks create the palette from the selected image.

Choosing the Color Depth

After determining the color palette, you can further optimize the document or slice by limiting the number of colors that are exported. When you modify the number of colors in the palette, you can preview the results using either the Preview window or the 2-Up or 4-Up preview modes. By previewing the document as you modify the color depth, you'll be able to see the affect the limited palette has on image quality and file size.

To choose the number of colors in the export palette:

1. Open the Optimize panel.

2. Click the triangle to the right of the Colors field and from the drop-down menu choose an option. You can choose between 2 and 256 colors. You can often export with fewer colors than one of the presets.

3. Click the Rebuild button to see the actual number of colors in the document, as shown here:

4. If you want, you can export the document with the number of colors shown after you click the Rebuild button by entering this value in the Colors field.

Note *When you click the Rebuild button, you rebuild the color table. For more information on the color table, refer to Chapter 8.*

Dithering an Image

If you choose an export method that uses an 8-bit (256 colors) color depth and have bitmap images in the document with more than 256 colors, you can dither the image to create a reasonable facsimile of any color not in the palette. Note that when you dither an image, you may end up with a significantly larger file size. If possible, create a slice for any bitmap images in the document and choose one the JPEG export setting.

To dither an image:

1. Choose Window | Optimize. Alternatively, click the arrow to the left of the word Optimize if you have the panel docked in the panel window.

2. Click the triangle to the right of the Dithering field and drag the slider to specify the percentage of dithering. Alternatively, enter a value between 0 and 100 in the Dithering text field.

Compressing GIF Images

You can compress GIF files to decrease the file size of the exported document. However, when you compress a GIF file, you lose data. The trick is to lose just enough data to decrease the file size without significantly degrading the quality of the images in your document. Typically, you can achieve good results when choosing a loss value of between 5 and 15.

To specify compression for a file exported in the GIF format:

1. Choose Window | Optimize. The Optimize panel opens.

2. Click the triangle to the right of the Loss field and drag the slider to specify a value. Alternatively, enter a value between 0 and 100 in the text field.

> **Tip** *When modifying export settings, always have one of the preview windows open so you can monitor the effect of your settings on the document or slice.*

Setting Transparency

If your document will be viewed on a Web page with a tiled background, you can specify one or more colors as transparent. When the document is exported and viewed in a Web browser, the color pixels you specify as transparent are not visible and the underlying Web page background color or tiled image shows through.

> **Note** *Even if you selected Transparent for the canvas color, you must still set transparency prior to exporting the document.*

1. In the Document Window, click the Preview, 2-Up, or 4-Up tab.

2. Choose Window | Optimize. The Optimize panel opens, as shown here:

Choose type of transparency

Remove color from transparency

Add color to transparency

Select transparent color

3. Click the triangle to the right of the Choose Type Of Transparency field, and from the drop-down menu choose Index. The canvas color pixels are set to transparent, as you can see by viewing the document in the Preview mode.

4. To set a different color as transparent, click the Select Transparent Color button, and your cursor becomes an eyedropper. You can now set a transparent color by doing one of the following:

   ■ Click a color in the document window.

   ■ Click a color in the Optimize panel color table.

After setting the transparency colors, you can set additional color pixels to transparent when the document is exported. You can also remove colors from transparency.

To add a color to transparency:

1. Click the Preview, 2-Up, or 4-Up tab. If you choose the 2-Up or 4-Up preview mode, click a window other than the original.

2. Click the Add Color To Transparency button.

3. Click a color from within the Preview window or from the Optimize panel color table. The color is added to the transparency, and all pixels of that color are hidden in the Preview window and the preview panes if you're previewing the document in the 2-Up or 4-Up preview mode. You can add colors as needed by clicking colors from within the Preview window or by selecting them from the Optimize panel color table.

Note *You can also select a transparent color from the original view; however you will not be able to see the results unless you select one of the preview modes.*

To remove a color from transparency:

1. In the document window, click the 2-Up or 4-Up tab.

2. Click the Remove Color From Transparency button and do one of the following:

   ■ Click a transparent color in the Optimize panel color table. Transparent colors in the color table are signified by a checkerboard background. Note that you cannot remove index transparency in this manner.

   ■ In the 2-Up or 4-Up preview mode, inside the original document pane, click an object that has the color you want to remove from transparency.

Interlacing a GIF Image

When you *interlace* a GIF image, it downloads in stages. The first stage shows a low-resolution image and gives the viewer an idea of how the final image will look. On succeeding passes, the image is revealed at higher resolution until the download is complete. Use this option when you don't want to lose your audience because of the amount of time it takes to download a large file. Most Web surfers are familiar with interlaced images and will wait for the image to download if the first stage of the download piques their interest.

To interlace a GIF image, choose Interlaced from the Optimize panel Options menu.

Removing the Halo from Anti-Aliased Objects

When you export a document with transparent colors and display the exported document in a Web page with a background image or color that is radically different from the canvas color of the Fireworks document, you see a visible halo around anti-aliased text and other objects. You can use a couple of methods to eradicate the halo from your exported documents.

To remove a visible halo from an anti-aliased object, do one of the following:

- Choose Modify | Canvas | Canvas Color and match the canvas color to the background color of the Web page on which your exported document will be displayed.

- Open the Optimize panel; click the Matte color swatch as shown in the following illustration; and from the pop-up palette, select the background color of the Web page on which your document will be displayed.

Matte color swatch

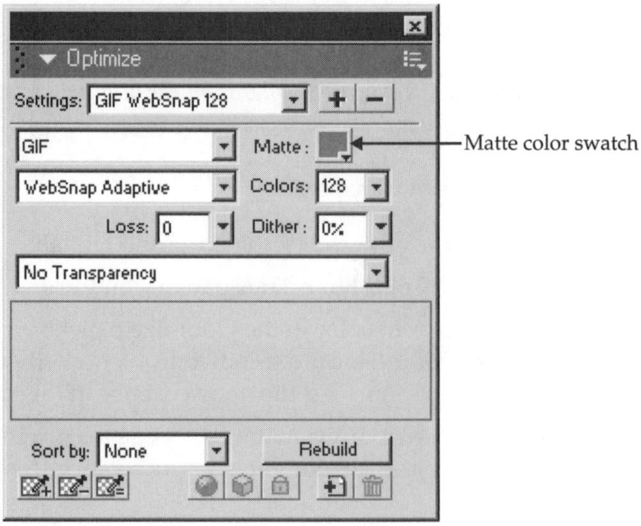

- Select the anti-aliased objects in your document, such as vector objects and text. Open the Property inspector and from the Edge drop-down menu, choose Hard. To ensure that the halo is totally removed, you can use this option in conjunction with changing the canvas color or matte color.

Using JPEG Optimization

When you export a bitmap image with millions of colors for use on a Web page, you'll achieve the smallest file size and highest quality image when you choose the JPEG export format. If the document is a combination of bitmap images, vector objects, and text objects, create a slice for each bitmap image and apply the JPEG export format to the slices with bitmap images.

Setting JPEG Quality

The JPEG format is known as a *lossy* format. When you compress a JPEG image, data is lost, which translates to a smaller file size. When you apply high levels of compression, you achieve a small file size at the expense of image quality. Your goal is to seek the middle road between file size and image quality. You do this by monitoring the image using one of the preview modes. By previewing the export as you apply compression, you'll know when you achieve the optimum compromise between image quality, file size, and download time. The following illustration shows three versions of a bitmap with different levels of compression applied.

To set JPEG quality:

1. Select the slice that contains the bitmap image. If the entire document is a bitmap image, proceed to step 2.

> **Tip**
> *If you want to apply the same export settings to several bitmaps in the document, select all bitmap slices and then choose an export setting. The setting you choose is applied to the selected bitmaps.*

2. Choose Window | Optimize. The Optimize panel opens.

3. Click the triangle to the right of the Export File Format field and from the drop-down menu, choose JPEG.

4. Click the triangle to the right of the Quality field and drag the slider to set image quality. Chose a high setting for the best image quality at the expense of a large file size. Choose a low setting to compress the image to a smaller file size at the expense of image quality.

> **Note**
> *If the image for which you are setting the quality was originally a JPEG image, you cannot enhance the image by choosing a higher quality setting.*

5. Click the triangle to the right of the Smoothing field and drag the slider to apply smoothing to the image. When you apply smoothing, you blur the transition between pixels of differing colors and hard edges. Smoothing an image will yield a smaller file size. However, if you go too far, the image will suffer a significant loss of detail due to the blurring that occurs when the image is smoothed.

> **Tip**
> *You can enhance an image with fine detail by choosing Sharpen Edges from the Optimize panel Options menu.*

Using Selective JPEG Optimization

When you have included several bitmaps in a document you intend to display on a Web page, you run the risk of a large file size and a lengthy download time. However, you can still control the file size of the exported document by using *selective* JPEG optimization.

Selective JPEG optimization enables you to apply different levels of compression to different areas of the image. Most images have a central area of interest. You create a mask for the area of interest and save the selection as a JPEG mask, as outlined in Chapter 6. You use a high quality setting on the masked area and a lower setting on the unmasked area, which yields a smaller file size when the document is exported.

The following illustration shows the original image at left and the image with a selective JPEG mask applied to the woman's face at right. The compression on the unmasked area has been exaggerated for the purpose of this illustration.

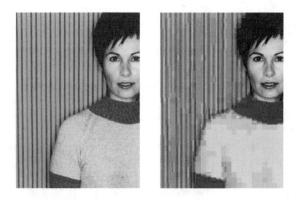

Using Progressive JPEG Optimization

You can also speed up download time by creating a *progressive* JPEG. A progressive JPEG downloads in stages. The first stage is low resolution, and each succeeding stage increases the quality of the image until it is fully downloaded. As a rule, a progressive JPEG fully downloads in three passes. This is a good option when you have no choice but to display a large JPEG at high quality on a Web page. Experienced Web surfers are familiar with JPEGs downloading in stages and will wait for the entire image to download if the first pass catches their attention.

To apply progressive JPEG optimization to an image:

1. Select the JPEG you want to optimize.

2. Choose Window | Optimize. The Optimize panel opens.

3. Click the triangle to the right of the Export File Format field and choose JPEG.

4. Select a quality setting.

5. Choose Progressive JPEG from the Optimize panel Options menu.

Using the WBMP Format

If the document you are creating will be displayed on a wireless device such as a personal digital assistant (PDA) or a cellular phone, you can use the Wireless Bitmap (WBMP) export format. This export format is monochrome (black-and-white). Only one setting is available with this format: dithering.

To optimize a document using the WBMP format:

1. Choose Window | Optimize. The Optimize panel opens.

2. Click the triangle to the right of the Export File Format field and choose WBMP.

OPTIMIZING AND
EXPORTING DOCUMENTS

3. Click the triangle to the right of the Dither field and drag the slider to set the dithering value. When you dither a monochrome image, you can approximate shades of gray.

The following illustration shows two versions of an image as optimized for WBMP export; the image on the left has 0 percent dithering, and the image on the right 60 percent dithering.

Optimizing for Print and CD-ROM Applications

When you optimize an image or document for a CD-ROM or for an application that will be printed by a service bureau, image quality is more of a factor than file size. In this regard, you can export the document with full color and no compression. For CD-ROM applications, you can choose PNG 24, PNG 32, TIFF 24, TIFF 32, or BMP 24. If you're exporting a file for print, choose TIFF 24 or TIFF 32. Although the TIFF format does have provisions for LZW (Lempel-Ziv-Welch) compression, Fireworks does not offer this option. To choose any of these file formats, open the Optimize panel, and choose the format form the Export File Format drop-down menu.

Saving Optimization Settings

When you find the ideal optimization settings for a particular type of document or image format you export frequently, you can save the settings. The settings will then appear on the Saved Settings drop-down menu in the Optimize panel and the Property inspector.

To save optimization settings:

1. Optimize a document or slice. Alternatively, you can open a document that you've already optimized.

2. Choose Window | Optimize. The Optimize panel opens, as shown here:

Save current settings

Delete current settings

3. Click the Save Current Settings button that looks like a plus sign (+). The Preset Name dialog box opens.

4. Enter a name for the preset and click OK. The preset is saved and appears at the bottom of the Saved Settings menu in the Optimize panel and the Property inspector.

After you save an optimization setting, you can use it by selecting it from the Saved Settings drop-down menu. If a saved setting outlives its usefulness, you can delete it. To delete a saved setting:

1. Open the Optimize panel.

2. Click the triangle to the right of the Saved Settings field and select the setting you want to delete. You cannot delete a Fireworks preset export setting.

3. Click the Delete Saved Settings button that looks like a minus sign (–).

Summary

In this chapter, you learned to optimize documents for the Web, CD-ROM, and print. You learned to choose a file export setting and then fine-tune the export parameters to suit the document and the intended destination. You learned to specify the number of colors to export and apply compression to images. You also learned to save export settings as a menu preset. In Chapter 22, you'll learn to export a document as images and an HTML document.

Chapter 22

Exporting Images
and HTML Code

The Fireworks workspace is well suited to the task of creating a document with vector objects and bitmaps images. The workspace also does a wonderful job of providing the tools you need to add interactivity to the document, but your ultimate goal for the document is to display it to an audience and not marvel at how well it looks in Fireworks. To get your document to your intended viewing audience, you must export it. In Chapter 21, you learned how to optimize the document, which boils down to nothing more than choosing the optimal export settings for the document's intended destination.

The result of the creative energy you used to build and optimize the document leads to the last stage in the process: exporting the document. In this chapter, you'll learn how to export a document as images and HTML. You'll also learn how to use a Fireworks wizard to optimize and export the document in one fell swoop. You'll also learn to use the Export Preview window to fine tune optimization and export the document. And for the times when you just need to edit a slice of the document, you'll learn how to export the edited slice.

Exporting Your Work from Fireworks

As you learned previously, you have only one option for saving your work in Fireworks, which is to save it in the program's native .png format. When you need to use an image you've edited, or an entire document you've created with graphics, buttons, and interactivity, you export the item from Fireworks. You can export an image you've edited for a specific application, a slice of a document, or the entire document. When you export a document, you can export it as an image or as images and HTML. When you export the document as images and HTML, you can edit the HTML file in an HTML editor, or if you've created an entire Web page in Fireworks, you can upload the images and HTML page directly to a Web site.

The format in which the image is exported in is determined by the export settings you chose when optimizing the document. As you learned in Chapter 21, you can preview your work in a primary or secondary Web browser prior to exporting it. After you've determined that everything is in order with your document, you can export it.

Exporting Images

If you use Fireworks to edit and optimize images for use in other applications, or for importing into an HTML editor, you export the document as an image. If the document contains slices, you can ignore the slices and export the document as a single image. This option is useful, for example, if you need to show a client a proof of a design you're creating.

To export a document as a single image:

1. Choose File | Export. The Export dialog box appears, as shown here:

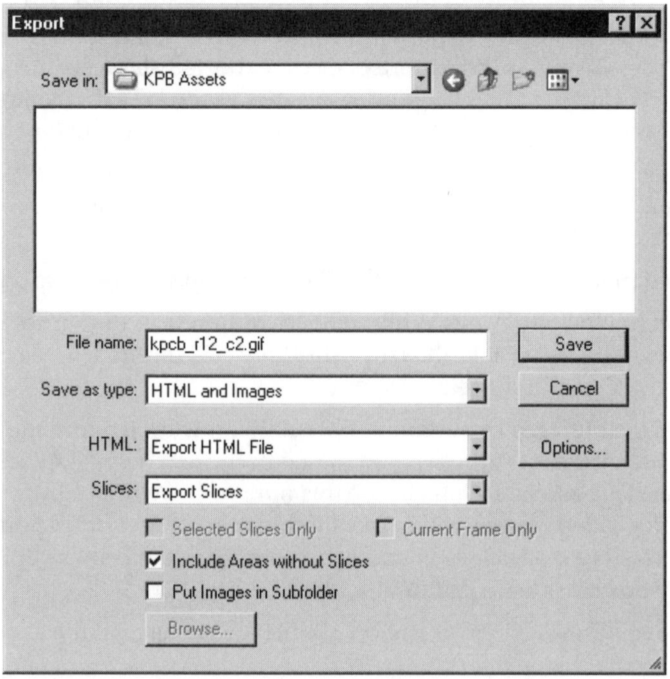

2. Navigate to the folder in which you want to store the image. If the image is part of a Web design, save it in the asset or images folder for your local Web site.

3. Enter a filename for the document. Fireworks automatically appends the filename with the proper extension for the export format you specified.

4. Click the triangle to the right of the Save As Type field and choose Images Only.

5. Click Save.

When you create a document with slices, Fireworks automatically defaults to exporting HTML and images. To create a proof for a client, you can choose Images Only, as outlined in the preceding steps. When you choose to export the document as images and HTML, you can modify the HTML options to suit the HTML editor that you use to edit your work.

To export a sliced document:

1. Choose File | Export. The Export dialog box opens.

2. Navigate to the folder in which you want to store the image files and HTML.

3. Enter a filename for the exported files. Fireworks will use this name for the HTML file, as well as the exported slices. Exported slices are appended by the location within the table Fireworks specifies in the HTML document. If you've named individual slices in the Property inspector, they will be exported with the names you selected.

4. Click the triangle to the right of the HTML field and from the drop-down menu choose Export HTML File. This is the default option.

5. Click the triangle to the right of the Slices field and choose Export Slices.

6. Deselect the Include Areas Without Slices option to export slices only. This option is selected by default. When this option is selected, areas without slices are exported as HTML cells.

7. Click the Put Images In Subfolder option if you want to store the image files in a subfolder. This is highly recommended because it helps you keep better track of your image assets. If you choose this option, Fireworks stores the image files in a folder called *images*, which is a subdirectory of the folder you specified in step 2. To store the images in another folder, click the Browse button to navigate to and select a different folder.

8. Click Save. Fireworks saves the HTML file and images in the specified folders.

Exporting Selected Slices

You also have the option of exporting only selected slices, which comes in handy when you reopen a document to edit individual areas of a document. You can edit a selected slice and then export it without re-creating the entire HTML document.

To edit a slice, select the slice and then click the Hide Slices button in the toolbox. You can then edit the image associated with the selected slice by using any of the tools or menu commands. It is recommended that you do not resize the graphic under the slice as it will not fit properly into the HTML table already created for it.

To export a selection of slices:

1. Select the slice you want to export. To add slices to the selection, click them while holding down the SHIFT key.

Tip   *If you have a hard time selecting small slices, open the Layers panel and select the desired slices from the Web layer. If you've named each slice, you'll be able to locate them easily.*

2. Choose File | Export. The Export dialog box opens.

3. Navigate to the folder in which you want to store the slices and enter a filename.

4. Click the triangle to right of the Save As Type field and choose Images Only.

5. Click the triangle to the right of the Slices field and choose Export Slices.

6. Select the Export Selected Slices checkbox and click OK. Fireworks exports the selected slices to the specified folder.

Tip   *To export a single slice, select it, right-click (Windows) or* CONTROL+*click (Macintosh), and then choose Export Selected Slice from the context menu. This option does not work with a slice over a symbol.*

Exporting Frames or Layers

Another export option you have available is exporting layers or frames as image files. When you export layers or frames, Fireworks creates a single image for each frame or layer in the document using the current export options applied to the document.

To export layers or frames:

1. Choose File | Export. The Export dialog box appears.

2. Navigate to the location in which you want the file saved and enter a filename.

3. Click the triangle to the right of the Save As Type field and choose either Layers To Files or Frames To Files.

4. If the Trim Images checkbox is checked (as it is by default), Fireworks sizes the exported document to encompass the objects on each frame or layer. Deselect this option, and the dimensions of the exported files are the same as the canvas.

5. Click Save. Fireworks exports each layer or frame of the document as an individual image file.

Exporting an Area of the Document

If desired, you can export an individual area of the document by using the Export Area tool to define the area you want to export and then using the Export Preview window to complete the export.

To export an area of the document:

1. Select the Export Area tool (shown next) from the toolbox. This tool is located in the same group as the Crop tool. If the Export Area tool is not selected, hold

your cursor over the Crop tool until the group flyout appears and select the Export Area tool.

2. Click an area on the canvas as the starting point for the area to export, and then drag down and across. As you drag, a bounding box defines the area you want to export. To move the export area as you're sizing it, press the SPACEBAR and drag the bounding box to a different location. Release the SPACEBAR to continue sizing the export area.

3. Release the mouse button when the area is the desired size. Eight handles appear around the edge of the selection. If the size and position of the export area isn't perfect, you can resize or reposition it by doing any of the following:

   ■ Click and drag any handle while holding down the SHIFT key to resize the marquee proportionately.

   ■ Click and drag any handle while holding down the ALT key (Windows) or OPTION key (Macintosh) to resize the marquee from the center outward.

   ■ Click and drag any handle while holding down ALT+SHIFT (Windows) or OPTION+SHIFT (Macintosh) to resize the marquee proportionately from the center outward.

   ■ Click the handle on the center top or center bottom and drag up or down to change the height of the marquee.

   ■ Click the handle on the middle right or middle left and drag in or out to change the width of the marquee.

   ■ Click inside the marquee and drag it to a new location.

4. When the marquee is the desired size and position, double-click inside the selection to open the Export Preview window, shown in Figure 22-1.

Note *The Export Preview window is also accessed when you choose File | Export Preview. The settings and options for this command and window will be covered in detail in "Using the Export Preview Window" later in this chapter.*

5. Modify the settings in the Export Preview window and then click Export. The Export dialog box appears.

6. Enter a filename and specify the location in which you want the file saved.

7. Click the triangle to the right of the Save As Type field and choose Images.

8. Click Save. Fireworks exports the area using the settings you specified in the Export Preview window.

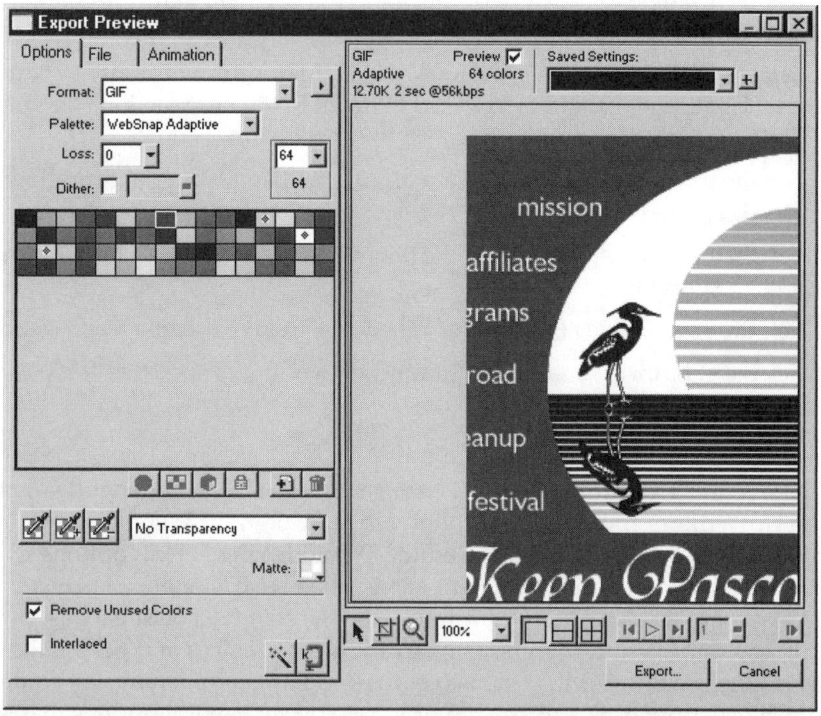

Figure 22-1.   *After you set the marquee to your preferences, double-click in the selection to open the Export Preview window.*

Exporting HTML

When you export a sliced document, by default you export HTML and images. When you export HTML, the resulting file is compatible with most popular HTML editors. HTML files exported from Fireworks contain all the elements needed for reconstructing the image slices in a table, as well as the JavaScript necessary for performing any behaviors you assign to a hotspot, such as image swapping or displaying a message in the browser's status bar. The exported HTML also includes any links to other Web pages or Web sites. When you export a sliced document, Fireworks also creates a file called spacer.gif. This is a 1 × 1-pixel, transparent GIF image that is used to correct any spacing problems that may occur when the slices cannot be reassembled in a traditional table with rows and columns.

To export HTML from your document:

1. Choose File | Export. The Export dialog box opens.

2. Navigate to the folder in which you want to store the file. If you've already created a folder for the Web site, choose this folder.

3. Click the triangle to the right of the Save As Type field and from the drop-down menu choose HTML And Images.

4. Click the Options button and choose the HTML editor you'll use to edit the files. HTML options will be covered in detail in the next section, "Setting HTML Options."

5. Click the triangle to the right of the HTML field and from the drop-down menu choose HTML (the default).

6. Click the triangle to the right of the Slices field and from the drop-down menu choose Export Slices.

7. Click the Save Images In Subfolder checkbox to save the images in a subfolder.

8. Click Save. Fireworks saves the file and images in the specified folder.

Setting HTML Options

When you export HTML from Fireworks, the generated HTML code works with most popular HTML editors and displays properly in most popular Web browsers. You can change HTML options to suit a specific editor. By modifying HTML options, you can modify the extension or export the document as an XHTML (Extensible Hyper Text Markup Language) file. XHTML will someday be the standard because this format works with standard Web browsers, as well as wireless devices and personal digital assistants (PDAs) that use XML (Extensible Markup Language) to display content.

Setting HTML options is a three-step process. You set general options that are specific to the HTML Fireworks generates, table options that are specific to the tables created in the HTML code to reassemble the slices properly, and document-specific options for which you can modify filenames for the slices, and so on.

To set HTML options:

1. Choose File | Export. The Export dialog box opens.

2. Enter a filename and location at which to save the file, and set the other parameters for the document export.

3. Click the Options button. The HTML Setup dialog box opens, as shown here:

4. Click the triangle to the right of the HTML Style field and from the drop-down menu choose one of the following:

■ **Dreamweaver HTML**   Generates HTML code tailored for Macromedia's Dreamweaver HTML editor

■ **FrontPage HTML**   Generates HTML code adhering to the preferences of the Microsoft FrontPage HTML editor

■ **Generic HTML**   Creates HTML code that can be deciphered by most popular HTML editors

■ **GoLive HTML**   Creates HTML that is suited for Adobe's GoLive HTML editor

■ **Dreamweaver XHTML**   Generates XHTML code for Macromedia's Dreamweaver HTML editor

■ **Generic XHTML**   Creates XHTML code that can be read by most popular HTML editors that support XHTML

■ **GoLive XHTML**   Creates XHTML code for Adobe's GoLive HTML editor

5. Click the triangle to the right of the Extension field and from the drop-down menu choose an option. For example, if you are going to create code for an ASP page in an HTML editor, choose the .asp extension option. (A detailed discussion of each extension is beyond the scope of this book. For more information on the specific file formats, refer to http://www.Osborne.com, where you can find books for your reference library on topics such as Active Server Pages, JavaScript, Cold Fusion, and more.)

6. Click the Include HTML Comments checkbox to export comments created by Fireworks relating to the placement of certain elements in the HTML document, such as the JavaScript for buttons, pop-up menus, tables, and so on. It's a good idea to include comments if you're going to further edit the document in an HTML editor. If desired, you can delete the comments in an HTML editor after editing the document. Comments are designated in code begin with < ! . . and end with . . ! >. Anything between these marks is not interpreted as HTML or JavaScript code.

7. Click the Lowercase File Name checkbox, and upon export Fireworks will lowercase the HTML filename and associated image filenames. The only exception to this rule is if you choose XHTML, HTM, or HTML as an extension name. In that case, choosing the lowercase option will lowercase everything in the filename except the extension.

8. Click the Table tab to open the Table section of the HTML Setup dialog box, as shown next. In this section, you set options specific to the HTML tables created upon export.

9. Click the triangle to the right of the Space With field and choose one of the following options:

- **Nested Tables No Spacers**   Re-creates document slices in nested tables without spacers. Choose this option only if you are sure that your slices are perfectly aligned and of the same size. If you choose this option with irregularly sized and spaced slices, they will not be aligned properly when displayed in a Web browser.

- **Single Table No Spacers**   Reassembles the slices in a single table with no spacers. This option is generally suited for a document in which you are exporting only a single row navigation bar.

- **1-Pixel Transparent Spacer**   Uses a 1 × 1-pixel spacer to reassemble the slices. The table has a 1-pixel spacer as the first row and a 1-pixel column on the right side. Additional spacers are added as needed and sized to realign the slices in the HTML table as they appear in the Fireworks document.

10. In the Empty Cells section, specify a color for HTML slices. By default, Fireworks uses the canvas color of the document. Click the checkbox to deselect this option and then click the color swatch to choose a color from the pop-up palette.

11. Click the triangle to the right of the Contents field and choose one of the following:

- **None**   Causes empty cells to remain blank upon export

- **Spacer Image**   Fills the cell with a 1-pixel transparent spacer

- **Non Breaking Space**   Places the `<td> </td>` tag in the empty cell

Note   *Empty cells occur only if you do not select the Include Areas Without Slices checkbox.*

12. Click the Document Specific tab to open the last section of the dialog box, shown here:

13. You can change the default slice and frame naming options by clicking the triangles and choosing options in each field. Many different options are available. As you change the naming conventions, an example of the new format is displayed at the bottom of the dialog box.

14. If desired, enter text in the Alternate Image Description field. The text you enter will be displayed as images downloaded into the user's browser. Some browsers also create a tooltip when a user's mouse passes over an image with an Alt tag.

15. Click the Multiple Nav Bar HTML Pages checkbox when exporting a document with a navigation bar. When you choose this option, Fireworks creates one page for each button in the navigation bar.

16. Click the Use UTF-8 Encoding (UTF-8 stands for Universal Character Set Transformation Format-8) checkbox when exporting a document with different character sets. For example, if your document includes Baltic text and English text on the same page, the different character sets will not display properly in a Web browser without this option selected.

17. Click the Set Defaults button to use these settings as your defaults for all exported documents.

18. Click OK to apply the settings and exit the HTML Setup dialog box. If desired, click the HTML Setup button to set HTML options, as discussed in the previous section.

Copying HTML to the Clipboard

You can copy HTML to your system clipboard and then paste the code directly into an HTML editor to create a Web page quickly. When you copy code to the clipboard, Fireworks exports the associated image files to the folder you specify. Unless you copy the code into Dreamweaver, you will lose some functionality, however. For example, when you copy HTML to the clipboard, you cannot specify a subfolder for images. When you paste the code into any application but Dreamweaver, the links and paths from pop-up menus are mapped to your hard drive. Another setback when using this option is that any JavaScript used for buttons, behaviors, and rollover image swaps may not function correctly unless the code is pasted into Dreamweaver or FrontPage.

To copy HTML code to the clipboard:

1. Choose Edit | Copy HTML. Alternatively, you can click the Quick Export button (it looks like the Fireworks logo in a yellow sphere) in the upper-right

corner of the document window and choose Copy HTML. Choosing either method launches the Copy HTML Code wizard, shown here:

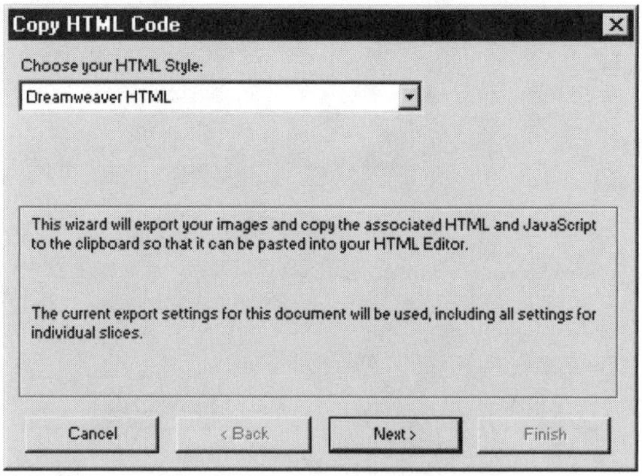

2. Click the triangle next to the Choose Your HTML Style field and select one of the following options: Dreamweaver HTML, FrontPage HTML, Generic HTML, GoLive HTML, Dreamweaver XHTML, Generic XHTML, or GoLive XHTML.

3. Click Next. The Copy HTML wizard reconfigures, as shown here:

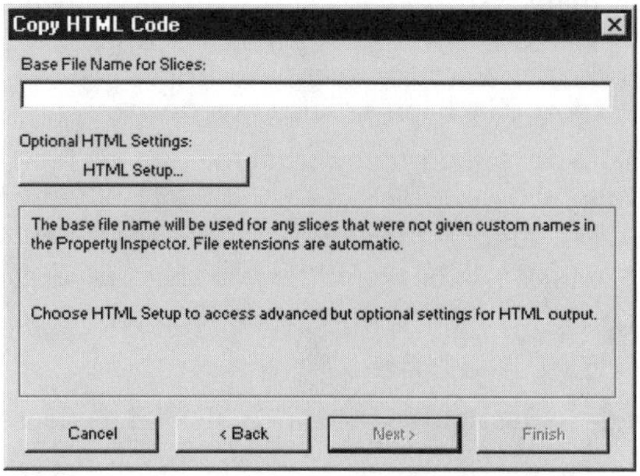

4. Enter a name for the image slices in the Base File Name For Slices field. To change HTML options, as discussed in the previous section, click the HTML Setup button.

5. Click Next to open the last screen of the dialog box, shown here:

6. Click the Browse button and navigate to the folder in which you want the images stored.

7. Click Finish. Fireworks copies the HTML to the clipboard and exports the images to the folder you specified.

An alternative method for copying HTML to the clipboard is to choose the option from within the Export dialog box. To copy HTML to the clipboard through the Export dialog box:

1. Choose File | Export. The Export dialog box opens.

2. Navigate to the folder in which you want to store the images. Note that this must be the same folder in which you store the HTML document after working with it in an HTML editor. When Fireworks copies the HTML to the clipboard, the path to the images will be the folder you select in this step.

3. Click the triangle to the right of the Save As Type field and from the drop-down menu, choose HTML And Images.

4. Click the triangle to the right of the HTML field and choose Copy To Clipboard.

5. Click the triangle to the right of the Slices field and choose Export Slices.

6. If desired, click the Options button to set up the HTML as outlined previously.

7. Click Export. Fireworks exports the images and copies the HTML to the clipboard.

After you copy the HTML code to the clipboard, you can paste it into a new or existing document in your favorite HTML editor. Each editor works a little differently, but the steps are similar.

To paste code into an HTML editor:

1. Launch your HTML editor and create a new document. Alternatively, open an existing HTML document into which you want to paste the copied code—which by the way is a quick and easy way to paste an element such as a Fireworks navigation bar into an existing page.

2. Place your cursor at the point at which you want to insert the copied HTML code. If you've created a new document, position your cursor after the <body> tag. (The actual tag will vary, depending on the HTML editor you use. The tag may include the background color and the text color, for example: <body bgcolor="#FFFFFF" text="#000000">.) Note that if you're working in a WYSIWYG HTML editor, you will have to switch to code view. (If you're not familiar with this terminology, *WYSIWYG* is an acronym for What You See Is What You Get. A WYSIWYG HTML editor such as Dreamweaver and FrontPage allows you to use a visual interface to create tables and insert text, images, and the like. The editor writes the underlying HTML code.)

3. Paste the code into the document. The method you use to paste the code will depend on the software you use to edit HTML. Refer to your software user manual for specific instructions.

4. After editing the document, save the document in the same folder to which you exported the images.

Using the Export Wizard

In the last chapter, you learned to optimize the entire document and slices. In the earlier parts of this chapter, you learned to export your work as HTML files and images. If you're ever in a pinch for time, or you are new to Fireworks and need a bit more practice before manually optimizing a document, you can optimize and export the document using the Export Wizard. When you use the Export Wizard, you launch a multiple-step process that guides you through the optimization process. After following the prompts, the wizard recommends export settings. At this stage of the process, you can accept the settings and export the document or launch the wizard again and arrive at different settings by supplying different answers to the prompts.

To optimize and export a document with the Export Wizard:

1. Choose File | Export Wizard. The first step of the Export Wizard prompts you for information in the dialog box shown here:

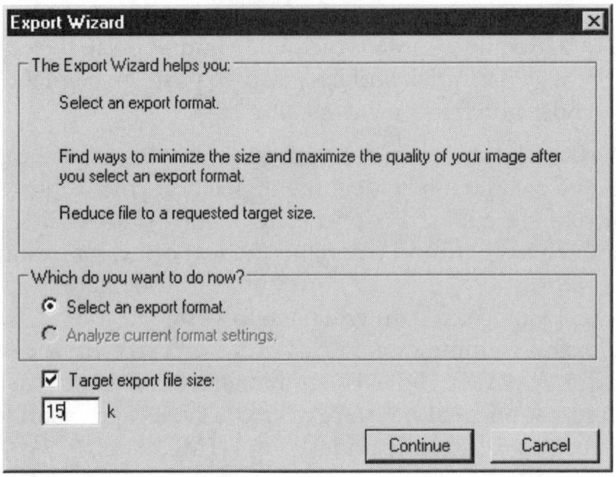

2. To optimize to a specific file size, click the Target Export File Size checkbox and then enter a value in the text field. In the preceding illustration, the user has requested a file size of less than 15K.

3. Click Continue to open the next dialog box for the next phase of the wizard, as shown here:

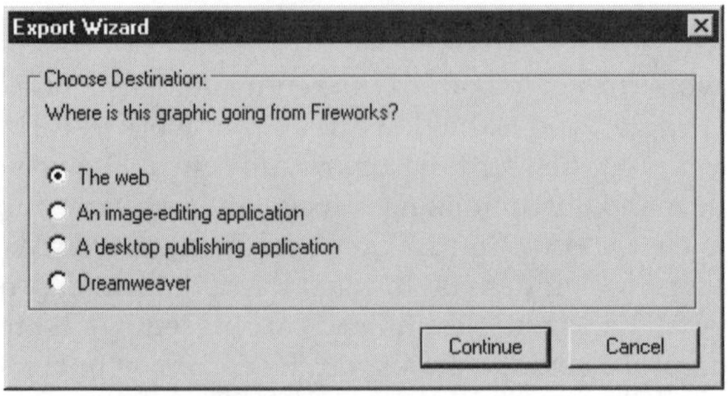

4. Choose one of the destination options and then click Continue. Fireworks processes the information you provided and then suggests a format, as shown here:

```
Analysis Results                                           [X]

 Fireworks Analysis Results:

   We recommend GIF or JPEG format, both of which are displayed in the
   preview. The first image is smaller.


   If your exported image has a transparent background, select the GIF
   format. JPEG does not support transparency.


   After selecting a format, you can choose Export Wizard again to fine-tune
   file size and image quality.


   Click Exit to view our recommendation in the preview window.


                                                      [  Exit  ]
```

5. Click Exit to view the suggested settings in the Export Preview window. You can then export the document or tweak the settings. The Export Preview window is covered in the next section.

Using the Export Preview Window

After you put the Export Wizard through its paces, the wizard suggests export settings and launches the Export Preview window. You can also access this window by choosing File | Export Preview. After the Export Preview window appears, you can choose to export the document using the settings recommended by the Export Wizard; or, if you used the Export Preview command to open the window, export the document using the current optimization settings. Alternatively, you can tweak the settings and then export the document.

To modify export settings using the Export Preview window:

1. Choose File | Export Preview or access the window through the Export Wizard as described in the previous section. After choosing either method, the Export Preview window appears, as shown in Figure 22-2.

2. In the area on the left side of the window, you can choose another export format, change the export palette, change the number of colors in the export palette, and set transparent colors. These controls are carbon copies of those contained in the Optimize panel discussed in Chapter 21. Figure 22-2 shows the Export Preview window with suggested export settings after using the Export Wizard to optimize a document for the Web with a file size of 15K or less.

3. Click the Launch Export Wizard button if you accessed the Export Preview window using the Export Wizard but are not satisfied with the export settings. This repeats the process outlined in the Using the Export Wizard section.

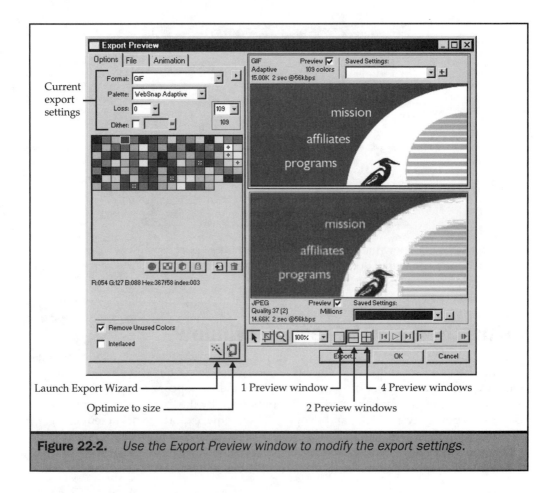

Current export settings

Launch Export Wizard

Optimize to size

1 Preview window

2 Preview windows

4 Preview windows

Figure 22-2. *Use the Export Preview window to modify the export settings.*

4. Click the Optimize To Size button to open the Optimize To Size dialog box. Enter a value and click OK. Fireworks arrives at new settings to optimize the document to the specified file size.

5. To compare the optimized document to the original, click the 2 Preview windows button. If you accessed the Export Preview window through the Export Wizard, you may be viewing different export settings in each window. To display the original document, click the Preview checkbox. To compare three optimized version to the original, click the 4 Preview windows button. To view only the optimized version of the document, click the 1 Preview window

button. These views work identically to the Preview, 2-Up, and 4-Up preview modes you used in Chapter 21, with the exception of the export settings in the left side of the Export Preview window. To view the original document when you choose the 4 Windows mode, click inside a window and deselect the Preview option.

6. Click Export if you're satisfied with the Export settings. The Export dialog box opens. Follow the steps in the Exporting HTML and Exporting Images sections to save the file as HTML and images. Alternatively, you can click the File tab to modify the File size and crop the document, as shown in Figure 22-3. If the document is an animation, you can open the Animation section of the Export Preview window, as shown in step 7.

7. Click the Animation tab if you're exporting an animation to open the window as shown in Figure 22-4. Within this window, you can fine-tune the frame time delay and modify the number of times the animation loops.

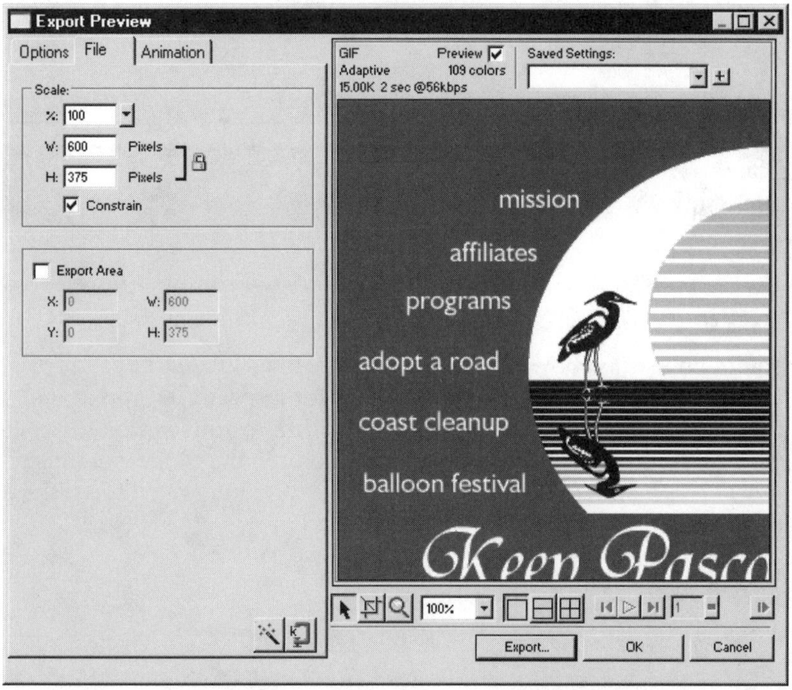

Figure 22-3.   You can also use the File tab to crop the document or modify the file size.

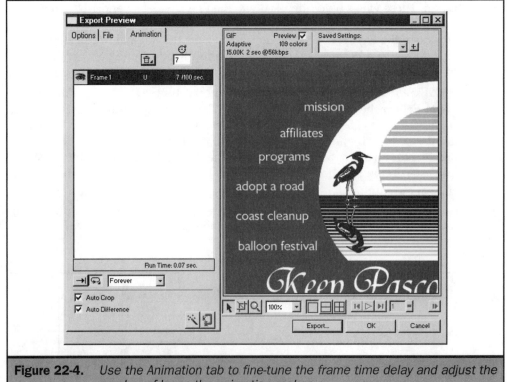

Figure 22-4. *Use the Animation tab to fine-tune the frame time delay and adjust the number of loops the animation makes.*

Summary

In this chapter you learned how to export a document as images or as images and HTML. You also learned how to tailor the HTML for a specific editor, as well as how to export a document using the Export Wizard. In addition, you learned to preview the document with the current export settings and fine-tune the export settings using the Export Preview command. In Chapter 23, you'll learn to integrate Fireworks with other Macromedia applications.

Chapter 23

Integrating Fireworks with Other Applications

W hen Macromedia launched Flash MX, their flagship product in the new MX series of software, they incorporated provisions for editing objects that were imported into Flash with other Macromedia software. When Macromedia produced other graphic-design software in the MX series, they added provisions for cross-program functionality as well. From within Fireworks, you can export files for use in Macromedia's other popular applications. For example, if you create an animation in Fireworks, you can export it as a Flash SWF movie. If you create a Fireworks document for use as a Web page, you can export it as HTML for use in Macromedia Dreamweaver. You can also launch Dreamweaver, Flash, Freehand, and Director from within Fireworks.

In this chapter, you'll learn to use this cross-program functionality to streamline your own workflow. You'll learn to edit graphics by launching Fireworks from within Dreamweaver or Flash. You'll also learn to export Fireworks documents for use in Dreamweaver, Flash, Freehand, or Director. You'll also learn to export a file for a specific application using the Export Launcher.

Integrating Fireworks with Other Graphics Software

As you've learned throughout the course of this book, you can use vector graphics and bitmaps to create documents in Fireworks. This flexibility makes it possible for you to create documents and edit images for use with other Macromedia software. In that regard, you can also create material for use with other software applications.

You reap the greatest benefits, however, when you integrate Fireworks with other Macromedia applications. Following are a few of the benefits you'll gain by integrating Fireworks with other Macromedia applications:

- You can launch Fireworks from within Dreamweaver or Flash. This functionality makes it possible for you to launch Fireworks, quickly edit a graphic, and then return to the host program. This is known as *round-trip editing*.

- When you export Fireworks documents to other programs, such as Dreamweaver, the behaviors you apply, such as image rollovers, interactive buttons, and pop-up menus, are preserved.

- If you import Fireworks PNG files into Flash, you can convert layers to frames, preserve frames, and preserve the ability to edit text. You can also flatten the PNG file into a single image. When you do this, you can still edit individual objects in the PNG file by launching Fireworks from within Flash.

In addition to the tight integration with other Macromedia software, you can also export documents that are tailored for Adobe GoLive, Adobe Illustrator, Adobe Photoshop, and Microsoft FrontPage.

Exporting Documents for Other Applications

In Chapter 22, you learned to export documents as images and HTML files. You also learned how to export slices and layers to files. You can also export documents for the following formats:

- **Dreamweaver Library (.lbi)**   Exports the document as a Dreamweaver Library item. Dreamweaver Library items are HTML and image files that can be used within a Dreamweaver document. For example, you can create a navigation bar and add it to the Dreamweaver Library. Library items are similar to symbols in Fireworks. You add them to a document as needed. You cannot edit the Library item within the Dreamweaver document; however, you can edit the master Library item, and all instances of it in the Dreamweaver document will be updated.

- **CSS Layers (.htm)**   Exports layers as a Cascading Style Sheet (CSS). CSS layers make it possible for you to define the appearance of certain elements such as buttons and headers in a Web design.

- **Director (.htm)**   Exports either layers or slices as .htm files for use in Director.

- **Lotus Domingo Designer**   Exports frames, layers, or slices for use in Lotus Domingo Designer.

- **Macromedia Flash (.swf)**   Exports the document as a Flash SWF movie. When you choose this export method, you can maintain editability and paths within the Fireworks document.

- **Illustrator 7**   Exports a document as an Adobe Illustrator AI file. When you choose this option, you can choose to make the exported file compatible with Macromedia Freehand.

- **Photoshop PSD**   Exports a document for use in Adobe Photoshop. When you choose this export method, you can control how layers, frames, and other objects are exported.

The most popular export methods will be covered in upcoming sections of this chapter. For further information, refer to the user's manual of the software program for which you are exporting the file.

Using The Export Launcher

The easiest way to integrate Fireworks with other applications is by using the Export Launcher. You trigger the Export Launcher by clicking an icon that looks like a round yellow sphere with the Fireworks logo in it, located in the upper-right corner of the document window. You can use a menu option from the Export Launcher to export files for a specific application or to launch a Macromedia application installed on your system.

To choose an option from the Export Launcher menu, follow these steps:

1. Click the Export Launcher icon in the upper-right corner of the document window, as shown in Figure 23-1.

2. Choose an option from the Export Launcher menu, shown here:

As you can see, each program has its own separate submenu. You access the submenu by clicking the arrow to the right of the program's name.

Figure 23-1. *Use the Export Launcher icon to view your options.*

Integrating Fireworks with Dreamweaver

Fireworks is used primarily for creating documents and images for the Web. Dreamweaver is an HTML editing program. As such, you experience enhanced interaction between the two programs. Links, behaviors, and other items you create in Fireworks are preserved in Dreamweaver. Slices you create in Fireworks are reassembled in tables within Dreamweaver. You can also edit images within Dreamweaver HTML designs directly in Fireworks.

Two common tasks you'll perform in Fireworks are exporting HTML and copying HTML to the clipboard. In Chapter 22, you learned to export HTML by choosing File | Export and then choosing Export as the HTML option. You learned to copy HTML to the clipboard by choosing Edit | Copy HTML Code and then following the prompts. You can perform the same tasks using the Export Launcher.

To export or copy HTML to the clipboard using the Export Launcher:

1. Click the Export Launcher icon.

2. Place your cursor over the word Dreamweaver, and from the submenu, choose one of the options shown here:

3. After you choose a command, the applicable dialog box opens. Refer to the instructions in Chapter 22 for specific information about each command.

Updating HTML Exported to Dreamweaver

If you've exported HTML to Dreamweaver for a Fireworks document such as a navigation bar, you can edit the document in Fireworks and update the HTML within Dreamweaver.

To update HTML:

1. Open the Fireworks PNG file from which you exported the HTML to Dreamweaver.

2. Edit the document as needed.

3. Choose File | Update HTML. Alternatively, you can click the Export Launcher icon and select Update HTML from the submenu. The Locate HTML dialog box opens.

4. Navigate to the folder in which you saved the HTML document and click Open. The Update HTML dialog box opens:

5. Choose one of the following options:

   ■ **Replace Images And Their HTML**   Replaces all images to reflect your edits, as well as updating any changes that will affect the HTML document.

   ■ **Replace Images**   Replaces images to reflect any changes you made to objects in the document.

6. Click OK. The Update HTML dialog box closes and the Select Images Folder dialog opens.

7. Navigate to the folder where the accompanying images are stored and click Open. Fireworks updates the HTML and replaces images as needed.

Launching Dreamweaver

You can also launch Dreamweaver from within Fireworks. This option is handy when you've just copied HTML to the clipboard. By launching Fireworks, you can quickly create a new Web page by creating a new document and pasting the copied HTML into the document.

To launch Dreamweaver from within Fireworks:

1. Click the Export Launcher icon.

2. Choose Dreamweaver | Launch Dreamweaver. Dreamweaver launches and you can create a new document or edit an existing document.

Exporting a Fireworks File as a Dreamweaver Library Object

Documents you create in Fireworks can be stored in Dreamweaver as Library items. A Dreamweaver Library item is similar to a symbol in Fireworks. You can use it repeatedly to create a Web site component such as a header that appears on every page of the site. You cannot edit individual instances of the Dreamweaver Library item. However, you can edit the master Library item and all instances of it will be updated.

To export a Fireworks document as a Dreamweaver Library item:

1. Choose File | Export. The Export dialog box appears.

2. Navigate to the root folder of the Web site on your hard drive and locate the Library folder.

3. Click the triangle to the right of the Save As Type field, and choose Dreamweaver Library (.lbi), as shown in Figure 23-2.

Note   *If you do not navigate to the Library folder, a dialog box appears prompting you to locate the Library folder.*

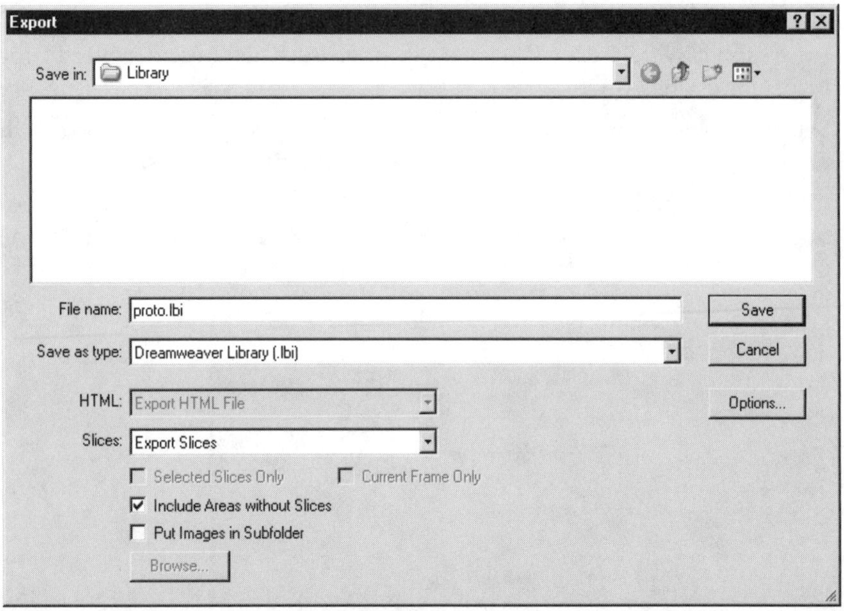

Figure 23-2.   *You can use the Export dialog box to export a file as a Dreamweaver Library item.*

4. In the File Name field, enter a name for the Library item.

5. Click the triangle to the right of the Slices field and choose Export Slices. If your document does not contain slices, this option is unavailable.

6. Click the Options button to set HTML options. Refer to Chapter 22 for specific instructions on setting HTML options.

7. Click Save. Fireworks exports the document as a Dreamweaver Library item.

Round-Trip Editing from Dreamweaver

When you're working in Dreamweaver, you'll often find it necessary to edit images. When you add images to a Dreamweaver design, you can immediately see the change in file size. If the file size increases drastically, you can select the image and then launch Fireworks to optimize the image. If you edit an image in Dreamweaver that was created from a Fireworks PNG file, the PNG file is automatically opened in Fireworks.

Items such as links, behaviors, and tables are shared between Fireworks and Dreamweaver. However, if you make wholesale edits to a Fireworks-generated table in Dreamweaver, you may encounter irreconcilable differences that cause your Dreamweaver edits to be overwritten when you edit the file in Fireworks. If you make considerable changes to a table in Dreamweaver, use the Dreamweaver Launch and Edit feature.

To launch Fireworks from within Dreamweaver:

1. In Dreamweaver, choose Window | Properties. The Dreamweaver Property inspector opens.

2. Select the object you want to update. If the object is a Fireworks object, the name of the source PNG file is displayed in the Property inspector.

3. Click Edit in the Property inspector. Fireworks launches. If Fireworks is already open, the source PNG file appears within Fireworks. An icon appears in the upper part of the document window, indicating the file is being edited from Dreamweaver, as shown here:

4. Edit the document in Fireworks as needed, and then click Done. The document is saved and then exported from Fireworks using the current export options. The image in Dreamweaver updates to reflect your changes.

If you select an image in Dreamweaver that was not created from a Fireworks document, you can still edit it in Fireworks by following these steps:

1. Select the image in Dreamweaver, and right-click (Windows) or CONTROL+click (Macintosh) and choose Edit In Fireworks from the context menu. Fireworks launches, and a dialog box appears asking whether you want to use a source PNG file to update the image.

2. Click No if the image was not the result of a Fireworks document, or if you do not want to edit a source PNG file. The image appears in Fireworks.

3. Perform the desired edits and then click Done. The image is updated in Dreamweaver to reflect your editing in Fireworks.

Note *When you round-trip edit from Dreamweaver to Fireworks, the Fireworks application does not close after you return to Dreamweaver. If your system just barely meets the minimum system requirements, consider exiting Fireworks to free up system resources.*

Note *HomeSite is an HTML editor that is distributed with Dreamweaver. You can quickly get Fireworks HTML into HomeSite using the Copy HTML To Clipboard command. Alternatively, you can click the Export Launcher icon and choose Copy HTML Code.*

Integrating Fireworks with Flash

Fireworks MX also shines when you integrate it with Flash. You can export vector objects directly to Flash, export Fireworks animations, export rollover buttons, and more. In addition, you can round-trip edit between Flash and Fireworks, a handy option when you need to resize or optimize a bitmap graphic in a Flash document.

Exporting Documents as SWF Files

When you create a document in Fireworks, you can export it as a Flash SWF movie. This option is useful, for example, when you create artwork for a Flash site such as an intricate user interface or you create an animation that you want to use as a Flash movie.

To export a Fireworks document as an SWF file:

1. Choose File | Export. Alternatively, you can click the Export Launcher icon, and then choose Macromedia Flash | Export SWF. The Export dialog box appears.

2. Navigate to the folder in which you want to save the file.

3. Click the triangle to the right of the Save As Type field, and from the drop-down menu, choose Macromedia Flash SWF.

4. Click the Options button to reveal the Macromedia Flash SWF Export Options dialog box shown here:

5. In the Objects section of the dialog box, choose one of the following options:

- **Maintain Paths**   (The default option) Allows you to edit vector objects within Flash. Any effects applied to the paths will be lost, as well as fill and stroke types selected from Fireworks stroke and fill categories.

- **Maintain Appearance**   Converts all vector objects into bitmaps, which will preserve the appearance of strokes and fills selected from Fireworks stroke and fill categories. However, you will be unable to edit vector objects in Flash.

6. In the Text section of the dialog box, choose one of the following options:

- **Maintain Editability**   Lets you edit text objects in Flash. However, any effect you apply to the text, such as kerning or paragraph indent, is not preserved.

- **Convert To Paths**   Converts text objects to bitmaps. Any kerning or spacing effects you applied in Fireworks are preserved when the text is converted to bitmaps. However, you will not be able to edit the text in Flash.

7. Click the triangle to the right of the JPEG Quality field and drag the slider to determine the amount of compression applied to any bitmaps in the document. The default value of 100 applies no compression to bitmaps, and they are exported with the same quality they have in the Fireworks document.

8. In the Frames section, accept the default option to export all frames; or click the radio button to the left of the From field, and in the From text field, enter the beginning frame to export. In the To text field enter the final frame you want to export.

9. Enter a value in the Frame Rate field. This is the number of frames used for 1 second of action when the movie is played in the Flash Player or imported into an existing Flash document. The default Flash frame rate is 12 FPS. If the document you are exporting will be imported into an existing Flash document, be sure to choose the same frame rate.

10. Click OK. Fireworks exports the document as a Flash SWF movie.

Importing an Exported Fireworks Document into Flash MX

When you export a Fireworks document as a Flash SWF file, you can play the exported file in the Flash Player. In many instances, you'll be creating content in Fireworks that you intend to incorporate in an existing Flash document, or you can use it as the basis for a new Flash movie. To use the exported Fireworks document as the basis for a Flash movie, you import the SWF file into Flash.

To import an exported Fireworks SWF file into Flash MX:

1. Launch Flash.

2. Create a new document.

3. Choose File | Import.

4. Navigate to the folder in which you exported the Fireworks document.

5. Select the file and click Open. Flash imports the file and creates keyframes for each frame exported from the Fireworks document. If you import the file to an existing document, Flash creates a new layer with enough frames to play the file at the beginning of the timeline. You can select each frame and then use the Cut Frames and Paste Frames commands to move the frames to the desired point on the Flash timeline.

Copying Vectors to the Clipboard

If you're working with Flash and Fireworks open at the same time, you can create vector or text objects in Fireworks and then copy them to the clipboard. After you copy the vector or text object to the clipboard, you can paste it directly into Flash. The vector or text object comes into Flash as a symbol and is added to the document Library.

To copy a vector or text object to the clipboard and paste it into Flash MX:

1. Select the object you want to copy with the Pointer tool. Remember that you can select more than one object by creating a marquee selection with the Pointer

tool or by holding down the SHIFT key while clicking additional objects you want to add to the selection.

2. Choose Edit | Copy. Alternatively, you can click the Export Launcher icon, and then choose Macromedia Flash | Copy. After choosing either method, Fireworks copies the vector objects to the clipboard.

3. Switch to Flash MX.

4. Choose Edit | Paste. The selected object or objects appear on the Flash Stage. The objects are movie clip symbols and are stored in the document Library in a folder named Fireworks Objects.

Launching Flash

If you're working in Fireworks with the express intent of creating vector objects for a Flash document, you can create the objects and paste them to the clipboard as outlined earlier in this chapter. You can then launch Flash from within Fireworks and paste the objects into a new document or an existing document. Working in this manner frees up system resources as you open Flash when you've finished created the vector objects rather than using system resources to keep both applications open while you create content in Fireworks.

To launch Flash from within Fireworks:

1. Click the Export Launcher icon.

2. Choose Macromedia Flash | Launch Macromedia Flash. Flash is launched and the Fireworks program is open in another window.

3. If desired, you can exit Fireworks to free up system resources.

Round-Trip Editing from Flash

You can use Fireworks to edit bitmaps or PNG files imported into a Flash document. This option is useful when you need to resample a bitmap. If the bitmap you are resampling was originally an imported PNG file, which you flattened, editing the bitmap in Fireworks opens the original document as a group, with all of the layers used to create the document. You can ungroup the bitmap in Fireworks and edit each object.

To round-trip edit a bitmap object in Flash:

1. Select the bitmap object you want to edit. You can either select the object on the Flash Stage or select it from within the Flash MX document Library.

2. If you selected the object on the Stage, right-click (Windows) or CONTROL+click (Macintosh), and from the context menu, choose Edit With Fireworks. If you selected the bitmap from the document Library, right-click (Windows) or CONTROL+click (Macintosh), and from the context menu, choose Edit With Fireworks. Alternatively, you can choose Edit With Fireworks from the

Flash MX document Library Options menu. After choosing one of these methods, Fireworks launches.

3. If you selected a flattened PNG bitmap, the original document appears in Fireworks. If the object was not a flattened PNG, the dialog box shown next appears, asking whether you want to find an existing Fireworks document to edit the selected bitmap.

4. Click Yes to open an existing Fireworks document, or click No to modify the image as it appears in Flash.

5. After editing the bitmap, click Done. The bitmap is updated in Flash to reflect your editing in Fireworks.

Integrating Fireworks with Director

When you export content from Fireworks to Director, you can preserve behaviors and slices. You can use behaviors and slices as interactive elements in your Director production. By optimizing the document in Fireworks, you're assured of the highest quality in Director.

Exporting Layers and Slices to Director

When you export layers or slices to Director, you export HTML as well. When you export slices, you export interactive elements such as buttons and rollover images, and the HTML that makes them interactive within Director. When you export layers, you can export a Fireworks animation.

To export a Fireworks document to Director:

1. Choose File | Export. The Export dialog box appears.

2. Navigate to the folder in which you want to store the exported document files.

3. Click the triangle to the right of the Save As Type field and choose Director (.htm).

4. Click the triangle to the right of the Source field and, from the drop-down menu, choose one of the following:

- **Fireworks Layers**   Exports each in the Fireworks document. Choose this option when exporting graphics organized in layers or an animation.

- **Fireworks Slices**   Exports each slice in the Fireworks document. Choose this option if the Fireworks document contains slices for interactive elements such as rollover buttons or images.

5. Select the Trim Images checkbox to resize the exported document to the objects on each frame.

6. Select the Put Images In Subfolder checkbox to store the images in a subfolder. When you choose this option, the Browse button becomes active. By default, Fireworks will create a subfolder called *images*. Alternatively, you can click the Browse button to select a different folder.

7. Click Save. Fireworks exports the document as an .htm file and stores the file and images in the specified folder.

Note *You can also export a Fireworks document to Director by clicking the Export Launcher button and then choosing Director | Source As Layers or Director | Source As Slices. Choosing either opens the Export dialog box with the proper option selected.*

Launching Director

You can launch Director from within Fireworks. This is a useful option when you've just exported a Fireworks document for Director and want to make sure it works properly.

To launch Director from within Fireworks:

1. Click the Export Launcher icon.

2. Choose Director | Launch Director. Director opens in a new window.

Note *To import an exported Fireworks document into Director, launch Director and then choose Insert | Fireworks | Images From Fireworks HTML. This option may differ depending on the version of Director you own. Refer to your user manual for specific instructions.*

Integrating Fireworks with Freehand

Fireworks and Freehand both use vector objects to create artwork. As such, you can use vector objects in Freehand that you create in Fireworks, and vice versa. When you export Fireworks objects to Freehand, you export them as Illustrator 7 files. The same techniques shown in this section can be used to export Fireworks documents for use in CorelDRAW and other vector illustration programs.

Exporting Objects to Freehand

When you create a document in Fireworks, you can export the document in a format that can be read by Freehand and other vector illustration programs. When you export a document with frames, you can convert frames to layers or export only the currently selected frame.

To export a document suitable for use in Freehand:

1. Choose File | Export. The Export dialog box opens. Alternatively, click the Export Launcher icon and then choose Freehand | Export To Freehand. When you choose this alternative method, the Export dialog box opens and Illustrator 7 is already selected as the file type.

2. Select the folder to which you want to export the document.

3. Click the triangle to the right of the Save As Type field and, from the drop-down menu, choose Illustrator 7. This step is not necessary if you opened the dialog box using the Export Launcher.

4. Click the Options button to open the Illustrator Options dialog box.

5. In the Frames section, choose one of the following options:

   - **Export Current Frame Only**   Exports the currently selected name while preserving layer names.

   - **Convert Frames To Layers**   Exports the document and converts each frame in the Fireworks document to a layer.

6. Select the Freehand Compatible checkbox to export the document for use in Freehand. When you choose this option, any bitmaps in the Fireworks document are excluded from the export, and gradient fills are converted to solid fills.

7. Click OK to close the Illustrator Export Options dialog box.

8. Click Save to export the document to the specified folder.

Copying Path Outlines

Another useful integration Fireworks provides with Freehand is the ability to copy paths to the clipboard. After you copy paths to the clipboard, you can paste them directly into Freehand.

To copy Fireworks paths to the clipboard:

1. Select the vector objects you want to copy to the clipboard.

2. Click the Export Launcher button and choose Freehand | Copy Path Outlines. Alternatively, you can choose Edit | Copy Path Outlines. Fireworks copies the selected vector objects to the clipboard.

To paste copies paths into Freehand:

1. Launch Freehand.
2. Create a new document, or open an existing document into which you want to paste the copied paths.
3. Choose Edit | Paste. The copied objects are pasted into Freehand.

Launching Freehand

In addition to being able to copy path outlines to the clipboard for use in Freehand and export documents for use in Freehand, you can also launch Freehand from within Fireworks. This option sidesteps the need to launch Freehand from the Start menu when you want to paste copied paths into a Freehand document.

To launch Freehand from within Fireworks:

1. Click the Export Launcher icon.
2. Choose Freehand | Launch Freehand. Freehand launches in a separate window.

Integrating Fireworks with Non-Macromedia Applications

In addition to the tight integration between Fireworks and other Macromedia applications, Fireworks artwork files and documents can be used with other software programs. The degree of integration varies from program to program. Certain features such as Live Effects are not supported by other software. Other features such as fill styles and texture may not be supported. The following is a list of Fireworks features not supported by other vector programs, including Freehand:

- Live Effects
- Blending modes
- Textures, patterns, Web dither fills, and gradient fills
- Slices and image maps
- Text formatting options such as kerning, baseline shift, horizontal scale, paragraph indent, and so on
- Guide lines, grids, and document canvas color
- Certain stroke styles

Exporting to Photoshop

You can export a file optimized for use in Photoshop. When you choose this export option, you can preserve editability of certain objects or convert objects to bitmaps maintain their appearance when the exported file is opened in Photoshop.

To export a file for use in Photoshop:

1. Choose File | Export. The Export dialog box appears. Alternatively, you can click the Export Launcher icon and choose Other | Export To Photoshop. When you choose this option from the Export Launcher menu, the Export options dialog box opens and Photoshop is already selected as the file type.

2. Navigate to the folder in which you want to save the file.

3. Click the triangle to the right of the Save As Type field and choose Photoshop. The Export dialog box is configured as shown here:

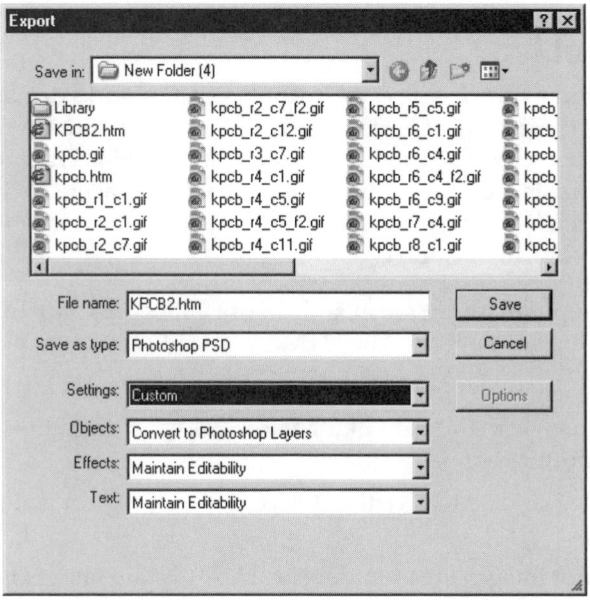

4. Click the triangle to the right of the Settings field, and choose one of the following options:

■ **Maintain Editability Over Appearance** Converts each object in the document to its own layer and converts all text objects to Photoshop text layers. This is your best choice if you plan to do extensive editing within Photoshop.

- ■ **Maintain Fireworks Appearance**   Converts vector and text objects to bitmaps. Choose this option to preserve the appearance of the Fireworks document in Photoshop.

- ■ **Smaller Photoshop File**   Converts each layer into a single bitmap object. This option is useful when the sheer volume of objects on each Fireworks layer would create a document with a large file size.

- ■ **Custom**   Enables you to choose specific export options for text, objects, and effects. When you choose this option, the Objects, Effects, and Text fields become active, as shown in the preceding illustration. In the Objects field, you can choose to Convert Objects To Photoshop layers or Flatten Objects. In the Effects field, you can choose to Render Effects or Maintain Editability. In the Text field, you can choose to Render Text or Maintain Editability.

5. Click Save. Fireworks saves the file as a Photoshop PSD file using the settings you specified.

Exporting to GoLive

If you use GoLive as an HTML editor, you can export a Fireworks document as HTML and image files. Exporting a document as HTML and images was covered in detail in Chapter 22. In a nutshell, you choose to export the document as images and HTML, and then set up the HTML, in which you can specify that Fireworks create HTML tailored to the GoLive HTML editor. However, there's a way you can achieve the same result more quickly.

To export a document to GoLive:

1. Click the Export Launcher icon and choose Other | Export To GoLive. The Export dialog box appears. The HTML is already set up for GoLive.

2. Navigate to the folder in which you want to store the HTML document.

3. Click the triangle to the right of the Slices field and, from the drop-down menu, choose Export Slices.

4. Choose the Include Areas Without Slice option to export non-sliced areas as HTML cells.

5. Select the Put Images In Subfolder checkbox to store images in a subfolder. When you choose this option, Fireworks creates a subfolder called *images*. If you want to store the images in a different folder, click the Browse button and navigate to the folder in which you want to store the images.

6. Click Save. Fireworks exports the document as HTML and images. The files are saved in the specified folder.

Exporting to FrontPage

If you use FrontPage to edit your HTML documents, you can quickly export a document as images and HTML with the HTML set up for Microsoft FrontPage. You can do this by manually setting up the HTML as outlined in Chapter 22, or you can do it quickly by using the Export Launcher.

To export a document as images and HTML for FrontPage:

1. Click the Export Launcher icon and choose Other | Export To FrontPage. The Export dialog box appears and the HTML options are set up for FrontPage.

2. Navigate to the folder in which you want to store the HTML document. Typically, this will be the root folder for the FrontPage Web site.

3. Click the triangle to the right of the Slices field and, from the drop-down menu, choose Export Slices.

4. Select the Include Areas Without Slices (the default option, which is selected by default) checkbox to export non-sliced areas as HTML cells.

5. Select the Put Images In Subfolder checkbox to store images in a subfolder. When you choose this option, Fireworks creates a subfolder called *images*. If you want to store the images in a different location on your hard drive, click the Browse button and navigate to the folder in which you want to store the images.

6. Click Save. Fireworks exports the document as HTML and images. The files are saved in the specified folder.

Exporting to Illustrator

If you use Adobe Illustrator to create vector illustrations, you can export a document as an Illustrator 7 file. You can do this manually by choosing File | Export and then choosing the appropriate choices in each field. This method was outlined in Chapter 22. Alternatively, you can export the document with all of the proper options for Adobe Illustrator selected.

To export a document for use in Adobe Illustrator:

1. Click the Export Launcher icon and choose Other | Export To Illustrator. The Export dialog box opens and Illustrator 7 is already selected as the file type.

2. Navigate to the folder in which you want to save the file.

3. Click the Options button to open the Illustrator Options dialog box.

4. In the Frames section, choose one of the following options:

   ■ **Export Current Frame Only**   Exports the currently selected name while preserving layer names.

   ■ **Convert Frames To Layers**   Exports the document and converts each frame in the Fireworks document to a layer.

5. Select the Freehand Compatible checkbox to export the document for use in Freehand. When you choose this option, any bitmaps in the Fireworks document are excluded from the export and gradient fills are converted to solid fills.

6. Click OK to close the Illustrator Export Options dialog box.

7. Click Save. Fireworks saves the document as an Illustrator 7 .ai file.

Summary

In this chapter, you learned to integrate Fireworks with other popular Macromedia applications. You learned to copy items to the clipboard and then paste them into other Macromedia software. You learned to do round-trip editing between Macromedia applications and Fireworks. You also learned to export Fireworks documents and objects for use in other programs using the Export Launcher.

In Appendix A, you'll find a list of the keyboard shortcuts for the Macromedia Standard keyboard shortcut set and the Fireworks keyboard shortcut set. In Appendix B, you'll find a list of Fireworks resources on the Internet. Each listing will have the URL to the site and a brief description of what you can expect to find there. In Appendix C, you'll find the URLs to Internet resources for Web design.

Where to Go from Here

Now that you've worked your way through this book, you can see the inherent power available with Fireworks. You can use the software as a full-fledged Web design tool, or use it to augment your other graphics-design software. To grasp a firm knowledge of the software, use it whenever you need to edit an image, edit a batch of images, create a graphic, create a vector object, or create an interactive object for a Web design. You should also make it a point to use Fireworks whenever you need to edit a bitmap image for a Web design. The advanced optimization methods make it possible for you to create a good-looking graphic with a smaller file size than possible with other image-editing software. At first glance, Fireworks can seem intimidating; but with persistence and practice, you'll be as comfortable working with Fireworks as you are when you curl up with a good book in your favorite easy chair.

The Complete Reference

Fireworks MX

Part VI

Appendixes

The Complete Reference

Fireworks MX

Appendix A

Keyboard Shortcuts

F ireworks has a wide diversity of built-in keyboard shortcut sets. In this appendix, the keyboard shortcuts for the default Macromedia Standard keyboard shortcut set are listed, as well as the Fireworks keyboard shortcut set.

Macromedia Standard Keyboard Shortcuts

The tables in this section list the keyboard shortcuts for the default Fireworks MX keyboard shortcut set: the Macromedia Standard keyboard shortcut set.

Command	Windows Keyboard Shortcut	Macintosh Keyboard Shortcut
New	CTRL+N	COMMAND+N
Open	CTRL+O	COMMAND+O
Close	CTRL+W	COMMAND+W
Save	CTRL+S	COMMAND+S
Save As	CTRL+SHIFT+S	COMMAND+SHIFT+S
Import	CTRL+R	COMMAND+R
Export	CTRL+SHIFT+R	COMMAND+SHIFT+R
Export Preview	CTRL+SHIFT+X	COMMAND+SHIFT+X
Preview In Browser	F12	F12
Preview In Secondary Browser	CTRL+F12, SHIFT+F12	COMMAND+F12, SHIFT+F12
Print	CTRL+P	COMMAND+P
Exit	CTRL+Q	COMMAND+Q

Table A-1. *Macromedia Standard File Menu Keyboard Shortcuts*

Command	Windows Keyboard Shortcut	Macintosh Keyboard Shortcut
Undo	CTRL+Z	COMMAND+Z
Redo	CTRL+Y, CTRL+SHIFT+Z	COMMAND+Y, COMMAND+SHIFT+Z
New Button	CTRL+SHIFT+F8	COMMAND+SHIFT+F8
New Symbol	CTRL+F8	COMMAND+F8
Hotspot	CTRL+SHIFT+U	COMMAND+SHIFT+U
Slice	ALT+SHIFT+U	OPTION+SHIFT+U
Find And Replace	CTRL+F	COMMAND+F
Cut	CTRL+X	COMMAND+X
Copy	CTRL+C	COMMAND+C
Copy HTML Code	CTRL+ALT+C	COMMAND+OPTION+C
Paste	CTRL+V	COMMAND+V
Clear	BACKSPACE, DELETE	BACKSPACE, DELETE
Paste Inside	CTRL+SHIFT+V	COMMAND+SHIFT+V
Paste Attributes	CTRL+ALT+SHIFT+V	COMMAND+OPTION+SHIFT+V
Duplicate	CTRL+ALT+D	COMMAND+OPTION+D
Clone	CTRL+SHIFT+D	COMMAND+SHIFT+D
Preferences	CTRL+U	COMMAND+U

Table A-2.   *Macromedia Standard Edit Menu Keyboard Shortcuts*

Command	Windows Keyboard Shortcut	Macintosh Keyboard Shortcut
Zoom In	CTRL+=, CTRL+NUM+, CTRL+SHIFT+=	COMMAND+=, COMMAND+NUM+, COMMAND+SHIFT+=
Zoom Out	CTRL+-, CTRL+NUM 0 -	COMMAND+-, COMMAND+NUM 0 -
50%	CTRL+5, CTRL+NUM 5	COMMAND+5, COMMAND+NUM 5
100%	CTRL+1, CTRL+NUM 1	COMMAND+1, COMMAND+NUM+1
200%	CTRL+2, CTRL+NUM 2	COMMAND+2, COMMAND+NUM 2
300%	CTRL+3, CTRL+NUM 3	COMMAND+3, COMMAND+NUM 3
400%	CTRL+4, CTRL+NUM 4	COMMAND+4, COMMAND+NUM 4
800%	CTRL+8, CTRL+NUM 8	COMMAND+8, COMMAND+NUM 8
1600%	CTRL+6, CTRL+NUM 6	COMMAND+6, COMMAND+NUM 6
Fit Selection	CTRL+ALT+0, CTRL+ALT+NUM 0	COMMAND+OPTION+0, COMMAND+OPTION+NUM 0
Fit All	CTRL+0, CTRL+NUM 0	COMMAND+0, COMMAND+NUM 0
Full Display	CTRL+K	COMMAND+K
Hide Selection	CTRL+L	COMMAND+L
Show All	CTRL+SHIFT+L	COMMAND+SHIFT+L
Rulers	CTRL+ALT+R	COMMAND+OPTION+R
Show Grid	CTRL+ALT+G	COMMAND+OPTION+G
Snap To Grid	CTRL+ALT+SHIFT+G	COMMAND+OPTION+SHIFT+G
Show Guides	CTRL+;	COMMAND+;
Lock Guides	CTRL+ALT+;	COMMAND+OPTION+;
Snap To Guides	CTRL+SHIFT+;	COMMAND+SHIFT+;
Slice Guides	CTRL+ALT+SHIFT+;	COMMAND+OPTION+SHIFT+;
Hide Edges	F9	F9
Hide Panels	F4, TAB	F4, TAB

Table A-3.   _Macromedia Standard View Menu Keyboard Shortcuts_

Command	Windows Keyboard Shortcut	Macintosh Keyboard Shortcut
Select All	CTRL+A	COMMAND+A
Deselect	CTRL+D	COMMAND+D
Superselect	CTRL+RIGHT	COMMAND+RIGHT
Subselect	CTRL+LEFT	COMMAND+LEFT
Select Inverse	CTRL+SHIFT+I	COMMAND+SHIFT+I

Table A-4. *Macromedia Standard Select Menu Keyboard Shortcuts*

Command	Windows Keyboard Shortcut	Macintosh Keyboard Shortcut
Trim Canvas	CTRL+ALT+T	COMMAND+OPTION+T
Fit Canvas	CTRL+ALT+F	COMMAND+OPTION+F
Animate Selection	ALT+SHIFT+F8	OPTION+SHIFT+F8
Convert To Symbol	F8	F8
Tween Instances	CTRL+ALT+SHIFT+T	COMMAND+OPTION+SHIFT+T
Flatten Selection	CTRL+ALT+SHIFT+Z	COMMAND+OPTION+SHIFT+Z
Merge Down	CTRL+E	COMMAND+E
Free Transform	CTRL+T	COMMAND+T
Numeric Transform	CTRL+SHIFT+T	COMMAND+SHIFT+T
Rotate 90° CW	CTRL+SHIFT+9	COMMAND+SHIFT+9
Rotate 90° CCW	CTRL+SHIFT+7	COMMAND+SHIFT+7
Bring To Front	CTRL+SHIFT+UP	COMMAND+SHIFT+UP
Bring Forward	CTRL+UP	COMMAND+UP
Send Backward	CTRL+DOWN	COMMAND+DOWN
Send To Back	CTRL+SHIFT+DOWN	COMMAND+SHIFT+DOWN
Left	CTRL+ALT+1, CTRL+ALT+NUM 1	COMMAND+OPTION+1, COMMAND+OPTION+NUM 1

Table A-5. *Macromedia Standard Modify Menu Keyboard Shortcuts*

Command	Windows Keyboard Shortcut	Macintosh Keyboard Shortcut
Center Vertical	CTRL+ALT+2, CTRL+ALT+NUM 2	COMMAND+OPTION+2, COMMAND+OPTION+NUM 2
Right	CTRL+ALT+3, CTRL+ALT+NUM 3	COMMAND+OPTION+3, COMMAND+OPTION+NUM 3
Top	CTRL+ALT+4, CTRL+ALT+NUM 4	COMMAND+OPTION+4, COMMAND+OPTION+NUM 4
Center Horizontal	CTRL+ALT+5, CTRL+ALT+NUM 5	COMMAND+OPTION+5, COMMAND+OPTION+NUM 5
Bottom	CTRL+ALT+6, CTRL+ALT+NUM 6	COMMAND+OPTION+6, COMMAND+OPTION+NUM 6
Distribute Widths	CTRL+ALT+7, CTRL+ALT+NUM 7	COMMAND+OPTION+7, COMMAND+OPTION+NUM 7
Distribute Heights	CTRL+ALT+9, CTRL+ALT+NUM 9	COMMAND+OPTION+9, COMMAND+OPTION+NUM 9
Join	CTRL+J	COMMAND+J
Split	CTRL+SHIFT+J	COMMAND+SHIFT+J
Group	CTRL+G	COMMAND+G
Ungroup	CTRL+SHIFT+G	COMMAND+SHIFT+G

Table A-5. *Macromedia Standard Modify Menu Keyboard Shortcuts* (continued)

Command	Windows Keyboard Shortcut	Macintosh Keyboard Shortcut
Smaller	CTRL+SHIFT+,	COMMAND+SHIFT+,
Larger	CTRL+SHIFT+.	COMMAND+SHIFT+.
Bold	CTRL+B	COMMAND+B
Italic	CTRL+I	COMMAND+I
Left	CTRL+ALT+SHIFT+L	COMMAND+OPTION+SHIFT+L
Centered Horizontally	CTRL+ALT+SHIFT+C	COMMAND+OPTION+SHIFT+C

Table A-6. *Macromedia Standard Text Menu Keyboard Shortcuts*

Command	Windows Keyboard Shortcut	Macintosh Keyboard Shortcut
Right	CTRL+ALT+SHIFT+R	COMMAND+OPTION+SHIFT+R
Justified	CTRL+ALT+SHIFT+J	COMMAND+OPTION+SHIFT+J
Stretched	CTRL+ALT+SHIFT+S	COMMAND+OPTION+SHIFT+S
Attach To Path	CTRL+SHIFT+Y	COMMAND+SHIFT+Y
Convert To Paths	CTRL+SHIFT+P	COMMAND+SHIFT+P
Check Spelling	SHIFT+F7	SHIFT+F7

Table A-6.   *Macromedia Standard Text Menu Keyboard Shortcuts* (continued)

Command	Windows Keyboard Shortcut	Macintosh Keyboard Shortcut
New Window	CTRL+ALT+N	COMMAND+OPTION+N
Tools	CTRL+F2	COMMAND+F2
Properties	CTRL+F3	COMMAND+F3
Answers	ALT+F1	OPTION+F1
Optimize	F6	F6
Layers	F2	F2
Frames	SHIFT+F2	SHIFT+F2
History	SHIFT+F10	SHIFT+F10
Styles	SHIFT+F11	SHIFT+F11
Library	F11	F11
URL	ALT+SHIFT+F10	OPTION+SHIFT+F10
Color Mixer	SHIFT+F9	SHIFT+F9
Swatches	CTRL+F9	COMMAND+F9
Info	ALT+SHIFT+F12	OPTION+SHIFT+F12
Behaviors	SHIFT+F3	SHIFT+F3
Find And Replace	CTRL+F	COMMAND+F

Table A-7.   *Macromedia Standard Window Menu Keyboard Shortcuts*

Tool	Windows Keyboard Shortcut	Macintosh Keyboard Shortcut
Pointer tool	V, 0	V, 0
Select Behind tool	V, 0	V, 0
Subselection tool	A, 1	A, 1
Marquee tool	M	M
Oval Marquee tool	M	M
Lasso tool	L	L
Polygon Lasso tool	L	L
Crop tool	C	C
Export Area tool	C	C
Magic Wand tool	W	W
Line tool	N	N
Pen tool	P	P
Rectangle tool	U	U
Rounded Rectangle tool	U	U
Ellipse tool	U	U
Polygon tool	U	U
Text tool	T	T
Pencil tool	B	B
Vector Path tool	P	P
Redraw Path tool	P	P
Brush tool	B	B
Scale tool	Q	Q
Skew tool	Q	Q
Distort tool	Q	Q
Freeform tool	O	O

Table A-8.   *Macromedia Standard Tools Keyboard Shortcuts*

Tool	Windows Keyboard Shortcut	Macintosh Keyboard Shortcut
Reshape Area tool	O	O
Eyedropper tool	I	I
Paint Bucket tool	G	G
Gradient tool	G	G
Eraser tool	E	E
Blur tool	R	R
Sharpen tool	R	R
Dodge tool	R	R
Burn tool	R	R
Smudge tool	R	R
Rubber Stamp tool	S	S
Knife tool	Y	Y
Rectangle Hotspot tool	J	J
Circle Hotspot tool	J	J
Polygon Hotspot tool	J	J
Slice tool	K	K
Polygon Slice tool	K	K
Hand tool	H	H
Zoom tool	Z	Z
Hide/Show Slices	2	2
Set Default Stroke/Fill Colors	D	D
Swap Stroke/Fill Colors	X	X
Toggle Screen Mode	F	F

Table A-8. *Macromedia Standard Tools Keyboard Shortcuts* (continued)

Command	Windows Keyboard Shortcut	Macintosh Keyboard Shortcut
Clone And Nudge Down	ALT+DOWN, CTRL+ALT+DOWN	OPTION+DOWN, COMMAND+OPTION+DOWN
Clone And Nudge Down Large	ALT+SHIFT+DOWN, CTRL+ALT+SHIFT+DOWN	OPTION+SHIFT+DOWN, COMMAND+OPTION+ SHIFT+DOWN
Clone And Nudge Left	ALT+LEFT, CTRL+ALT+ LEFT	OPTION+LEFT, COMMAND+OPTION+LEFT
Clone And Nudge Left Large	ALT+SHIFT+LEFT, CTRL+ALT+SHIFT+LEFT	OPTION+SHIFT+LEFT, COMMAND+OPTION+SHIFT+LEFT
Clone And Nudge Right	ALT+RIGHT, CTRL+ALT+RIGHT	OPTION+RIGHT, COMMAND+OPTION+RIGHT
Clone And Nudge Right Large	ALT+SHIFT+RIGHT, CTRL+ALT+SHIFT+RIGHT	OPTION+SHIFT+RIGHT, COMMAND+OPTION+SHIFT+RIGHT
Clone And Nudge Up	ALT+UP, CTRL+ALT+UP	OPTION+UP, COMMAND+OPTION+UP
Clone And Nudge Up Large	ALT+SHIFT+UP, CTRL+ALT+SHIFT+UP	OPTION+SHIFT+UP, COMMAND+OPTION+SHIFT+UP
Edit Bitmap	CTRL+E	COMMAND+E
Exit Bitmap Mode	CTRL+SHIFT+E	COMMAND+SHIFT+E
Fill Pixel Selection	ALT+BACKSPACE, ALT+DELETE	OPTION+BACKSPACE, OPTION+DELETE
Next Frame	PAGE DOWN, CTRL+PAGE DOWN	PAGE DOWN, COMMAND+PAGE DOWN
Nudge Down	DOWN	DOWN
Nudge Down Large	SHIFT+DOWN	SHIFT+DOWN
Nudge Left	LEFT	LEFT
Nudge Left Large	SHIFT+LEFT	SHIFT+LEFT
Nudge Right	RIGHT	RIGHT
Nudge Right Large	SHIFT+RIGHT	SHIFT+RIGHT
Nudge Up	UP	UP
Nudge Up Large	SHIFT+UP	SHIFT+UP

Table A-9. *Macromedia Standard Miscellaneous Command Keyboard Shortcuts*

Command	Windows Keyboard Shortcut	Macintosh Keyboard Shortcut
Paste Inside	CTRL+SHIFT+V	COMMAND+SHIFT+V
Play Animation	CTRL+ALT+P	COMMAND+OPTION+P
Previous Frame	PAGE UP, CTRL+PAGE UP	PAGE UP, COMMAND+PAGE UP

Table A-9. *Macromedia Standard Miscellaneous Command Keyboard Shortcuts (continued)*

Macromedia Fireworks Keyboard Shortcut Set

In this section is a handy reference to the Macromedia Fireworks keyboard shortcut set. Use these keyboard shortcuts if you've selected the Fireworks keyboard shortcut set from Keyboard Shortcuts dialog box as outlined in Chapter 3. Note that some of the tools have two shortcuts and some of the tools have the same keyboard shortcut set, which makes it possible for you to quickly toggle from one tool to another by pressing the same keyboard shortcut.

Command	Windows Shortcut Key	Macintosh Shortcut Key
New	CTRL+N	COMMAND+N
Open	CTRL+O	COMMAND+O
Close	CTRL+W	COMMAND+W
Save	CTRL+S	COMMAND+S
Save As	CTRL+SHIFT+S	COMMAND+SHIFT+S
Import	CTRL+R	COMMAND+R
Export	CTRL+SHIFT+R	COMMAND+SHIFT+R
Export Preview	CTRL+SHIFT+X	COMMAND+SHIFT+X
Preview In Browser	F12	F12
Preview In Secondary Browser	SHIFT+F12	SHIFT+F12
Print	CTRL+P	COMMAND+P
Exit	CTRL+Q	COMMAND+Q

Table A-10. *Fireworks Keyboard Shortcuts for the File Menu*

Command	Windows Keyboard Shortcut	Macintosh Keyboard Shortcut
Undo	CTRL+Z	COMMAND+Z
Redo	CTRL+SHIFT+Z	COMMAND+SHIFT+Z
Insert New Symbol	CTRL+F8	COMMAND+F8
Insert Hotspot	CTRL+SHIFT+U	COMMAND+SHIFT+U
Insert Empty Bitmap	CTRL+ALT+Y	COMMAND+OPTION+Y
Cut	CTRL+X	COMMAND+X
Copy	CTRL+C	COMMAND+C
Paste	CTRL+V	COMMAND+V
Clear	BACKSPACE, DELETE	BACKSPACE, DELETE
Paste Inside	CTRL+SHIFT+V	COMMAND+SHIFT+V
Paste Attributes	CTRL+ALT+SHIFT+V	COMMAND+OPTION+SHIFT+V
Duplicate	CTRL+ALT+D	COMMAND+OPTION+D
Clone	CTRL+SHIFT+C	COMMAND+SHIFT+C
Crop Selected Bitmap	CTRL+ALT+C	COMMAND+OPTION+C

Table A-11. *Fireworks Keyboard Shortcuts for the Edit Menu*

Command	Windows Keyboard Shortcut	Macintosh Keyboard Shortcut
Fit Selection	CTRL+0	COMMAND+0
Fit All	CTRL+ALT+0	COMMAND+OPTION+0
Full Display	CTRL+K	COMMAND+K
Hide Selection	CTRL+M	COMMAND+M

Table A-12. *Fireworks MX View Keyboard Shortcuts*

APPENDIXES

Command	Windows Keyboard Shortcut	Macintosh Keyboard Shortcut
Show All	CTRL+SHIFT+M	COMMAND+SHIFT+M
Rulers	CTRL+ALT+R	COMMAND+OPTION+R
Show Grid	CTRL+'	COMMAND+'
Snap To Grid	CTRL+SHIFT+'	COMMAND+SHIFT+'
Edit Grid	CTRL+ALT+G	COMMAND+OPTION+G
Show Guides	CTRL+;	COMMAND+;
Lock Guides	CTRL+ALT+;	COMMAND+OPTION+;
Snap To Guides	CTRL+SHIFT+;	COMMAND+SHIFT+;
Edit Guides	CTRL+ALT+SHIFT+G	COMMAND+OPTION+SHIFT+G
Slice Guides	CTRL+ALT+SHIFT+;	COMMAND+OPTION+SHIFT+;
Hide Edges	CTRL+H	COMMAND+H
Hide Panels	TAB, CTRL+SHIFT+H	TAB, COMMAND+SHIFT+H

Table A-12.   *Fireworks MX View Keyboard Shortcuts* (continued)

Command	Windows Keyboard Shortcut	Macintosh Keyboard Shortcut
Select All	CTRL+A	COMMAND+A
Deselect	CTRL+D	COMMAND+D
Superselect	CTRL+UP	COMMAND+UP
Subselect	CTRL+DOWN	COMMAND+DOWN
Select Inverse	CTRL+SHIFT+I	COMMAND+SHIFT+I

Table A-13.   *Fireworks MX Select Menu Keyboard Shortcuts*

Command	Windows Keyboard Shortcut	Macintosh Keyboard Shortcut
Convert To Symbol	F8	F8
Tween Instances	CTRL+ALT+SHIFT+T	COMMAND+OPTION+SHIFT+T
Group As Mask	CTRL+SHIFT+G	COMMAND+SHIFT+G
Flatten Selection	CTRL+ALT+SHIFT+Z	COMMAND+OPTION+SHIFT+Z
Merge Down	CTRL+E	COMMAND+E
Free Transform	CTRL+T	COMMAND+T
Numeric Transform	CTRL+SHIFT+T	COMMAND+SHIFT+T
Rotate 90° CW	CTRL+9	COMMAND+9
Rotate 90° CCW	CTRL+7	COMMAND+7
Bring To Front	CTRL+F	COMMAND+F
Bring Forward	CTRL+SHIFT+F	COMMAND+SHIFT+F
Send Backward	CTRL+SHIFT+B	COMMAND+SHIFT+B
Send To Back	CTRL+B	COMMAND+B
Left	CTRL+ALT+1	COMMAND+OPTION+1
Center Vertical	CTRL+ALT+2	COMMAND+OPTION+2
Right	CTRL+ALT+3	COMMAND+OPTION+3
Top	CTRL+ALT+4	COMMAND+OPTION+4
Center Horizontal	CTRL+ALT+5	COMMAND+OPTION+5
Bottom	CTRL+ALT+6	COMMAND+OPTION+6
Distribute Widths	CTRL+ALT+7	COMMAND+OPTION+7
Distribute Heights	CTRL+ALT+9	COMMAND+OPTION+9
Join	CTRL+J	COMMAND+J
Split	CTRL+SHIFT+J	COMMAND+SHIFT+J
Group	CTRL+G	COMMAND+G
Ungroup	CTRL+U	COMMAND+U

Table A-14.   *Fireworks MX Modify Menu Keyboard Shortcuts*

Command	Windows Keyboard Shortcut	Macintosh Keyboard Shortcut
Plain	CTRL+ALT+SHIFT+P, F5	COMMAND+OPTION+SHIFT+P, F5
Bold	CTRL+ALT+SHIFT+B, F6	COMMAND+OPTION+SHIFT+B, F6
Italic	CTRL+ALT+SHIFT+I, F7	COMMAND+OPTION+SHIFT+I, F7
Underline	CTRL+ALT+SHIFT+U	COMMAND+OPTION+SHIFT+U
Left	CTRL+ALT+SHIFT+L	COMMAND+OPTION+SHIFT+L
Centered Horizontally	CTRL+ALT+SHIFT+C	COMMAND+OPTION+SHIFT+C
Right	CTRL+ALT+SHIFT+R	COMMAND+OPTION+SHIFT+R
Justified	CTRL+ALT+SHIFT+J	COMMAND+OPTION+SHIFT+J
Stretched	CTRL+ALT+SHIFT+S	COMMAND+OPTION+SHIFT+S
Editor	CTRL+SHIFT+E	COMMAND+SHIFT+E
Attach To Path	CTRL+SHIFT+Y	COMMAND+SHIFT+Y
Convert To Paths	CTRL+SHIFT+P	COMMAND+SHIFT+P
Check Spelling	SHIFT+F7	SHIFT+F7

Table A-15.   *Fireworks MX Text Menu Keyboard Shortcuts*

Command	Windows Keyboard Shortcut	Macintosh Keyboard Shortcut
New Window	CTRL+ALT+N	COMMAND+OPTION+N
Tools	CTRL+F2	COMMAND+F2
Properties	CTRL+F3	COMMAND+F3
Answers	ALT+F1	OPTION+F1
Layers	CTRL+ALT+L	COMMAND+OPTION+L
Frames	CTRL+ALT+K	COMMAND+OPTION+K

Table A-16.   *Fireworks MX Window Keyboard Shortcuts*

Command	Windows Keyboard Shortcut	Macintosh Keyboard Shortcut
Styles	CTRL+ALT+J	COMMAND+OPTION+J
URL	CTRL+ALT+U	COMMAND+OPTION+U
Color Mixer	CTRL+ALT+M	COMMAND+OPTION+M
Swatches	CTRL+ALT+S	COMMAND+OPTION+S
Info	CTRL+ALT+I	COMMAND+OPTION+I
Behaviors	CTRL+ALT+H	COMMAND+OPTION+H

Table A-16.   *Fireworks MX Window Keyboard Shortcuts* (continued)

Tool	Windows Keyboard Shortcut	Macintosh Keyboard Shortcut
Pointer tool	V, 0	V, 0
Select Behind tool	V, 0	V, 0
Subselection tool	A, 1	A, 1
Marquee tool	M	M
Oval Marquee tool	M	M
Lasso tool	L	L
Polygon Lasso tool	L	L
Crop tool	C	C
Export Area tool	C	C
Magic Wand tool	W	W
Line tool	N	N
Pen tool	P	P
Rectangle tool	U	U
Rounded Rectangle tool	U	U

Table A-17.   *Fireworks MX Tool Keyboard Shortcuts*

Tool	Windows Keyboard Shortcut	Macintosh Keyboard Shortcut
Ellipse tool	U	U
Polygon tool	U	U
Text tool	T	T
Pencil tool	B	B
Vector Path tool	P	P
Redraw Path tool	P	P
Brush tool	B	B
Scale tool	Q	Q
Skew tool	Q	Q
Distort tool	Q	Q
Freeform tool	O	O
Reshape Area tool	O	O
Path Scrubber tool - additive	O	O
Path Scrubber tool - subtractive	O	O
Eyedropper tool	I	I
Paint Bucket tool	G	G
Gradient tool	G	G
Eraser tool	E	E
Blur tool	R	R
Sharpen tool	R	R
Dodge tool	R	R
Burn tool	R	R
Smudge tool	R	R
Rubber Stamp tool	S	S
Knife tool	Y	Y
Rectangle Hotspot tool	J	J

Table A-17.   *Fireworks MX Tool Keyboard Shortcuts* (continued)

Tool	Windows Keyboard Shortcut	Macintosh Keyboard Shortcut
Circle Hotspot tool	J	J
Polygon Hotspot tool	J	J
Slice tool	Z	K
Polygon Slice tool	K	K
Hand tool	H	H
Zoom tool	Z	Z
Hide/Show Slices	2	2
Set Default Stroke/Fill Colors	D	D
Swap Stroke/Fill Colors	X	X
Toggle Screen Mode	F	F

Table A-17. *Fireworks MX Tool Keyboard Shortcuts* (continued)

Command	Windows Keyboard Shortcut	Macintosh Keyboard Shortcut
Exit Bitmap Mode	CTRL+SHIFT+D	COMMAND+SHIFT+D
Fill Pixel Selection	ALT+DELETE	OPTION+DELETE
Group As Bitmap Mask	CTRL+SHIFT+G	COMMAND+SHIFT+G
Next Frame	CTRL+PAGE UP	COMMAND+PAGE UP
Nudge Down	DOWN	DOWN
Nudge Down Large	SHIFT+DOWN	SHIFT+DOWN
Nudge Left	LEFT	LEFT
Nudge Left Large	SHIFT+LEFT	SHIFT+LEFT
Nudge Right	RIGHT	RIGHT

Table A-18. *Fireworks MX Miscellaneous Keyboard Shortcuts*

Command	Windows Keyboard Shortcut	Macintosh Keyboard Shortcut
Nudge Right Large	SHIFT+RIGHT	SHIFT+RIGHT
Nudge Up	UP	UP
Nudge Up Large	SHIFT+UP	SHIFT+UP
Paste Inside	CTRL+SHIFT+V	COMMAND+SHIFT+V
Previous Frame	CTRL+PAGE DOWN	COMMAND+PAGE DOWN

Table A-18. *Fireworks MX Miscellaneous Keyboard Shortcuts* (continued)

The
Complete
Reference

Fireworks
MX

Appendix B

Fireworks Resources

Y ou can find almost anything on the Internet, including resources for popular software applications. In this appendix, you'll find the URLs for Web sites that support Fireworks or offer information about Fireworks. The list is by no means all inclusive, as the Internet is in a constant state of flux. The URLs for these sites are accurate as of May 27, 2002.

The following sections list sites that contain information you can use to further your knowledge of Fireworks. You'll also find sites that are devoted to resources and tutorials for Fireworks. As you explore these Web sites, you may find links to additional information about Fireworks and references to new sites. The more information you can find on an application in today's burgeoning information age, the better off you'll be.

Macromedia Designer & Developer Center

http://www.macromedia.com/desdev/

With the release of the MX product line, Macromedia makes it possible for designers to use MX software products as a suite, one product complementing the other. With MX software, it is possible to handle the vast majority of your Web design tasks. To better serve their customers, Macromedia created a Designer & Developer Center on its Web site. At this portal you'll find information on the following:

- Java
- Databases
- 3D
- XML
- CSS (cascading style sheets)

In addition, you'll find articles and tutorials from Web designers and developers. You'll also find links to other Macromedia resources.

The Edge

http://dynamic.macromedia.com/bin/MM/hub/edgeLogin.jsp

The *Edge* is Macromedia's monthly newsletter. You can follow the above link to sign up for the newsletter at no charge. After you sign up for the newsletter, it is delivered to you via e-mail. If you prefer, you can view it online by following the link at Macromedia's Designer & Developer Center.

The *Edge* features the latest information on Macromedia products, a toolbox section that shows you how to get the most out of your software, a tips section, and a section called "Sites That Inspire," where you can view the latest work of prominent Web designers.

Macromedia Fireworks Support Center

http://www.macromedia.com/support/fireworks/

In the Macromedia Fireworks Support Center, you'll find the latest tech tips, as well as any patches or updates that may be available for Fireworks. You'll also find links to other Fireworks information on the Web, as well as links to Fireworks user groups.

Macromedia Exchange

http://www.macromedia.com/exchange/

At the Macromedia Exchange, you'll find extensions for Macromedia software. Extensions are automated features that you can use to perform complex tasks. To use Macromedia Extensions, you download the free Extension Manager. After you install the Extension Manager, you can download extensions for your software. When you install an extension, the Extension Manager links the extension with the proper application. Once an extension is installed, it appears as a menu command. Fireworks MX supports extensions; however, as of this writing, no Fireworks extensions are available. This is sure to change in the upcoming months after Fireworks users and developers have had a chance work with Fireworks and create extensions to streamline workflow and enhance the usability of the software.

Macromedia Showcase of Sites Designed with Fireworks

http://dynamic.macromedia.com/bin/MM/showcase/scripts/showcase_cs_listing_by_query.jsp?product=Fireworks

Macromedia Showcase is devoted to stellar examples of Web sites created with Macromedia software. This URL is the link to the Fireworks section of the showcase that boasts several links to showcase Web sites created with Fireworks. Click any of the links to learn more about the Web site and the designer's needs and goals for the Web site. After reading this information, you can click a link to visit the actual site. If you're ever stuck for inspiration, the Macromedia Showcase is a good place to start.

The Macromedia Showcase features links to Macromedia's Web sites in the following international regions:

- Asia Pacific
- Brazil
- Canada
- France

- Germany
- Italy
- Japan
- Latin America
- Scandinavia
- Spain
- United Kingdom

The sites may be in a language you don't speak, but you'll be able to glean some ideas from the sites. After all, tasteful Web design knows no language barriers.

Macromedia's Showcase also has a "Site of the Day" section, where you'll find sites created with Flash, as well as other Macromedia software. When you view a Site of the Day, a link to the Web designer's site is usually supplied—yet another source for examples of stellar Web design.

Lynda.com

http://www.lynda.com/tips/

This section of lynda.com is devoted to tips and tutorials related to Web design. Here you'll find tutorials for most popular Macromedia software products, as well as tutorials for Adobe products and more. The tutorials are QuickTime movies that you can view online.

Macromedia Fireworks

http://epaperpress.com/fireworks/index.html

At this site, you'll find a collection of useful tutorials about Fireworks. The tutorials are viewed online as *viewlets*, animated tutorials of the software in action. As of this writing, you'll find tutorials related to the following Fireworks topics:

- Working with transparency in Fireworks
- Creating outline masks
- Creating grayscale masks
- Creating photo effects
- Creating photo borders
- Creating metallic effects
- Simulating 3D

The topic list is bound to expand as the site owners gain experience with the new features of Fireworks MX.

Project Fireworks

http://www.projectfireworks.com/

Project Fireworks is an Internet portal of information devoted exclusively to Fireworks. The site is divided into the following sections:

- **Classroom** This section has tutorials for Fireworks, as well as Dreamweaver. The Dreamweaver tutorials are still under construction at this writing.
- **Voices** An online newsletter to which you can subscribe.
- **Gadgets** Commands, patterns, symbols, and textures you can download.
- **Library** Features links to other Fireworks Web sites.

SmartWebby

http://www.smartwebby.com/web_site_design/fireworks_tips.asp

Here's a Web page chock-full of Fireworks tips and tricks. From the "Fireworks Tips and Tricks" page, you can follow links to additional information about Web design with a variety of products. You'll also find individual sections with the following information:

- Web site design ideas
- Web design tips
- Web site navigation tips
- Web graphics design ideas and tips
- Tips for designing a fast-loading Web site
- HTML table tricks and tips
- Designing Web sites for different monitor resolutions
- Dreamweaver tips
- Creating text effects with CSS

FW MX Zone

http://www.fwzone.net/

This site features information related to Fireworks MX. The site is divided into several sections. All the information is useful. In particular you'll want to browse the "News" section, where you'll find up-to-date information about Fireworks and related issues.

Another area sure to spark your interest is the "Tutorials" area. Currently the information in this section is for Fireworks 4. However, as the Web design community embraces Fireworks MX, you can export to find tutorials devoted to Fireworks MX.

In the "Extensions" area of this site, you'll find a number of commands you can add to Fireworks to add custom features to your work.

Phireworx

http://www.phireworx.com/

Here is another Web site where you can download some free Fireworks goodies. The site features a collection of commands called Keap. Keap features the following commands: Filler Text 2.0, Mode Switcher 1.0, Pseudo Browser 1.0, Pseudo Browser 1.0, Select and Shift 1.0, Twist, and Fade 2.0.

Appendix C

Web Design Resources

647

It's only fitting that the World Wide Web should be an inexhaustible source of information for Web design, and it is—almost. In this appendix, you'll find links to Web design resources. Some sites listed here contain information or resources devoted to a specific phase of Web design, while other sites offer support for Web design software. Still other sites in this section offer extensive tutorials on Web design and the various programming languages used in conjunction with Web design. These sites are all active as of May 2002. However as the Internet is in a constant state of change; what is here today may be gone tomorrow.

Macromedia Dreamweaver Support Center

http://www.macromedia.com/support/dreamweaver/

If you use Dreamweaver in conjunction with Fireworks, you'll find all the information you need to support the Dreamweaver application at this page, including updates, patches, and technical support for the product, as well as links to other Dreamweaver information.

Adobe GoLive Support

http://www.adobe.com/support/products/golive.html

If GoLive is your HTML editor of choice, you'll find support information, training, tutorials and other information at this URL. In addition, you can glean information about a particular aspect of GoLive from Adobe's Support Knowledgebase, which features a search engine.

Microsoft Support

http://support.microsoft.com/

If you use Fireworks and FrontPage as a one-two combination for Web design, you'll find support information for FrontPage, as well as other Microsoft products, at this Web site. Enter your query into the search engine or browse through the database of information.

Project Cool

http://www.devx.com/projectcool/developer/default.asp

Here's a useful site with information about many aspects of Web design. If you'd like to learn more about ASP (Active Server Pages), DHTML (Dynamic Hyper Text Markup Language), or XML (Extensible Markup Language), you'll find useful information and tutorials here. On the site's home page, you'll find links to articles about HTML, tutorials about Web design, reference libraries for HTML code, tags, and so on, as well as a section devoted to Web design tools and components.

W3C Technical Reports and Publications

http://www.w3.org/TR/

Here's a resource at the World Wide Web Consortium Web site that lists documents and articles for code written in HTML 3.2. Here you'll find links to information on XML, XHTML, the PNG graphics format, and more.

HTML 4.0 Specification

http://www.w3.org/TR/WD-html40-970708/cover.html

Here's another resource at the W3C Web site that lists everything you could possibly want to know about HTML 4.0. After viewing the home page, you can go to the table of contents to find specific information. Another section lists the differences between HTML 3.2 and 4.0.

Internet.com

http://www.internet.com/home-d.html

This site features a diverse and eclectic portal of information related to Web design and the Internet. The site is divided into 16 sections. When you move your cursor over each section's menu, a pop-up menu appears to provide additional choices. The site's home page features interesting articles about Web design and the Internet. If you're developing content for wireless devices, you may find useful links in the "Wireless Internet" section. Use the site's search engine to cut to the chase and quickly find the information you're looking for.

Java and JavaScript Resources

http://www.web-hosting.com/javalinks.html

If JavaScript is your cup of tea, you'll find information to interest you at this Web page. The page features links to several JavaScript resources.

A Beginner's Guide to JavaScript

http://www.geocities.com/SiliconValley/Park/2554/index.html

If you enjoy working with the JavaScript elements in Fireworks and would like to find out how to write your own JavaScript code, this Web site provides a useful guide to get you pointed in the right direction. You'll find a section devoted to tips and another to examples.

PageResource.com

http://www.pageresource.com/

Here's another useful collection of information for Web masters and developers. At this site, you'll find information about Active Server Pages (ASP), cascading style sheets (CSS), HTML, PHP, JavaScript, XML, and more. If you can't find what you need at this site, check out the links page, which lists several sources for information about Web design and the Internet.

HotSyte

http://www.serve.com/hotsyte/

Here's another Web design resource with links to all manner of information about JavaScript, DHTML, and related topics. The site is divided into sections that contain links to Web sites that contain information pertaining to a specific Web design topic.

CGI Resources

http://www.cgi-resources.com/Programs_and_Scripts/

If you've ever had the desire to branch out and add interactivity to your site in the form of common gateway interface (CGI) scripts, you owe it to yourself to visit this Web site. Here you'll find a list of resources for scripts that record the number of visitors to a site, enable you to set up a chat room, let you create a rotating ad banner, and more.

Index Dot HTML

http://www.blooberry.com/indexdot/html/index.html

You can never get enough information, especially when information about your field of endeavor is constantly changing. At this Web site you'll find information dedicated to HTML.

Web Wonk

http://www.dsiegel.com/tips/index.html

Here's an interesting site with information on using images, text, and other elements in your Web designs. You'll also find information on using a single-pixel transparent GIF image to space elements in your design. This is similar to the Fireworks spacer, but here you learn how to use it as part of your HTML code to create paragraph indents and so on.

WebMonkey

http://hotwired.lycos.com/webmonkey/

This valuable resource features tutorials and articles about Web design. The site is divided into a "How-To Library" and a "Quick Reference" section.

In the "How-to Library," you'll find tutorials on the following topics:

- **Authoring** Features sections on HTML, XML, tables, frames, browsers, and more. Each section features several tutorials on the given topic.

- **Design** Features sections on site building, graphics, and fonts. Select a section for detailed tutorials about a given topic.

- **Multimedia** Features several sections devoted to adding multimedia elements to your Web designs. Individual sections feature tutorials devoted to Shockwave/Flash, MP3 music, video, and more.

- **E-Business** Features three sections devoted to building an e-commerce site, marketing an e-commerce site, and tracking visitors to your e-commerce site.

- **Programming** Features several sections devoted to the popular code languages used in Web design. Here you'll also find two excellent articles on programming in general.

- **Backend** Features information about incorporating databases with a Web site, setting up a network, security, and so on.

- **Jobs** Features information about finding Web design jobs, freelancing, and more.

The "Quick Reference" section of the WebMonkey site is divided into the following categories:

- **JavaScript Code Library** A code library with bits of code and ideas of how you can use JavaScript code for your designs.

- **HTML Cheatsheet** Shows a list of the commonly used HTML tags and a description of what each tag is used for.

- **Special Characters** Shows a list of special characters and the proper HTML formatting for the character.

- **Color Codes** Features a color chart and the hexadecimal value for each color.

- **Browser Chart** Features a chart of the popular Web browsers in use, as well as the features supported and not supported by each.

- **Stylesheets Guide** Shows how to use CSS for controlling the look of your Web pages. This guide is divided into several sections including properties and examples of style sheets.

- **Unix Guide**   Shows the basic commands used for file management on a Unix server.
- **Glossary**   Provides an alphabetical glossary to terms commonly used in Web design.
- **Domain Registries**   Provides links to domain registration services.

Index

I

INTERNATIONAL CONTACT INFORMATION

AUSTRALIA
McGraw-Hill Book Company Australia Pty. Ltd.
TEL +61-2-9415-9899
FAX +61-2-9415-5687
http://www.mcgraw-hill.com.au
books-it_sydney@mcgraw-hill.com

CANADA
McGraw-Hill Ryerson Ltd.
TEL +905-430-5000
FAX +905-430-5020
http://www.mcgrawhill.ca

GREECE, MIDDLE EAST,
NORTHERN AFRICA
McGraw-Hill Hellas
TEL +30-1-656-0990-3-4
FAX +30-1-654-5525

MEXICO (Also serving Latin America)
McGraw-Hill Interamericana Editores S.A. de C.V.
TEL +525-117-1583
FAX +525-117-1589
http://www.mcgraw-hill.com.mx
fernando_castellanos@mcgraw-hill.com

SINGAPORE (Serving Asia)
McGraw-Hill Book Company
TEL +65-863-1580
FAX +65-862-3354
http://www.mcgraw-hill.com.sg
mghasia@mcgraw-hill.com

SOUTH AFRICA
McGraw-Hill South Africa
TEL +27-11-622-7512
FAX +27-11-622-9045
robyn_swanepoel@mcgraw-hill.com

UNITED KINGDOM & EUROPE
(Excluding Southern Europe)
McGraw-Hill Education Europe
TEL +44-1-628-502500
FAX +44-1-628-770224
http://www.mcgraw-hill.co.uk
computing_neurope@mcgraw-hill.com

ALL OTHER INQUIRIES Contact:
Osborne/McGraw-Hill
TEL +1-510-549-6600
FAX +1-510-883-7600
http://www.osborne.com
omg_international@mcgraw-hill.com